ULTIMATE
Adventures

AUSTRALIA

ANDREW BAIN

Hardie Grant

EXPLORE

Introduction	iv
Adventure types	vi
Adventure time	x
Map of Australia	xii

NEW SOUTH WALES & ACT — 1

Burrawa Climb, Sydney Harbour Bridge	3
Kayaking, Sydney Harbour	6
Canyoning, Blue Mountains	13
Beyond Skyway, Blue Mountains	17
Hang gliding, Bald Hill	23
Horse riding, Boambee Beach	27
Stand-up paddleboarding, Solitary Islands Marine Park	30
Surfing, Byron Bay	37
Backcountry skiing, Guthega, Snowy Mountains	43
Climbing to the top of Australia, Mount Kosciuszko	48
Ballooning, Canberra/Ngambri/Ngunnawal	55

VICTORIA — 59

Swimming with dolphins and seals, Port Phillip	61
Surfing, Bells Beach	64
Rock climbing, Mount Arapiles/Dyuritte	71
Canoeing, Glenelg River	76
Cycling the 7 Peaks, High Country	80
Abseiling, Mount Buffalo	87
Sleeping on a portaledge, Mount Buffalo	91
Snow camping, Mount Hotham	97
HeliSUP-ing, Gippsland Lakes	103

SOUTH AUSTRALIA — 107

RoofClimb, Adelaide Oval	109
Kayaking, Adelaide Dolphin Sanctuary	113
Cycling, Barossa and Clare valleys and McLaren Vale	117
Biking and boarding, Little Sahara, Kangaroo Island	120
Diving with great white sharks, off Neptune Islands	127
Hiking the Arkaba Walk, Ikara-Flinders Ranges	132
Hiking with camels, Ikara-Flinders Ranges	138
Sinkhole snorkelling, Mount Gambier	145
Caving, Naracoorte Caves National Park	151

WESTERN AUSTRALIA   155

Matagarup Zip+Climb, Perth/Boorloo	157
Cycling, Rottnest Island/Wadjemup	162
Sandboarding, Lancelin	168
Kayaking, Shark Bay	173
Swimming with whale sharks, Ningaloo Reef	178
Diving, Exmouth Navy Pier	183
Exploring gorges, Karijini National Park	187

NORTHERN TERRITORY   193

Swimming with a crocodile, Crocosaurus Cove	195
Canoeing, Nitmiluk National Park	199
Hiking the Larapinta Trail, Tjoritja/West MacDonnell National Park	204
Helibiking, Alice Springs/Mparntwe	211
Cycling, Uluṟu	215

QUEENSLAND   219

Rock climbing, Kangaroo Point, Brisbane/Meanjin	221
Snorkelling, Tangalooma Wrecks, Moreton Island/Mulgumpin	225
Cycling, Brisbane Valley Rail Trail	231
Kayaking, Noosa River	234
Kayaking, Whitsunday Ngaro Sea Trail	239
Stand-up paddleboarding, Cobbold Gorge	244
Hiking the Thorsborne Trail, Hinchinbrook Island/Munamudanamy	251
Rafting, Tully River	256
Bungy jumping, Cairns/Gimuy	260
Diving and swimming with minke whales, Ribbon Reefs	265

TASMANIA   271

Kayaking, Turrakana/Tasman Peninsula	273
Rafting, Franklin River	279
Hiking the Overland Track, Cradle Mountain-Lake St Clair National Park	285
Canyoning, Cradle Mountain	291
Whitewater sledding, Meander River	297
Mountain biking, Derby	300
Hiking the wukalina Walk, Larapuna/Bay of Fires	305
Climbing the Abels, across Tasmania	309

Index	314
About the Author	321
Acknowledgements	321

INTRODUCTION

Australians have never been shy of adventure. We've grown up with a harsh outback seemingly at most of our backs, flooded off to wars on the other side of the planet, and travelled the globe in pursuit of experiences. But some of the world's best adventures are right here, within our borders.

I've been travelling the globe in pursuit of adventure for 25 years, and over that time the range and breadth of adventure possibilities here in Australia has broadened beyond anything I could have imagined. To our bedrock of Aussie adventure classics – bushwalking, four-wheel driving and surfing – has been added a wealth of diverse experiences and activities.

In this book alone, you'll find bushwalks, cycling tours, mountain-bike rides, canyoning, caving, abseiling, hang gliding, hot-air ballooning, kayaking, canoeing, snorkelling, diving, river sledding, surfing, stand-up paddleboarding (SUPing), First Nations–led cultural adventures, horse riding, bungy jumping, backcountry skiing, snowshoeing, rock climbing, snow camping, zip-lining, fat biking, cage diving with great white sharks, swims with a crocodile, whale shark, dolphin and seal encounters, sandboarding blasts and a trek with camels. Phew.

To that, you can add adventures that defy categorisation and sometimes even the imagination. In the pages ahead, you'll vicariously sleep out for a night on a cliff-hanging portaledge, climb onto the roof of a cable car 270m above the earth, and stand-up paddleboard home at the end of a helicopter flight.

This book brings together gentle adventures, a few aspirational head-turners, and some true outdoor immortals such as hiking the Overland Track, rafting the Franklin River and swimming with whale sharks at Ningaloo Reef.

The emphasis is largely on adventures within the capabilities of as many people as possible, and most of them are possible as guided experiences. Some of the activities might push you out of your comfort zone, but testing and reshaping your comfort zone is half the fun and reward of adventures. Most of the activities in this book don't require a military-style fitness regime to have you ready and capable, though you also wouldn't want to step out on something like the Larapinta Trail – two weeks through the desert on foot – without adequate preparation and training.

The adventures ahead are unquestionably some of the most exciting, most beautiful and quirkiest outdoor experiences in the country, and still they only scratch the dusty surface of what an adventurous spirit can experience in Australia. Are you up for an adventure?

ANDREW BAIN

Opposite Abseiling down Mount Buffalo's North Wall in Victoria for an evening on a portaledge

ADVENTURE TYPES

Adventures come in so many forms and shapes, and often defy categorisation – one person's adventure is often another person's I-don't-dare-venture. They can be activities as simple as a walk along a cliff-edge, or a bike ride on a rail trail, or they could mean stepping backwards over that cliff-edge, attached to a rope with a 200m drop beneath, or barrelling down a rocky, root-splayed mountain-bike trail.

Loosely grouped, the adventures in this book fit the following themes.

Adventures on foot

The oldest form of adventure is also the simplest: walking. Throwing your entire life for a few days or a couple of weeks onto your back, armed only with a map and compass, is an act of self-sufficiency and acceptance of the unknown that can be as mentally and physically challenging as any high-octane, adrenaline-fuelled activity.

In Australia, the walking opportunities are as varied as our landscapes. You can spend a fortnight on foot through desert mountains on the Larapinta Trail (*see* p.204), hop from tropical beach to tropical beach along the Thorsborne Trail (*see* p.251), or indulge in a dozen-or-so luxury guided hikes that do most of the walk for you, other than the steps. Prepare and pack well and there's nothing more rewarding than the sense of journey that comes with the slowest form of travel.

There are thousands of places to walk in Australia, but a few trails and experiences are recognisably first among equals. In this book, I've chosen a representative selection of the country's best multi-day walks. Thread through one of the most beautiful collections of mountains in the country along the Overland Track (*see* p.285), and take to deserts or island beaches on the Larapinta and Thorsborne trails.

To this, there's a taster of luxury guided walking with the Arkaba Walk in South Australia's Flinders Ranges (*see* p.132), and a cultural hike in First Nations footsteps along Tasmania's wukalina Walk (*see* p.305).

Come to any hike well prepared. Wear in your hiking boots or shoes before you travel, invest in good raingear and warm clothing, take adequate food, water and a first-aid kit, know all of your gear and check conditions before you start out. If hiking independently, ensure people know your intended itinerary, take a Personal Locator Beacon (PLB) with you and be proficient and confident in your map and compass skills.

Left Crossing Frog Flats on the Overland Track, Tasmania
Opposite Kayaking in Shark Bay, WA

Adventures on water

We're girt by sea, right, so it makes sense that so many Australian adventures involve water, and there are almost as many possibilities as there are waterways. In this book alone, you'll find surfing, kayaking, diving, snorkelling (in the ocean and in sinkholes), rafting, stand-up paddleboarding (SUPing) and river sledding, as well as marine encounters with the likes of great white sharks, crocodiles, whale sharks, dolphins and seals.

A country bookended by the world's largest coral system (Great Barrier Reef) and the largest fringing reef on the planet (Ningaloo Reef) is naturally one of the planet's great diving locations, and in these pages we slip beneath the ocean's surface at Ribbon Reefs (see p.265) for the twin thrill of dwarf minke whales and vibrant corals. Close to shore, at Western Australia's Navy Pier (see p.183), there's the unusual combination of an operational naval base open to divers.

Two of surfing's big names – Bells Beach (see p.64) and Byron Bay (see p.37) – are featured here, from the big waves of the world-famous former to the chilled vibes of the latter.

Kayaks and canoes nose through the Whitsundays (see p.239) and across the mirrored surface of the Noosa River (see p.234) in Queensland, among dolphins in Adelaide's Port River (see p.113), into beauty and First Nations' culture in WA's Shark Bay (see p.173), beneath Australia's tallest sea cliffs on Turrakana/Tasman Peninsula (see p.273), and through a deep limestone gorge along the Victoria–South Australia border on the Glenelg River (see p.76).

In rivers that pour down from mountains, Australia has world-class rafting, be it a short squirt through high-octane Tully Gorge (see p.256) in north Queensland or an eight-day epic along Tasmania's almost mythical Franklin River (see p.279). The former was once named in the world's 10 best rafting rivers, while the latter was declared the world's best river journey by a leading US adventure magazine.

Want a more intimate form of river 'rafting'? River sledding on Tasmania's Meander River (see p.297) is rafting's little sibling, shrinking the adventure to a li-lo-like inflatable sled-for-one through less punishing rapids.

Stand-up paddleboards (SUPs) are the new black in water sports, and Australia has some incredible possibilities. If you've ever wanted to paddle through the outback, or with the oldest paddling culture in the world, or even out of a helicopter, you've come to the right spot with respective adventures in the Queensland savannah at Cobbold Gorge (see p.244), at Solitary Islands Marine Park (see p.30), and heliSUP-ing at Victoria's Gippsland Lakes (see p.103).

Adventures in the air

There's no more calming moment in this book than a Canberra/Ngambri/Ngunnawal dawn in the basket of a hot-air balloon (*see* p.55). And yet even this gentle act of floating over the earth beneath a bag of air is such an act of trust and trepidation that it truly qualifies as an adventure.

Other aerial adventures require even more faith. Tossing yourself off NSW's Bald Hill (*see* p.23) strapped to a hang glider (and thankfully also to a pilot who knows what they're doing) is another step into thin air, while it takes a cool mind to leap off a 50m-high metal frame above the Cairns/Gimuy rainforest on Australia's only bungy jump (*see* p.260).

You may as well be in the air if you decide to spend an evening atop the Southern Hemisphere's largest aerial cable car, suspended above a 270m drop in the Blue Mountains (*see* p.17), or zip-lining across the Swan River in Perth/Boorloo after you've scaled Matagarup Bridge (*see* p.157). And who knew that mountain biking and stand-up paddleboarding could take you to such heights? In this book you'll uncover heli-mountain biking out of Alice Springs/Mparntwe (*see* p.211) and heliSUPing in Victoria's Gippsland Lakes (*see* p.103).

Adventures on wheels

Bike sales in Australia gathered momentum faster than a downhill mountain biker during the Covid pandemic – 1.7 million bikes came into the country in 2021 – and there are myriad places now to ride them.

The last decade has seen a mountain-biking revolution across the country, and it can pretty much be carbon dated to the launch of Blue Derby, the trail network around the Tasmanian town of Derby (*see* p.300) that has now hosted a round of the Enduro World Series – the pinnacle of world mountain biking – three times, and yet still offers fun, flowing riding for all abilities.

Alice Springs/Mparntwe (*see* p.211) is another of my favourite mountain-bike trail networks, providing natural desert lines, solitude and the option to drop in on the trails by helicopter.

The cycling renaissance is perhaps best exemplified by rail trails, of which there are now more than 100 across the country. Some are as short as a handful of kilometres, while the longest in the country, the Brisbane Valley Rail Trail (*see* p.231), stretches for 161km along the Brisbane River. It's this trail that I've focussed on as an example of the genre in this book.

The breadth of cycling possibilities in Australia shines through in the book's other cycling selections. Go from the parched pedalling of a lap around Uluru (*see* p.215), to wetting your whistle on a ride through three of SA's wine regions (*see* p.117). Pedal around WA's Rottnest Island/Wadjemup (*see* p.162) in your swimmers, barely encountering a bump, or notch up more than 7000m of climbing as you tackle cycling's greatest mountain challenge – the 7 Peaks (*see* p.80) in Victoria's alpine region.

Having your own bike is the best and easiest way to take any of these rides, but popular trails and regions now typically also have bike hire available.

Left Hot-air ballooning above the National Library in Canberra/Ngambri/Ngunnawal

Adventures on a rope

Whether going up them or down them, Australian cliffs are a heady place to be. We're a country that once sported the world's toughest rock-climbing route – Mount Arapiles's Punks in the Gym – and now boasts the world's highest commercial abseil on Mount Buffalo (see p.87), both in Victoria. This book takes you down the rope of the latter, and up climbs a little easier, but no less spectacular, on the revered Arapiles (see p.71). Elsewhere, you don't even need to leave the city to find brilliant climbing on the cliffs at Kangaroo Point in Brisbane/Meanjin (see p.221). Then it's back to the cliffs of Mount Buffalo for one of the most unusual/exciting/confronting/paralysing (choose according to your perspective) adventures of all – sleeping out on a portaledge 250m above the ground on what's billed as the world's highest cliff camping experience (see p.91).

Canyoning is a melange of activities in one – it usually takes swimming, wading, leaping, scrambling and abseiling to navigate through these deep slots, of which you'll find two – Empress Canyon in the Blue Mountains (see p.13) and Dove Canyon at Tasmania's Cradle Mountain (see p.291) – in this book.

All of these activities require dedicated gear – climbing harness, helmet, rope, carabiners and the like (and a lifejacket in the case of canyoning) – and without expertise, you should only partake in them as part of guided trips.

Adventures with wildlife

There's something about the sight of ocean that makes so many of us want to interact with what's beneath. It entices us into scuba gear, shark-proof cages or just snorkels and fins to witness a world otherwise alien to land mammals such as us.

In this book there are swimming adventures with dolphins and seals (see p.61), whale sharks (see p.178), dwarf minke whales (see p.265), even crocodiles (see p.195) and great white sharks (see p.127). They're encounters that are delightful and disarming, reminding us that the 70 per cent of the planet we typically don't see is just as beautiful as the 30 per cent above.

As ever with wildlife encounters, be aware of the ethics and guidelines around your interactions. Almost all wildlife tourism has regulations to protect the animals you've come to enjoy. Be mindful of the distance you should keep from an animal (it varies according to the encounter and activity), and take it as a blanket rule that you should never touch a creature during a wildlife encounter.

Many wildlife tourism operators also run citizen science–type programs, collecting data for research, so keep an eye out for these if you want your visit to be about more than a good time. For example, Great Barrier Reef minke whale dive trips (see p.265) help collect data and monitor behaviour and risks to these creatures.

To learn more about guidelines around wildlife tours and interactions, a good starting point is the Wildlife Tourism Australia website (wildlifetourism.org.au/about/guidelines).

Adventures in holes

Opportunities for proper caving are few and far between in Australia, but spelunking is about the most exciting thing you can do inside the earth. Caving requires dexterity and is not for the claustrophobe. It forces you to squirm, bend and squeeze to advance your way through a cave, often crawling on hands and knees (or even flatter, on your stomach) to push through dark tunnels. The reward is in the remarkable cave formations and the thrill of the adventure itself.

There's one caving trip in this book, in South Australia's World Heritage–listed Naracoorte Caves (see p.151), and it's well suited to novice cavers, featuring an entry-level cave, with the chance to progress to more challenging caves under the guidance of rangers. There are other guided caving adventures in Australia, such as around the Mole Creek caves in northern Tasmania, the Capricorn Caves near Rockhampton, and the Jenolan Caves in NSW.

Adventures on snow

When winter hits, the fun is just beginning in the mountains. Almost any snow activity has an adventurous quality, be it downhill skiing at one of the alpine ski resorts, touring on skis across the ranges, or just tobogganing with kids.

The snow activities covered in this book peer beyond the normal, taking you out into the NSW Snowy Mountains backcountry on skis (see p.43), and into a snow dome or igloo for a sleep-out on Victoria's Mount Hotham (see p.97).

Dress to suit, and watch the weather, and a winter wonderland of adventure awaits.

ADVENTURE TIME

Time to get out there. Onto the trail, into a kayak, down a rope or up into the sky. So much awaits. Each adventure is an experience that begins with an idea before growing into nervous energy, anticipation, preparation and finally participation – the plunge, the pedal, or the paddle.

By nature, there's an unknown to any adventure, but the uncertainties are lessened by the fact that the majority of the activities in this book can be done as guided adventures – indeed, for all but readers experienced in the particular activity in question, it's the recommended way to undertake the adventure. It not only increases the safety of the experience, it also provides a chance for you to test drive the activity and perhaps find yourself a new outdoors love under the watch of an experienced and passionate guide.

Planning

The first step in planning is now in your hands – this book. Use it to plant the seeds of an adventure or 60. Hopefully the chapters ahead will inspire ideas and adventurous dreams of big days out in the mountains, on the water, in caves, sinkholes and canyons, or soaring beneath a hang glider.

When taking a guided tour, don't just leave everything (including all the thinking) to the pros showing you the way. Think about the sort of fitness that might be needed to get you through the particular adventure, and the mindset you might require to enjoy, rather than endure, it. To assist with that, each of the adventures in this book features a rating system, looking at the fitness requirements, the fear factor and the level of expertise required. Each one is assigned a rating from 1 to 5, with 1 being the easiest and 5 the most difficult or challenging. Guided adventures are typically marked down the scale to reflect the comparative ease they bring to that particular activity. These are inevitably subjective judgments, especially around the fear factor, but plenty of thought and care has gone into making them realistic and consistent. Individual thresholds will, however, ultimately decide the fear factor of any activity.

All the guided adventures in this book require advance booking, so be sure to visit the operators' websites ahead of your visit to secure your place. Costs of guided adventures naturally vary, and are often dictated by the amount of equipment a company requires for an activity, or the number of guides needed to ensure its safety.

Tour company websites will also provide more detailed practical information than has been included in this book, with the chapters here intended to give you a sense of what it's really like to be out there on that rope or in that canyon. The websites often contain details about what you should bring on the day of the adventure (or this may be emailed to you after the booking is complete), and might sometimes also provide criteria for any fitness and health requirements.

Safety

All adventures have some inherent risk, and safety can never be guaranteed. The majority of adventures in this book, however, tend to be at the easier, more achievable, end of things. Prepare ahead and keep your wits about you, and you won't regret any of the adventures you'll find in these pages.

Guided adventures take place under the watch of well-trained guides, proficient in first aid and medical emergencies. Ultimately, however, the only person who can keep you fully safe is yourself – don't outsource common sense just because you're in the comforting company of a guide. Be smart and alert, taking heed of all safety instructions and directions. Stay on trails, ride within your limits, don't poke a hand outside that shark cage.

Part of the safety requirement for any guided adventure is the completion of a waiver form, which you'll likely fill out online before you arrive at the activity, or complete at the operators' office. In these waivers, you typically outline any medical issues, potentially your fitness level (and such things as swimming ability if undertaking an adventure on water), and details of an emergency contact in event of an accident. In signing a waiver, you acknowledge the inherent risks involved in the activity, and accept responsibility for whatever may come.

Independent adventures of course require more forward planning, so think ahead about any fitness training that might be needed, test any equipment you'll be using (and be sure that you know how to use it), and refresh your first-aid knowledge if you haven't done so in a while.

Family adventures

A number of adventures in this book are family friendly – fun for the adults and the kids – and have been marked as such in the chapters. When this icon appears in a chapter, it's an adventure that I think kids will likely love, though there are a lot of variables with children's skills, abilities and confidence. Some adventures will require kids to be strong swimmers, for instance. It's no good throwing kids in the real or proverbial 'deep end' as it jeopardises their safety and that of the group.

It's worth remembering that tour operators usually have a minimum age requirement. Check the operator's website, where minimum ages are often listed. Some adventures are suited only to adults, or perhaps teenagers also, but the company might also run a similar trip suited to younger children. For instance, the canyoning trip through Dove Canyon (*see* p.291) in this book has a minimum age requirement of 15 years, but the operator also runs a Lost World Canyon trip higher up the waterway that has a minimum age of eight years.

A very common minimum age among the family-friendly adventures in this book is eight years of age, but be certain to check with operators before booking.

Talk to your kids before you embark on an adventure to build excitement, but also manage their expectations. For example, tell them whether it's guided, about the location and the environment, how long the drive to get there will take, details about the adventure itself and safety aspects – such as any special clothing or equipment they might need to wear.

By embarking on a family adventure and challenging yourself, you might well discover a new activity or passion you can all share and pursue.

Good for you, good for nature

If you can't see the forest for the adrenaline, pause, take a breath and look around. However challenging the adventure, you're only getting half the experience if you don't also create moments in which to take in and enjoy the world around you. Almost every activity in this book has a framework of natural beauty – sure, you might be hanging off 200m of cliffs but ain't the view great!

No visit to the outdoors comes without responsibility, especially to the environment and cultural sites. Tread lightly, be respectful. The reasons that you're here are the same reasons that you want to leave the place in the same condition as when you arrived.

The seven principles of Leave No Trace were created with hikers in mind, but they're relevant to anyone in the outdoors:

1. Plan Ahead and Prepare
2. Travel and Camp on Durable Surfaces
3. Dispose of Waste Properly
4. Leave What You Find
5. Minimise Campfire Impacts
6. Respect Wildlife
7. Be Considerate of Other Visitors.

Check them out online (lnt.org.au/programs/7-principles).

Right Stand-up paddleboarding through Cobbold Gorge, Queensland

MAP OF AUSTRALIA

NEW SOUTH WALES & ACT
1. Burrawa Climb, Sydney Harbour Bridge
2. Kayaking, Sydney Harbour
3. Canyoning, Blue Mountains
4. Beyond Skyway, Blue Mountains
5. Hang gliding, Bald Hill
6. Horse riding, Boambee Beach
7. Stand-up paddleboarding, Solitary Islands Marine Park
8. Surfing, Byron Bay
9. Backcountry skiing, Guthega, Snowy Mountains
10. Climbing to the top of Australia, Mount Kosciuszko
11. Ballooning, Canberra/Ngambri/Ngunnawal

VICTORIA
12. Swimming with dolphins and seals, Port Phillip
13. Surfing, Bells Beach
14. Rock climbing, Mount Arapiles/Dyurrite
15. Canoeing, Glenelg River
16. Cycling the 7 Peaks, High Country
17. Abseiling, Mount Buffalo
18. Sleeping on a portaledge, Mount Buffalo
19. Snow camping, Mount Hotham
20. HeliSUP-ing, Gippsland Lakes

SOUTH AUSTRALIA
21. RoofClimb, Adelaide Oval
22. Kayaking, Adelaide Dolphin Sanctuary
23. Cycling, Barossa and Clare valleys and McLaren Vale
24. Biking and boarding, Little Sahara, Kangaroo Island
25. Diving with great white sharks, off Neptune Islands
26. Hiking the Arkaba Walk, Ikara-Flinders Ranges
27. Hiking with camels, Ikara-Flinders Ranges
28. Sinkhole snorkelling, Mount Gambier
29. Caving, Naracoorte Caves National Park

WESTERN AUSTRALIA
30. Matagarup Zip+Climb, Perth/Boorloo
31. Cycling, Rottnest Island/Wadjemup
32. Sandboarding, Lancelin
33. Kayaking, Shark Bay
34. Swimming with whale sharks, Ningaloo Reef
35. Diving, Exmouth Navy Pier
36. Exploring gorges, Karijini National Park

NORTHERN TERRITORY
37. Swimming with a crocodile, Crocosaurus Cove
38. Canoeing, Nitmiluk National Park
39. Hiking the Larapinta Trail, Tjoritja/West MacDonnell National Park
40. Helibiking, Alice Springs/Mparntwe
41. Cycling, Uluru

QUEENSLAND
42. Rock climbing, Kangaroo Point, Brisbane/Meanjin
43. Snorkelling, Tangalooma Wrecks, Moreton Island/Mulgumpin
44. Cycling, Brisbane Valley Rail Trail
45. Kayaking, Noosa River
46. Kayaking, Whitsunday Ngaro Sea Trail
47. Stand-up paddleboarding, Cobbold Gorge
48. Hiking the Thorsborne Trail, Hinchinbrook Island/Munamudanamy
49. Rafting, Tully River
50. Bungy jumping, Cairns/Gimuy
51. Diving and swimming with minke whales, Ribbon Reefs

TASMANIA
52. Kayaking, Turrakana/Tasman Peninsula
53. Rafting, Franklin River
54. Hiking the Overland Track, Cradle Mountain-Lake St Clair NP
55. Canyoning, Cradle Mountain
56. White-water sledding, Meander River
57. Mountain biking, Derby
58. Hiking the wukalina Walk, larapuna/Bay of Fires
59. Climing the Abels, across Tasmania/Lutruwita

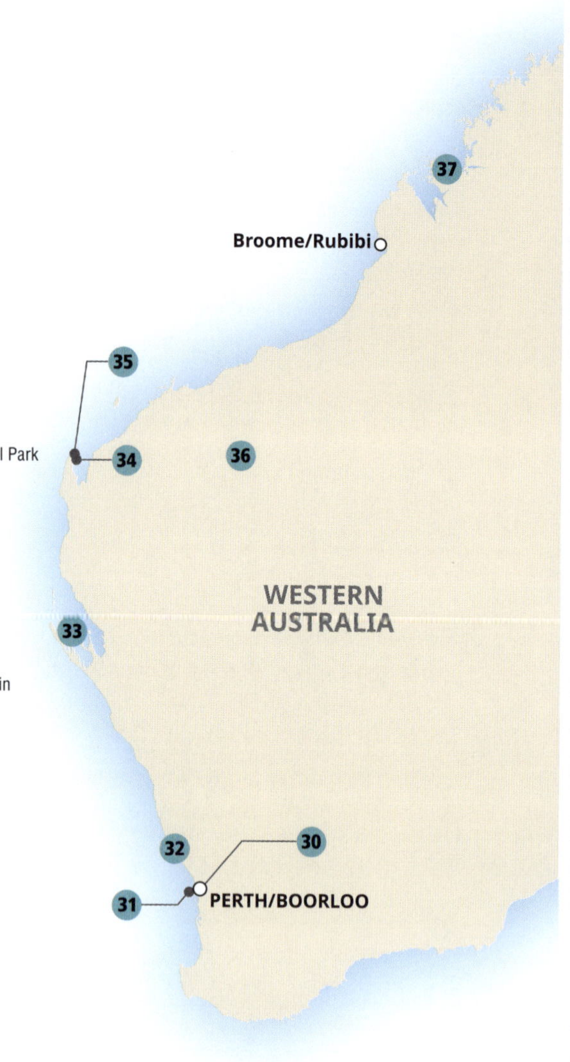

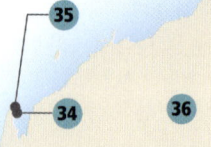

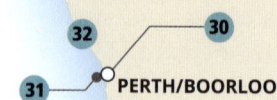

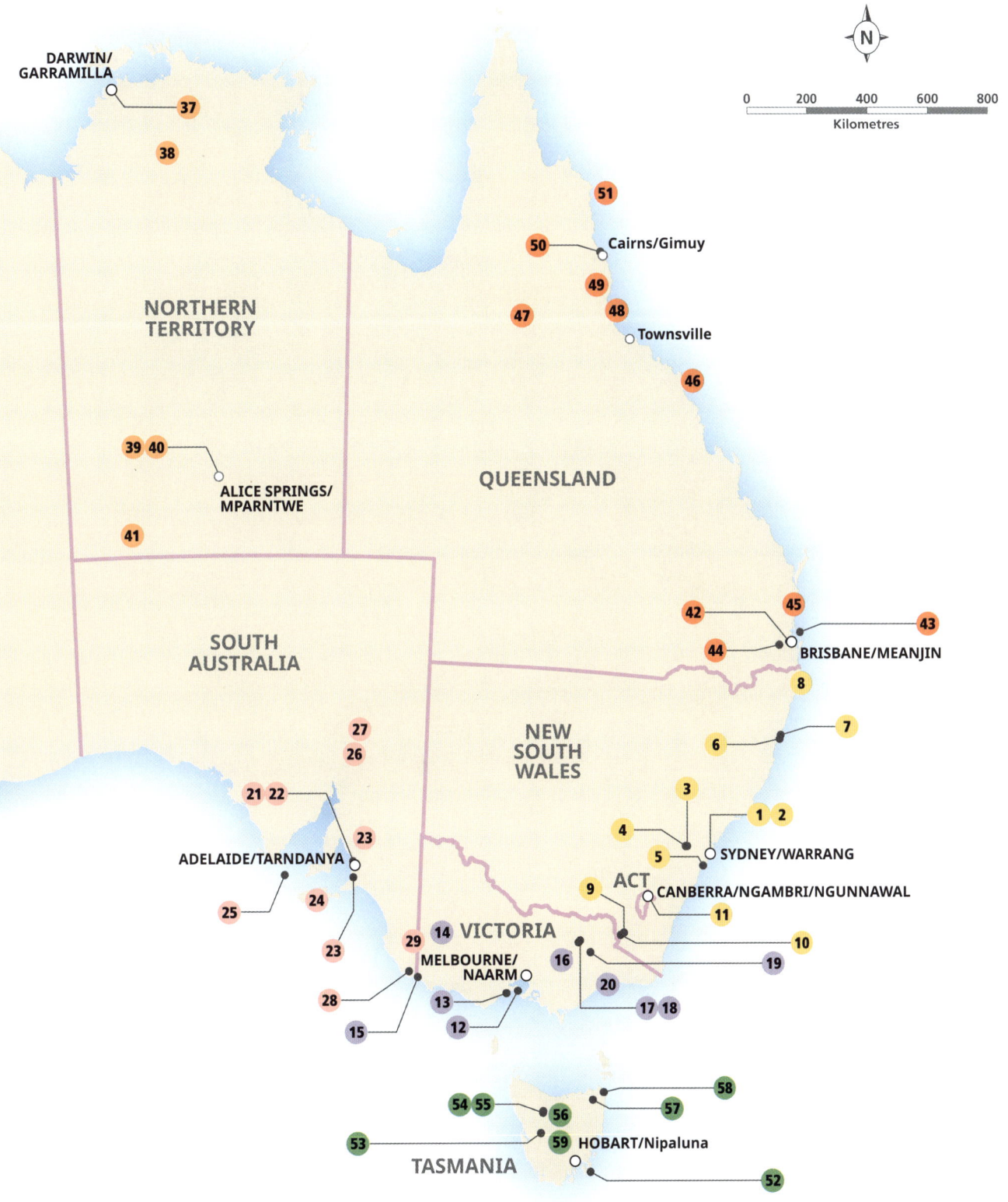

New South Wales & ACT

From the country's highest mountain to some of its deepest canyons, NSW presents an incredible array of adventure experiences.

Ascend Australia's most famous bridge and see Sydney/Warrang from a First Nations perspective.

Burrawa Climb, Sydney Harbour Bridge

Gadigal Country

WHY IT'S SPECIAL

The view from atop the Sydney Harbour Bridge, 134m above the water, is vast, but there's far more in this scene than you can see with the eye. Stretching beyond the city buildings and the sprawl of suburbs is a human history that spans tens of thousands of years, when the people of the Eora Nations live and hunted here, caring for Country since time immemorial.

Today, hundreds of visitors look over this view every day on BridgeClimb tours, but twice a week the standard tour comes with a rich cultural overlay on the Burrawa Climb, teaming Sydney/Warrang's finest view with its most enduring story – that of the First Nations People who preceded European settlement and later interacted with it.

The Burrawa Climb combines all the challenging qualities of the BridgeClimb – the exposure, the ladder climbs, the vertiginous ascent and descent of the arch – with a modern city view that provides a surreal background to millennia-old stories.

Where
All BridgeClimb tours start from the climb office on Cumberland St, The Rocks.

When
Burrawa Climbs run every Wed and Sat.

Do it
Book online (bridgeclimb.com).

Fitness ●●○○○

Fear factor ●●●○○

Expertise required ●○○○○

Family friendly

Opposite Ascending above the Sydney Harbour Bridge traffic
Previous Canyoner descending through Empress Falls in Empress Canyon

THE ADVENTURE

In the BridgeClimb office, tucked into a cavernous concrete arch beneath the Sydney Harbour Bridge, there are people already admitting to their terror of heights. As they step into overalls and harnesses, blow into breathalysers – don't drink and climb! – and simulate the climb and the use of the 'sliders' (the devices that keep you attached to the bridge) on a replica set of stairs, the air is a cocktail of nervous energy.

In this room, one group stands apart from the others, with each member holding a takeaway espresso cup partly filled with ochre. Dipping their fingers into the ochre, they smear it across their foreheads, faces, even their overalls, in a ceremony signifying togetherness. They are ready to begin the Burrawa Climb.

Preparations to climb take around 45min before you step through a door and immediately into sight of the familiar metal innards of the bridge. A song plays over a speaker – a song that Eora man Bennelong wrote in 1792 and then performed for King George III when he was one of the first two Aboriginal men, along with companion Yemmerawanne, to travel to Europe. (Both men suffered poor health while in Britain, with Yemmerawanne dying while overseas. Many viewed the voyage as grossly exploitative.) It's a song that was heard and written down by an English musician, but then lost for almost 200 years.

Attaching your slider to a cable – to which you'll be umbilically connected for the next two hours – you walk out along a wooden platform along the bridge's lowest girders. The Opera House and the city make their first appearances, and while there are chances to ask about and ponder the bridge's own history and stories, the urge to know these modern details seems to fade as the First Nations' history unfolds.

Climbers are encouraged to brush their hands across the bridge's granite pylon, a traditional Gadigal gesture of luck around granite, and then you begin the most difficult part of the climb, ascending a series of four long ladders. At the top of the first flight, you pop through the road deck, cars whirring past on both sides, before continuing up and emerging partway along the bridge's famous arch.

Far below now, ferries and pleasure craft squirt about like ducks on Sydney Harbour. Jet boats carve patterns on the water and, the morning I was on the bridge, an enormous cargo ship sailed beneath us, blasting its horns as it went, accompanied by tugboats like a shark surrounded by remoras. The airspace was only marginally less busy, filled with planes and helicopters, a few of which buzzed low overhead, almost giving us a haircut.

As you slowly ascend the famous arch, with the city and Opera House gradually shrinking below, you're witness to arguably the most impressive and famous urban outlook in Australia, but they're scenes often overwritten by history and stories. Instead of 70-storey buildings, there's the memory of a three-storey high midden that the First Fleet observed near Bennelong Point, and of the stream that flowed down what is now Pitt St (and which remains beneath the street), where Gadigal People gathered to eat, drink and socialise. The Opera House almost morphs into the sails of the First Fleet ships when you're immersed in this narrative.

They are tales told by a First Nations guide or 'storyteller', who on my day here was Quandamooka woman Shona. 'Sydney has a very dark history, but it's also a beautiful history,' she said.

Though the stories span thousands of years, the early days of European settlement fill the bulk of the narrative, from the early, hopeful years of contact to the wars that followed.

They are stories populated by familiar historical figures such as Bennelong, Barangaroo and Pemulwuy, the Bidjigal warrior who spent 12 years fighting the invaders for his land and people.

Reaching the top of the bridge, 134m above sea level, you suitably stop beneath the Australian and Aboriginal flags, and the Gadigal People's creation story for the Parramatta River is told.

The bridge is crossed here, in readiness to descend on the opposite side, and there's a moment to pause and savour this most heady of views. The city rises like a series of toy towers, and traffic blurs past 85m below your feet. Luna Park grins crazily across the water, and the Blue Mountains smudge the horizon. Other BridgeClimb groups shuffle up and down the bridge, but having now undertaken both climbs – Burrawa and the Summit climb – I'm convinced it's not the view that's the most memorable thing here. It's the insight of Burrawa, seemingly returning Sydney/Warrang to the place it was 250 years ago and beyond.

Sydney's BridgeClimb might be the original and most famous in the land, but it isn't Australia's only bridge climb. In Perth/Boorloo, you can scale Matagarup Bridge (and zip-line off; *see* p.157), while the Story Bridge Adventure Climb ascends to the top of Brisbane/Meanjin's 74m-high signature bridge.

Top Sydney's finest view of the Opera House *Opposite* Dwarfed by iconic structures

See Sydney/Warrang at its most dazzling, lit by the dawn sun, from the seat of a kayak.

Kayaking, Sydney Harbour
Gadigal Country

WHY IT'S SPECIAL

At 5am, Sydney Harbour is like a freeze-frame image of itself. As the city slumbers and first light leaks across the sky, the only traffic on the water is often a small fleet of kayaks setting out silently from a tiny beach in Lavender Bay. For kayakers, this is the most beautiful time of day on the harbour, and also the safest. Sydney/Warrang's ferries have yet to begin their day, and if the dawn conditions are calm – as they customarily are – the city and Harbour Bridge will likely be admiring their own reflections in the harbour. The only thing that stirs is the water around your paddle.

On Sydney by Kayak dawn tours, the scarcity of harbour traffic means there's the chance to paddle beneath the bridge, peering up to the deck of one of Australia's iconic structures. Across the water, the bridge's companion piece, the Sydney Opera House, rises in white waves.

I'd always thought that my favourite views of this city came from atop the bridge, but paddling beneath it caused me to wonder – seeing the city centre, the underbelly of the bridge and the Opera House from this low angle might well be my new favourite perspective.

Where
Tours depart from the boat ramp in Lavender Bay, near the end of Lavender Crescent, immediately across the harbour from The Rocks.

When
Sydney by Kayak's 2hr Sunrise & Coffee kayaking tours run daily.

Do it
Kayaking trips are run by Sydney by Kayak. Book online (sydneybykayak.com.au).

Fitness: ●●●○○

Fear factor: ●●○○○

Expertise required ●●○○○

Family friendly

Above **Dawn calm** *Opposite* **Paddling beneath the Harbour Bridge**

THE ADVENTURE

On the shores of Lavender Bay, just 1km as the fish swims from the Sydney Harbour Bridge, the approaching day is still a rumour as kayakers fit lifejackets, grab paddles and (most importantly at this time of morning) fit pre-ordered travel mugs of coffee into holders set into the small kayaks that line a sliver of beach beside the boat ramp.

One by one, the kayaks slide into the dark water and the equally dark morning, weaving through the bay's yacht moorings and into one of Australia's most famous urban scenes. Kayaking beneath the empty gangway of the McMahons Point ferry terminal, the kayaks gather in a loose group beside Blues Point, with the landmark Blues Point Tower rising above. When this 25-storey apartment block was built in 1962, it was the tallest residential building in Australia, and though it's heritage-listed, it's often been called Sydney/Warrang's ugliest building. But on mornings in a kayak, this point often also has the city's best view.

As the kayaks pause (and if cloud permits), the sun rises over the pylons of the Harbour Bridge, with the spiked hairdo of the Sydney Opera House crouched beneath. As the first rays catch the windows of the Opera House, igniting them like flares, you can't help but feel that you're being treated to a rare and unique moment. The morning I was here, a fog rolled down the Parramatta River, covering and uncovering the city in cloud. Skyscrapers peeped above the fog and were then blotted from view.

The kayaks used are small recreational kayaks – singles rather than the doubles traditionally used on kayaking tours – that are easily manoeuvrable, and it's a quick crossing from Blues Point towards the dawn yawn of Luna Park's entrance gate. From here, it's just a few paddle strokes until you're beneath one of the world's most famous bridges, its traffic deck 49m overhead and its famous arch reaching to 134m. Dimpled with six million rivets, the 52,800-tonne bridge features not a single weld.

Left Settling into sunrise

Kayaking, Sydney Harbour

Popping back out of the bridge's shadow, you paddle on to Kirribilli Point, drifting around the point to pause beneath Admiralty House and Kirribilli House, the Sydney/Warrang residences of the governor-general and prime minister, respectively.

Often, the water around the low Kirribilli cliffs is also the home of turtles, while the Martello tower of Fort Denison casts an ominous silhouette on the horizon. Here, and at various other stops, the kayaking guides spin tales, fast facts and figures about this incredible city and harbour, from the laundry that occupies the penthouse space in Blues Point Tower, to the story of Vincent Kelly, the riveter who somehow survived a fall from the Sydney Harbour Bridge during its construction.

Returning towards Lavender Bay, the kayaks edge along the shores and back beneath the bridge. The first ferries of the day are waking from their slumber, and now crisscross the harbour as you paddle back across Lavender Bay, a small inlet known to the Dharug People as Gooweebahree, a name believed to mean 'freshwater'. The name is a record of the Traditional Owners' long connection to the area, referring to a spring that poured from the ground here before the bay was covered by the sea after the last Ice Age.

Turn around in the kayak and take a final look at the city as it now rubs the sleep from its eyes and begins its day. See the bridge seemingly holding two lands together, the bar graph of city towers, and the galah-like crest of the Opera House. The city has never woken looking better.

> To venture further into Sydney/Warrang's waterways by kayak, there are a couple of good options. Set out from Middle Harbour, hiring a kayak or joining a tour with Sydney Harbour Kayaks (sydneyharbourkayaks.com.au) to watch the urban sprawl slip behind as you paddle into bush-tangled Garigal National Park. Further afield, set out on the Hawkesbury River (scene of the annual, two-day, 111km Hawkesbury Classic Paddle), paddling between riverside campsites or to the likes of the Berowra Inn for a degustation lunch. Hire single and double kayaks from Hawkesbury River Kayaks (hawkesburyriverkayaks.com.au).

Right Contemplative moments under the Harbour Bridge

Kayaking, Sydney Harbour

Hike, swim, leap and abseil your way through the Blue Mountains's most accessible canyon.

Canyoning, Blue Mountains

Dharug and Gundungurra Country

WHY IT'S SPECIAL

If any single natural feature defines the Blue Mountains, it's canyons. The soft sandstone of the World Heritage–listed range at Sydney/Warrang's western edge is fractured and split by around 900 slot canyons, turning the 'Blueys' into Australia's premier canyoning destination. Many of these canyons are committing, challenging endeavours (or ordeals, depending on your perspective), but some yield more easily. Empress Canyon is prime among the latter.

There's no better introductory canyon in Australia than this short and narrow chasm. It has every feature you want of a canyoning trip – scrambling along rock walls, swimming, leaping into pools, dramatic beauty and a 30m abseil beside and through a waterfall. Empress is also one of the shortest canyons in the Blue Mountains – around 500m in length – and one of the most accessible, reached along a popular walking trail out of Wentworth Falls, making it one of the few canyons you can complete in half a day.

The most popular canyoning outing in the Blue Mountains, Empress shot to even greater prominence in late 2022 when Zac Efron's 'Down to Earth' Netflix series featured the canyon in the first episode of its second season.

For all that, Empress Canyon is still a technical route, particularly the concluding abseil, so for all but experienced canyoners a guided trip is the only safe way through. It's an experience that's both cold and cool: it's scrambling meets walking meets rockpool swimming meets the high diving board.

Where
Guided canyoning trips typically depart from Katoomba, 100km west of Sydney/Warrang. Katoomba can be reached on Sydney/Warrang's suburban rail network.

When
Empress Canyon is a wet and cold canyon, and guided trips run from around Sept to April.

Do it
Blue Mountains Adventure Company (bmac.com.au) runs daily trips into Empress Canyon, along with a range of other Blue Mountains canyons.

Fitness: ●●●○○

Fear factor: ●●●●○

Expertise required
●○○○○ (for guided trips)
●●●●● (independent trips)

Opposite The long way down: Empress Falls

THE ADVENTURE

Empress Canyon has become such a popular canyoning route that the NSW National Parks and Wildlife Service now assigns time slots to commercial groups heading into the canyon. These slots are in the early afternoon, so guided groups spend the morning on abseil instruction, learning or practicing the techniques and trust of lowering yourself down a cliff on a rope. Options vary, but the morning might begin with a gentle 5m abseil, building up to a 30m drop off an adjoining cliff. Confidence invariably comes quickly – by the third abseil of my visit, it had turned into races: two people on ropes side by side, plunging in a controlled descent.

The walk to the canyon begins at the edge of the Wentworth Falls township, from where it's a steep 30min descent to Lillian's Glen. Here, beneath an overhang beside the stream, canyoners change into wetsuits, harnesses and helmets, and the real fun begins.

On the day I was here, water poured fast into the canyon after recent rain, though even in dry times there are flows here, with water seeping out of sponge-like 'hanging swamps' on the slopes above.

Entering the canyon is a literal leap of faith. A few steps inside its narrowing cliffs and you come to the first jump. It's around 3m in height, but with a rock in the water that has to be cleared. The best way to take this leap is backwards, facing back up the canyon and springing so that you splash into the pool on your back.

The first section of the canyon continues in this vein – leap, wade, walk. Rinse and repeat. The canyon is so narrow that above one pool you can make a bridging manoeuvre, with your feet on one cliff and your hands against the other, before pushing off to leap into the next pool downstream.

Each pool and jump requires a short swim, typically laying on your back and using your backpack as a virtual flotation aid. It's a position that has the twin benefit of directing your gaze high through the canyon, where the cliffs all but pinch the sky shut.

It's an energetic and exciting start, but soon enough you're stepping out into a wider section of the canyon – and perhaps into a brief moment of sunlight – at so-called Heapy Beach. In the early days of Blue Mountains' tourism, a wooden boardwalk extended down to this point of the canyon, and above the small beach there's still the name of 'Mr and Mrs Heapy' scratched into the cliffs.

Empress is very much a journey in three parts, and this point marks the end of the first section. Most of the leaps from pool to pool are done – the early moments of chaos are over – and for a time the canyon relents, flattening and slowing. It becomes a gentle wade downstream to the top of Empress Falls, a chance to slow and absorb the surrounds. The cliffs are covered in moss, with ferns sprouting from them and the likes of sassafras trees straining towards the distant sunlight. These trees are remnants of Gondwanan forests that were here when dinosaurs roamed the land.

Look up and you'll see a footbridge straddling the canyon. This is Lillian's Bridge, part of the popular walking trail down to the base of Empress Falls, and itself a remnant of the Blue Mountains' early settler activity – the bridge's handrails are made from the tramway tracks that ran through here to a coal mine in the 19th century.

It's at Empress Falls that this canyon, named for Queen Victoria, has its crowning moment, and the third, most challenging, part of the canyon begins. To exit the canyon, you must abseil 30m beside and through the waterfall. At its top, secured to two ropes, you step out from an overhang, a tricky first manoeuvre before an airy drop onto a ledge a few metres below. From here, you join the flow of the waterfall, descending as it thunders onto your helmet and shoulders, filling your vision with water as your feet try to maintain purchase on a cliff as slippery as ice. It's a far trickier abseil than anything in the morning's practice runs, but it's also more exciting. Stand and watch from the pool's edge below and it can look like drunken manoeuvres, as feet slip and bodies twist and crunch into the cliffs, though always held safely by the rope and the belayer above.

Dropping into the pool, you begin to unclip the ropes as you tread water. And then it's over and your body calls for warmth – a sunny spot to help counter the darkness and chill of the short canyon – ahead of the climb back to the carpark.

Above Wading through Empress Canyon *Opposite* Abseiling through Empress Falls

If the canyoning bug bites after this fun descent through Empress Canyon, as it often does, there's good news. There's another 899 or so canyons slicing through the Blue Mountains. Other slots revered among canyoners include Twister and Rocky Creek canyons (typically done together in one trip), Grand Canyon and the more challenging Claustral Canyon and Butterbox Canyon.

Turn the concept of a cable car on its head by climbing out onto its roof, suspended above a 270m drop.

Beyond Skyway, Blue Mountains

Dharug and Gundungarra Country

WHY IT'S SPECIAL

Cable-car rides have their own shock value – these virtual tin cans that hang in the air above chasmic drops, held aloft by a thread of cable. Now imagine climbing out of a cable car and standing atop its roof, with a drop almost the height of the Eiffel Tower beneath you. The wind is likely blowing, and the cable car sways in the breeze. What you're imagining is Beyond Skyway.

Strung between escarpments in the World Heritage–listed Blue Mountains, and staring out over the Jamison Valley and the Blue Mountains' signature Three Sisters, Scenic Skyway was Australia's first cable car (opened in 1958) and remains the largest aerial cable car in the Southern Hemisphere.

Most visitors are content to stay inside its confines, taking in the views from behind the windows, but the more exposed and exciting Beyond Skyway experience will have you harnessed and climbing through a manhole in the ceiling and seemingly hovering above the valleys, waterfalls and cliffs of the Blue Mountains as you wander about on the roof. It's far from just another day in the mountains.

Where
Scenic World sits at the edge of Katoomba, 100km east of Sydney/Warrang.

When
Beyond Skyway runs three times a day.

Do it
Book Beyond Skyway and other Scenic World tickets online (scenicworld.com.au).

Fitness: ●○○○○

Fear factor: ●●●●○

Expertise required ●○○○○

Opposite Suspended reality atop Scenic Skyway

THE ADVENTURE

Inside the Scenic World building, which clings to the cliff-edge in Katoomba, harnesses and helmets are fitted before glass doors slide back and you step inside the Scenic Skyway cable car. Moments later, it begins inching across the valley, floating low over ferns before the earth suddenly tumbles away below.

The Scenic Skyway cable car line stretches for 384m between cliffs, but on this journey it stops halfway between stations, where a hatch in the ceiling is popped open. The true adventure begins after the guide concludes preparations and you and the others in the group are harnessed and ascend a garden-variety ladder through the hatch, stepping out onto the roof of the cable car, with one of the Blue Mountains' most recognisable scenes laid out like a canvas before you. The Three Sisters protrude from the escarpment like horns, Mount Solitary stands, well, solitary, beyond the Jamison Valley, and Katoomba Falls pours over the escarpment immediately below the cable car. Near to hand also is Orphan Rock, now an almost forgotten Blue Mountains feature, though it was once more famous than the Three Sisters – look around Katoomba and you'll notice its image etched into old windows.

With your harness tethered to the cable, you can step right up to the edge of the cable car, as well as walk around it – the roof is carpeted for greater grip. If you're feeling brave, you can also lean out over the edge, poised above the valley and view.

The view is a dynamic one. As I stood at the edge, a man stepped out onto the rock shelf at the base of Katoomba Falls and stripped to his underwear, the water thumping into his shoulders and head. Further around the cliffs, a pair of rock climbers ascended a route known as Wally World, a grade 22 climb that's one of the most revered in the area. Suddenly this standing-atop-a-cable-car thing didn't seem quite so crazy in comparison.

The most challenging view is down, with the Kedumba River and surrounding rainforest a vertiginous 270m beneath the cable car. This is twice the height of the Sydney Harbour Bridge – so far down that it's like looking onto broccoli florets rather than trees.

'I've skydived, and this is more frightening,' the woman standing beside me muttered as she peered over the edge.

Right Hanging out above the Jamison Valley

Beyond Skyway, Blue Mountains

'Ask any engineer and you're safer out here than almost anywhere back there on land,' guide Peter explained. The Skyway's cable has a breaking strain of 189 tonnes, and even fully loaded with 85 people, the cable car weighs no more than 19 tonnes. On the Beyond Skyway tour, only five people – four visitors and one guide – are in and on the cable car.

Standing here, you are at the whim of the weather, which is fickle and fluky in the mountains. Ten minutes before I stepped into the cable car, a powerful hailstorm blew through, chased by a rainbow arching into the valley – the full heavenly welcome. But by the time we'd climbed onto Skyway's roof, the wind had eased to a breeze that gently rocked the cable car. In higher winds, the experience can be like surfing on air. 'I've seen this get to about a 45-degree angle,' Peter said. On this trip, on this cable, however, a rocking cable car is just as safe as a motionless one, so enjoy the ride.

Like most good adventures, this one involves a thermos. Atop the cable car, hot chocolates are poured, and a mug is tethered to your wrist by an elastic strap – it may be the airiest place in which you've ever drunk a hot chocolate.

By the time you're sipping chocolate goodness on the evening tour, the sun will have set. As twilight edges towards night, lights along the walking paths flicker into life, and it's like looking into a glow-worm grotto. Flood-lighting illuminates Katoomba Falls, Orphan Rock and the Three Sisters and, in between them all, a cable car hangs suspended like an eye in the sky. For a final few minutes, it remains the best view for kilometres.

Above The view down onto Katoomba Falls *Opposite top* Hot chocolate in the sky *Opposite bottom* Eye to eye with the Blue Mountains cliffs

Head to the Northern Hemisphere and cable cars are prolific, running like zippers up and down mountains but, outside of ski fields, they are rare accessories to the landscape in Australia. There are chairlifts such as the one at Launceston's Cataract Gorge and gondolas like Arthurs Seat in Victoria, but the only other major cable car is Skyrail (skyrail.com.au), skimming over the top of the World Heritage-listed Wet Tropics rainforest as it climbs from Cairns/Gimuy's northern suburbs to the Atherton Tablelands town of Kuranda. The 7.5km cable car can be combined with a return journey on the Kuranda Scenic Railway.

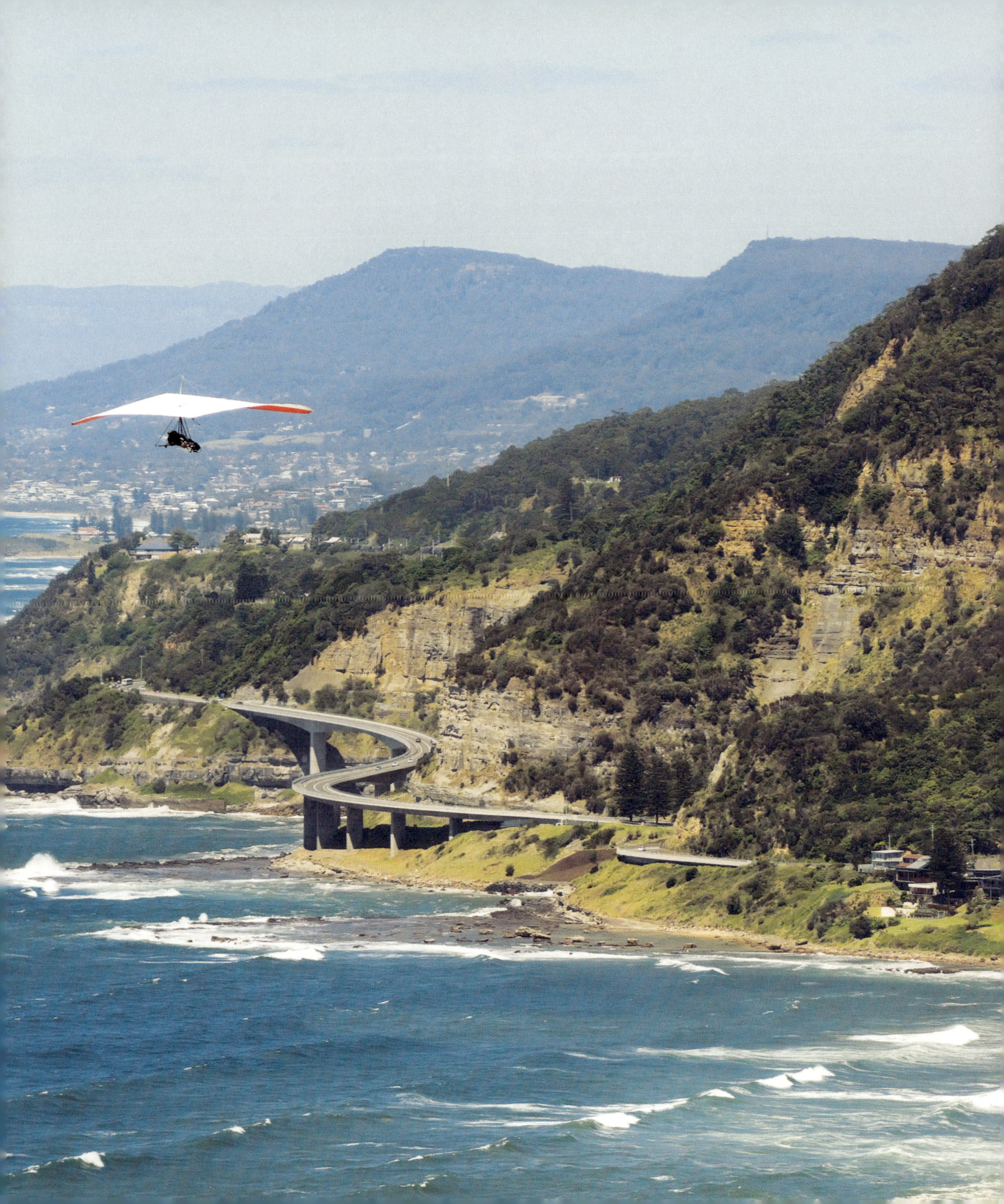

Soar like a bird on a tandem flight at one of the world's great coastal hang gliding sites.

Hang gliding, Bald Hill

Wodi Wodi Country

WHY IT'S SPECIAL

Among hang gliders, there's a reverence to the name Bald Hill. When the winds are blowing through the Illawarra at around 15 knots from between the south and east, there's almost no better site on the planet at which to take to the sky.

From the moment the wind lifts you off the grassy hilltop, until the final seconds of flight as you're swirling down towards Stanwell Park Beach, it's all beauty, silence and grace, gliding hundreds of metres above the Pacific Ocean and coast.

There's no more personal way to fly than on a hang glider, and getting airborne is simple, with tandem flights delivering all of the thrill with none of the requirement to know what you're doing. Clipped to an experienced pilot, you can literally take wing from this celebrated hill for a god-like view of a gorgeous slice of coast. The only disappointing bit might be the return to earth.

Where
Bald Hill is at the northern end of Stanwell Park, 60km south of Sydney/Warrang and 35km north of Wollongong.

When
Flights are dictated by wind speed and direction, with hang gliders able to fly at Bald Hill in around 10 to 25 knots of wind, blowing from the south to east. Weekends can be very busy with flyers and spectators, with up to 60 hang gliders and paragliders in the air, so weekdays are a good time for tandem flights.

Do it
Tandem hang-gliding flights can be arranged through HangglideOZ (hangglideoz.com.au).

Fitness: ●○○○○

Fear factor: ●●●○○

Expertise required ●○○○○

Opposite A glider's-eye view of Sea Cliff Bridge

THE ADVENTURE

On a fine weekend at Bald Hill, there's traffic on the roads and in the air. Cars spill beyond the large carpark, and the sky can be filled with dozens of hang gliders and paragliders. The parachute-like paragliders swirl and swing like pendulums, carving patterns across the sky. Beside them, hang gliders look so large – the alpha birds in the sky. Step to the edge of the hill and you're looking down onto the rooftops and beach of Stanwell Park, a small coastal surfing town set beneath an amphitheatre of hills, but in just a few minutes you'll be looking down at them from an even greater height.

Preparations for take-off are reassuringly quick – you're ready to fly as soon as you're fitted into a flying harness and helmet – giving you little time to ponder the 300m of air about to yawn open beneath you.

Amid a customary crowd of spectators, you step over the triangular control bar of the hang glider, and your harness is clipped to the frame (with a second strap also clipped to the frame as an additional safety line). A looped strap hangs off each hip of the pilot beside you, with your hands each gripping a loop. The skies await.

If the idea of hang gliding creates visions of hurling yourself off a cliff-edge at the end of a mad sprint, let Bald Hill ease your mind. This hill's great gift to flyers is its position and rounded shape. Its bald summit, ringed by bush, and round profile create excellent airflows, while it also faces a number of different directions for launch, making it possible to take off in a wider range of winds than at most sites. Often, as on the day I was here, it's a simple matter of taking three strides and the wind has lifted you from the earth. With the wind blowing against the hill, deflecting upwards, you're quickly soaring into the air. You're a bird now.

Even when the wind is whipping at you on Bald Hill, it seems to disappear once you're airborne, as the hang glider sails on its currents. As the world drops away beneath your feet, cliffs appear below, with small, rounded beaches seemingly scooped into them. A wrecked car lies mangled in the bush and, away to the south, the instantly recognisable, 665m-long Sea Cliff Bridge wriggles along the cliffs. Offshore, you peer down into turquoise shallows and rockpools as intricate as artworks. Once up in the air, you reach down with your left hand and release a metal bar, onto which you place your feet, trailing them behind you as you skate across the sky.

In the coastal winds, the flight is surprisingly smooth, due to a combination of conditions and the experience of pilots like Tony Armstrong. The owner of locally based HangglideOZ, Tony has been flying at Bald Hill for 43 years, and operating tandem flights for 41 years. He once flew a hang glider 400km (still well shy of the world-record flight of 764km) and was a footnote to a Guinness World Record when he took 94-year-old Veronica Adams on a flight, making her the oldest person to ever tandem hang glide. To a pilot like Tony, a few loops around the Illawarra coastline is a figurative breeze.

Each flight is unique – you might circle near the hill to begin, or glide out to sea – but once you're comfortable in the air, Tony releases the bar and you can have a short time controlling the glider, turning your body to steer it, pushing the bar down to gain speed.

'Faster, faster, faster,' Tony calls, until the bar is almost in against your stomach and you're angling in towards the land or ocean like a diving seabird.

Much of the flight will be spent over the top of Stanwell Park, where rooftops turn to LEGO blocks. Among the waves the waves rolling into Stanwell Park Beach, surfers resemble colourful turtles. What else these 20min in the air bring is random luck. The day I was here, a white-bellied sea eagle flew directly beneath us, followed later by the larger, more imposing figure of a military helicopter.

The hang glider soars and dips almost imperceptibly until you begin to prepare for the landing, making ribbon-like turns as you swoop down towards Stanwell Park Beach. Beside a lagoon, you finally straighten and plump gently down onto the sand at its edge. It's as casual as a bird landing.

Bald Hill might be considered Australia's top hang-gliding site, but there are other locations where you can take to the sky. Rex Point Lookout, north of Cairns/Gimuy, is a favourite launch site, with tandem flights available through Air Play Hang Gliding (airplayhanggliding.com.au). Other hang-gliding locations with tandem flights include Byron Bay and the Gold Coast Hinterland. Tandem paragliding flights are also available at Bright in Victoria and the Great Ocean Road.

Few people will want to tangle with them, but one of the great hang-gliding sights in Australia is the turbulent Morning Glory clouds that roll in across the Gulf of Carpentaria around Oct; they're legendary among gliders.

Top and opposite Coasting, in every sense

Hang gliding, Bald Hill

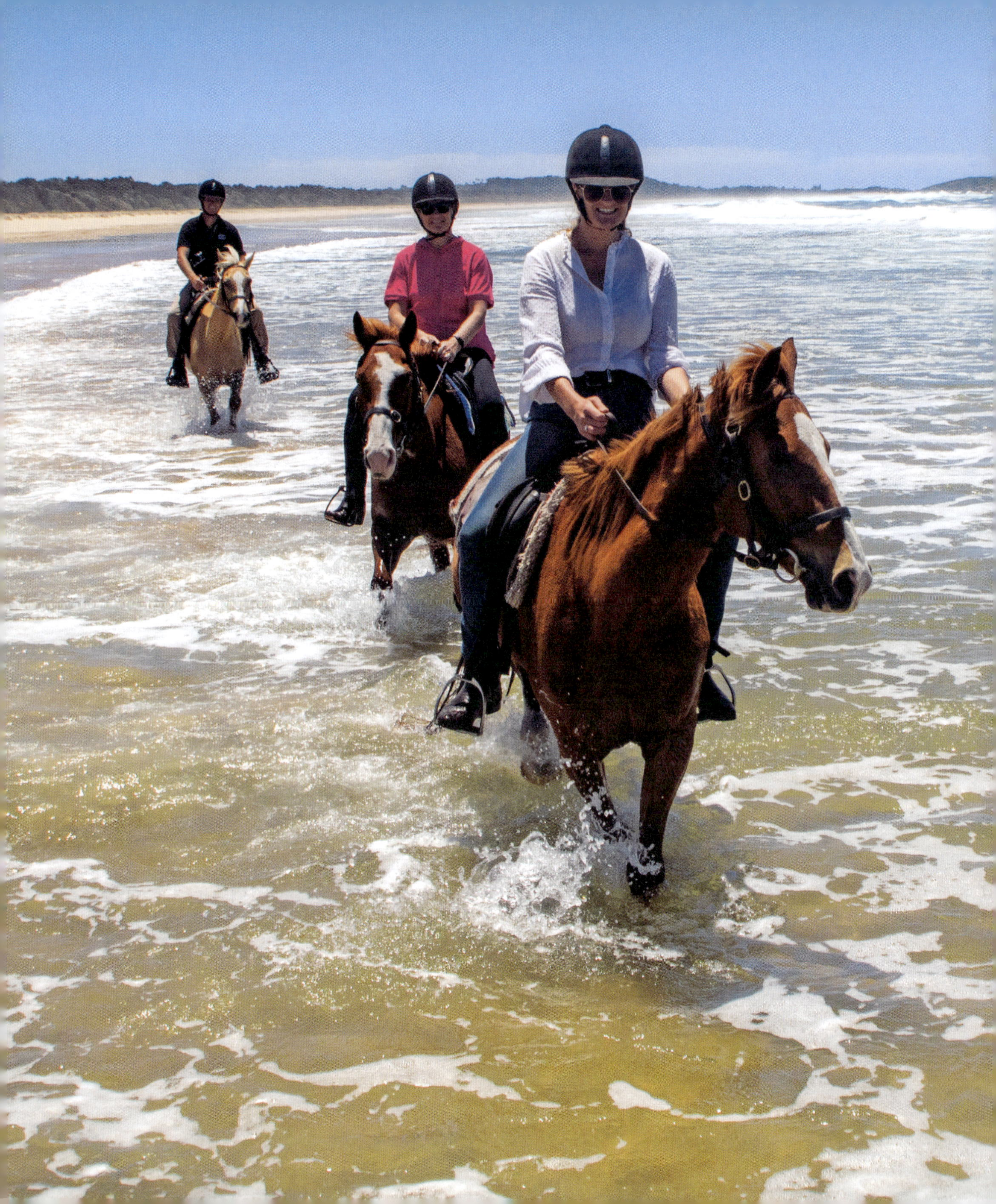

Discover the freedom of a horse ride along a Coffs Harbour beach, through the surf and into a beautiful lagoon.

Horse riding, Boambee Beach

Gumbaynggirr Country

WHY IT'S SPECIAL

There are lifelong horse riders who still get starry-eyed at the mention of a beach ride – the surf rolling in, sand rising in white clouds from the hooves of their mount. And yet it's something every rider, skilled or novice, can experience on Boambee Beach at the southern edge of Coffs Harbour.

This 7km-long beach is the idyllic backdrop for trail rides with HWH Stables. The sand is the trail and the water is the playground, with horses encouraged into the surf and the clear waters of the lagoon at the mouth of Boambee Creek. Unlike many trail rides, which compel you to ride in single file, follow-the-leader style, the beach setting gives you the liberty to wander in and out of the sea, to trot or canter at will, and to choose your own sandy course to the end of the beach.

Where
Boambee Beach is at the southern edge of Coffs Harbour, 540km north of Sydney/Warrang and 385km south of Brisbane/Meanjin.

When
HWH Stables' beach rides run year-round.

Do it
Beach rides range from one hour to 3.5 hours, with the longer ride including the lagoon dip in Boambee Creek. Sunrise and sunset beach rides are also available. HWH Stables also runs a 'River Ride' along the Urumbilum River, with riders able to jump directly from their saddle into the water for a swim. Book online (hwhstables.com.au).

Fitness: ●●○○○

Fear factor: ●●○○○

Expertise required ●○○○○

Family friendly

Above Cantering on the beach *Opposite* Walking through the shallows

THE ADVENTURE

Boambee Beach reaches its northern finish beside the prominent Corambirra Point near the centre of Coffs Harbour, and it's here that rides begin, clopping down a short access track onto its sands. A World War II observation bunker sits propped on a low hill above, and 7km of sand stretches out ahead.

Part of the thrill of riding on an east coast beach is the presence of surf – an ocean of water throwing itself towards your horse – and instead of turning along the beach you'll likely step straight towards the sea. Invariably, it rolls ashore in lines of whitecapped waves, breaking before you, water rising to the knees of your horse. It's a chance for both you and the animal to become accustomed to this uncommon trail-riding element.

Turning back to the sand, the journey begins, and it's one that will take you the length of Boambee Beach, a wide white strip of sand that's all things to all people: 4WD track, off-lead dog beach, and now horse trail. Stretching behind it is Coffs Harbour's airport, from where RAAF jets spiralled noisily into the sky on the day I rode down the beach.

At the head of the mob, and moving gracefully around it, will be Chris Fenech, the owner of HWH Stables, who returned to his hometown of Coffs Harbour a decade ago after 14 years working as a manager on Kimberley stations El Questro and Home Valley. Though he didn't grow up among horses, Fenech says he always gravitated to the animals and, at age 15, using money earned from part-time jobs, purchased his first horse at saleyards in Sydney. When the seller asked him which float to put the horse in, Chris shrugged – he'd travelled to the sale by train. It would be a year before his parents even knew he'd bought the horse.

Today, Fenech has 10 horses in the HWH stable, each one with its own personality and quirks. My mount was Brandy, a former harness racer that Fenech purchased from a slaughterhouse, and now the leader of the herd. I'm no horseman, but with the slightest bit of rein work and a squeeze of the heels, we were soon trotting gently, even as more experienced riders burst out of the group intermittently like jockeys entering a home straight.

This autonomy to trot or canter off the front, returning and settling back into walking pace, is one of the great delights of the ride, equalled only by the occasional venture into the water. Surf conditions obviously vary, but this day waves were soon splashing around us as we stepped out into the sea several times.

Above Lagoon dip in Boambee Creek *Opposite* Boambee Beach

The best dip, however, is at the very end of the beach, where Boambee Creek flows out into the ocean beneath Boambee Headland. The estuary is an inviting blue-green lagoon – the sort of vivid colour on which a tropical resort would market itself – and it presents the most confronting and memorable moment of the ride. From the beach, the horses step into a shallow ledge of water, and then down off the ledge into the main body of the creek. Water rises to the horses' chests, submerging your feet and shins. You'll likely emerge dripping wet but, hey, you've just been in a lagoon with a horse. What's not to like?

The pace picks up as you retrace your hoof prints back along Boambee Beach, with the horses knowing this is now their home straight. Partway along the beach, the ride turns off the sand, heading in behind the dunes to a path through the coastal scrub. At times this trail is a wide set of wheel tracks; other times it narrows to the equivalent of a mountain-bike singletrack.

Ducking beneath branches and dodging around trees that intrude over the track, the ride slowly returns towards Coffs Harbour. Goannas skitter into the bush, cockatoos creak in the distance, and there's one tree that's become known to Chris as the 'barking owl tree' for the regularity with which he's spotted the namesake bird sitting in it. The ocean is now a sound rather than a sight, but this day that you saddled up by the sea will be long lodged in your memory.

> The quintessential Australian companion piece to a beach horse ride is a High Country horse ride, as immortalised by *The Man from Snowy River* poem and movies. Fittingly, many of the trail rides on offer in the High Country focus on locations from the films, such as the famously steep jump scene and Craig's Hut, the cattlemen's hut built as a film set on the slopes of Mount Stirling in Victoria. High Country trail-ride operators include Watsons' Mountain Country Trail Rides (watsonstrailrides.com.au) and McCormacks Mountain Valley Trail Rides (mountainvalleytrailrides.com.au).

Horse riding, Boambee Beach

Paddle with a First Nations guide to a beautiful beach with an equally compelling Gumbaynggirr story.

Stand-up paddleboarding, Solitary Islands Marine Park

Gumbaynggirr Country

WHY IT'S SPECIAL

Moonee Beach might once have been named Australia's finest mainland beach in the annual 101 Best Australian Beaches list, but there are things here that are far more significant than what meets the eye. It's only as you paddle towards the mouth of Moonee Creek with Gumbaynggirr guide Clark Webb, skimming over fish and sting rays on a stand-up paddleboard (SUP), that you realise that behind this beauty there are stories just as spectacular – creation stories that speak of the momentous nature of this very spot. As you step off the board onto the beach, you're suddenly aware that you are walking on more than sand.

Moonee Creek forms part of the Solitary Islands Marine Park, north of Coffs Harbour, the estuaries of which are described by the NSW National Parks and Wildlife Service as among the most pristine in the state. To this impressive natural history can be added an equally significant cultural history. And while the origins of SUPing are typically credited to Hawaii, Webb quickly contends that the first stand-up paddlers might have been closer to home.

'Who were the first people to stand-up paddle?' he asks. 'Australia has the oldest cultures in the world, and we made canoes in which you could sit or stand. So, we were the original stand-up paddlers.'

This is unquestionably a special place to paddle.

Where
Moonee Creek is 15km north of Coffs Harbour, 550km north of Sydney/Warrang and 370km south of Brisbane/Meanjin. There are direct flights to Coffs Harbour from Sydney and Melbourne.

When
Trip times and locations are determined by the tides, with Wajaana Yaam Adventure Tours operating on three local waterways: Moonee Creek, Red Rocks Creek and Coffs Creek.

Do it
Book through Wajaana Yaam Adventure Tours (wajaanayaam.com.au), where you'll also find details of cultural and walking tours.

Fitness: ●●○○○

Fear factor: ●●○○○

Expertise required ●○○○○

Family friendly

Opposite SUPing on Moonee Creek

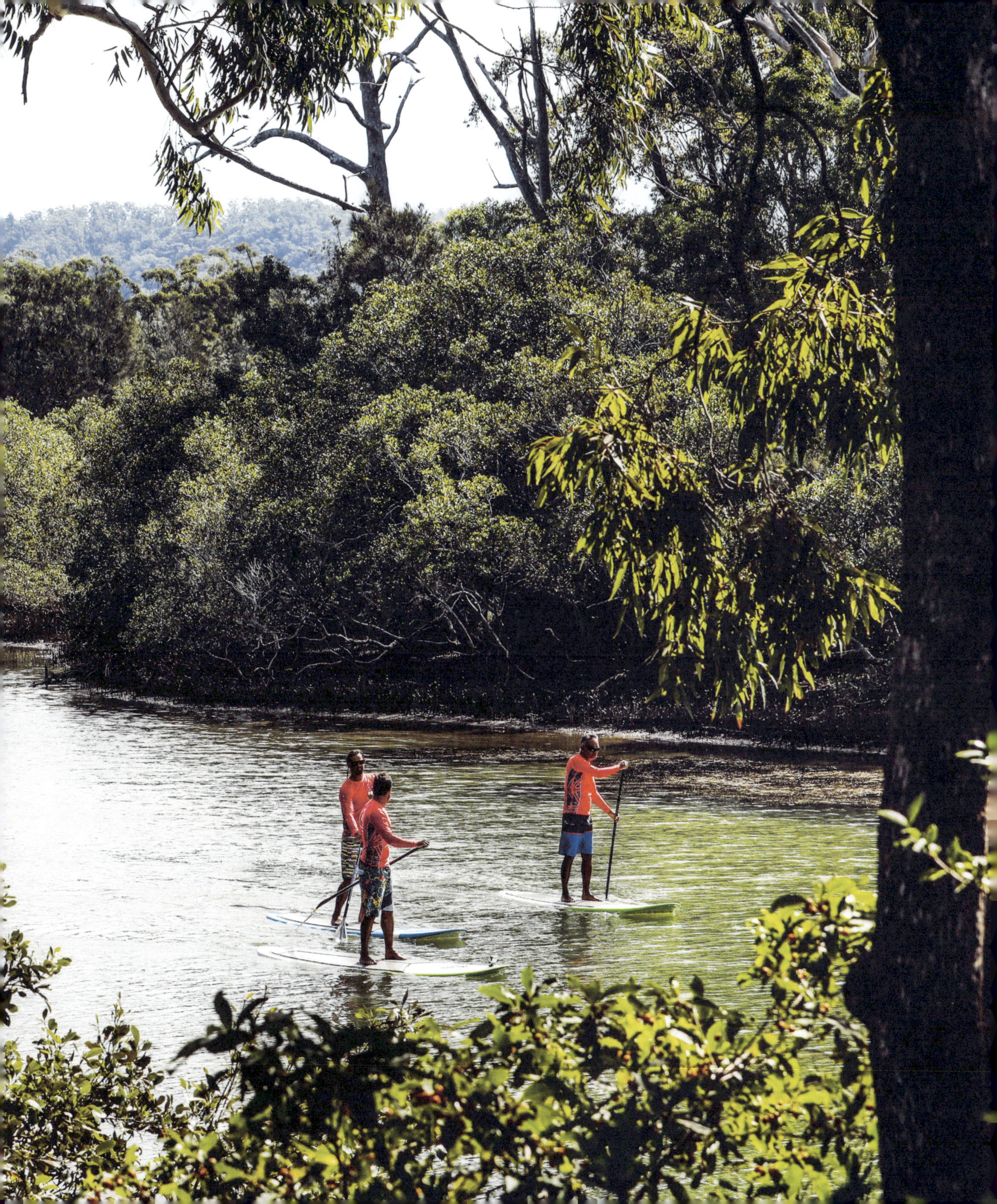

New South Wales & ACT

THE ADVENTURE

On the bank of Moonee Creek, prior to taking to the water, Clark Webb taps his SUP and makes the declaration that 'this is a cultural tour on modern equipment'. It's a promise well fulfilled over the coming couple of hours, with stories and knowledge flowing as easily as the stream on which the SUPs will travel.

Typically, the creek is swollen with high tide when trips begin – at low tide, Moonee Creek can suck almost dry – and from a boat ramp at the edge of a housing estate (your send-off might well be the sound of lawnmowers), you glide out into the creek on your knees before rising to your feet and beginning the paddle downstream. Moonee Creek is usually placid, flowing sluggishly towards the coast, and it takes little time to get your balance, even with the forces of wind and tide at play. From the first moments of paddling out on your knees, you're quickly up on your feet, with the gentle flow doing little to rock this particular boat. Unlike SUPing in surf or on fast-flowing rivers, you can paddle smoothly and focus almost entirely on the surrounds. The banks are lined with mangroves, giving the creek the appearance of a Top End river – you half expect to see crocodiles, even though no crocs exist here. Also along the water are low cliffs of coffee rock, a form of rock composed of sand cemented together by organic matter that filters out the salt from the estuary.

A deep channel carves its way towards the sea, but at its sides, the creek is shallow and clear. Fish dart about beneath the boards, and sting rays lie sprawled on the creek bed. At times it's so shallow that, when I was here, I had to stop paddling at one point so that I didn't accidentally brain a ray that was no more than 30cm beneath my board. Above the water, sea eagles, ibises and cockatoos are often sighted, along with the occasional spoonbill.

The boards weave on downstream, turning through a couple of large bends and beneath trees that have long provided tucker to the Gumbaynggirr People: the paperbarks, with their leaves that can be boiled for bush tea (and their yellow flowers that serve as a cultural indicator, blooming when the mullet are running north looking for warmer waters); the sweetness of the honeysuckle banksia; and the fallen casuarinas, containing a worm with a similar texture to oysters.

Left Board games

A caravan park appears on the right, and an expanse of bush on the left. 'In the 1970s, this area was a big sand mine and they dug up so many artefacts,' Webb says, pointing into the bush. 'I've heard that they even found bones. This whole area is an enormous cultural landscape.'

It's a statement evidenced by signs ahead, near the creek mouth, announcing the presence of a cultural site. In this eroded, sandy spot, discovered by Webb and his cousin in 2015, more than 150 artefacts – tools, axes and the like – have been found, along with human bones, which have been relocated and reburied away from the erosion.

It was two years after this discovery that Webb began his company, Wajaana Yaam Adventure Tours, stirring together adventure activities and culture, and in 2022 it won gold in the Excellence in Aboriginal and Torres Strait Islander Tourism category at the NSW Tourism Awards.

Drifting on past the cultural site, you glide ashore onto Moonee Beach, pinched between the sea and the final sweep of the creek. Waves explode ashore, spraying in steam-like plumes, and you set out wandering a short distance along the beach until Split Solitary Island peeps into view from behind Green Bluff. In the Gumbaynggirr creation story recounted by Webb, Moonee Beach is the spot where two sisters departed on a journey that created the oceans and Australia's coast. The two islands now visible – Split Solitary and the lighthouse-topped South Solitary – are also the place where the sisters rested their digging sticks at the end of their journey, turning to stone and becoming two of the stars in the Pleiades (Seven Sisters) constellation. Geographically, this is also the spot where the warm waters of the East Australian Current meet colder waters from the south, stirring together temperate, tropical and subtropical marine life. It's a significant place in every sense.

Returning to the SUPs, the paddle begins back upstream, skimming over sea grasses and along the depths of the channel. It's a chance to slow and reflect on this journey through the oldest culture in the newest (and yet still oldest) of ways.

Above The mouth of Moonee Creek *Opposite* SUPers prepare to paddle on Moonee Creek

Clark Webb estimates that he's one of only about 20 people who fluently speak the Gumbaynggirr language – 'I've worked hard over about 16 years to learn it', he says – but that's very likely to be on the increase, thanks to a new school in Coffs Harbour. Twenty per cent of Wajaana Yaam Adventure Tours' profits go to the Gumbaynggirr Giingana Freedom School, NSW's first bilingual school of an Aboriginal language, which opened in Coffs Harbour in 2022.

Stand-up paddleboarding, Solitary Islands Marine Park

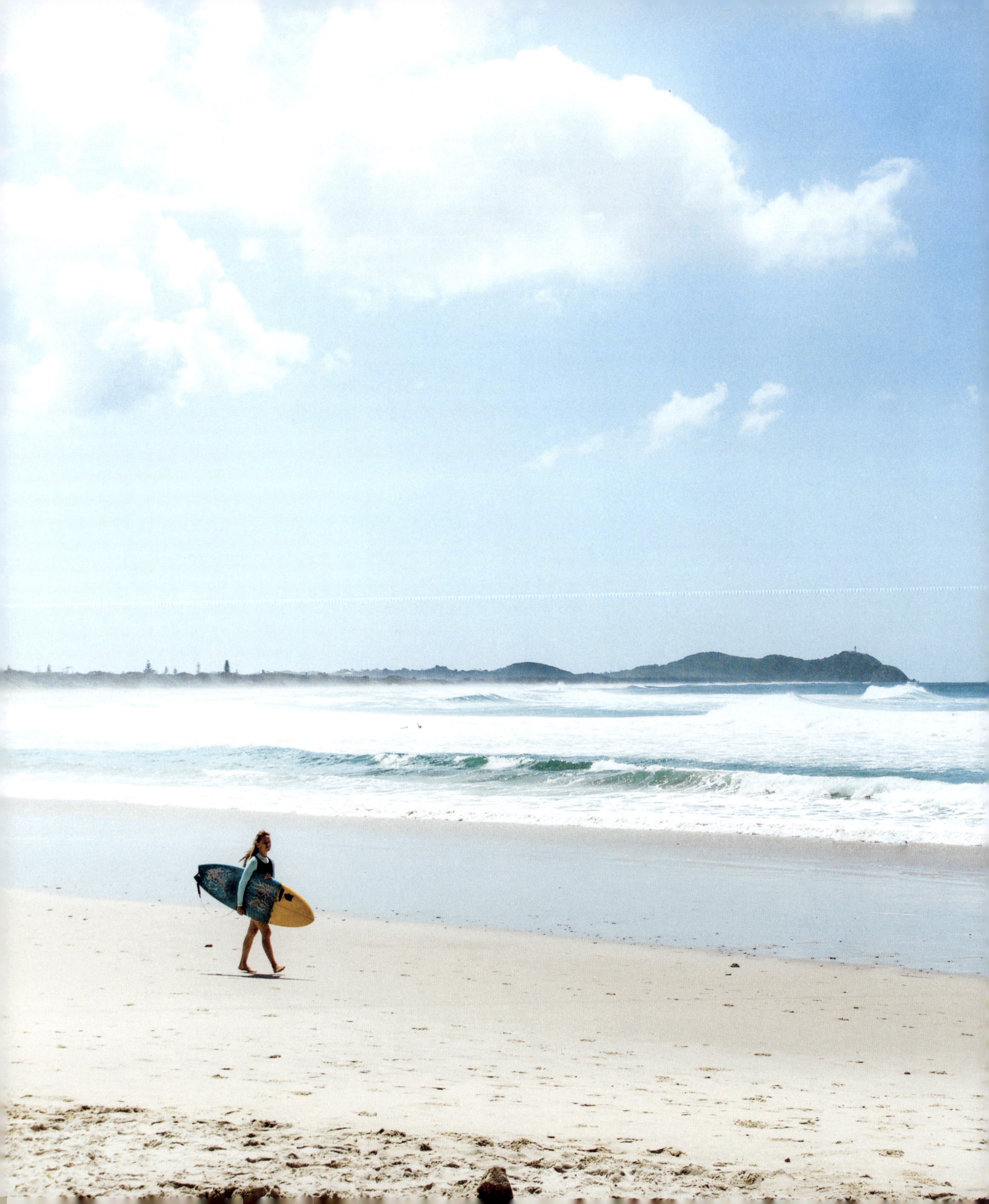

Take to the waves around one of Australia's great surf towns.

Surfing, Byron Bay

Arakwal and Bundjalung Country

Contributed by Louise Southerden

WHY IT'S SPECIAL

There's a lot for a surfer to love about Byron Bay – and the coastline either side of it. There are literally dozens of great surf breaks between Yamba in the south and Tweed Heads to the north, many of which originally put northern NSW on the surfing map back in the 1960s and '70s. But there's something special about 'the Bay', as locals used to call Byron. The water's warm enough for swimming year-round, and Byron bulges further east than anywhere else in Australia, copping swell from all directions. At the same time, Cape Byron, the towering headland that is officially mainland Australia's most easterly point, shelters the town's north-facing beaches, so there's surfing for all levels at Main Beach, Clarkes and Wategos.

Then there's the vibe – despite its working-class roots and more recent hippie and influencer reputation, Byron is a surfers' town through and through. It's all sun-bleached hair and sandy feet, bikinis and boardshorts in the main street (even in winter), surf shops on every corner and an attitude that's every bit as laid-back as the 'Cheer up, slow down, chill out' sign on the road into town would have you believe.

Where
Byron Bay is in northern NSW, about 750km north of Sydney/Warrang, 165km south of Brisbane/Meanjin and an hour's drive south of the Gold Coast.

When
You can surf Byron Bay any time of the year, but the waves are less crowded very early in the morning and around lunchtime (a local's tip).

Do it
Local surfing legend Rusty Miller (rustymillersurf.com) was Byron's first surfing instructor in the 1970s and he and his daughter Taylor run private surfing lessons and coaching sessions at Wategos and The Pass.

Let's Go Surfing (letsgosurfing.com.au) also offers group, private, women-only and family surf lessons right in Byron Bay.

Avoid parking fees at some of Byron's beaches by buying an annual pass from NSW National Parks and Wildlife Service (nationalparks.nsw.gov.au/passes-and-fees).

Fitness: ●●●○○

Fear factor: ●●○○○

Expertise required ●○○○○

Family friendly

Opposite Heading out for a splash

Above Sharing a wave at The Pass *Opposite* Surfing Wategos with Julian Rocks/Nguthungulli behind

THE ADVENTURE

To get your 'surfing in Byron' bearings, start at Main Beach, Byron's main swimming beach, which is patrolled by lifesavers year-round, though you can surf there too, outside the flagged zone. To your right, the beach curves around the bay to become Clarkes, where the waves tend to be tamer than anywhere else in the Bay.

Keep going and you reach The Pass, which is without a doubt the choice spot – a right-hand point break famous for its long, peeling, sometimes barrelling, rides. It's about as popular as a surf spot can be – and highly egalitarian (except maybe when the waves are serious in size; then it's every surfer for herself). Some mornings it can feel as if the whole town is out there – grommets and grandmas and everyone in between – on all kinds of boards. A friend of mine loves to say that when the sun's shining and the waves are good, you could almost walk on water from the beach to the line-up, across everyone's surfboards, without getting your feet wet. You might even find yourself surfing with a pod of dolphins there.

The paddle-out spot at The Pass is next to the boat ramp (dive boats sound a siren when they're coming or going), which is next to a small rocky outcrop called Spectator 'Speccies' Rock that's prime surf-check territory. Climb the stairs to the platform at the top and you can take in all the surfing action at The Pass, all the way back to Main Beach, Clarkes and Wategos.

Surfing, Byron Bay

No board? No problem! Bodysurfing is the ultimate freedom

Further along, Wategos is the place to hang ten with the local longboarders on Sunday mornings – or any day of the week, for that matter (does anyone actually work in Byron?). It can be fickle, as it's more exposed than The Pass, but it's also a beautiful place just to hang out, with its wide beach, grassy picnic area and shady trees, nestled at the base of Cape Byron.

Around the corner from Wategos, there's another gem of a beach: Little Wategos, the easternmost beach on the Australian mainland. It's accessible only on foot (across the wet sand from Wategos at low tide or, at other times, via the high timber boardwalk that leads to the lighthouse), so it's mostly surfed by those willing to put in a bit of extra effort to avoid the crowds. Keep your eye out for wallabies, which have displaced the feral goats that used to dot the grassy flanks of the cape.

From there, the walking track leads steeply up to Cape Byron Lighthouse and a view south to Tallow Beach, which stretches seemingly forever to Broken Head. The northern end of 'Tallows' is called Cosy Corner and it's a great summer surf spot when the northerlies and nor-easters are blowing.

Back on Main Beach, head in the other direction (west), past the seawall at the top of Jonson St, where drumming circles pop up like magic mushrooms most evenings, and you'll come to Belongil Beach. The first surf spot is called The Wreck after the rusting hulk of the *Wollongbar*, a steamship that carried passengers and cargo between Byron and Sydney/Warrang until it ran aground in 1921 and created a nice surf break (and, on calm days, a good snorkelling spot). You can still see part of its hull and its rudder some days, depending on the tide.

Beyond The Wreck, Belongil is beach-break country so where you surf will depend on the day – as well as the tide, the wind, the sandbanks and the swell.

For all the joy and exhilaration of surfing, sometimes it's the moments between waves that make a surf session memorable, and that's particularly true in Byron. No matter where you surf, sitting on your board in gin-clear water on a sunshine-y day in the company of dolphins and sea turtles, looking at the volcanic hills to the north, including the sacred Wollumbin (Mount Warning), those gorgeous beaches following the curve of the bay, the steep green flanks of Cape Byron and the lighthouse – there's nowhere else quite like it.

Check the surf from a different angle on the coast-hugging 3.7km-loop walk from The Pass to Tallows via the lighthouse (remember to look out for dolphins and turtles, and humpback whales from July to Oct). Arakwal Bundjalung Elder Delta Kay (explorebyronbay.com) leads tours along part of this track, covering First Nations' culture in and around 'Cavvanbah' (Byron's original name, meaning 'meeting place').

For more water-based action, you can kayak with dolphins (capebyronkayaks.com), go snorkelling or diving at Julian Rocks Nguthungulli Nature Reserve (snorkellingbyronbay.com.au, sundive.com.au) or explore the Brunswick River, just north of Byron, on a stand-up paddleboard (byronstanduppaddle.com.au).

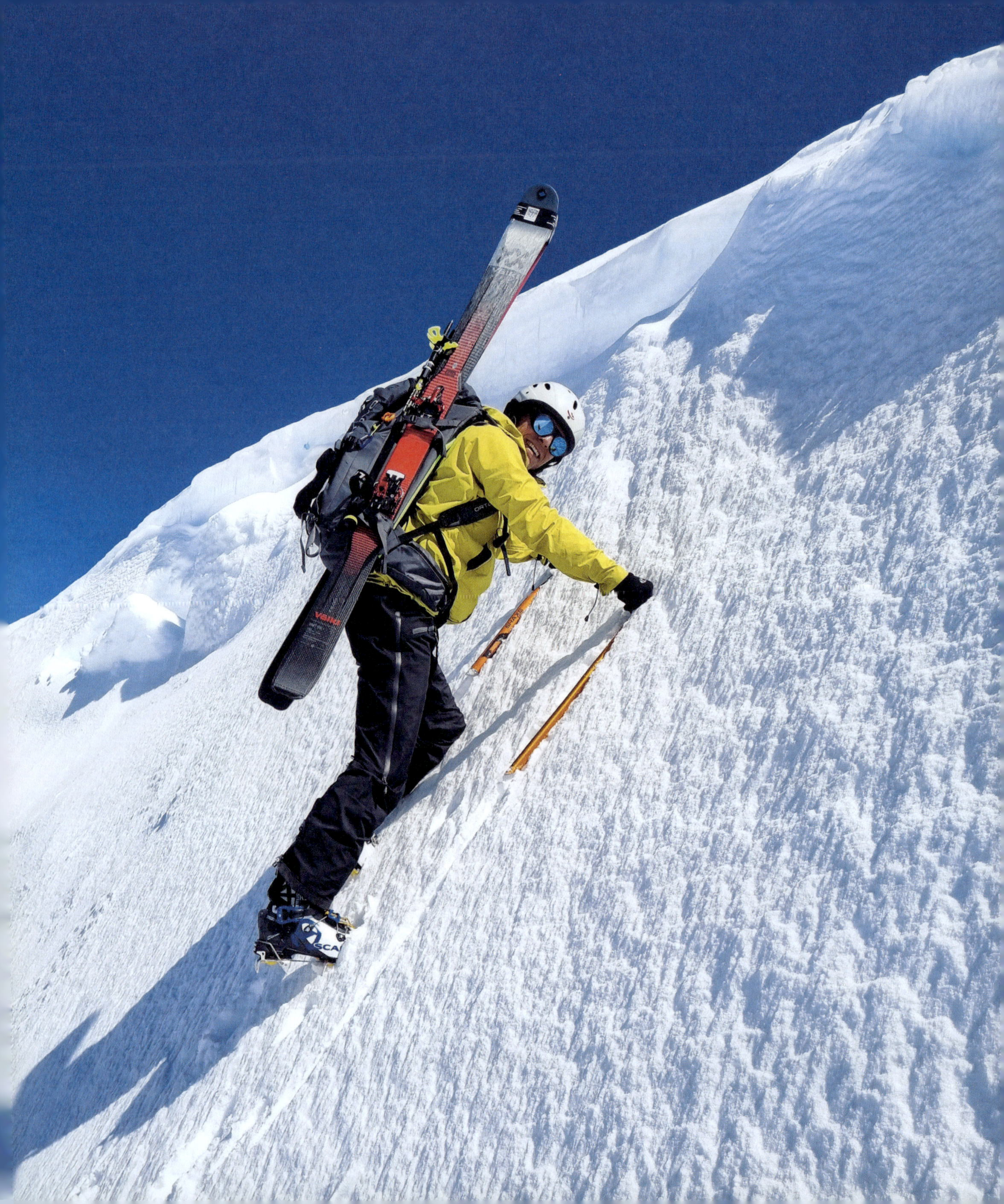

Off the slopes and into the wilderness for backcountry touring.

Backcountry skiing, Guthega, Snowy Mountains

Ngarigo Country

Contributed by Jim Darby

WHY IT'S SPECIAL

Imagine yourself on the highest mountain in Australia. Snow has fallen fresh overnight, and the day dawns cold and crisp, meaning the snow will stay light and dry. You could point your skis one way, riding the lifts and fighting the ski-resort crowds for fresh tracks, or you could head into the mountains from Guthega under your own steam, having most of the terrain to yourself and your small group, choosing the angle and aspect to best suit the snow cover and snow quality. No queues and no crowds. That's the lure of backcountry ski touring in the Snowy Mountains.

Where
Guthega is about a 45min drive from Jindabyne along the Kosciuszko and Guthega roads. SMBC is located just above the carpark, at the base of the Guthega Car Park Chairlift.

When
The ski season runs from around June to the end of Sept.

Do it
Snowy Mountains Backcountry Tours runs tours for beginner and experienced backcountry skiers and snowboarders (on split boards). Overnight and extended tours are also available. Equipment hire is available and there's also a well-stocked gear shop at SMBC headquarters. Book online (snowymountainsbackcountry.com.au).

Fitness: ●●●●○

Fear factor: ●●●○○

Expertise required ●●●○○

Above Skiing the east ridge of Mount Tate on the Main Range of the Snowy Mountains *Opposite* Earn your turns – climbing on the slopes of Mount Tate using crampons and an ice axe for grip

THE ADVENTURE

Adventure-central at the small mountain village of Guthega is at the headquarters of Snowy Mountains Backcountry Tours (SMBC), just across the way from the Basecamp Café. SMBC owner and head guide Doug Chatten brings decades of experience in these mountains, and in the office he runs through a mandatory gear check, giving his group of skiers a clear and detailed safety briefing. After all, he's taking them in his charge into a wilderness area.

Gearing up for backcountry skiing is different than for downhill, and if going it alone it's a pursuit for experienced skiers only. Skis and boots for backcountry skiing are built much lighter, and bindings give the versatility to free the heels for walking and climbing and locking them in for a delightful downhill run. Poles are telescopic to make them higher for an uphill push while also account for traversing slopes, where the downhill pole can be lengthened and the uphill pole shortened for balance and momentum. For grip on uphill stretches, nylon 'skins' are strapped to the base of the skis, their bristles smooth on the slide forward and rough against the slide back, so none of the climbing effort is wasted.

Guthega is well located for backcountry adventures, serving as a trailhead for the vast snowfields beyond, especially the Snowy Mountains Main Range, with peaks such as Mount Tate and Mount Twynam rising in the distance, above the Snowy River and Guthega Dam.

This dam was one of the first components of the vast Snowy Mountains Hydro Scheme, many builders of which came from Norway, bringing their love of winter sports with them. On a slope above the dam there are remnants of an old ski tow built by the Norwegians – according to legend – from parts purloined from the Hydro Scheme.

Backcountry skiers on this trip, however, won't be using any lifts; they'll be making their way across the dam wall, beginning a steady climb through the snow gums, then up above the tree line – zig-zagging up ridges and making long traverses across the slopes.

Right Doug Chatten, Snowy Mountains Backcountry head guide, skiing the slopes of Watsons Crags, deep in the Snowy Mountains

Backcountry skiing, Guthega, Snowy Mountains

New South Wales & ACT

After maybe an hour of heading uphill, they'll be ready for the first run down. With the snow light and dry, the skiing is very easy: short turns off the ridge at the top, long turns over a vast open slope and then quick turns as they scoot around among the snow gums, which are sparse at first, then thicker the lower the skiers go.

Once at the base of the slopes, the skiers will start the climb all over again, and while it's physically taxing, there's an easy rhythm along the snow track set by Chatten, a steady click-clack as skis and boots slide forward. He'll issue some tips – the best angles to climb, about sliding skis rather than lifting them, and maybe even on the execution of the comical kick turn. This latter move is a more-than-handy component of ski technique, where one leg kicks around to be 180 degrees away from the other, then that one follows to execute a complete direction change, but it's the kind of manoeuvre Charlie Chaplin might employ if he were filming on snow.

Chatten also keeps his charges in tune with the risks in the backcountry. Australia doesn't have the avalanche danger of the alpine nations, or even Aotearoa New Zealand, but the risk, like sudden weather changes or negotiating icy slopes, is something to be aware of and prepared for.

Another couple of runs and it might be time for lunch, sheltered among some trees and with views out to the mighty Snowy Mountains Main Range. Maybe that's the scene of your next ski tour. The only way from here is up.

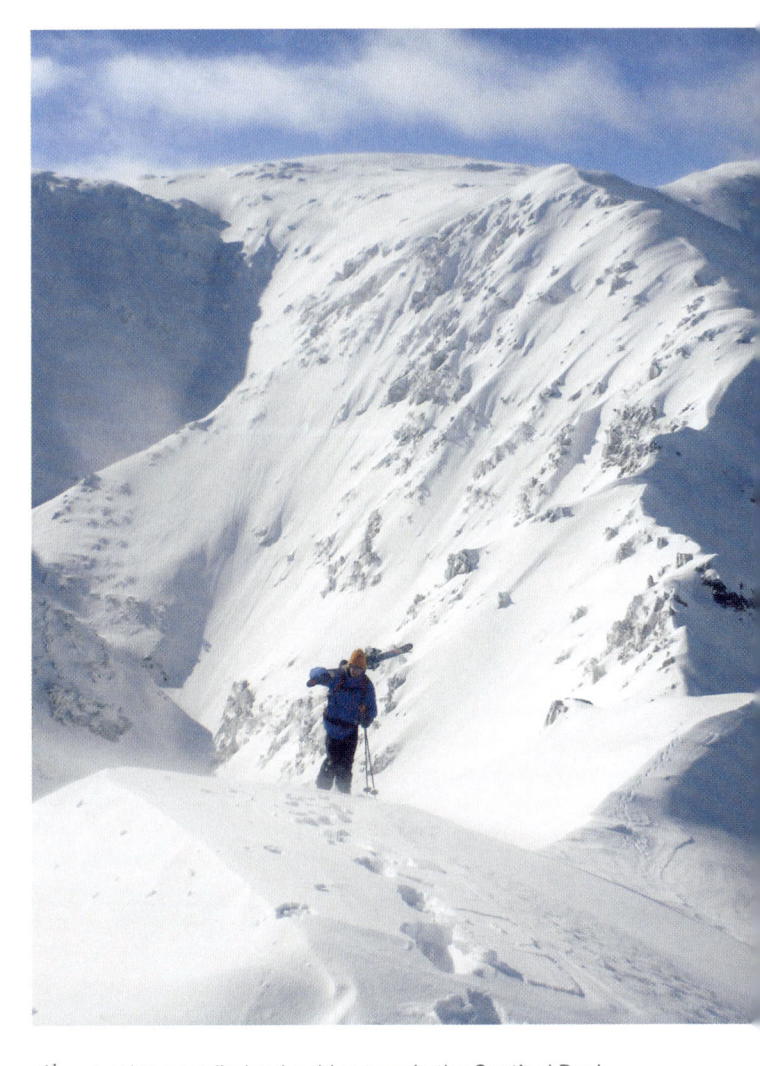

Above A ski tourer climbs the ridge to gain the Sentinel Peak
Opposite Fully-equipped ski tourers making their way towards Mount Twynam

Wherever there's snow, there's scope for backcountry skiing, but guided backcountry skiing for a day or sometimes overnight, along with equipment hire, is also available in NSW at Thredbo (threbo.com.au) and in Victoria at both Falls Creek (fallscreekguides.com.au) and Mount Hotham (mthotham.com.au).

Hike to the tip of Australia's highest mountain on gentle alpine paths.

Climbing to the top of Australia, Mount Kosciuszko

Ngarigo and Walgalu Country

WHY IT'S SPECIAL

Highs come easily on Mount Kosciuszko. Though it stands 2228m above sea level – taller than any other mountain in Australia – the physical reality of Australia's highest peak is that it rises little more than 100m above the main ridgeline of the Snowy Mountains. And with most of the climbing work done by a chairlift from Thredbo, the tallest mountain of all is also one of the easiest summit experiences in the Australian Alps.

A hike to the summit of 'Kozzie' is about more than just ticking off the highest point of land in the country. It's a brush with the mighty Snowy Mountains, in the company of Australia's 10 highest mountains, on one of the most straightforward alpine outings in the country. Small effort, big reward.

Where
The walk begins at the highest station on Thredbo's Kosciuszko Express chairlift. Thredbo is 210km south-west of Canberra/Ngambri/Ngunnawal, and 500km south-west of Sydney/Warrang.

When
Summer is the ideal time to be along the heights of the Snowy Mountains - wildflowers will be blazing and snow's likely to have melted. Expect the mountains to be snow covered from around June to October. Year-round, check forecasts and emergency warnings ahead of time and be prepared for all weather as alpine conditions change suddenly.

Do it
In summer, the Kosciuszko Express chairlift runs from 8.30am to 5pm. A Park Pass is required for any activity in Kosciuszko National Park; they can be purchased at vehicle entry stations along the Alpine Way.

Thredbo operates guided hikes, including to the summit of Mount Kosciuszko (thredbo.com.au/activities/hikes).

Fitness: ●●●○○

Fear factor: ●○○○○

Expertise required ●●○○○

Family friendly

Above Snow gum below the slopes of Mount Kosciuszko *Opposite* View from the summit of Mount Kosciuszko to Mount Townsend

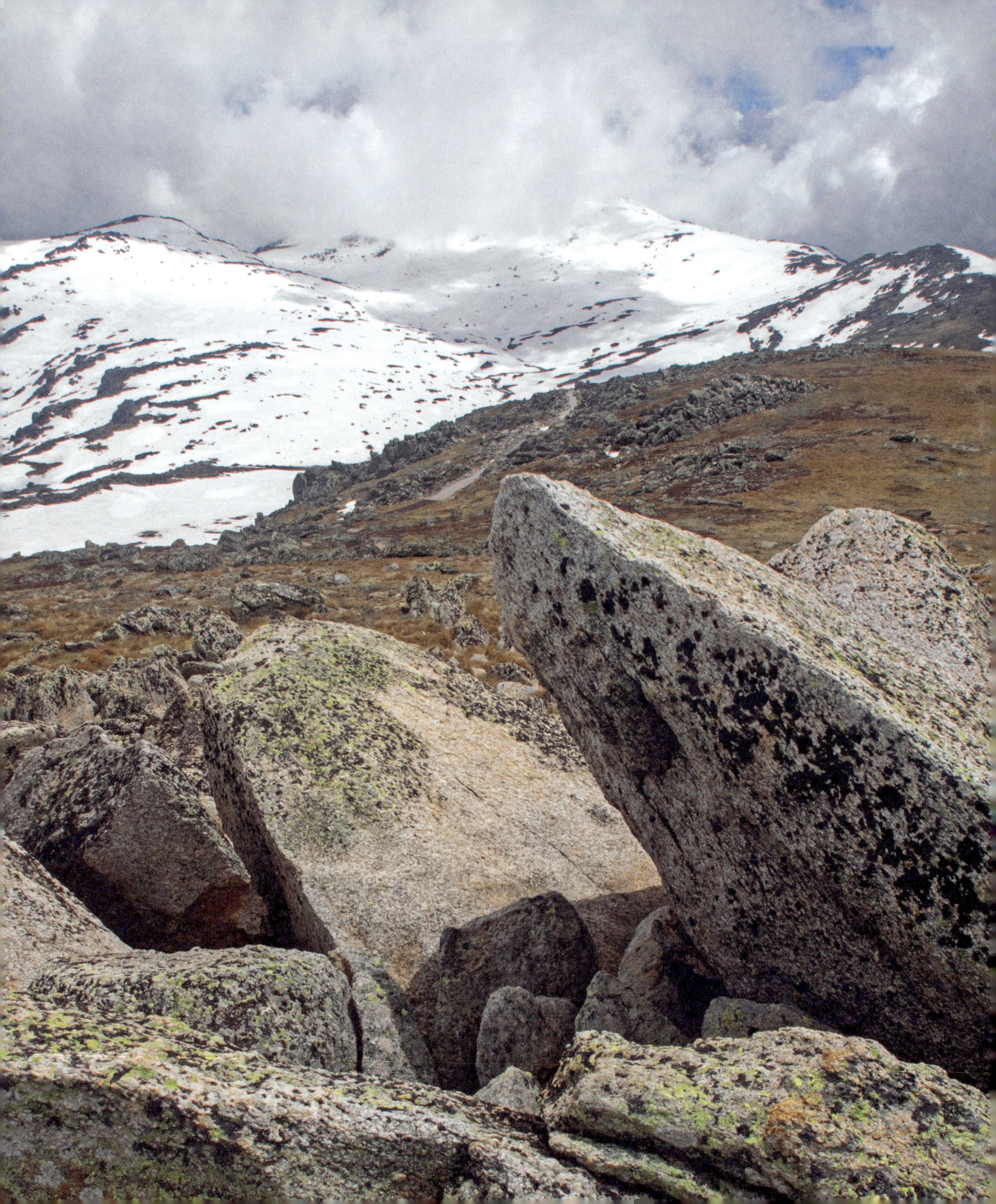

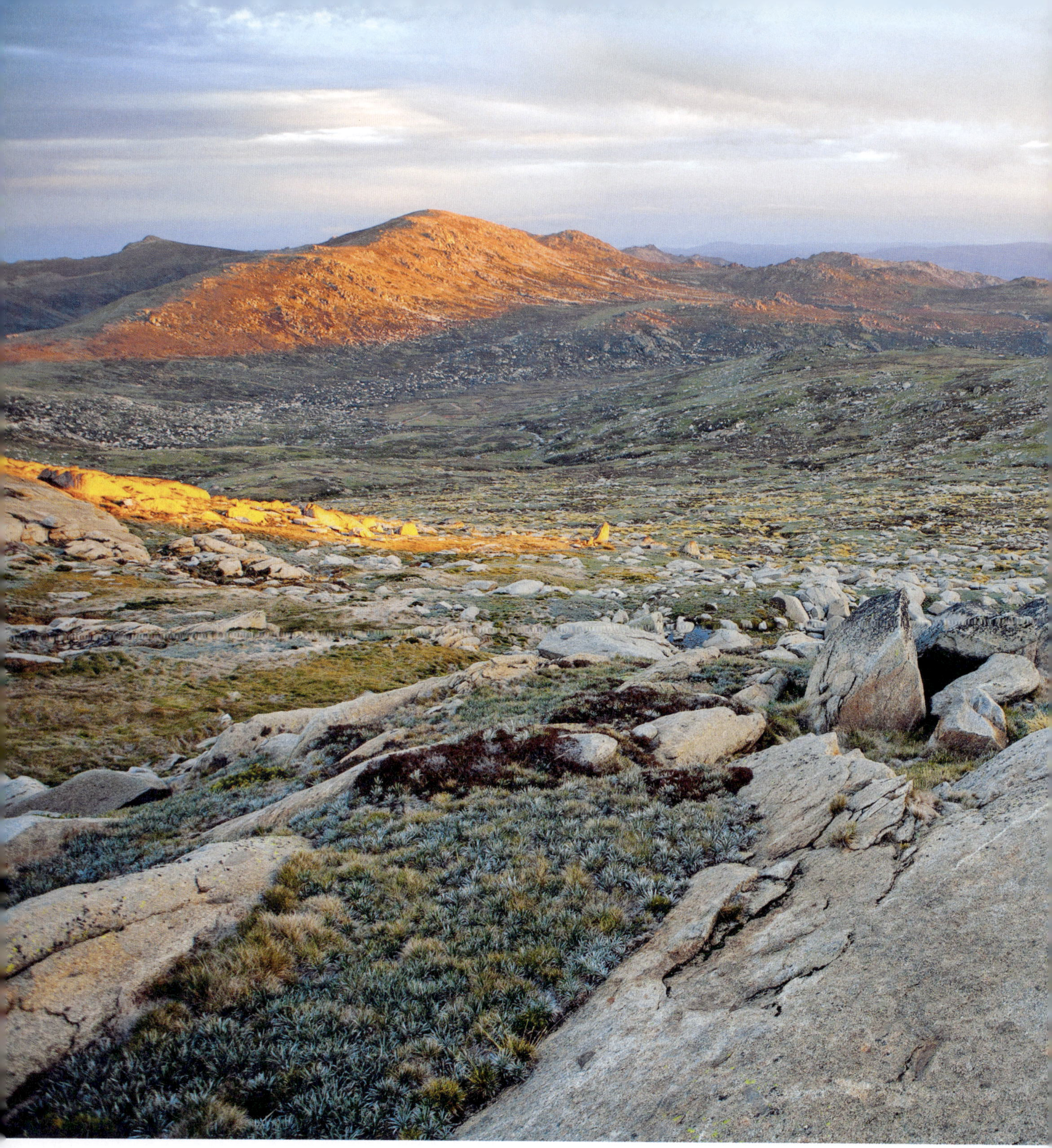

THE ADVENTURE

There are several approaches to Mount Kosciuszko on foot, including an 18.6km-return walk from Charlotte Pass, and the long and grinding climb from Thredbo village, which weaves steeply through the bare ski runs, with mountain bikers likely bombing down the slopes around you.

The most popular approach, though, is to begin (and end) the walk at the top of Thredbo's Kosciuszko Express chairlift, following a steel mesh walkway to Rawson Pass and then curling gently up onto the summit. It's a 13km signposted return walk, with around 500m of cumulative ascent. The going is straightforward throughout, mostly on the walkway and then well-graded paths beyond Rawson Pass.

Alpine conditions demand that you carry warm clothing and wet-weather gear, regardless of the forecast – weather can change fast and unexpectedly in the Snowy Mountains. The walk is long enough that you should have food and water on board also.

The chairlift's base station is far below Kosciuszko, on the bank of the Thredbo River, immediately opposite Thredbo's Village Square. It's 600m of climbing done effortlessly as you step back out at the Eagles Nest – the chairlift's terminal station – 1930m above sea level. The walk sets out on a paved pathway, immediately into alpine terrain, dipping after 500m to cross a stream and transforming into a steel mesh walkway elevated above the alpine grasses and wildflowers. There may even be snow beneath (or over) the walkway, with snow patches lingering on the slopes through spring and even into summer.

For the next 1.5km, the walk ascends gradually to Kosciuszko Lookout where, in the right conditions, the rounded summit of Australia's highest mountain appears for the first time, peering through a gap in the ridge of the Snowy Mountains Main Range. Away to the west, rising immediately above the lookout, in the Ramshead Range, with a wonderland of tors and tarns hiding out of sight atop the range.

As the trail dips again, there are views down onto a high alpine plain and the squiggle of Australia's most poetic river, the Snowy River, just beginning its journey towards the coast at faraway Marlo in Victoria.

Left First light on Mount Kosciuszko

The walkway continues tucked in beneath the ridgeline, finally rising to cross it, emerging above Lake Cootapatamba. Pooled at the base of Mount Kosciuszko's summit mound, Cootapatamba is the highest lake in Australia (2048m) and one of only five mainland lakes to have been formed by glacial action – look at the valley's U-shape and you'll be able to detect the footprint of the long-gone glacier. The red spot down the valley is Cootapatamba Hut, an emergency shelter for which I've had cause to give particular thanks, having once been caught out overnight here in a storm.

Contouring around the head of the cirque, the walkway rises onto Rawson Pass, immediately beneath Kosciuszko's summit. Here, the walk intersects with the trail from Charlotte Pass, which follows the line of the dirt road that, until 1976, ran all the way to the tip of Kosciuszko. In a world where mountaineers battle to the summits of the highest peaks in countries across the world, Australia's highest mountain could once be reached in a car.

This history speaks volumes about the gentility of the terrain, which continues beyond Rawson Pass as the trail wraps easily around the back of the mountain and up onto the summit, which is topped by a rectangular cairn.

There are days on the summit when there's no view, there are days when the view is endless, and there are those classic mountain days when it's one thing one minute and the other the next. When your luck is in, the view is enormous, looking out across a vast sweep of mountains and beyond, while closer to hand, the Snowy Mountains form a piebald world of fractured boulders, alpine tussocks and snow patches. Stay a while and savour the moment – for these few minutes, you might well be the tallest person in Australia.

> Peer north from Mount Kosciuszko and the first peak in the view is Mount Townsend. Standing just 19m lower than Kozzie, it is Australia's second highest mountain and, with its summit of fractured granite tors, it is in many ways more dramatic and impressive than its infinitely more famous neighbour. By virtue of being second, Mount Townsend sees little of the hiking attention that's focussed on Mount Kosciuszko, and it's a significantly more challenging outing – a 22km return hike from the chairlift, over more difficult terrain. The faint trail to the second highest point in the country departs the Main Range walking track at Mueller Pass (the saddle between Mount Kosciuszko and Mueller Peak), skirting Mueller Peak and ascending to Townsend for a striking view back onto Mount Kosciuszko.

Stream pouring beneath the Ramshead Range
Opposite top The metal walkway to Mount Kosciuszko
Opposite bottom Tors on the Ramshead Range

Climbing to the top of Australia, Mount Kosciuszko

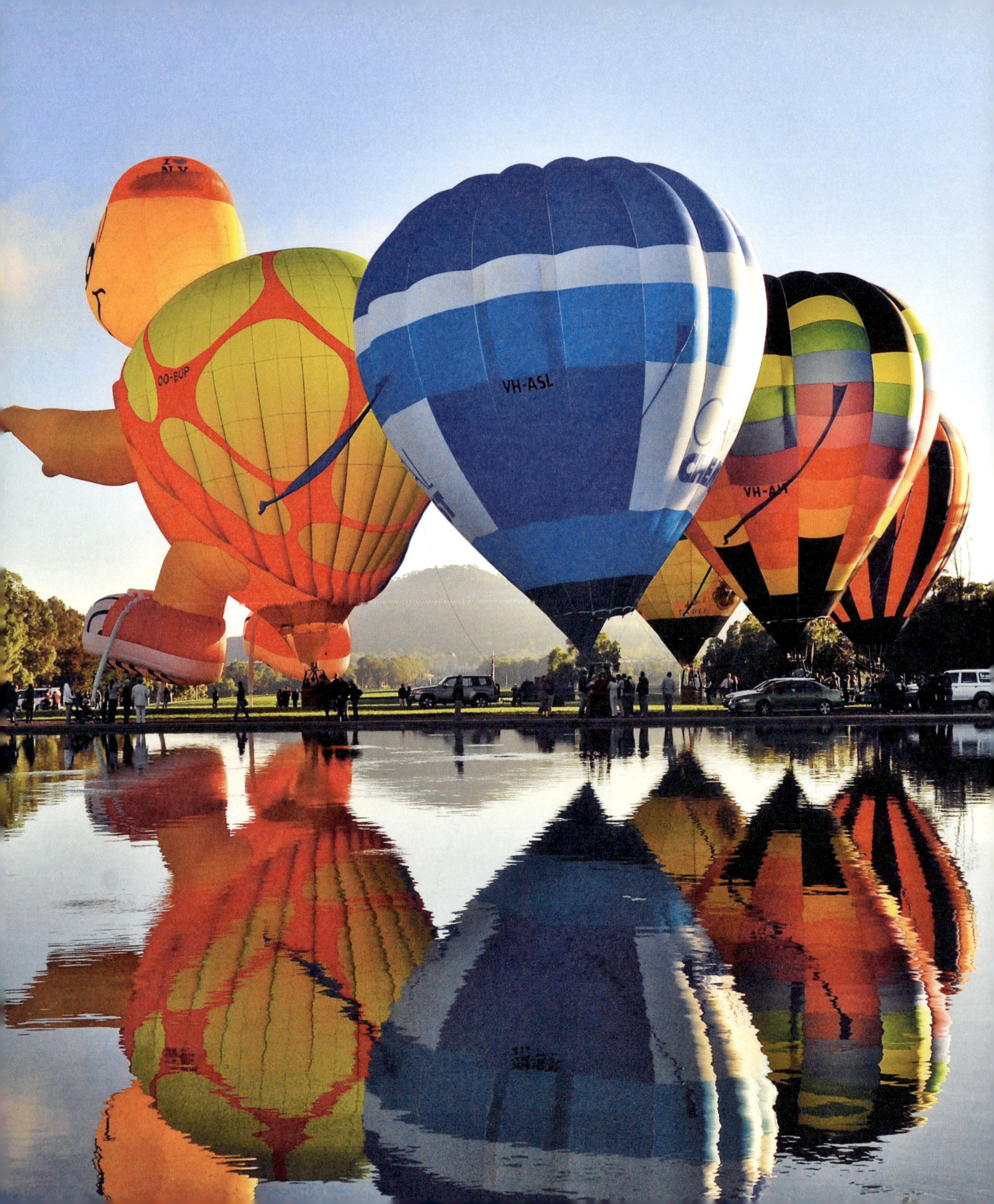
OO-BUP
VH-ASL

Float over the national capital at dawn, peering down onto Lake Burley Griffin and the architectural masterpieces that ring it.

Ballooning, Canberra/ Ngambri/Ngunnawal

Ngunnawal Country

WHY IT'S SPECIAL

There are few places in the world where you can stand in the basket of a hot-air balloon and peer straight down into the heart of a city, but look to Canberra/Ngambri/Ngunnawal's sky on any fine morning and it's likely to be decorated with balloons. Drifting over Lake Burley Griffin, the view from a balloon is filled with national treasures and icons: Parliament House, the National Library, the National Museum and a host of other monumental national structures, looking like LEGO constructions from overhead.

On a breathless morning, the lake can be like a mirror laid out on the ground, reflecting the dawn colours of the sky. Look around and it's likely that other balloons will speckle the view – sometimes one, sometimes two, drifting in tandem across the lake.

These dawn flights are the gentlest of adventures, but still require an act of faith – stepping into a basket and letting a bag of air lift you into the sky, propelled only by the wind for one of the best city views in the country.

Where
Passengers meet at the Hyatt Hotel on Commonwealth Ave, pinched between Parliament House and Lake Burley Griffin.

When
Flights operate year-round; autumn brings the spectacle of Canberra's changing colours.

Do it
Book flights through the operator, Balloon Aloft Canberra (balloonaloftcanberra.com.au).

Fitness: ●○○○○

Fear factor: ●●○○○

Expertise required ●○○○○

Family friendly

Opposite Reflections on a serene adventure

THE ADVENTURE

In pre-dawn darkness, a group of passengers gathers at a hotel near the shores of Lake Burley Griffin. From here, they'll disperse to a ballooning launch site, of which there are around a dozen possibilities dotted around the lake and beyond, depending on the morning's conditions. Even as the group mills, the balloon pilots are sending up smaller balloons, running micro-scale weather checks on wind direction and speed to determine the best launch site.

The prevailing winds around Lake Burley Griffin at this time of day are easterlies (even when there's a westerly blowing up higher), so most launches take place on the eastern side of the lake. In the faintest of first light, the balloon is filled first with cold air and then hot – the burners blasting into action for the first time – until the balloon stands tall. You climb into the basket and physics irrepressibly take over, with the hot air lifting you off the ground. Though this is the morning's greatest moment of trepidation – it's common to be nervous at this point – the take-off is gentle, almost imperceptible.

Close your eyes and you might not even know you're airborne. Open your eyes and you'll find the sun rising over the horizon almost in tandem with the balloon.

In moments, the lake at Canberra's heart comes into view, soon expanding to take in the rest of the city. Depending on the wind, the lake and city might be as far as 300m below, or as near as 20m. The National Gallery drifts beneath, then the columned National Library, with the flag post atop Parliament House rising as if in competition with the tall sculptural loop on the National Museum across the lake.

'I can't think of another Parliament House in the world that you could actually fly right over the top of, and nobody would stress about it,' says Balloon Aloft Canberra chief pilot John Wallington.

Away to the west, beyond the city's long sprawl, rises the Brindabella mountain range, while immediately beneath you, walkers, joggers and cyclists swirl like electrons around the lake's shore. If it's autumn, the shores will be glowing with colour. Wherever you look, there's something monumental and something happening.

Inside the basket, there's the curious feeling of the day being wind-free, regardless of the conditions, since the balloon moves on the breeze, aided by a blast of flame from the burner every 30 seconds or so – a loud exhale briefly disturbing the silence.

After around 45min, the balloon approaches the western end of Lake Burley Griffin, and it's time to get out of the sky. Landing sites can be anywhere large and open enough to fit a balloon – ovals, even schools – but typically you might come back to earth in parkland beside the lake. On calm days, the basket will touch and settle in the one spot; on a windy day, it might tip to its side and drag briefly along the ground for a more exciting finish.

Air is released from the balloon, diminishing its lift, and out you climb, back on Canberra soil. You're free to help fold up the balloon, or you can just tuck into the champagne or orange juice that welcomes you back to planet Earth.

Above Flying above the National Museum of Australia
Opposite Lift off

Canberra's big ballooning moment comes in March, when the city hosts the Canberra Balloon Spectacular. For nine days, balloons hover above the city like Christmas baubles, launching each morning (at around 6.45am) from the Patrick White Lawns in front of the National Library. To watch them rise at once over Lake Burley Griffin is a beautiful sight. You can join the party with special Spectacular flights from Balloon Aloft Canberra. The Spectacular is held as part of the Enlighten Festival.

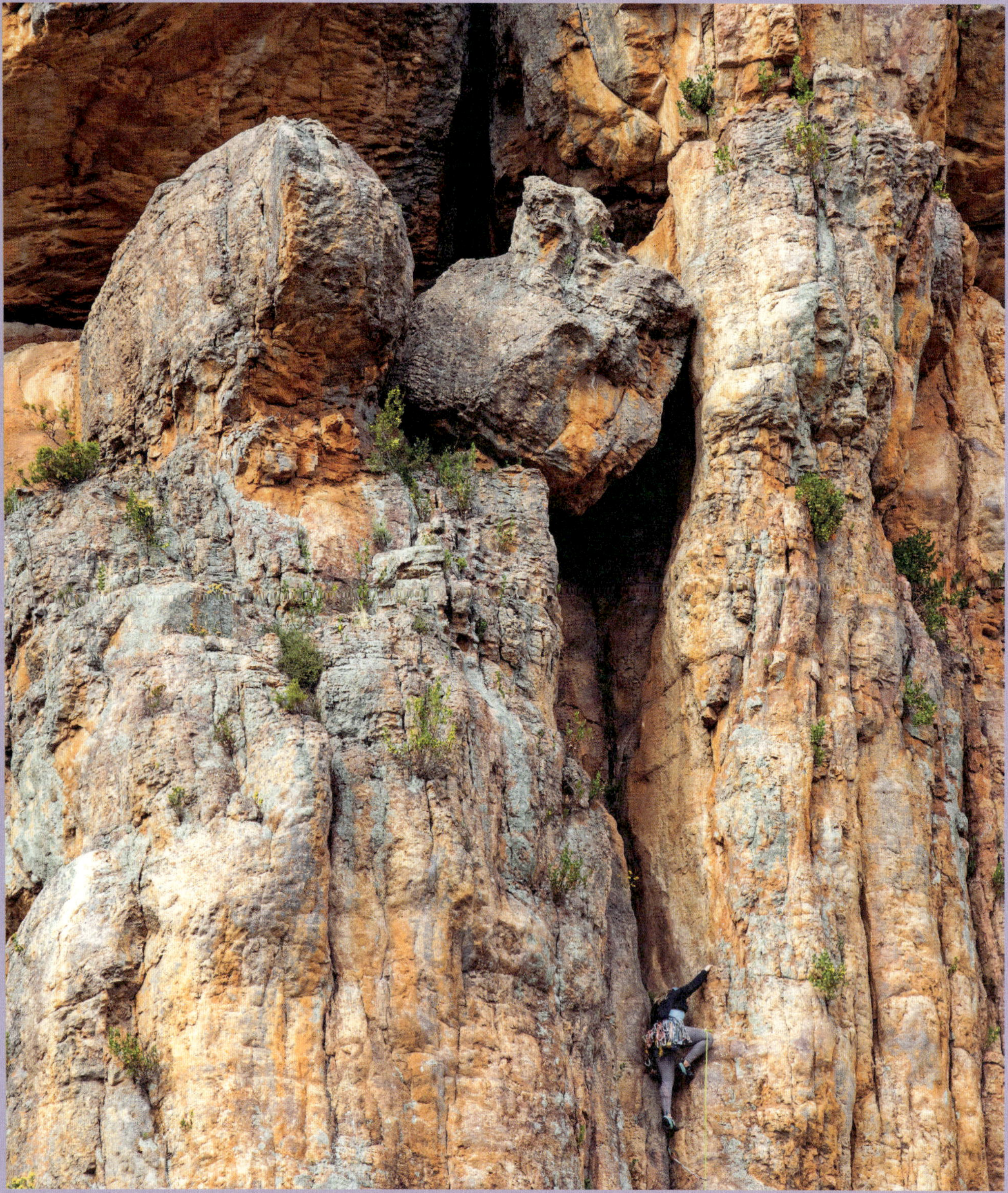

Victoria

High Country high jinks and the nation's best rock climbing are just the start of the Victorian adventure.

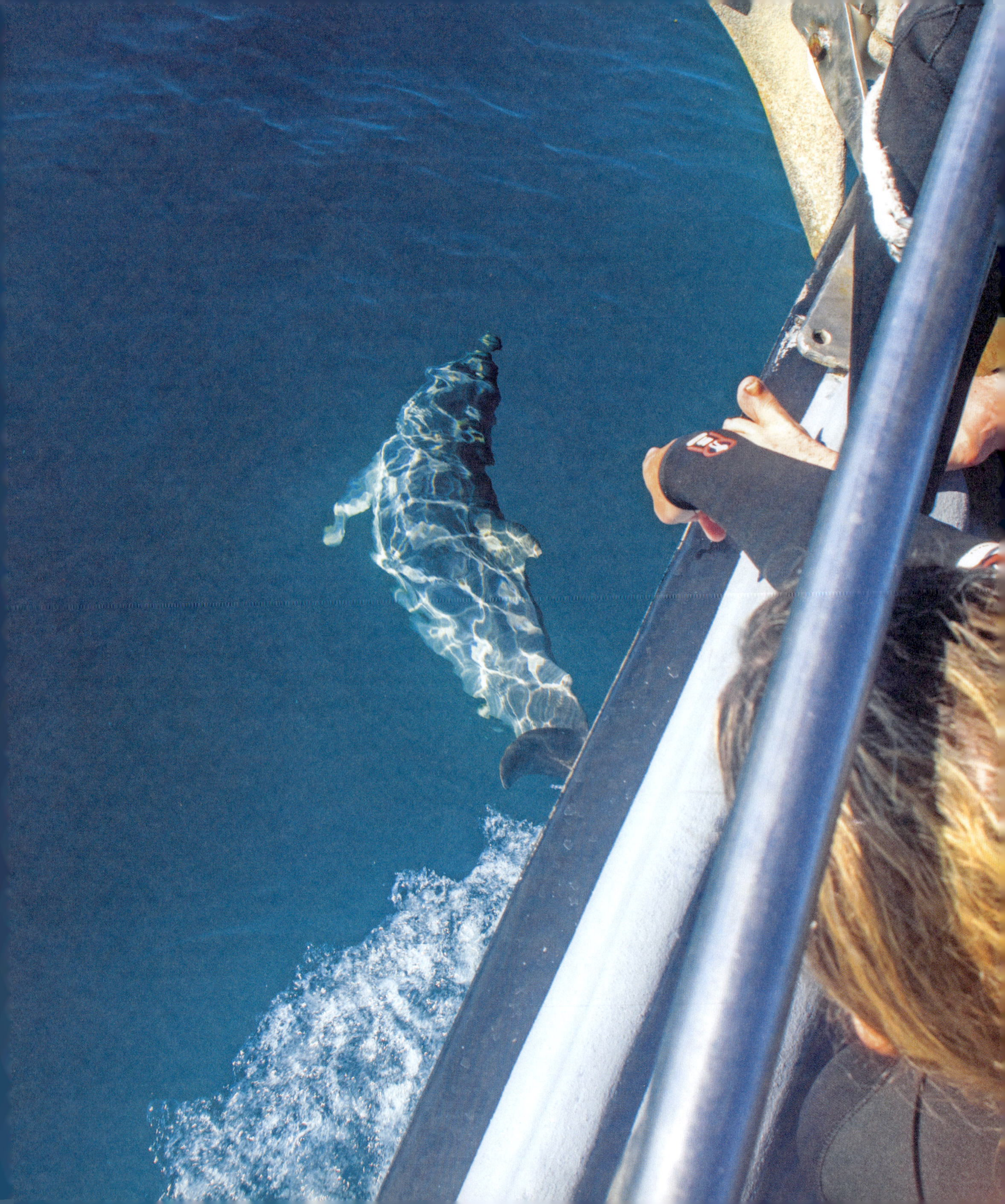

Snorkel among wildlife just a few minutes from shore in Melbourne/Naarm's backyard bay.

Swimming with dolphins and seals, Port Phillip

The Bellarine Peninsula is Wadawurrung Country, while Sorrento is on the Traditional lands of the Boon Wurrung/Bunurong People.

WHY IT'S SPECIAL

Just 50km from the centre of Melbourne/Naarm, inside Port Phillip, there's a patch of water that is the capital city's true wild side. Pinched between Queenscliff and Sorrento, it's an underwater world occupied by seals and dolphins, in an environment conducive to interactive marine wildlife encounters.

Roll off a boat here and you can be watching dolphins glide gracefully beneath or beside you, and swimming among curious Australian fur seals. And unlike most marine wildlife trips, which involve long sails in search of the animals, you can be among these creatures just a few minutes after motoring out into the bay from Queenscliff or Sorrento.

Where
Dolphin and seal swims operate from Queenscliff and Sorrento. Queenscliff is on the Bellarine Peninsula, 105km south-west of Melbourne/Naarm; Sorrento is on the Mornington Peninsula, 100km south of Melbourne.

When
The Dolphin and Seal Swim Tour, operated by See All Dolphin Swims, departs twice daily.

Do it
Sea All Dolphin Swims is based at Queenscliff Harbour. Book online (dolphinswims.com.au). Sorrento-based operators are Moonraker Dolphin Swims (moonrakerdolphinswims.com.au), Watermaarq (watermaarq.com.au) and Polperro Dolphin Swims (polperro.com.au).

Fitness: ●●○○○

Fear factor: ●●○○○

Expertise required ●●○○○

Family friendly

Above The *Maureen M Opposite* Dolphin company *Previous* Scaling the cliffs at Mount Arapiles/Dyuritte

THE ADVENTURE

On the Queenscliff side of Port Phillip, an old fishing boat weaves its way out of the marina, pausing as the far larger Queenscliff-Sorrento ferry pulls rank and begins its short journey across this narrowest point of the bay.

Onboard the smaller *Maureen M*, there's a tight squeeze of people, requiring order and system. Fins are neatly racked together, and snorkels and masks hang from bars overhead. With the ferry on its way, the *Maureen M* leaves the marina, setting out into the bay in search of two of the ocean's most beautiful of creatures – regal dolphins and playful seals.

Within minutes, the skipper calls for all on board to don their wetsuits. The first stop is just minutes ahead. I'm on the Dolphin and Seal Swim Tour with Sea All Dolphin Swims, and the first stop is usually Popes Eye, a near-complete circle of rocks laid down in the 1880s as the foundation for a never-built fort to guard the entrance to Port Phillip. But wildlife experiences are one of the most dynamic forms of adventure – no two days and no two trips are the same. The day I was here, the boat hadn't even reached Popes Eye, just 2.5km offshore from Queenscliff, when a feeding frenzy of seabirds was spotted in the distance. A host of Australasian gannets speared into the sea, feasting on a bait ball and signalling the likelihood of dolphins in the area, also chasing the tiny fish. Sure enough, fins were soon sighted, rising and falling in arcs across the surface of the sea.

The dolphins sighted in Port Phillip are Burrunan dolphins, a species found only in Victoria, and even then, the Port Phillip animals are one of only two resident populations (the other being found in the Gippsland Lakes, see p.103).

On reaching such a dolphin pod, the skipper and crew pause to assess the animals. If there are no calves in the pod, visitors can snorkel freely among the dolphins, but if there are calves, two ropes – mermaid lines – are set out from the boat, drifting on the surface of the sea. Snorkellers enter the water, holding onto the lines, letting the dolphins come to them. On my day here, the pod was intent on feeding, and sightings were fleeting, but they did come, with four dolphins weaving gracefully just a couple of metres from where I floated off the rope. Even as we left, the animals fell in beside the boat, riding its bow wave across the bay.

The most certain company on this trip into Port Phillip are the seals. Rising out of the bay, almost equidistant between Queenscliff and Sorrento, is a gazebo-like shelter known by the outdated name of Chinaman's Hat that serves as a haul-out point for Australian fur seals. At any one time, there might be 30 to 40 seals beneath the shelter, basking like tourists at a tropical resort, or swimming in the waters around it. Comically, there's the occasional tussle for space, with seals jostling and shoving others off the shelter and into the sea, most times with success. It's for this reason – to prevent 200-plus kilograms of seal from dropping onto your head – that there's a 5m snorkelling exclusion zone around the shelter.

That said, Chinaman's Hat is effectively a seal bachelor pad, filled only with young and old males. It's not a breeding colony, which reduces the aggression among the seals and makes this a particularly good spot to swim and interact with the animals.

The boat stops just offshore from the shelter, and snorkellers again slide off the boat into the sea, which here is just a few metres deep. The dolphins might be the stars of the day, but the seals are typically more interactive and memorable. As you snorkel over the sandy seabed, young seals can be as playful as puppies, darting around you and then shooting away like torpedoes. It's hard not to think they're having as much fun as you.

Not all the fun of this day on the water in virtual sight of Melbourne is in the critters. Even before you reach the seals or dolphins, it's customary for the skipper to stop the *Maureen M* and encourage passengers to climb a ladder onto the boat's roof and leap into the sea – a jump of around 4m. A boom also lowers off the side of the boat, holding a net into which you can scramble and lie down, skimming centimetres above the surface of the sea. There's also a chance to be towed behind the boat, clinging to the stern by your fingers, as it heads back towards Queenscliff. And, finally, there's another chance on the return to ascend the ladder for more leaps into the sea – a concluding moment of playtime before the *Maureen M* weaves back into Queenscliff's crowded harbour.

Dolphins and seals aren't all that Melbourne/Naarm brings to the adventurous.

Melbourne Skydeck is the Southern Hemisphere's highest observation deck, peering down onto the city's highest rooftops from almost 300m above the ground - its Edge Experience puts you into a glass cube overhanging the city.

Melbourne Airport might be the last place you'd expect to find surf, but it's just down the road from URBNSURF, Australia's first surf park. Learn to surf, or test yourself on 2m barrels in its perfect, machine-controlled waves.

Stretch your climbing arms on the Burnley Bouldering Wall, set beneath the Monash Fwy in inner-suburban Burnley.

Walk tight ropes and ride zip-lines high in the canopy of the Dandenong Ranges at Treetops Adventure in Belgrave.

Top Sealing the deal *Opposite* The seal bachelor pad of Chinaman's Hut

Ride your luck on the famed waves that inspired a Hollywood movie and one of the world's great surfing contests.

Surfing, Bells Beach

Wadawurrung Country

Contributed by Larissa Ham

WHY IT'S SPECIAL

The spectacular twists and turns of the Great Ocean Road draw visitors from around the globe. But for surfers, there's one stop that really gets the adrenaline firing: the world-famous waves of Bells Beach.

With legendary swells coming from the Southern Ocean, protected by large cliffs, many Bells days have gone down in folklore, including 'Big Saturday' during the Easter of 1981. On that famous day, surfers took their lives in their hands to battle thundering waves ranging – depending who you ask – from 15 to 20ft.

But you don't have to be Mick Fanning or Stephanie Gilmore, or take a jetski out the back on a massive day, to enjoy a visit to Bells. There's something about the raw, almost otherworldly beauty of this place that's difficult to forget. And that's the case whether you experience it in your Ugg boots from the lookout, while walking or cycling along the cliff-top tracks, or potentially scoring the best ride of your life.

Adding to Bells' mystique is the presence of the Rip Curl Pro, which brings some of the world's best surfers to the beach each Easter, for what is the world's longest continuously running surf competition (it was cancelled for two years during Covid, but returned in 2022).

Long before it became a sacred place for surfers, Bells held deep connections for the local Wadawurrung People, who gathered and traded here for thousands of years, and hunted for crayfish and abalone.

Where
Bells Beach is about a 10min drive from Torquay along the Great Ocean Road, or about 100km south-west of Melbourne/Naarm.

When
To see the world's best surfers in action, join the crowds at the Rip Curl Pro at Easter. Or visit year-round for sheer natural beauty.

Do it
Find more details online (torquaylife.com.au/explore/bells-beach).

Fitness: ●●●○○

Fear factor: ●●●○○

Expertise required
●●●○○ (depending on conditions)

Opposite **Contemplating the surf at Bells**

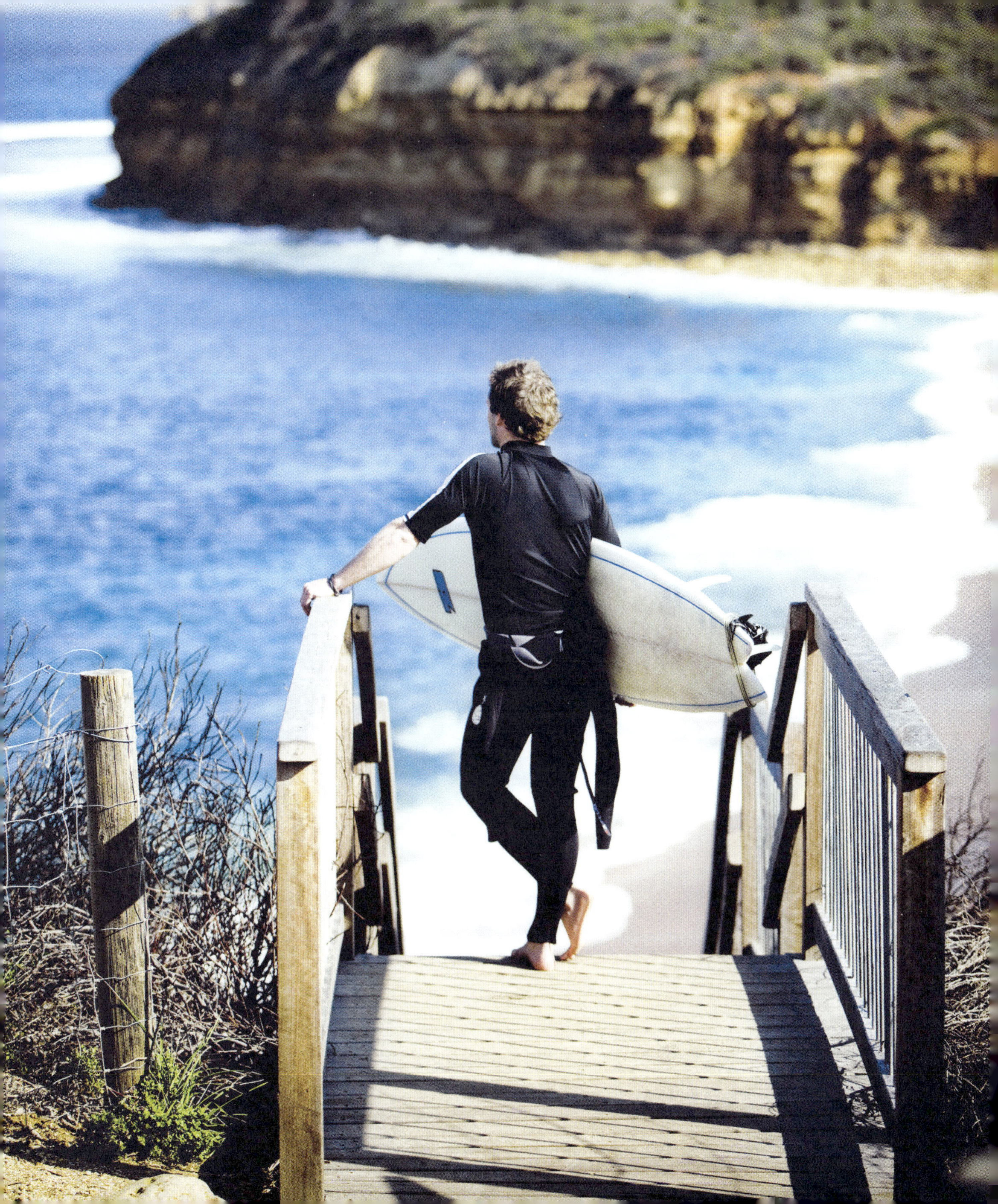

Victoria

THE ADVENTURE

No two days at Bells are exactly the same. Visit when the Southern Ocean is flat and uncooperative (and the winter beanies are out in full force), and you might wonder why so many people flock to this often cold, but ruggedly beautiful part of the world.

But then there are the days when the carpark is alive with salty anticipation. Locals greet each other with some surf chit-chat, and there's a scratching soundtrack of boards being waxed. It's not uncommon to see a frothing surfer jogging down the stairs to hurry to the action, later calmly returning with wet hair and a twinkle in the eye.

If it had been the '90s, you could have been forgiven for thinking the lead character of the classic movie *Point Break*, Bodhi (played by Patrick Swayze), had visited these parts and come to grief in an impressive 50-year storm. But that Bells scene, pine trees and all, was filmed many thousands of kilometres away.

When you arrive at the actual Bells Beach, you'll want to drive to the far-right end of the car park, and check out the natural amphitheatre from the wooden lookout. At this point, it's worth taking your skills into consideration, as Bells can serve up a humbling experience. I found this out when I once optimistically dared to paddle out with some mates on a day beyond my capabilities. After being held down by several large waves in a row, I felt as if I had swallowed the entire Southern Ocean. It was the longest, and saltiest, coughing fit of my life.

Tragically, there have been numerous drownings at Bells over the years. So if you're not sure about the conditions, ask an experienced local – and be aware that the shore break can suck you up and spit you out if you don't time your entry and exit carefully.

A smaller day at Bells is far less intimidating. Even so, beginners shouldn't surf here and would be wise to join a surf school in Torquay, or head to nearby Torquay Point or Point Addis instead.

Left Heading for the waves

There are two main reef breaks at Bells – Rincon and The Bowl. Both are reef breaks and right-handers, and are usually at their best during autumn and winter. With the water dipping to around 13°C from about July to Sept, this is definitely not Noosa or Bali. So pick up a 4/3 'steamer' wetsuit at one of the surf shops in Torquay, and add booties and perhaps a hood during the coldest parts of the year.

While a winter surf at Bells is, well, a little hypothermic, it pays to remember that the surfers of yesteryear were doing it without the comfort of modern wetsuits. It's said that some particularly dedicated young surfers used to paddle all the way here from Torquay. Others would light a fire on the beach, before braving the conditions in footy jumpers and shorts, and then take a break for a sustaining can of baked beans warmed by the flames.

In 1960, local character Joe Sweeney bulldozed the first bumpy, muddy track through the scrub to Bells Beach, charging surfers £1 a pop for the privilege of driving through. It wasn't long until more and more surfers converged on Bells, and by the late 1960s, local surf breaks had inspired the beginnings of two of Australia's most famous surf brands, Rip Curl and Quiksilver, with many of the products tested at Bells.

These days, there's no shortage of vans, utes and roof-racked cars making their way to the famous break, as well as the popular neighbouring Winki Pop, a right-hander reef break. Like many surf breaks, they can both be a wee bit territorial.

During Covid-19 lockdowns, when the surf was pumping, local police checked number plates for surfers unable to resist the siren call of the waves in breaking the 5km-radius rules. A shark that latched on to a French surfer's leg in May 2020 at Southside, around the corner from Bells, might have put off one or two surfers from trying their luck too, but maybe not for long.

If you'd rather stay on land, the 3km Bells Track, stretching from Bird Rock lookout in Jan Juc to Bells, is a ripper of a walk along the cliff-tops, with panoramic views of the surf dotted all the way along.

Or you could start at Bells Beach and head inland to the sheltered forest of the Ironbark Basin, before eventually popping out at stunning Point Addis. Along the way, you'll likely spot echidnas and wallabies along the Koorie Cultural Walk, and find out more about the Traditional First Nations lifestyles in this area.

Back at Bells, watching the feats of highly experienced surfers unfold from the safety of the carpark can prove inspiring. When veteran, mostly male big-wave chargers took on 10- to 12ft waves at Bells in July 2017, two talented teenage girls, Angela Ball and Bella Wilson, were spotted among them. The girls, then just 14 and 15 years of age, later described their athletic feats as 'no big deal'.

Humble or not, there have been plenty of big deals at Bells over the years, including those who've had the chance to ring the famous bell after winning the Rip Curl Pro.

The place itself is a huge deal, and yet on a quiet day, it's almost as if you're the only person experiencing its true magic. And if you're doing so at sunrise or sunset, when the sky can light up in a kaleidoscopic show of pinks, purples and oranges, it's just about the best place to be in the world.

Prefer a bird's-eye view? Southside, around the bend from Bells, is one of the most popular launch sites along this coast for paragliders. On a calm day, you might be lucky enough to see a handful of paragliders taking off and soaring above the cliffs - or better yet, be up there yourself. In the right conditions, you can glide to Jan Juc or, in the other direction, to Anglesea and beyond. You might even spot some ocean life from above.

Top Game time

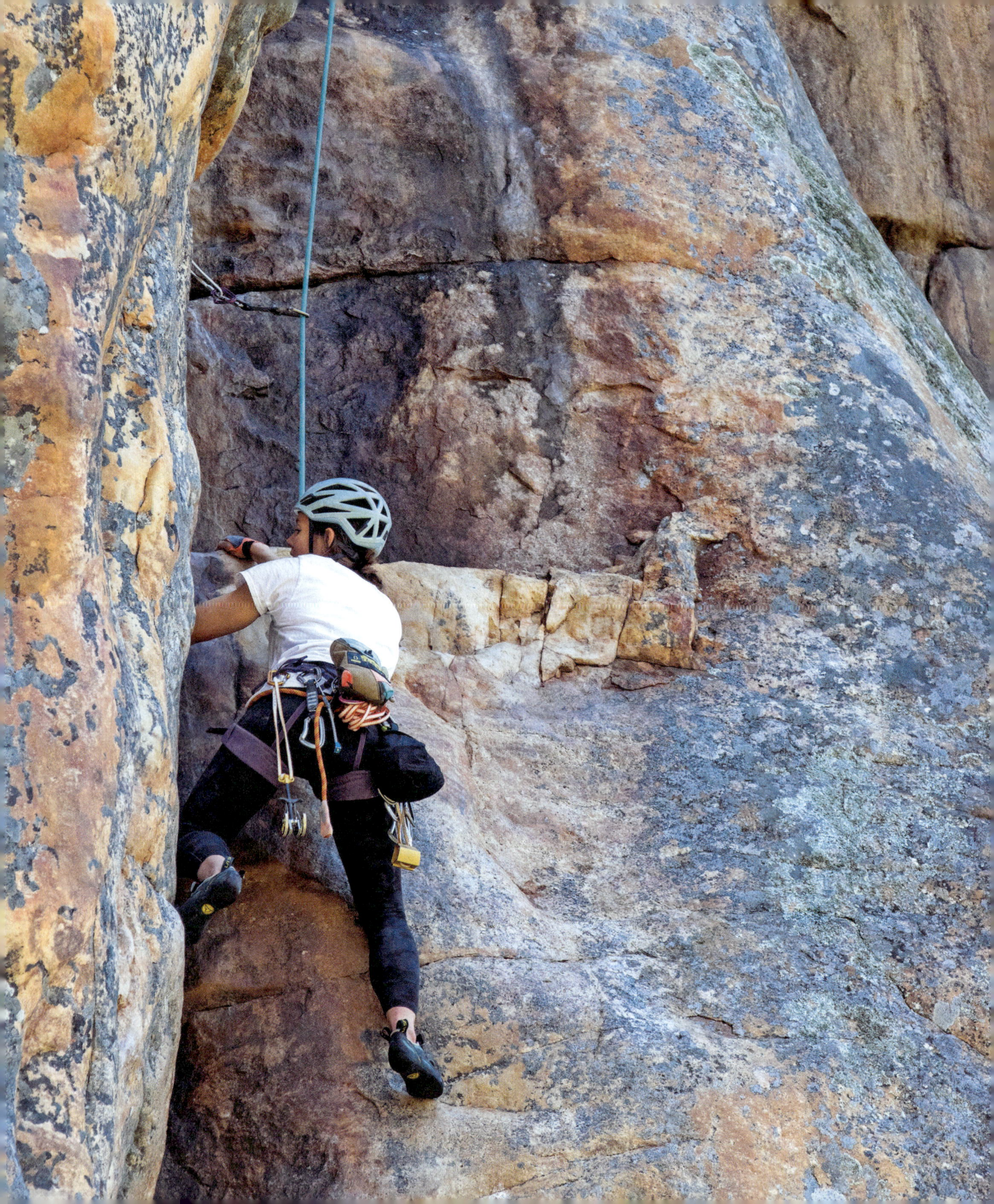

Australia's legendary climbing site has a wealth of wonderful routes catering to everyone from beginners to rock pros.

Rock Climbing, Mount Arapiles/Dyuritte

Wotjobaluk, Jaadwa, Jadawadjali, Wergaia and Jupagulk Country, known as the Dyuritte Traditional Owners

WHY IT'S SPECIAL

In the climbing world, there's no greater Australian rock star than Mount Arapiles/Dyuritte. A low hill that's high on possibility, it rises as a rack of cliffs from the rolling-pin-flat farmland of Victoria's Wimmera Plain to form a globally known climbing site.

The first climbers here were the Dyuritte Traditional Owners, who scaled the mountain to quarry sandstone from which to make tools. Modern climbers stumbled upon its orange rock in the 1960s, when a father and son were drawn to the area by a photo in a tourist brochure of Mitre Rock. What they found was the small outcrop of Mitre Rock and, to their greater surprise, the far-larger 'Araps' immediately beside it.

Today, there are more than 3000 climbing routes throughout these remarkable cliffs, from airy but exposed classics to a climb that was once considered the hardest in the world.

No place in Australia does climbing quite like Arapiles/Dyuritte, and no place has quite this climbing culture.

Where
Mount Arapiles/Dyuritte is just west of Gariwerd/Grampians, 335km west of Melbourne/Naarm

When
Climbing is good year-round – hunt out shaded climbs in the full blast of summer.

Do it
The guidebook *Arapiles Selected Climbs* by Simon Mentz and Glenn Tempest is a good starting point for climbers, listing more than 1300 of Araps' routes.

Learn to climb, or lead climb, or simply hire a guide from Natimuk-based Arapiles Climbing Guides (arapiles.com.au).

Fitness: ●●●○○

Fear factor: ●●●●○

Expertise required ●●●●○

Opposite Climbing in Central Gully

THE ADVENTURE

The customary way to plan a visit to Mount Arapiles/Dyuritte is to camp in the Pines, one of three basic campgrounds at the base of the cliffs. It's the camp to which climbers gravitate, creating the closest thing Australia has to Yosemite's Camp 4, the legendary climbers' campground inside the natural cathedral of the Yosemite Valley, one of the world's great climbing destinations.

At Araps, you'll find tents strewn like rubble through the campground, with slacklines and hammocks often strung between the namesake pine trees. Immediately behind it is the dramatic backdrop of the orange and grey cliffs of this almost unexpected mountain towering out of the wheatfields.

After setting up camp, the cliffs are calling. Approach trails set out from the rear of the camp, running to the likes of the Organ Pipes, Central Gully and along the main face of cliffs to the north. For so long, this entire cliff line was a natural climbing gym. Several recent rediscoveries of Aboriginal cultural heritage have closed some areas to climbing. At the time of writing, Pharos Gully Boulders, Chicken Boulder, Plaque Rock, Castle Crag, Tiger Wall and Taylors Rock were off-limits; check the official Mount Arapiles-Tooan State Park webpage (parks.vic.gov.au and click on 'Things to do' and 'Rock climbing') for any updates.

With 3000 routes staring back at you, most of them between a 5min and 30min walk of camp, one of the toughest moves of the day might be in choosing where you climb. Potentially the most popular route of all, The Bard (grade 12 – *see* p.75 for grading information)), is in one of the closed areas, but one of the things that's great about Araps is the vast number of classic climbs in its chalk bag, even at low grades.

High among them is Tiptoe Ridge, which was one of the first routes climbed on the mountain in 1963. Ascending a prominent ridge on Pinnacle Face, immediately below Arapiles' highest point, Tiptoe Ridge is only a grade 5 climb – not a whole lot more than a scramble – but it's considered among the best routes of its grade in the world and has a high sense of exposure that adds immeasurably to the challenge.

Right Hanging about on the Organ Pipes

Rock Climbing, Mount Arapiles/Dyuritte

Victoria

To reach Tiptoe Ridge from the Pines campground, you walk past the Pharos, a tall, island-like pinnacle rising in isolation beside the main cliffs. To get a sense of the variety of challenges on Araps, peep around the Pharos's corner to find Punks in the Gym, a route that when first climbed by Wolfgang Gullich in 1985 was considered (for about the next year) to be the toughest climb in the world. It was the first grade 32 climb on the planet (it's since been downgraded to 31), and it would be 10 years before anyone succeeded in climbing it again. Today, it's not even the hardest route at Araps, with the nearby Somalia (33) having surpassed it.

Chances are you'll never climb Punks in the Gym or Somalia – few will – but the Pharos is strung with more classics per square metre of rock than perhaps any other climbing areas here, including Slopin' Sleazin' (27), Judgement Day (19) and Lamplighter (14).

Close to camp, the Organ Pipes and neighbouring Atridae climbing areas are long-time crowd favourites. On the fluted columns of the Organ Pipes is a route named D Minor (15), said to have once been voted the best climb in Victoria, and its companion, D Major (10). Atridae is home to Muldoon, another immortal route pegged at grade 13 but held by many to feel more difficult, despite the jug-like holds, or you can climb deep in a narrow chimney on Agamemnon (11).

For pure wow factor, it's hard to beat Kachoong (21), with its dramatic protruding roof peering out over Mitre Lake and the Wimmera Plains. If you've only ever seen one photo of Araps, it's likely to have been from this climb, with someone dangling from its roof by their fingers and toes … or maybe just their fingers. It's the most photographed climb in the country.

In the evenings, climbers straggle back into camp, part energised, part wearied, but there's climbing life even beyond the Pines and the cliffs. The town of Natimuk is around 10km from Mount Arapiles/Dyuritte, with a climbing culture suitable to its location. With its wide main street, general store and pub, it looks like most other country towns, until you spy its climbing shop (with an extensive selection of climbing gear for sale, and ready knowledge of Araps and its climbs), or visit on a Sunday afternoon when its climbing museum is open. Step into the National Hotel, better known as the Nati Pub, and climbing photos line one wall.

Around this mountain, climbing is life, and life is climbing.

Opposite top The quartzite cliffs of Mount Arapiles/Dyuritte *Opposite bottom* The Pines campground

How to tell the difficulty of a rock climb? It's a game of numbers, with every climbing route in the country given a numeric grading, from 1 (easiest) currently through to 35, which represents the toughest climb in Australia (presently the Retired Extremely Dangerous route in the Blue Mountains). Confusingly, other grading systems are used elsewhere around the world – at least 10 different systems exist. Most commonly seen is the Yosemite Decimal System used in the United States, with climbs ranging from 5.0 to 5.15d.

The toughest rock climb in the world? Right now, it's Silence, located in Hanshelleren Cave among the fiords of central Norway. It was climbed in 2017 by Czech Adam Ondra, considered the world's best sport climber and, at the time of writing, has never been repeated. In Australian terms, Silence would be graded at 39.

Paddle through a deep gorge, staying each night in exclusive canoeing campsites, with plentiful wildlife and solitude.

Canoeing, Glenelg River

Gunditjmara Country

WHY IT'S SPECIAL

Deep in a limestone gorge near Victoria's border with South Australia, the Glenelg River settles towards dusk. The day's wind has blown itself out, and the only things that disturb the mirrored waters are the brief appearance of a platypus and the soft tinkle of a rope trailing behind a canoe.

Meandering through Lower Glenelg National Park, the Glenelg River Canoe Trail is one of Australia's best flatwater paddles. Its wide, gentle flow is encased in bush and cliffs, with a gorge up to 50m deep as its centrepiece. The river is lined with campgrounds, including seven reserved exclusively for canoeists, making it a simple task to piece together days along the river.

Where
The border town of Nelson is 400km west of Melbourne/Naarm and 470km southeast of Adelaide/Tarndanya.

When
Conditions are best through summer and early autumn.

Do it
Rent canoes from Nelson Canoe Hire (nelsoncanoehire.com.au) or Paestan Canoe Hire (canoehire.com.au) in Winnap. Both companies can drop you off at a launch site along the river for an additional charge

Fitness: ●●●○○

Fear factor: ●●○○○

Expertise required ●●●○○

Family friendly

Opposite Paddle perfect on the Glenelg River

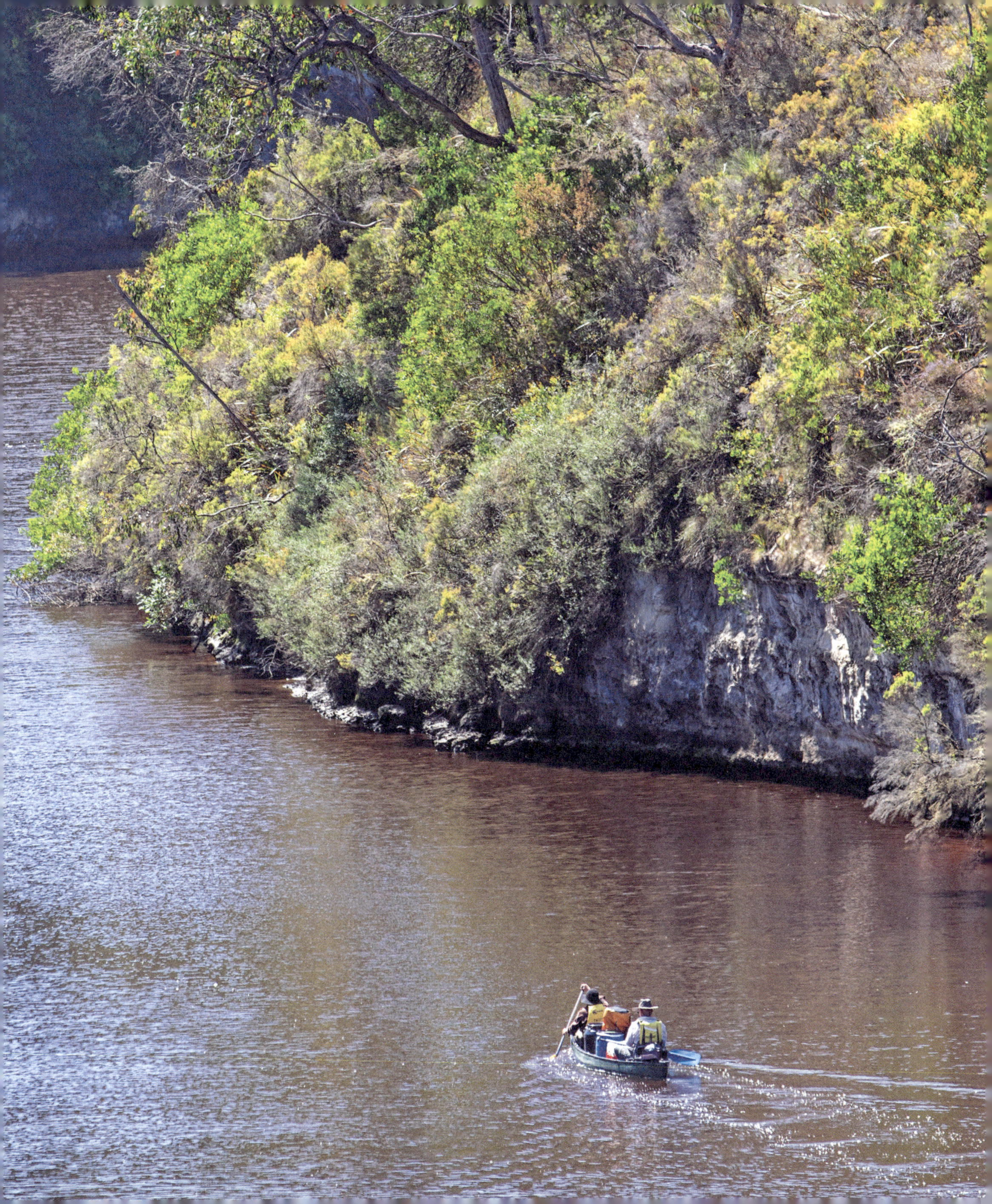

Above The Glenelg River near Pines Landing *Opposite* Shacked up at Donovans

THE ADVENTURE

The Glenelg River, known to the Gunditjmara People as Bocara, begins its 400km journey on the slopes of Gariwerd/Grampians, but the canoe trail officially begins in Dartmoor, almost 100km to the west of the headwaters.

With the river accessible by road at many points, there are, however, numerous possible launches, and few canoeists set out from Dartmoor, which sits outside the national park, above a stretch of the river noted for snags. A more popular start, ideal for a four-day paddle to Nelson, is Pines Landing, just beyond the point at which the Glenelg River enters Lower Glenelg National Park. From here, it's 56.6km by water to the river mouth, and 54.4km to Nelson.

The recommended first night's camp, Moleside Landing, is just 4km downstream from Pines Landing, making it possible to set out late in the afternoon (or to paddle upstream for a while before heading for Moleside Landing). In once doing so, I spied my first platypus in the river, drifting along as kangaroos grazed at the river's edge, disturbed only when my canoe brushed against the reeds.

Along river bends here, limestone cliffs rise high overhead, though the gorge is still far downstream. At Moleside Landing, a small pier on the left bank leads up to twin campgrounds: one for canoeists and one for hikers on the Great South West Walk, which runs beside the river from here to the sea. Empty your canoe, flip it over (to keep out any overnight rain), set up camp and take a 5min walk upstream to Moleside Falls, so tiny – little more than a step in a staircase – that you might wonder how they earned the name 'falls', and yet still beautiful when running with recent rain.

Leaving Moleside Landing, you're setting out on the trail's longest stretch between canoe campgrounds – 13.7km to

Skipworth Springs. It's a chance to settle into river rhythms and existence. As you paddle downstream, cormorants perch on overhanging trees, black swans sail about oblivious to your presence, and swamp hens provide occasional comic relief, bursting out of the banks to dash across the river, seeming almost to run on water.

One of canoeing's greatest appeals, particularly on a stretch of river like this, is the complete sense of removal. When driving or walking in a national park, there are always signs of human presence – in the roads you drive, the paths you walk, the markers that point the way. But along this stretch of the Glenelg River, you might well be in an original Australian paradise. There's a road nearby, but it's blocked from view; the Great South West Walk is on the bank, but you can't see it.

The canoe trail's most beautiful stretch comes beyond Skipworth Springs and Georges Rest. By the time you pass Forest Camp, you've slipped into the gorge, with white limestone walls rising dozens of metres above you. This thin white line of gorge runs almost all the way to Nelson, giving most canoeists two days of tunnel-like paddling beneath cliffs that are sometimes sheer and smooth, and other times eroded like Cappadocian formations.

The centrepiece of the gorge used to be Princess Margaret Rose Cave, complete with its own river landing, but at the time of writing, the cave had been closed to visitors for two years due to safety risks – check online for any updates.

The final canoe campground, Lasletts, is 2km before the cave and worth a night's stop, not just for the chance to linger in the gorge, but to save some energy for what can be a challenging final stretch into Nelson, 14.6km ahead. Park brochures note that 'the last day of canoeing can be affected by incoming tides and winds, which may slow progress', and they're not exaggerating. The winds that blow through this final section can make it feel as though you're stuck on a rowing machine, paddling but going nowhere, so try to set out early from Lasletts to counter as much of this sea breeze as possible.

Past Princess Margaret Rose Cave, the river sweeps into its biggest, longest bend, crossing the border into South Australia and an immediate, stark change in landscape. Lower Glenelg National Park ends at the state border, and the banks instantly fill with corrugated-iron shacks and boathouses at Dry Creek and then Donovans, before the river turns back into Victoria and the national park. It's like a meditative inhale before the final few kilometres to the highway bridge at Nelson. The river flows on, out into the sea, but the journey finishes here.

The landlubber's companion to the Glenelg River Canoe Trail is the Great South West Walk (GSWW, greatsouthwestwalk.com), which makes a 250km loop along Victoria's south-west coast and beside the Glenelg River. Setting out from Portland, it heads inland to meet the Glenelg River just above Moleside Landing, following the waterway to its mouth beyond Nelson - if you're canoeing, the GSWW is pretty much your unseen companion the entire way. Along Discovery Bay, the walk follows the coast or, alternatively, turns up onto Mount Richmond, before rounding Cape Bridgewater (with its seal colony and Petrified Forest) and Cape Nelson back into Portland.

Pedal seven of Australia's most challenging mountain roads in a European-style cycling quest.

Cycling the 7 Peaks, High Country

The High Country is the Country of many Traditional Owner groups, including the Dhudhuroa, Gunai Kurnai, Taungurung, Waywurru and Jaithmathang peoples

WHY IT'S SPECIAL

Cycling's loftiest moments come in the mountains. It's where Europe's Grand Tours – the Tour de France, Giro d'Italia and Vuelta a España – are won, lost and immortalised, and where legs truly experience the baptism of cycling.

Australia has few mountain rides to rival Europe's grand alpine climbs, at least until you set wheels on the 7 Peaks Ride. Ascending through Victoria's High Country, this collection of seven rides to seven summits is Australia's literal peak cycling challenge, luring road cyclists across the summer months. As on European mountains roads, climbs here are even specifically signposted for cyclists – an indication of their popularity – with markers noting distances and gradients as you ascend.

Riding one peak will put sting in your legs; riding all seven, climbing more than 7000m over 160km, will put you in exclusive cycling company.

Where
The 7 Peaks are sprinkled through the High Country, from Lake Mountain, 120km north-east of Melbourne/Naarm, to Mount Buffalo and Falls Creek in the state's north-east.

When
The season for the 7 Peaks Ride is from around late Oct through to April. Nov to March typically bring the best conditions.

Do it
Research at the 7 Peaks Ride website (ridehighcountry.com.au/7-peaks). The Climbing Cyclist website (theclimbingcyclist.com) is also a good resource for detailed descriptions of each ascent.

Fitness: ●●●●●
Fear factor: ●●○○○
Expertise required ●●●●○

Above Almost there ... *Opposite* Climbing towards the summit of Mount Hotham

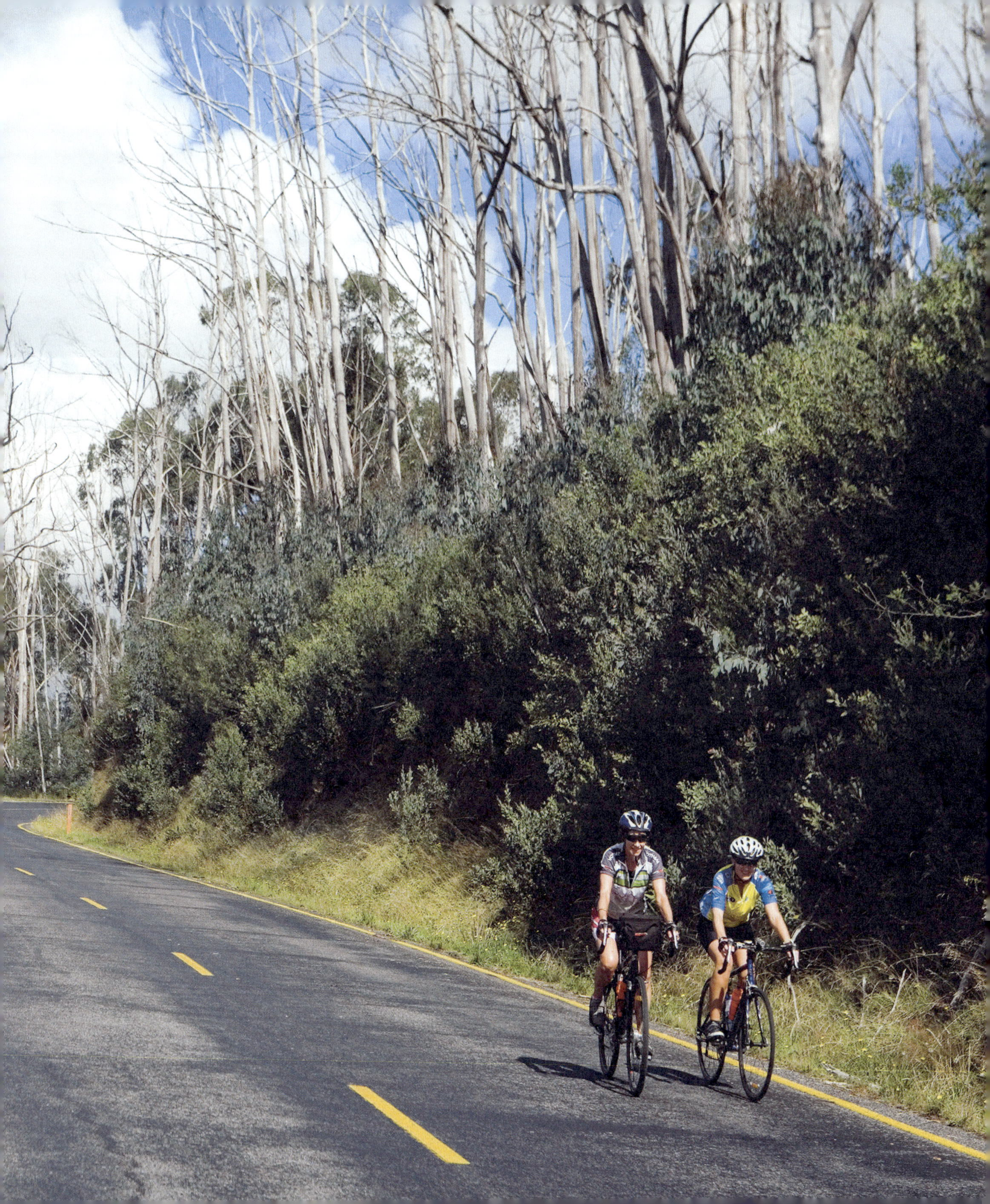

Victoria

THE ADVENTURE

When the ski season melts across Victoria's High Country, its alpine resorts turn their thoughts predominantly to bikes. Mountain-bike trails snake through the snow gums and ski runs, and roads beckon cyclists into a summer of scaling slopes. Each year, a determined faction of road cyclists set their sights on the 7 Peaks Ride, aiming to pedal to the top of seven of the highest mountain roads in the country. A few will complete it in as little as seven days; others might space it out over seven years.

In years past, 7 Peaks cyclists carried a 7 Peaks passport, getting it stamped in the ski villages atop the climbs, though the onset of a certain pandemic slammed the passports shut. Satisfaction (and a decent set of thighs) is now the only prize.

By nature, the mountain roads on the 7 Peaks Ride are narrow and twisting, but that also means that vehicle traffic is intermittent and slow, presenting few problems to cyclists.

In ascending order of vertical metres climbed, the rides are Mount Baw Baw (741m), Mount Buller (921m), Lake Mountain (932m), Dinner Plain (943m), Mount Buffalo (1015m), Falls Creek (1129m) and Mount Hotham (1321m), though the numbers are an unreliable measure of challenge and difficulty.

The lowest of the ascents, the revered (or feared) Mount Baw Baw, is the most gruelling of the 7 Peaks, and one of the toughest climbs in Australia. The ride from the Gantry extends over just 6.5km, but with an average gradient of more than 11% to Mount Baw Baw village. The thigh-busting climbing begins immediately, never relents and almost halfway up, around notorious Winch Corner, it exceeds 20%. That's likely exhausting just to read.

Fair to say that Baw Baw is probably not the climb on which to begin a 7 Peaks attempt – that should be nearby Lake Mountain, the closest peak to Melbourne/Naarm, though it too starts with a punch, setting out at around 8% for the first 4km through the tall mountain ash forest on Robley Spur, and then settling into a gentler morning out for the rest of the 21km ascent.

Left Snow poles line the heights of Mount Hotham

Cycling the 7 Peaks, High Country

Drive north and you come to Mount Buller and what feels like the first of the big-name alpine ascents. Buller rises clear and tall, as if trying to intimidate, as you approach Mansfield, disappearing again as you continue to the climb's start by the Delatite River in Mirimbah. It's a 15.3km climb, and for the first 10km the road ribbons across the mountain slopes, the gradient consistent and manageable enough to allow riders to settle into a rhythm.

I first climbed Mount Buller in the company of Phil Anderson, the first Australian to wear the leader's yellow jersey in the Tour de France (and a five-time top-10 finisher in the race). Along the way, I asked him how these Australian climbs compared to the punishing passes and peaks of Europe.

'It could be compared to some of the Alpine or Pyrénéan climbs they do in the Tour de France, except that in the Tour you might have two or three climbs like this in a day,' he said.

Only 6km from the top of Mount Buller, the road suddenly coils up a spur, hair-pinning through Unnamed Corner and Dump Inn Corner before climbing on to the most suitably named bend of all, Hell Corner – the ride's steepest moment (13%) saved until its very end.

The remaining four peaks – Buffalo, Dinner Plain, Falls and Hotham – sit clustered at the northern end of the state. On a Saturday or Sunday morning, there can be almost as many bikes as cars on the slopes of Mount Buffalo, betraying the fact that this is the most popular of all the peak climbs. And with good reason. Though it ascends 1015m, it does so at a fairly consistent 5%, with the road making wide, sweeping bends as it rises up the slopes. Distraction from the effort comes in the deep valley views, the thick bush shielding riders from the sun, and glimpses up the slopes to the narrow granite cleft of the Gorge. The climb tops out at the edge of the Gorge, beside its glass lookout platform, for suitably heroic photos of a climb well done.

Dinner Plain is the longest of the rides (42.8km from Omeo), essentially ascending the back of Mount Hotham (fight the urge to claim a Dinner Plain ascent by descending to it from Hotham's summit ...), while the Falls Creek climb rolls out relentlessly from the town of Mount Beauty – such is the altitude variation that you set out in tall timber and finish in alpine openness. It's a test of endurance, stretching on for 29.5km, climbing steadily for 4km then settling into 12.5km of undulations – these are moments of relief or frustration, depending on your frame of mind (some days you just hate losing hard-gained vertical metres). The climb is at its steepest – an average of around 6% – over the final 4km.

If you really want to get beaten up by Falls Creek, you can ascend instead from the other side – the Back of Falls – where getting started is the toughest part of the day. From the Omeo Highway, the Bogong High Plains Road begins at a 10% gradient, rising immediately into the infamous WTF Corner (yes, it's well named) and remaining brutal for another 9km, climbing around 700m in that short distance. From there, things get easier. Phew.

With almost 200m more vertical ascent than the next highest ride, Mount Hotham is the challenge's pinnacle and a true climber's climb. Out of Harrietville, the ascent begins almost immediately, rising in three distinct sections over 30km: short, sharp climbs that break any sense of rhythm over the first 10km; flattening out across a fire-scarred ridge over the next 10km; then hitting you with its biggest and toughest climbs – the seemingly endless CRB Hill and finally, most cruelly, the concluding 9% pull to the summit – just when you don't want them, across the final 10km.

Then, like all cycling climbs, the real fun is in getting back down ...

Above Mist rolls over the summit of Mount Hotham *Opposite* Wallace Hut near Falls Creek

Take the Peaks idea one step further - or shorter - by packing three of the High Country's revered climbs into a one-day mission at the Peaks Challenge Falls Creek. Held each March, this mountain monster is a 235km loop ride on roads, beginning and ending in Falls Creek. It starts out happily enough - descending the 1129m to Mount Beauty - before climbing through Tawonga Gap and over Mount Hotham. Rolling down into Omeo, there's just the crux to come: the lung-splitting Back of Falls climb. As the event website suitably notes, 'With 200km in your legs, the back of Falls will hit you like a tonne of bricks …'

You have 13 hours to complete the challenge, totalling up more than 4000m of climb.

Find details online (bicyclenetwork.com.au and click on 'Rides & Events').

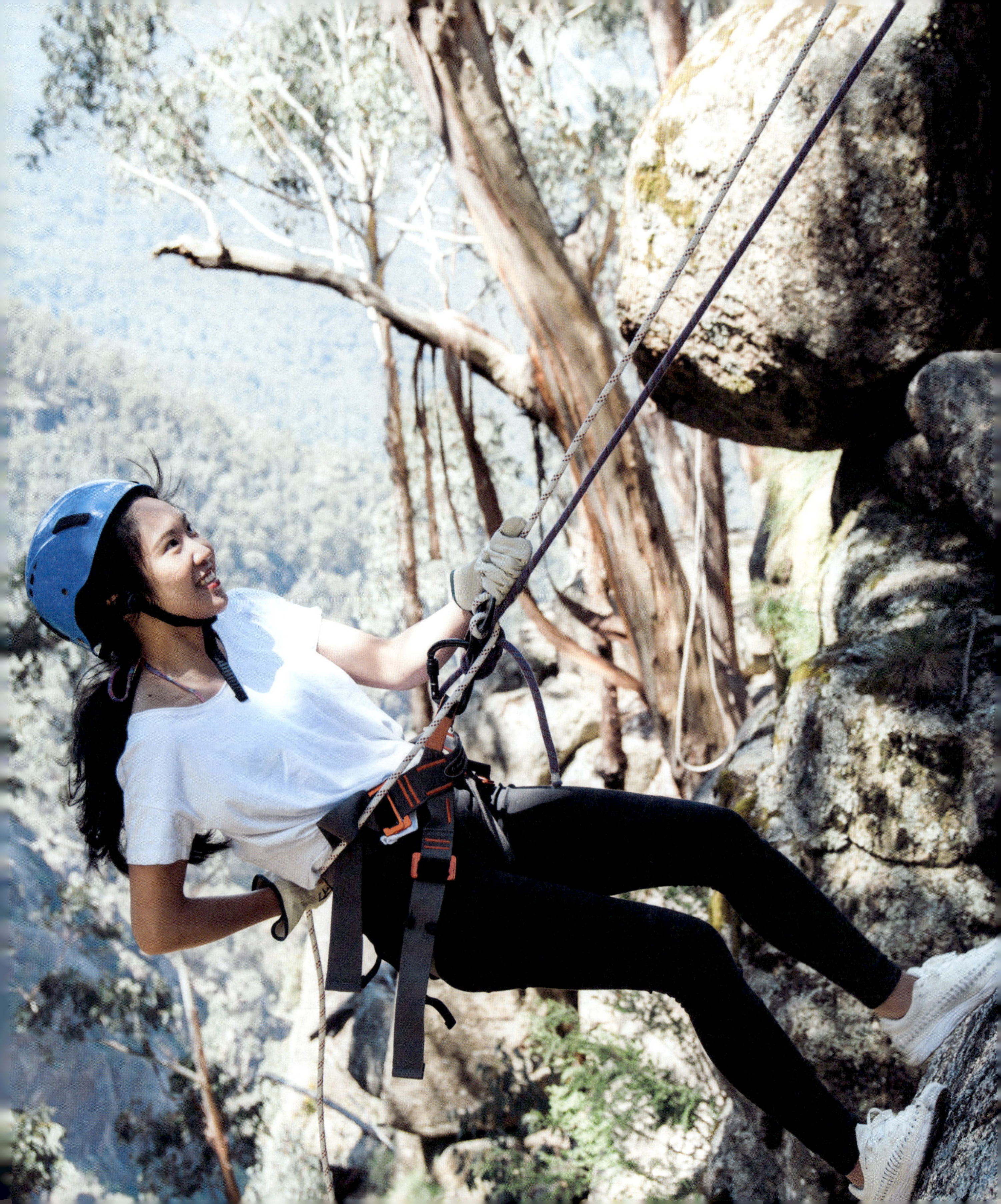

Tackle the world's highest commercial abseil, dangling from the cliffs of a mighty granite gorge.

Abseiling, Mount Buffalo

Taungurung Country

WHY IT'S SPECIAL

Even when you're not about to dangle off its cliffs like a teabag, the Gorge on Mount Buffalo is a colossal and daunting place. Stand near its edge and the world seems to tumble into an abyss, with granite cliffs that just keep going down and down and then down some more. Now imagine standing atop those cliffs, turning your back and stepping backwards over their edge, held only by a thin thread of rope, with the ground 220m below. It's about the equivalent of abseiling off the 35th-tallest building in Australia (Circle on Cavill North Tower on the Gold Coast, in case you're wondering).

This is the formidable prelude to what is believed to be the world's highest commercial abseil, launched in 2023 by the Bright Adventure Company, descending the Gorge's imposing North Wall, with glorious views out over the Ovens Valley and beyond ... if you can bring yourself to look up from the task.

Consider this for perspective on the magnitude of this abseil: the now-defunct abseil on Tasmania's Gordon Dam long laid claim to being the world's highest commercial abseil, at 140m in height. This Mount Buffalo abseil is more than 50 per cent higher again.

Where
The meeting point for the abseiling tour is the carpark at the Gorge day-visitor area, in front of the Mount Buffalo Chalet. It's 33km from Bright and a 4hr drive north of Melbourne/Naarm.

When
Abseiling trips on the Gorge at Mount Buffalo operate from late spring through to autumn.

Do it
Bright Adventure Company operates the North Wall abseil (brightadventurecompany.com.au).

Fitness: ●●●●○

Fear factor: ●●●●●

Expertise required ●●○○○

Above Going down *Opposite* Hard at work on the training wall

THE ADVENTURE

You don't step up to something as formidable as a 220m abseil without first testing your capability and your head for heights on something less dizzying. On this North Wall adventure, that means a morning of shorter abseils elsewhere around the Gorge rim with the Bright Adventure Company (BAC). One of the possible training grounds is so-called Sewer Wall, lowering yourself down a 25m cliff beside an old pipe through which, in its earliest days, the nearby Mount Buffalo Chalet would pour its sewage straight into the Gorge.

This low cliff looks directly across to the North Wall, making it easy to get psyched out by a view of cliffs so tall and imposing that you can't even see their base. For BAC owner Rowan Blakers, the particular view was always more inspiring than intimidating – it was while sitting here belaying abseilers on the Gorge's southern cliffs that he first wondered about the abseiling possibilities on the North Wall. Later, while climbing on Ozymandias, one of the Gorge's classic rock-climbing routes, he settled on the idea that this particular section of wall would indeed make a great abseil. It just happened to be one of the most daunting cliffs in Australia, described by one climbing website as 'the premier Australian big-wall test piece', and typically taking climbers several days to ascend. Coming down on a rope is a much quicker affair.

After a morning in the training ground of the lower cliffs, the big drop beckons. From the Chalet, a walking trail sets out atop the rim of the gorge, passing Mount Buffalo's quirky mountain-top cricket pitch and crossing Crystal Brook just before it tips over the cliffs as a 200m-high waterfall. Look into the stream and you'll probably discover that it's well named, with fish swimming about in its clear water just metres from the big drop.

Further along the cliff-edge, you come to Wilkinson's Lookout, where the North Wall abseil is soon anchored. A 300m-long rope, weighing around 20kg, dangles over the cliff-edge, and you step back, trusting your weight to the rope. Crystal Brook Falls roar in the distance, and the gorge yawns beneath.

With so much weight of rope behind you, it takes effort even to move as you begin stepping down the cliffs. But as the descent progresses, it becomes easier and (if you wish) faster. The pace of the movement is in your hands, literally, with a braking device on the rope working to control your speed. Pinch it between your fingers and it releases, allowing you to slide down the rope; release the pinch and the device holds you firm on the rope.

For the first 20m or so of the descent, your feet are against the cliffs. Sat back in the rope, you step down the wall like Spiderman on a city tower. But then you reach an overhang, and the cliffs disappear from beneath your feet. Your next steps are out into air, where you will hang for the next 100m. This instant of separation from the cliffs was probably the most confronting moment I experienced in researching this book, suddenly hanging above a 200m drop, with no points of contact on the mountain, held only by an 11mm-thick rope.

Quickly, the adrenaline passed. Within another 20m I'd stopped, suspended above 180m of air, absorbing the view of the cliffs, the waterfall, the Ovens and Buckland valleys and distant High Country peaks such as Mount Bogong and Mount Feathertop, the two highest mountains in Victoria. The colourful helmet of Tom, my belayer, was a distant speck far below at the base of the cliffs, while across the gorge a school group had stopped its own smaller abseil adventures to watch me dangle from this massive cliff, spinning in the breeze as though I was Australia's highest ceiling fan.

The sensation is like hovering. You're in the mountains, but not on the mountains, suspended from them by a rope little thicker than one of your fingers. As the descent gains pace, it's like being in some kind of mountain elevator without walls, ceiling or floor. Climbers might be heading up Ozymandias just a few metres away as you head down – the climbers might spend three days scaling this cliff, but you'll be down in less than 30min.

After 100m of nothing but air, your feet return to the granite cliffs and you can begin again to step down the mountain until you finally hit horizontal ground, unclipping around 220m below where you last stood upright.

The satisfaction of having abseiled off one of the highest cliffs in the country is immense, but the most tiring bit is still to come – the climb back out, crossing Crystal Brook and ascending on faint climbers' trails back to the cliff-top Chalet. What goes down must come up.

To dangle off Mount Buffalo, you don't have to pitch yourself straight into the world's highest abseil. Bright Adventure Company has three other possibilities in its rope bag: a family abseiling adventure that has a range of abseil options up to 25m in height; the 45m Dragon's Foot Abseiling Adventure, which includes a rock squeeze or climb to get back to the top; and the North Wall Mega Abseil, which involves a string of four abseils to descend 300m through the Gorge.

Deeper into the mountain you can try the Underground River Caving Adventure, exploring a 350m-long infill cave with a stream flowing through it. And there's always the prospect of sleeping out on the Gorge's cliffs (see p.91).

Top View over the Ovens Valley from the Gorge

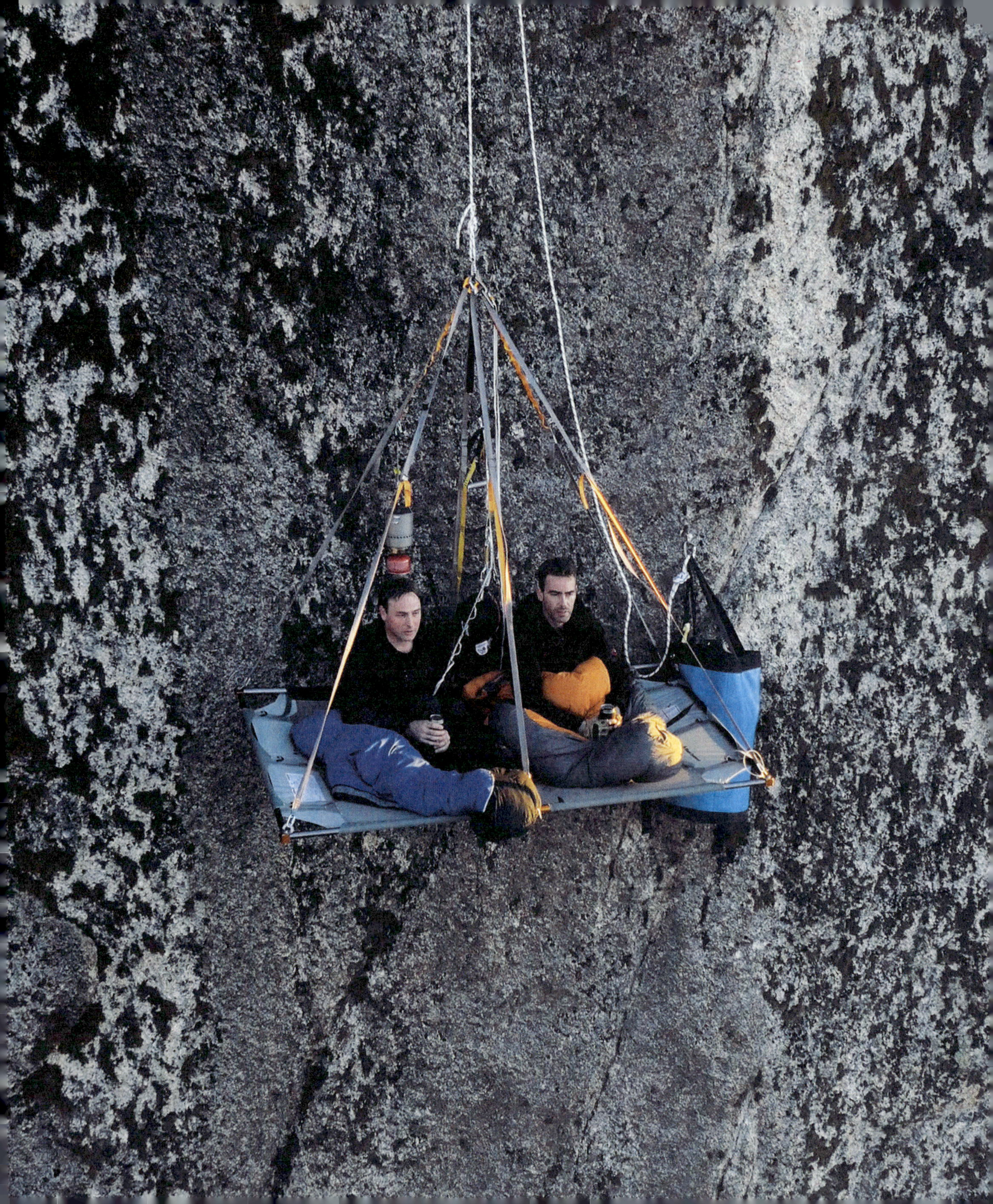

Spend a night sleeping on air on this dizzying experience usually reserved for big-wall rock climbers.

Sleeping on a portaledge, Mount Buffalo

Taungurung Country

WHY IT'S SPECIAL

On towering rock walls across the world – the likes of El Capitan and Half Dome in Yosemite National Park, needlepoint Cerro Torre in Patagonia, and Pakistan's Trango Towers – hot-shot climbers spend days scaling single cliffs, inching towards the top and sleeping out each night on portaledges anchored to the rock.

Australia has little such big-wall climbing, but it does have what most other countries don't – the adventure of a night spent out on a portaledge without the necessity of scaling hundreds of metres of vertical rock to get there. Billed as the world's highest cliff camping experience, Beyond the Edge has you abseiling down the North Wall of Mount Buffalo's vertiginous Gorge before spending the night on a tiny portaledge, suspended over a drop of around 250m. Holding you there is a thread-thin sheet of nylon inside an aluminium frame. Peer down and ask yourself, are you brave enough to roll over in your sleep?

Where
The meeting point for the abseiling tour is a stone hut at the base of the carpark at the Gorge day-visitor area in front of the Mount Buffalo Chalet. It's 33km from Bright and a 4hr drive north of Melbourne/Naarm.

When
Beyond the Edge trips run from Nov to May, and are weather dependent.

Do it
Beyond the Edge is operated by Unleashed-Unlimited. Book online (unleashed-unlimited.com.au).

Fitness: ●●●○○

Fear factor: ●●●●●

Expertise required ●●○○○

Opposite Home sweet home

THE ADVENTURE

There are so many breath-catching moments in this overnight adventure, and the first one is immediate as Howie Dawson, the creator of Beyond the Edge, stands on the south rim of the Gorge and points across to the monstrously high North Wall. It's one of the tallest mountain cliffs in Australia, and dangling from it, around 30m beneath the lip of the cliffs, is a tiny white triangle with nothing but cliffs and air beneath it. It's your home for the night, hanging above a 250m drop. It's a sight so audacious and confronting that there have been tears from past participants at this moment of reveal.

Like all adventures that involve abseiling, instruction comes before induction, except that on this experience you also need to learn the art of getting yourself back off the portaledge.

On a granite outcrop, in sight of Mount Buffalo's Cathedral and Hump summits, a 12m-high training ground is created, allowing you to learn, refresh or refine your abseiling skills. Comfortable with that? Now it's time to learn to jumar.

To get off the portaledge, you need to scale the cliffs, and the cliff immediately above the ledge is beyond the abilities of even many very good climbers. Instead, you'll use jumars, or climbing ascenders – a pair of hand grips that slide up the rope but don't slide back down. They are connected by a strap to foot loops, so that as your right hand moves higher, so does your right foot. Then the left hand and left foot. And so you ascend, rocking and rolling your weight between the two sides. The layman's version of rock climbing.

Victoria

Having packed a haul bag with your gear for the night, it's a short walk out to Wilkinson's Lookout. About 5m around from where the world's highest commercial abseil pitches over the edge (*see* p.87), another abseil is rigged. You shuffle back over the rock, secured to the mountain by rope, and take the backward step of faith over the edge of the cliffs. If you're not feeling any trepidation at this moment, you're a cool cat indeed.

From the cliff-edge, it's about a 20m abseil down to a natural rock ledge, then it's all exposure and awe. Beyond this ledge, the world seems to disappear into a void. As you continue, you're hanging over a drop of more than 250m, though you only have to abseil another 10m before you step into the portaledge.

Arriving at the portaledge is not the immediate moment of relief you might anticipate. The portaledge is effectively the floor of a (very strong) tent, pulled tight and taut between an aluminium frame. When you move, the frame often moves, jolting and scraping against the cliffs (no, you're not about to plunge to your death).

And then slowly everything settles. For the next 12 to 15 hours, this is your home. They're blessed hours of solitude and precarious peace, with the world and the light changing by the hour, and you safely clipped to the cliffs by your harness. Soon enough, you'll be getting your space organised like any campsite (albeit one that's very limited in places to go for a walk …). Gear hangs from carabiners, and the haul bag that you've packed with your sleeping bag, mat and warm clothing hangs beside the portaledge like bedside drawers. The portaledge also has tent-style flaps that can be zipped around you in the event of rain.

If a portaledge can have a version of glamping, this is it. By the time you arrive onto the ledge it's typically around 90min to sunset, and soon canapés of crackers and cheese (complete with cheese board and cheese knife) are lowered down the rope in an Esky bag, followed by a home-cooked dinner delivered the same way. Mount Bogong, Hotham and Feathertop crown the horizon in a who's who of Victorian mountains beneath changing, colouring skies, and the Buckland Valley is partitioned into neat fields far below.

Right Big wall, tiny figure *Opposite* The abseil begins

Sleeping on a portaledge, Mount Buffalo

The portaledge is wide enough to accommodate two people – a romantic night hanging off a cliff, anyone? – and there have even been proposals on it. 'I always ask people to propose in the morning,' Howie jokes, 'because if they ask in the evening and the answer is no, it can be an awkward place to be.'

If there are two of you, the biggest decision is around who sleeps on the cliff-side and who sleeps on the airside. No side is any safer or different, but mentally they're worlds apart. On the airside, without the perceived security of the cliffs beside you, there's a heightened sense of exposure. When I lay down on the airside on the night I spent on the portaledge, I needed only to shift my head and neck to peer down into infinity.

In this area of low light pollution, the night skies are dazzling. Satellites and the International Space Station might buzz past overhead, Porepunkah glitters like a Christmas tree in the valley, and Bright casts a glow over an intervening ridge.

The trepidation of the situation never abates entirely, for there's a low-level acceptance that hanging from a cliff like this isn't normal human behaviour. But it's also the most dramatic camp I've ever stayed in. The solitude is absolute, and with 200m-high Crystal Brook Falls pouring down the cliffs nearby, it's a 'room' with a water feature that no resort in the world has ever been able to surpass.

A wake-up call (if you want one) from Howie comes before dawn on the UHF radio, allowing you to watch the sky warm up ahead of the sun's arrival. When it does rise, it shines directly onto the North Wall and the portaledge, bathing you in dawn light. Breakfast comes down the rope, you pack your gear and begin the process of jumaring up the cliffs. Pause as you near the top, look around and take it all in once more – it's a huge world from here and you've been one tiny part of it, clipped to the cliffs for a night.

Above The natural penthouse *Opposite* Life on the ledge

Not all cliffs require extreme measures to be appreciated. Australia's tallest sea cliffs - 300m in height - stretch along the southern edge of Tasmania's Turrakana/Tasman Peninsula and can be viewed on a Pennicott Wilderness Journeys' Tasman Island Cruise (pennicottjourneys.com.au).

If there's any conjecture about the Tasman Peninsula's claim to be Australia's highest sea cliffs, it comes from Ball's Pyramid, offshore from Lord Howe Island. Rising 550m out of the Pacific Ocean, it's considered the world's tallest sea stack. Climbing on the Pyramid is banned (except with special permission from parliament), but Reef N Beyond Eco Tours (visitlordhowe.com.au) runs snorkelling trips to Ball's Pyramid from Lord Howe.

Sleeping on a portaledge, Mount Buffalo

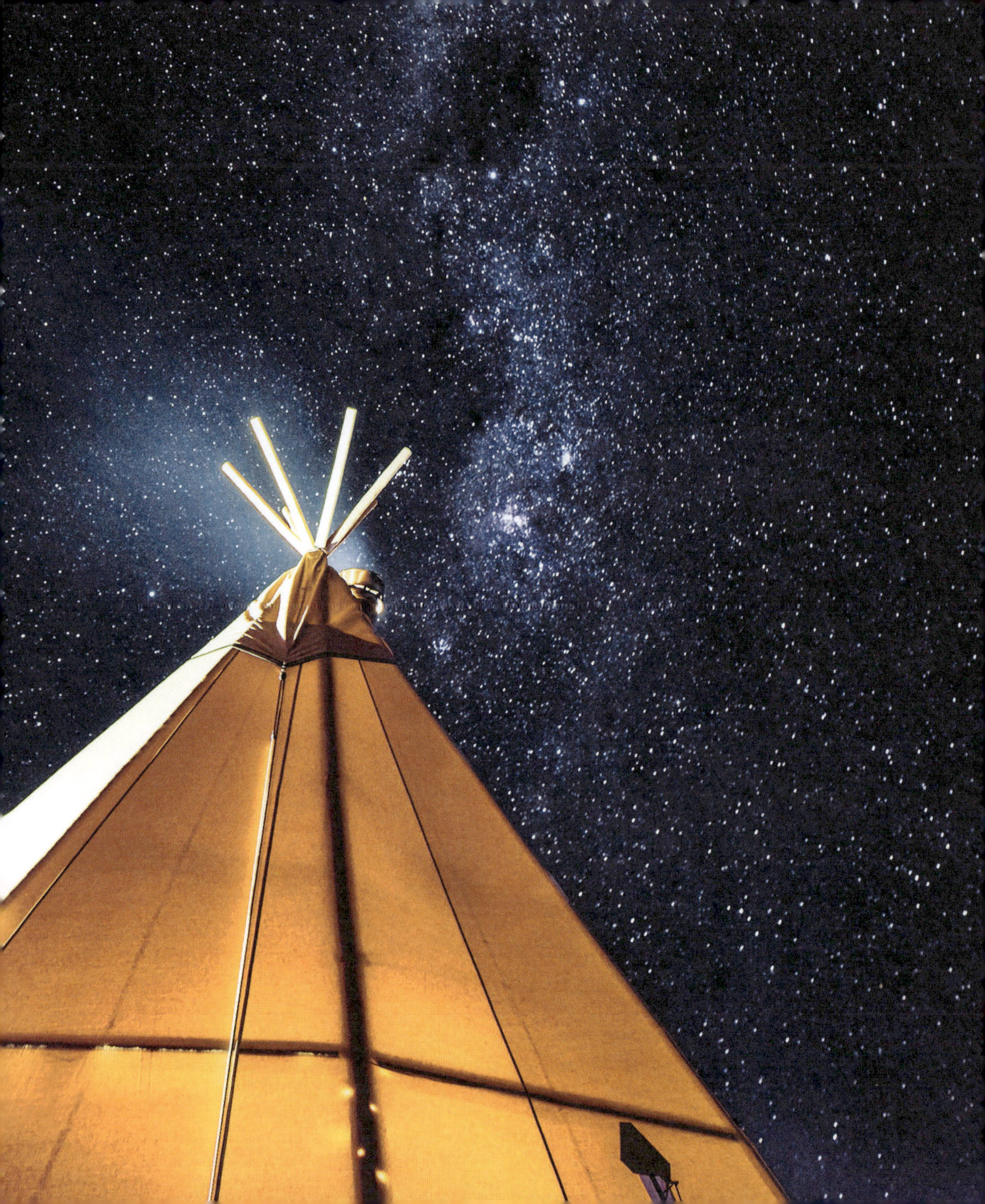

Experience a winter wonderland of snow domes or igloos, snowshoeing, mulled wine and fondue.

Snow camping, Mount Hotham

Gunaikurnai, Taungurung Country

Contributed by Jim Darby

WHY IT'S SPECIAL

Head to the alpine resorts of Victoria's High Country and there's a wealth of sleeping options, from high-end lodges to backpacker hostels, but you've come for the snow, so why not sleep in the snow? Alpine Nature Experience is a unique opportunity to camp in comfort in the snowfields.

After an adventurous guided ramble on snowshoes through snow gum forests in the heart of the mountain country around Mount Hotham, there's dinner waiting in true alpine style. Happily wearied by the day, and lit by a heavenly ceiling of stars, you end the day lying back in a snow dome, watching the stars, or snowflakes falling around you. When conditions are right, there's even a chance to stay overnight in an igloo.

Where
Wire Plain and the Dargo Lookout are about halfway between Hotham Heights and Dinner Plain villages on the Great Alpine Road.

When
Trips run Wed to Sun between June and Sept.

Do it
The winter Alpine Nature Experience can be taken at a few levels: just the snowshoe tour; snowshoeing and dinner; or the full overnight package of tour, dinner, bed and breakfast. Find more details online (alpinenatureexperience.com.au).

Fitness: ●●●○○

Fear factor: ●●○○○

Expertise required ●●○○○

Above Inside an Alpine Nature Experience igloo *Opposite* Under the stars and under a snowy roof: The central Nordic tipi

THE ADVENTURE

There's nothing subtle about the name – the Dargo Lookout – just as there's nothing subtle about the views. They stretch forever over the Dargo Valley and beyond, where the ridges and ranges of the Victorian Alps interlock like giant forested fingers. If you've booked ahead, you might be lucky enough to admire those views from your hot tub, warm with the knowledge that this is Australia's highest wood-fire-heated hot tub.

It's all part of the Alpine Nature Experience, which sits inside the Mount Hotham Resort area, surrounded by the Alpine National Park. At the centre of the experience is an off-the-grid, fully sustainable village with a communal, Nordic-style tipi at its heart and snow domes, or even an igloo, for accommodation. The village is the creation of Jean-Francois Rupp, who grew up skiing the French Alps but found himself drawn to Australia's mountains.

Unsurprisingly, the Alpine Nature Experience only takes place in winter. You gather at Wire Plain, on the Great Alpine Road between Mount Hotham and Dinner Plain village. From there, you don snowshoes for a half-hour wander through snow gum forests, with Rupp revealing some of the history of the region, explaining the intricacies of the surrounding flora and fauna, and some of the differences between the Australian mountains and those around Tignes and Val d'Isere, the giant French ski resorts of his childhood.

Then you'll reach the Eco Village at Dargo Lookout and take some time to absorb the views over the Dargo Valley one way and across to Mount Hotham the other, before hopping into the tipi with a fire crackling and some mulled wine to warm up on the inside.

Staying with the alpine theme, dinner is a fondue prepared by Rupp – all the ingredients are sourced locally, except for the cheese, which comes from France.

'We use two particular cheeses but you'd have to come for dinner for me to tell you what they are,' he says. 'It's a family recipe. We actually run it as a bit of a masterclass, where I teach you to make the perfect fondue. We have a lot of nice local wine, mostly from Rutherglen, where I used to work in the wine industry.'

Just as warming, there's also some schnapps available, again in the French style – an alpine liqueur called *genepy,* infused with flowers from the Alps for flavour.

Right A serene moment amongst the snowy landscape

Snow camping, Mount Hotham

After dinner, those guests who aren't staying the night at the Eco Village are guided back to the road, with those remaining having some time to linger in the tipi, downing a few more drinks and then heading to their snow domes for the night.

The domes are wood-framed structures covered in canvas, but with clear ceilings to enable you to watch the stars or the falling snow. Inside, there's a fireplace, a comfortable bed, sheepskins for extra warmth and a sink in which to freshen up.

In winters that deliver enough snow, igloos might also be part of the Eco Village. Made entirely of snow and ice, they have the same set-up as the snow domes, except for the fireplace. In the morning there's breakfast, a chance for a bath and then a tour on a snowmobile.

At the village and surrounds, you might see wombats, even a wallaby or High Country marsupials such as antechinus and possibly a mountain pygmy possum. 'The birds are amazing,' Rupp says. 'We get king parrots, gang gang cockatoos, rosellas and currawongs. Unfortunately, the birds are coming back earlier and leaving later – good for the guests but a bad sign for the snowfall.'

At the end of each winter, the village is dismantled to give the vegetation a chance to grow and recover. It returns in summer, but in the form of tree tents. 'We strap tents into trees,' Rupp says. 'They're exceptionally comfortable and cool to sleep in, and they have no impact on the environment, like leaving a dead patch of grass on the alpine region.'

The summer program extends to hikes along the Falls to Hotham Alpine Crossing, one of the High Country's premier multi-day bushwalks, connecting the two alpine resorts along a 37km trail, with guides carrying your gear, setting up camp and cooking for you along the way.

> Other remote but catered camping experiences can be found as far afield as Bungle Bungle Wilderness Lodge (aptouring.com.au/experiences/wilderness-lodges/bungle-bungle) and El Questro (elquestro.com.au) in WA's Kimberley region; at Bamurru Plains (bamurruplains.com) near Kakadu National Park in the NT; and in Tasmania at the Tasmanian Walking Company's Crescent Bay Camp (taswalkingco.com.au/tasman-long-weekend).

Left Snowshoeing over the plains *Opposite top left* One of the winter-warm snow domes *Opposite top right* Around the campfire *Opposite bottom* The eco-village from the air – surrounded by snow gums at Wire Plain, between Mount Hotham and Dinner Plain

Snow camping, Mount Hotham

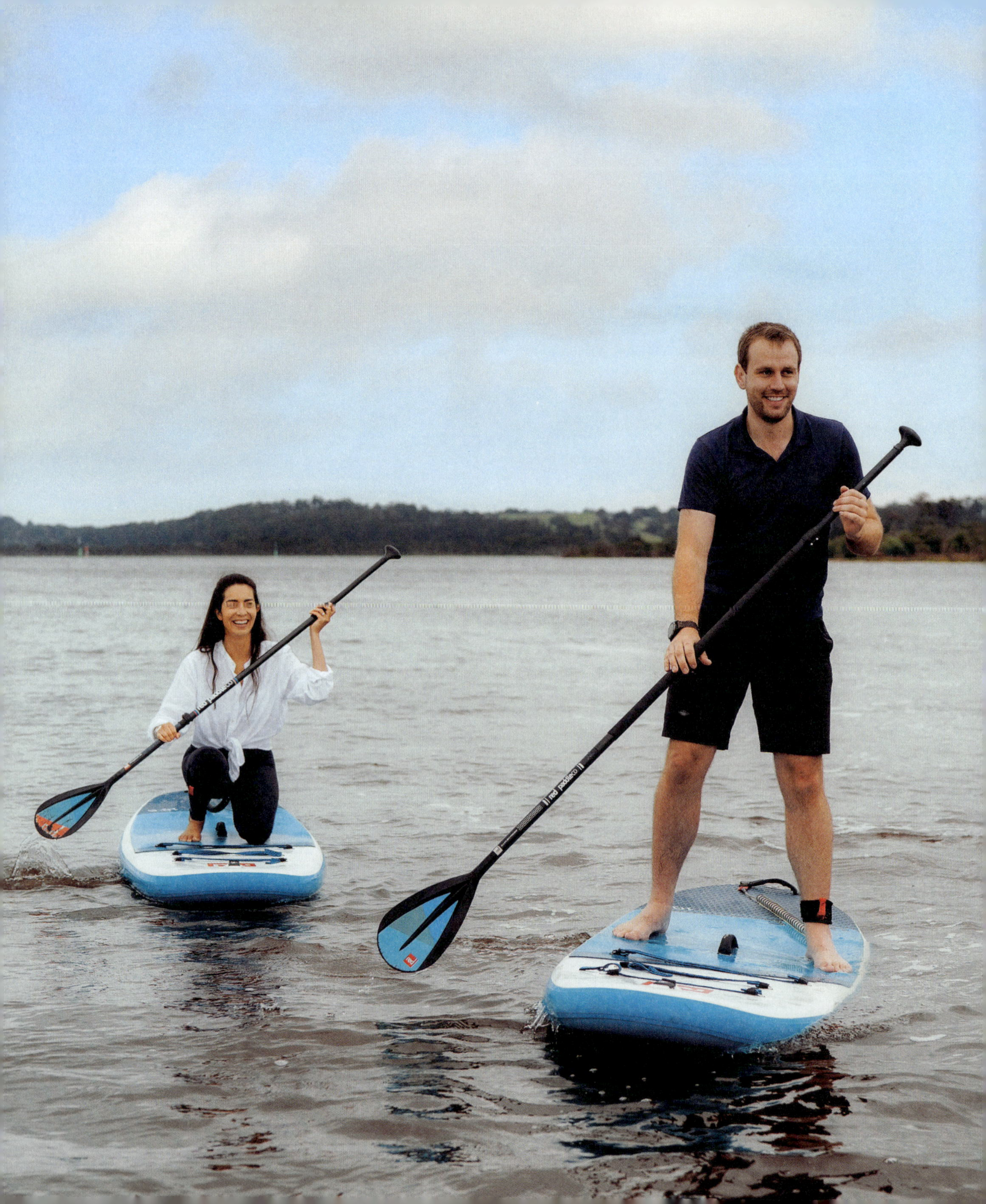

An elemental adventure – air and water – helicoptering to a private island and paddling back along the shores of a bird-filled island.

HeliSUP-ing, Gippsland Lakes

Gunaikurnai Country

WHY IT'S SPECIAL

From the sky, the Gippsland Lakes seem to slumber behind the dunes that separate them from the sea. Lines of waves roll ashore on one side, while the long and narrow lakes look like spills of paint as the helicopter banks over the 'entrance' – the artificial channel, carved through the dunes in the 1880s to connect the lake system to the sea – that gives Lakes Entrance its name. It's a spectacular meeting of waters, but the view is just the prelude to your day as you fly towards a rendezvous with Australia's first heli stand-up paddleboard (heliSUP) tour.

More familiar in the mountain regions of North America and Aotearoa New Zealand, where helicopters fly SUPs to remote alpine lakes, this tour out of Lakes Entrance brings a coastal flavour to the activity. A short but scenic helicopter flight lands paddlers on an island in the Gippsland Lakes, from where it's a SUP journey of around two hours back into Lakes Entrance, paddling in waters protected by the barrier dunes and Ninety Mile Beach, shielded from the waves and swell that assault the coast just a few hundred metres away.

Where
Trips depart from the Lakes Entrance Airfield at Kalimna West, 6km north of Lakes Entrance. Lakes Entrance is about a 3.5hr drive east from Melbourne/Naarm.

When
Trips run on demand; note that they do not run during the height of summer school holidays, when boat traffic on the lakes is at its heaviest.

Do it
The heliSUP tour is operated by Lakes Entrance-based Venture Out. For info and bookings, head online (ventureout.com.au).

Fitness: ●●●○○

Fear factor: ●●○○○

Expertise required ●○○○○

Opposite Paddling through the Gippsland Lakes

THE ADVENTURE

From almost the moment the helicopter takes to the air from an airstrip north of Lakes Entrance, tiny Fraser Island (no, not that one), the paddle's starting point, is visible, though the chopper doesn't head directly to the island. Instead, it makes a 30min scenic loop above the lakes, flying west over Metung and turning east to follow Ninety Mile Beach back to the 'entrance'. It's like looking down onto a mud map of the coming couple of hours.

The chopper touches down near the southern tip of Fraser Island, a private 31ha island anchored by an 11-bedroom Edwardian mansion with tennis court, pool and nine-hole golf course. It was originally the holiday home of the Syme family, the founders of Victoria's *The Age* newspaper, and at the end of 2022, it was offered up for sale for a mere $79 million, so if you have some loose coins jangling around in your pocket ...

Beside the landing, a water taxi arrives with the SUPs and Sarah Carlisle, the owner of local outdoors store and tour operator Venture Out. The boards are unloaded, instructions issued, and soon you're slipping off the shores to begin the 5km paddle into Lakes Entrance.

Fraser Island is the second of three islands all but clipped together at the eastern end of the Gippsland Lakes, and the bulk of the trip follows the shores of larger Rigby Island, which stretches almost all the way back to Lakes Entrance.

The 3m inflatable SUPs are as stable as barges, and as you push off from the shores of Fraser Island, the water is knee-deep ... until it's quickly not. In just a few minutes you're crossing Reeves Channel, the deep main channel that winds through the lake to the entrance. Around midsummer, don't be surprised if you have to pause before the channel in a Gippsland Lakes version of a traffic jam, waiting for a queue of boats to pass before you roll over their wakes (potentially on your knees at this point as you figure out the balance of the board) and across to the shores of Rigby Island. The southern edge of this island, along Hopetoun Channel, will be your guiding line for the next hour or so.

At Rigby's western end, the island is covered in typical coastal scrub – low, woolly, unkempt. Seals and dolphins are regularly sighted – there's a population of around 65 Burrunan dolphins in the Gippsland Lakes (one of only two known resident populations in Australia, the other being found at Port Phillip, see p.61) – and shoals of fish swim beneath the boards. And those dark shadows you'll spot in the shallows could just as easily be rays as weed. Then there's the occasional surprise visitor.

'Around four years ago, we had a whale and her calf come in through the entrance into the lakes,' Carlisle says.

Pelicans drift overhead, looking as heavy as cargo planes, and at times there might be hundreds of fairy terns and cormorants along stretches of beach on Rigby Island. It's a reminder that the Gippsland Lakes is one of Australia's 67 Ramsar-listed wetlands of international importance, providing habitat for an estimated 20,000 water birds. For at least 24,000 years they've also been the home of the Gunaikurnai People, providing them with an abundance of seafood. Even today, the local fishing industry is worth around $50 million a year.

Boats continue to pass in the channels but, now that you have your board legs, their wakes are almost certainly less unbalancing. Slowly you advance east on your SUP, skirting the island and gliding over water the colour of amber, with the Gippsland Lakes fed by seven rivers that wash tannins into the three lakes.

Somewhere approaching the eastern end of the island, at an indeterminate spot not filled with sea birds on that particular day, you step ashore onto the beach, pausing for a break and

Above Paddling along the shores of Rigby Island *Opposite* The helicopter-eye view

snack. At this end of the island, Rigby's bare, dune-like landscape almost resembles a coral cay. It's not a natural environment, with the island here built up of sand dredged from the entrance over decades and deposited in this spot. It's such a contrast to the island's scrubby western end that it feels almost as though you've paddled from temperate lands to tropical in just 2.5km.

Setting out on the board again, you cross another boating channel, beside the spot where North Arm pours into the lake, bringing with it an armada of boat traffic. Crossing the channel towards Bullock Island can, at busy times, feel a bit like trying to drive around the Arc de Triomphe, with boats, jetskis and water skiers seeming to come from every direction. You might pause, paddle and pause again in a game of water Frogger, but soon you're across the channel and turning towards the entrance that continues to be regularly dredged – around 250,000 cubic metres of sand a year – to keep it open and safe for boat traffic.

Instead of heading through the entrance, with its rising swells, you paddle to a small beach tucked behind its eastern breakwater. Here, a boardwalk follows the entrance to the sea, where the view has a lively edge, with Australian fur seals darting about in the channel, hunting for fish on the turn of the tide.

Back at the boards, it's about a half-hour paddle into Lakes Entrance, slipping back across the channel and gliding along beside the town's fishing fleet before finally pulling into shore across the road from Venture Out's Esplanade office – a grounding finish after such a flying start.

If Gippsland excels at one adventure activity, it's rail trails. Victoria has more than 30 of these disused railways-turned-cycling-trails, of which a dozen are in Gippsland. Popular choices include the Great Southern Rail Trail, stretching for 109km between Nyora and Port Welshpool; the 100km East Gippsland Rail Trail from Bairnsdale to Orbost; and the scenic coastal trundle of the 17km Bass Coast Rail Trail. The Gippsland Lakes Discovery Trail is a 17km ride along an old tramway that connects the East Gippsland Rail Trail to Lakes Entrance.

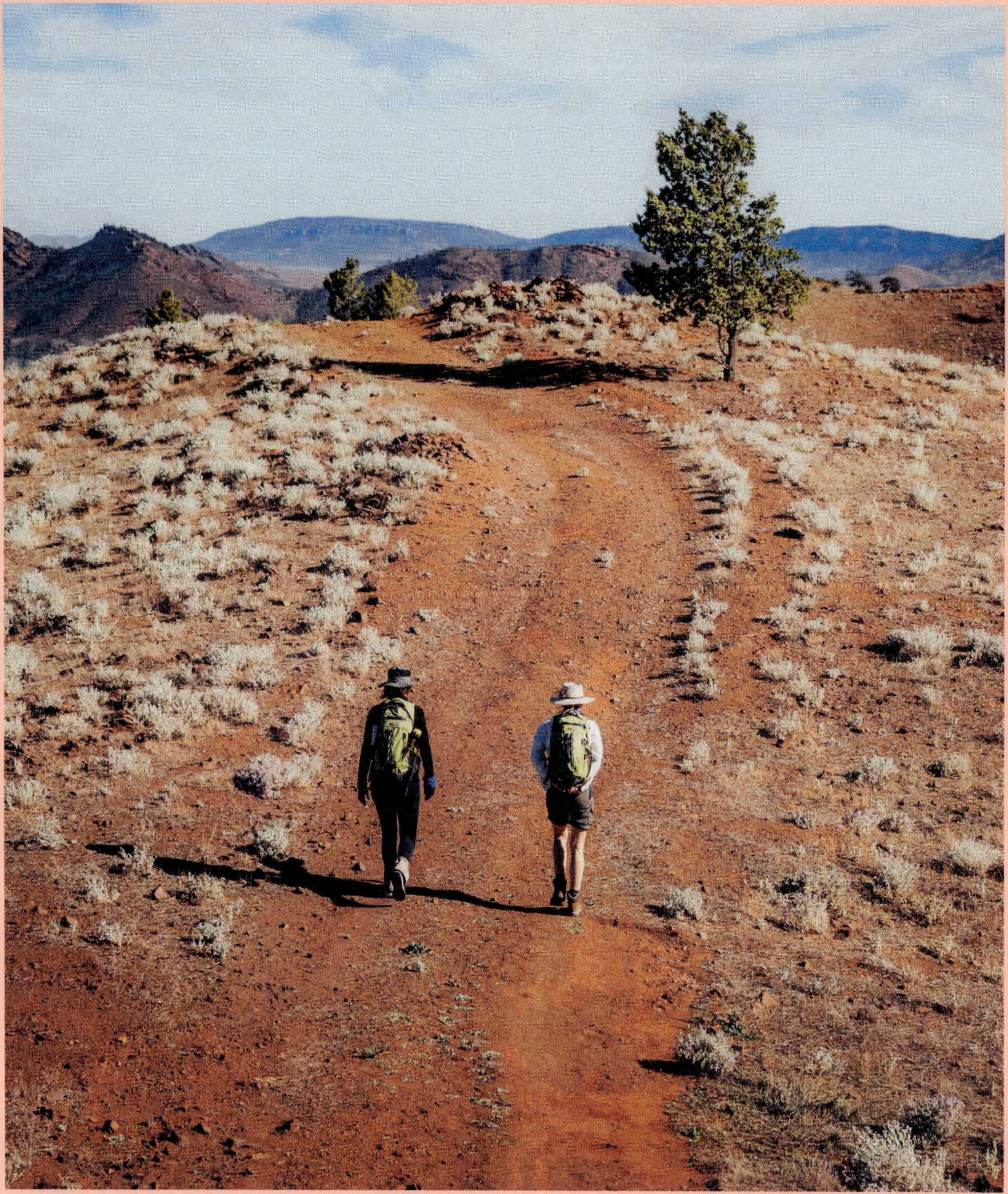

South Australia

*Plunge into the some of the clearest water on Earth,
or set out across the desert's edge.*

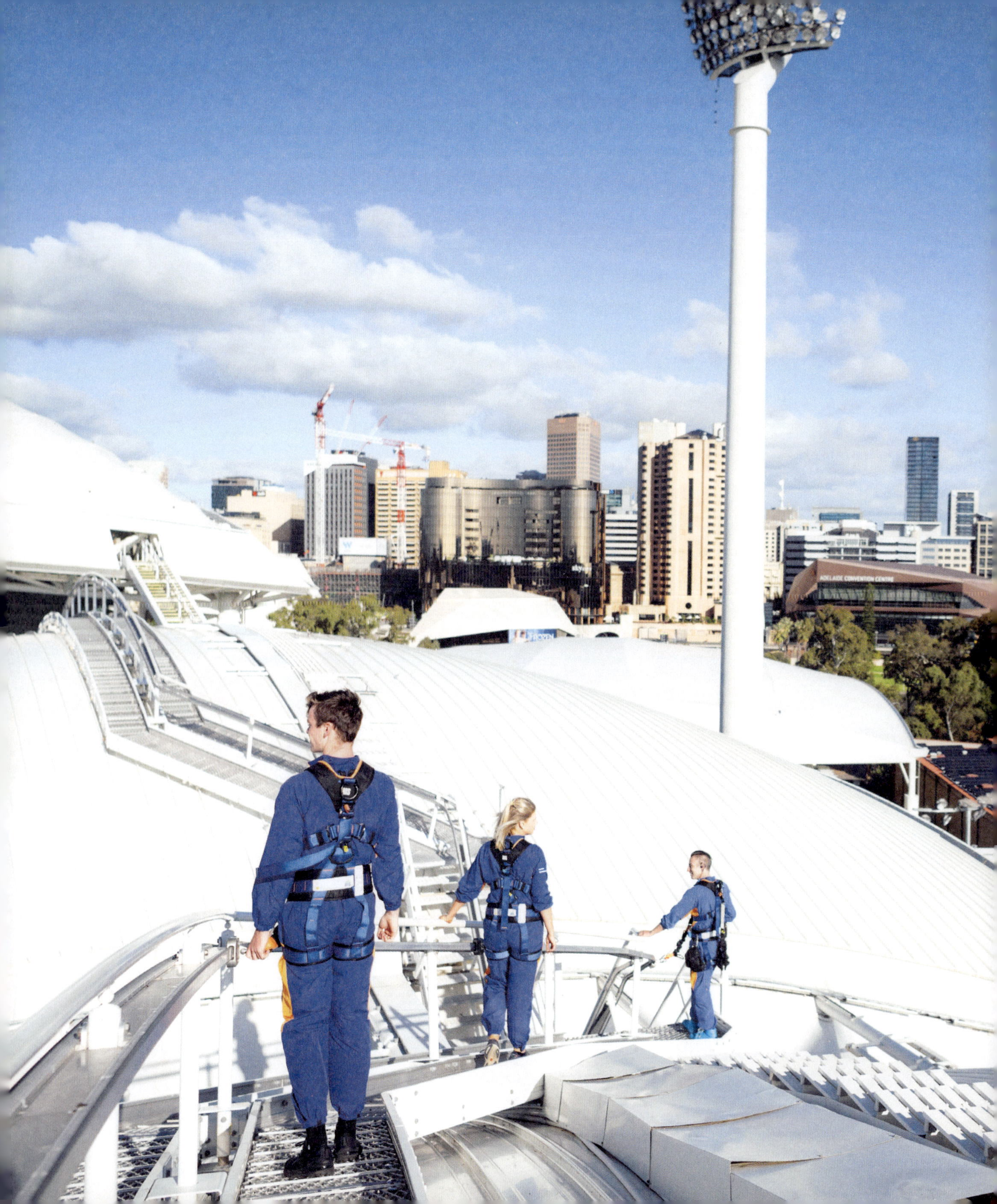

Find a new sporting high, strolling atop the roof of the Adelaide Oval, perhaps even during an AFL or Test cricket match.

RoofClimb, Adelaide Oval
Kaurna Country

WHY IT'S SPECIAL

Adelaide/Tarndanya has traditionally been known as the City of Churches, but in this sport-loving capital, the most revered of all cathedrals might easily be Adelaide Oval. Often called the most picturesque oval in the world, the venerable stadium has sat on the northern bank of the River Torrens since 1871.

Tradition runs strong at the oval – the century-old, hand-operated scoreboard was retained when the oval underwent a $500-million makeover in 2012–14 – but so too does innovation. Look up to the roof of the grandstands at any time of day or evening and you might spy a line of human silhouettes walking around atop them. This is the Adelaide Oval RoofClimb, a vertiginous experience mixing heritage and heights. From 50m above the playing surface, the oval comes into sharp relief and there are views across the Adelaide/Tarndanya plains to the hills, the coast and the city centre.

Where
Adelaide Oval is a short walk across the River Torrens from the Adelaide/Tarndanya city centre.

When
The 2hr climbs run daily, with the option of daytime, twilight and night tours.

Do it
Book online (roofclimb.com.au).

Fitness: ●●○○○

Fear factor: ●●●○○

Expertise required ●○○○○

Family friendly

Above Setting sail in the sunset *Opposite* Roof with a view *Previous* Striding out on the Arkaba Walk

THE ADVENTURE

Within the stadium's inner workings, things begin with a wardrobe change, as climbers are fitted out like skydivers, slipping into RoofClimb overalls and a complicated but reassuring harness system.

The first climb is the easiest, ascending the Western Stand in an elevator, where a hidden door then pops open, and a ladder leads onto the roof. At the base of this ladder, climbers are connected umbilically to a railing by a trolley cable system. From here until the RoofClimb's finish, they are never detached from the security of this cable.

There's an Opera House–like quality to walking across the tin top of the Western Stand, with its flowing white roofline. There's also ingenuity beneath your feet, with this modern stand designed to almost balance atop its preserved predecessor – the heritage-listed George Giffen Stand, which was built in 1882 – without putting any pressure or weight onto it. Atop the stand come the first views out beyond the oval, across Adelaide/Tarndanya's rolling-pin-flat western suburbs to the sea, and east to the Adelaide Hills.

With planes skimming low overhead as they take off from Adelaide Airport, 6km to the west, the climb first crosses to the northern end of the Western Stand. From this edge, there's more heritage in sight – Adelaide Oval's famous Edwardian scoreboard and the signature line of Moreton Bay figs behind it. These trees were planted early last century to stop the hoi polloi from watching sporting matches from outside the stadium for free. Behind it all, St Peter's Cathedral completes one of world cricket's classic scenes, while the statue of Colonel Light – Adelaide's original designer – stands on Montefiore Hill, its right index finger seemingly pointing out this strange line of people wandering atop the grandstand.

Returning along the roof, the Western Stand ends at a floating link bridge built specifically for the RoofClimb. Connecting the Western Stand to the Riverbank Stand, the bridge provides one of the RoofClimb's most exposed moments. The view of the oval widens through the gap between the two stands, but look down at your feet and you're suddenly peering through open grating to the concrete ground far below. It's almost like walking on air.

At the top of the link bridge, the climb steps in beneath the Riverbank Stand's taut canvas roof, walking on a high platform clipped into the ceiling. A few moments later, it steps back out again, passing through an opening in the roof to a platform overhanging the oval. Immediately beneath the platform during the AFL season (March to Sept), and again visible through the grating, the goalposts rise like stakes at the bottom of a pit.

On match days, the tours pause here, with climbers treated to the highest seats in the house as they watch a quarter of an AFL match or a few overs of a cricket game, perched high above the players as they scurry about like ants.

Regardless of the day, this elevated platform also becomes the climb's most confronting challenge, for you are encouraged to inch to the edge of the platform, turn your back on the oval and lean back as far as you can go. Still clipped to the railing, you're held firm to the stand, but it feels like being suspended in air,

Above Crossing the floating link bridge between stands

poised as if about to fall onto the goalposts – they really feel like stakes now.

The return walk circuits beneath the roof of the Riverbank Stand, looking over the River Torrens to the city centre. Behind the angular Festival Centre rises what one guide describes as 'Adelaide's best collection of brown buildings', and, further east, the city's tallest structure, the 135m Frome Central Tower.

Back across the link bridge and atop the Western Stand roof once again, the oval remains like a patch of suburban lawn far below, but the vertiginous sense of exposure has likely long dissipated. To be walking atop one of Australia's great stadiums suddenly feels as normal as a walk in a park.

> Riding the coat-tails of Adelaide's RoofClimb is a similar experience at Perth/Boorloo's Optus Stadium. Opened in 2018, the riverside oval has a couple of rooftop meanders on the menu: Halo, which is a walking tour around the stadium roof; and Vertigo, which adds the chance to lean back over the oval (similar to the RoofClimb lean-out) from a semi-circular walkway. Optus Stadium also runs Warrang Bridil's Aboriginal Cultural Tours, providing a perspective on the site's Noongar heritage.

RoofClimb, Adelaide Oval

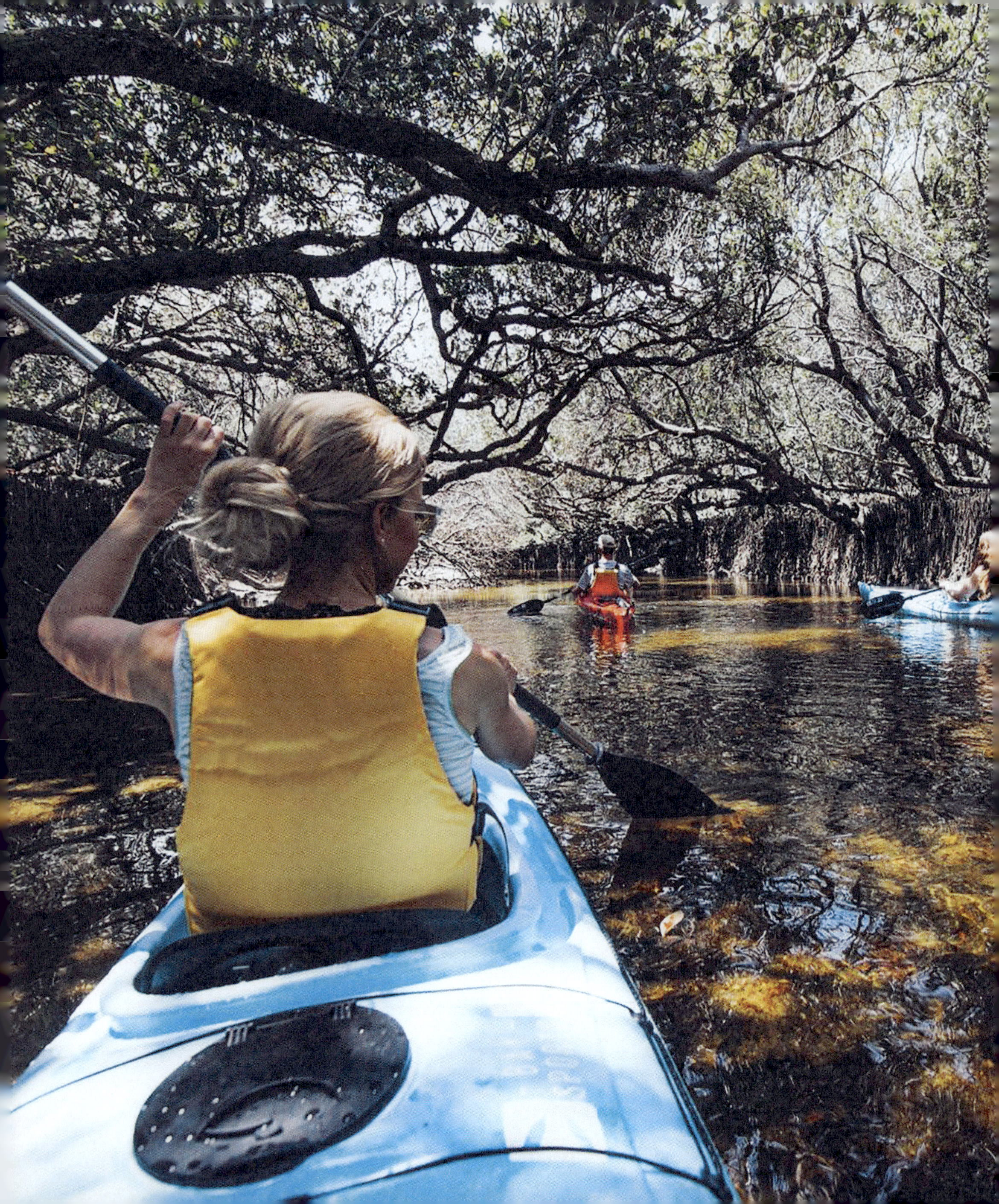

Paddle in the company of dolphins among an ancient mangrove forest and a ship graveyard.

Kayaking, Adelaide Dolphin Sanctuary

Kaurna Country

WHY IT'S SPECIAL

The Port River is a place of surprising natural significance, given that it fringes South Australia's largest port and is less than a 30min drive from Adelaide/Tarndanya's city centre. A 10,000-year-old mangrove forest covers the river's banks as it flows into St Vincent Gulf at Port Adelaide, and bottlenose dolphins cruise its waters.

This wide stretch of the river is protected as the Adelaide Dolphin Sanctuary, a marine park that's home to more than 30 resident bottlenose dolphins, with several hundred transient dolphins known also to visit. It's also the site of Australia's largest ship graveyard, where early last century more than 25 ships were scuttled and abandoned, their hulls lying in the mudflats like rusting monuments to shipping's glory days.

The best way to experience the dolphin sanctuary is in a kayak, paddling among the river's playful inhabitants and into the mangrove-lined estuaries that flow into it. Bring your own kayak and you can also paddle through the ship graveyard. If hiring a kayak on Garden Island, as most people do, you're limited to an area downstream from the graveyard.

Where
The Adelaide Dolphin Sanctuary is best accessed from Garden Island, a 22km drive from Adelaide/Tarndanya's city centre.

When
Take to the river at any time. Operating days for kayak hire and guided paddles vary, but are most reliable around weekends.

Do it
Dolphin Sanctuary Kayak Tours hires out kayaks and operates guided tours from Garden Island. Book ahead (dolphinsanctuarykayaktours.com.au).

Fitness: ●●○○○

Fear factor: ●●○○○

Expertise required ●●○○○

Family friendly

Opposite Paddling through a mangrove-lined tributary

THE ADVENTURE

The best launch point for kayaking in the Adelaide Dolphin Sanctuary is the boat ramp on the northern shores of Garden Island. From here, it's a simple paddle around the island's northern tip and into the estuaries that vein the neighbouring Torrens Island.

The most likely place to encounter dolphins is in the main body of the Port River, though wildlife viewing always comes with a caveat – animals can be unreliable company. Your kayak might be surrounded by dolphins, or there might be none. It's dolphin lottery, albeit with very good odds.

Even if the dolphins aren't at home, there's ample here to enjoy. Birdlife is plentiful, with the Adelaide International Bird Sanctuary National Park – Winaityinaityi Pangkara immediately to the dolphin sanctuary's north. This national park is a 60km slice of coastline at the southern end of the East Asian-Australasian Flyway that's home to thousands of birds. In the language of the Traditional Owners, the Kaurna People, 'Winaityinaityi Pangkara' means 'a country for all birds and the country that surrounds these birds'. On the Port River, pelicans drift overhead, and herons, egrets and ibises typically strut along the banks.

Rounding Garden Island's northern tip, there's the incongruous sight of the Torrens Island Power Station towering into view, its tall chimneys looking like two upturned legs of a chair. Stretching out from the power station's edges are the trees of an ancient mangrove forest, their roots resembling a natural bed of nails.

Reaching into this forest on Torrens Island are two narrow estuaries that are worth exploring in the kayak. With mangroves covering the banks and reaching across the creek, the paddle is like a gentle slalom course, requiring you at times to duck, bend and lean to get around or beneath the trees, with the streams narrowing the deeper you head into the island. Though you're in South Australia, the estuaries' muddy banks more resemble something from the tropics – you might half expect mud crabs scurrying about, or a crocodile sunning itself, but there's only silence as even windy days calm to a hush inside this tightly latticed forest. It's peace at the Port.

Back at the Port River, the tributaries pour out opposite the Garden Island marina. At their edge, in the middle of the river, lies an overturned yacht, keeling at 45 degrees and providing a taster of the ship graveyard – even if you're unable to paddle to the other side of the island. To reach the graveyard, which is in the river's North Arm, you need to kayak back upstream and around to Garden Island's south coast. Three on-water interpretive signs, beside the main group of wrecks, offer backgrounding on the graveyard, where around 26 ships were scuttled between 1909 and 1945.

Above Showing off *Opposite top* Paddling the Port *Opposite bottom* Passing a wreck in the Port River

> Dolphins abound in Australian waters, and so too do opportunities to interact with these fascinating marine creatures. Swim-with-wild-dolphin experiences can be found at Port Phillip (Victoria, *see* p.61), Glenelg and Baird Bay (SA), Rockingham and Koombana Bay (WA). In Port Stephens (NSW), you can be towed beneath a catamaran (hanging onto a rope) to effectively swim at dolphin speed, or you can head to the water's edge at Monkey Mia (WA) and Moreton Island/Mulgumpin (Queensland) to watch wild dolphins being fed.

Kayaking, Adelaide Dolphin Sanctuary

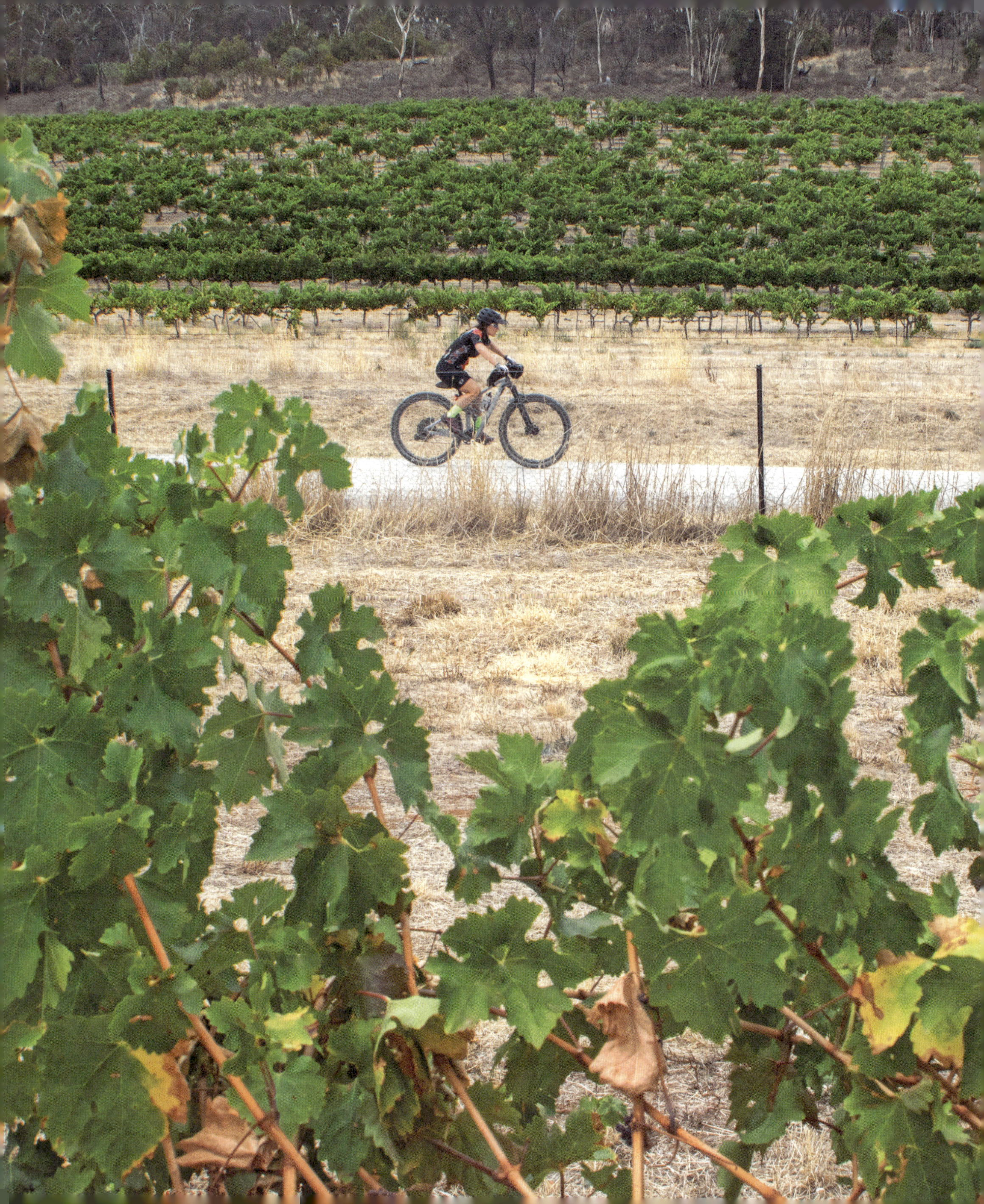

Pause for tastings as you pedal through the vines of SA's top wine regions on gentle rail trails.

Cycling, Barossa and Clare valleys and McLaren Vale

Ngadjuri, Kaurna Country

WHY IT'S SPECIAL

Trying to name Australia's top wine state is a fool's game beset by parochialism, but trying to name Australia's best state for winery bike rides is simplicity itself. With the Barossa Valley, Clare Valley and McLaren Vale wine regions threaded with rail trails, South Australia, which contains more than half the land under vine in Australia, is by far the best state in which to combine a ride and a riesling.

With all three wine regions within a 2hr radius by car of Adelaide/Tarndanya, this is the perfect vineyard triathlon: Clare's Riesling Trail, McLaren Vale's Coast to Vines Rail Trail, and the Barossa Trail. Ride one or ride the set – quality ~~drinking~~ cycling time is guaranteed.

Where
Distances from Adelaide/Tarndanya: Clare is 150km north, Gawler is 50km north, and McLaren Vale is 40km south of the city.

When
There's good riding year-round on these trails, though winter means bare vines. Autumn brings a splash of gold to each region.

Do it
Plot your course (and your wine list) at Walking SA (walkingsa.org.au) - the website is pitched at walkers but is just as handy for cyclists.

There are bike-hire options along each trail; try Riesling Trail Bike Hire (rieslingtrailbikehire.com.au), Barossa Bike (barossabikehire.com) and McLaren Vale-based SA eBikes (sa-ebikes.com.au).

Fitness: ●●●○○

Fear factor: ●○○○○

Expertise required ●●○○○

Family friendly

Above Archway along the Riesling Trail *Opposite* Vine times on the Riesling Trail

THE ADVENTURE

South Australian wine regions tend to live in the shadow of the Barossa Valley, but it's the Clare Valley's Riesling Trail that has the highest profile of the state's wine rides. Named for the region's star varietal, the Riesling Trail stretches for 27km between Clare and Auburn (with little-pedalled extensions south to Riverton and north to, well, nowhere particular), and few wine trails in the country can match it for single-minded focus on the grapes and wine.

Whichever direction you cycle the Riesling Trail (and there's nothing that really favours either direction), it begins as it intends to continue: with a cellar door.

At the southern end in Auburn, the old railway station beside the trailhead has been transformed into the Mount Horrocks Wines cellar door, while as you roll out of (or into) Clare, it's just a few pedal strokes to Mr. Mick.

What sets this wine ride apart from most others are the exclusive bike entrances from the trail – at the likes of O'Leary Walker Wines and Tim Adams Wines, you don't even have to share driveways with vehicles. The most elaborate of these entrances is at Sevenhill Cellars, where a dedicated side trail cuts past beautiful red gums to the valley's oldest vineyard, established by Jesuit brothers in 1851. Taking its name from the seven hills of Rome, the winery has a long tradition of Jesuit brothers as winemakers – ever since 1852 – and it remains framed around the Gothic Revival St Aloysius Church, beneath which is a crypt in which 41 Jesuits are buried.

The design of the trail is simple – whether you ride from Clare or from Auburn, the ride ascends gently to its highest point near Penwortham, midway along the trail, and then descends just as gently to its finish, with one of those bookending cellar doors at which to celebrate your arrival.

Closer to Adelaide/Tarndanya's northern edge, the Barossa Trail has two very likeable features: one, it's in the Barossa; two, it can be accessed on Adelaide/Tarndanya's suburban train network. The southern start of the trail is at the eastern edge of Gawler, meaning you need only weave through the town's streets from its train station to find the path at Sunnydale Ave.

The 37km ride gets into its wine stride around Lyndoch, 13km out of Gawler, from where it runs beside the Barossa Valley Way all the way to Roland Flat, crossing cellar door driveways that disappear like temptation into the vines. At Rowland Flat, the trail goes its own way for a while, leaving the road to embark on its most interesting section, guided instead by the meanders of the North Para River. Back here, away from the world for much of the time, you'll find wineries such as Jacob's Creek and St Hugo nestled into the bush.

There's barely a bump in the landscape to interrupt the cycling (or the tastings) as you pedal through Tanunda and on to Nuriootpa and finally Angaston, leaving you undistracted from the wine and Australia's most famous wine region.

Suburban trains can similarly be used to access the Coast to Vines Rail Trail, which includes a thirst-inducing approach to the McLaren Vale wine region through Adelaide/Tarndanya's southern suburbs. Alighting at Marino Rocks (on the Seaford train line), the 39km ride to Willunga at first feels light years from a wine region, but by the time you reach Old Reynella, just 10km along the trail, the first of the vineyards appear – quite suitably, since this was also the very spot where Australia's first vineyard was planted in 1841 by John Reynella.

The ride really changes flavour as it approaches the town of McLaren Vale, suddenly curling through vines and olive trees rather than suburban blocks. If it's just the vineyard bits you want from this ride, you can always start at McLaren Vale, pedalling the 8km to Willunga. This shorter section doubles as the Shiraz Trail, and is the most vine-dense stretch of the ride, with the bitumen path forming a virtual corridor between vineyards.

McLaren Vale's biggest and quirkiest attractions – the d'Arenberg Cube, the vine-wrapped Salopian Inn, the double-decker-bus cellar door at Down the Rabbit Hole – aren't directly on the trail but they're all easy detours (the Cube is the furthest from the trail, at 3km).

Across Australia, there are as many wine-themed bike trails as there are wine varietals.

In NSW, the Cycle Hunter Valley map (huntervalleybicyclerentals.com.au) details 20 routes around the namesake wine region, where the centrepiece is the Hermitage Road bike path, passing some of the valley's best wineries. Head inland too, where Orange and Mudgee publish cycling maps with rides that take in local cellar doors.

Victoria's Murray to Mountains Rail Trail, combined with its offshoots into the Milawa Gourmet Region, Beechworth and Rutherglen, might be the ultimate wine on wheels experience.

The 34km Stanthorpe to Ballandean Bike Trail passes through Queensland's premier wine region.

It just takes a few detours to find a wine fix as Western Australia's 23km Wadandi Track brushes past Margaret River.

Top The vine-striped slopes of the Barossa Valley *Opposite* Cellar door stop on the Riesling Trail

Ride a fat bike between tall sand dunes, then hurtle down them on a sandboard.

Biking and boarding, Little Sahara, Kangaroo Island

Kartan, Ramindjeri, Ngarrindjeri, Kaurna and Barngalla Country

WHY IT'S SPECIAL

Kangaroo Island, or KI as it's commonly known, has so many phenomenal landscapes, from the wind-scoured Remarkable Rocks, to a rock arch sheltering fur seals, and a beach (Vivonne Bay) once named the best in Australia. Less familiar, but no less impressive, is an inland field of sand dunes rising up to 70m above sea level. Known as Little Sahara, it's an ocean setting without an ocean – the coast is 4km to the south of this rare white-sand inland dune system pinched between Vivonne Bay and Seal Bay.

The dunes sit on private land, which operates as the Little Sahara Adventure Centre, running the likes of buggy tours, sandboarding and fat-bike tours across the dunes and surrounding bush. It's a rare chance to propel yourself through dunes in different ways – gliding down them on a board or toboggan, and pedalling between the sand hills on tyres so broad they seem almost to float atop the sand.

Where
Little Sahara is 40km south-west of Kangaroo Island's airport in Kingscote, and 85km west of the ferry terminal at Penneshaw.

When
Little Sahara Adventure Centre opens daily year-round. Avoid wet days, when the sand becomes slower and stickier.

Do it
Book ahead for bike tours and board hire at Little Sahara (littlesahara.com.au).

Fitness: ●●●○○
Fear factor: ●●○○○
Expertise required ●●○○○
Family friendly

South Australia

Above Speeding down the dunes *Opposite* Fun board games

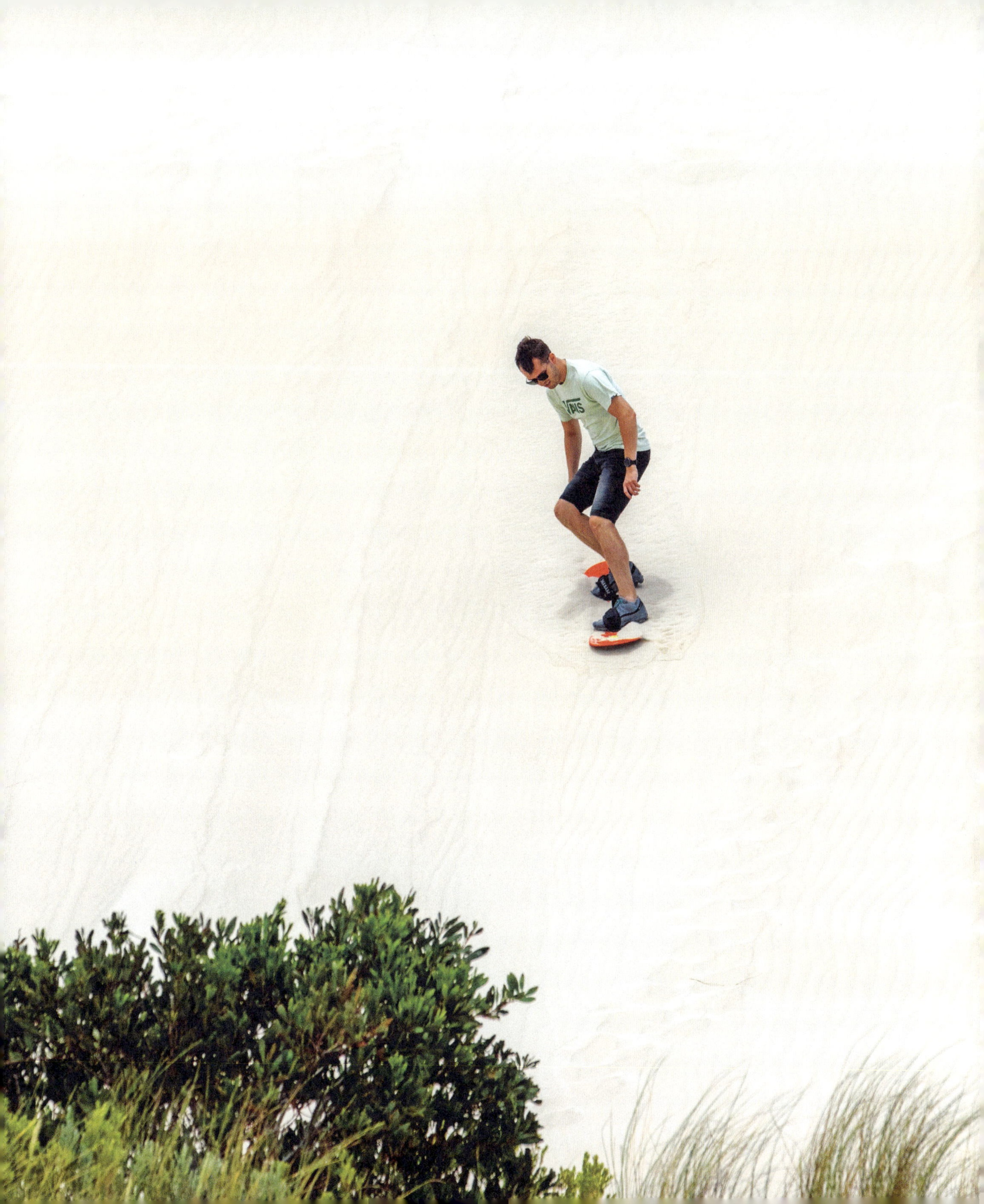

South Australia

THE ADVENTURE

As you cross Kangaroo Island from north to south, the Little Sahara dunes aren't visible from the road, but as you turn into the Adventure Centre's carpark, their size and scale become evident – you might wonder how you could ever not have seen them as they rise like a small mountain range before you.

Setting out on a fat-biking tour gives you the widest perspective on the property, so it's the best starting point. Before heading onto the dunes, these tours head out around the property, pedalling away from the sand hills and spinning through heath and then mallee bush to the bank of the Eleanor River, the waterway with the second largest catchment on KI. Along the riverbanks, tall old eucalypts provide grandstands for koalas, which peer down lazily from their branches and forks. It's not an unusual sight on this island named for another marsupial, with more than 8000 koalas inhabiting KI – there were almost 50,000 koalas here before the catastrophic bushfires of 2019–20 burned almost half the island.

Little Sahara escaped the fires, and the bush through which you ride beside the river is tall and lush. On the day I was here, we passed a couple of native beehives, draped inside the hollowed trunks of two large eucalypts. Ligurian bees were brought to the island in the 1880s, and it was quickly declared a bee sanctuary, with no other bees subsequently brought here. This has resulted in the island possessing what's considered the world's purest strain of Ligurian bees.

Above Pedalling towards the dunes *Opposite* Fat biking through the Little Sahara bush

On these bush tracks, the fat-bike tyres sound as heavy as tractor tyres, but the going is easy and soon the bush fades to nothing as you arrive at the edge of the dunes. The way ahead is only sand, and it's on sand that the fat bikes come into their own. On any other bike, riding on sand is the cycling equivalent of trying to run in mud – heavy, laborious, exhausting – but fat bikes are so named because of the width of their tyres. The bikes at Little Sahara run on 4.5-inch tyres – around double the width of traditional mountain-bike tyres – with low inflation to spread their footprint even wider across the sand, creating a balloon-like effect over the dunes, and making progress easier (especially if you take the e-bike tour).

The unquestioned highlight of the riding tours is this crossing of the 2.5sqkm dune field. Much of the wind-groomed sand is unmarked by anything except kangaroo and bird tracks, and now briefly your wheel tracks, which blow away quickly, while ripples in the sand provide a soft saddle massage. The riding is largely flat as you weave between and around dunes before skirting low beneath a dune that rises around 30m overhead, like a storm wave about to break over the bikes.

These dunes formed during the last Ice Age when, as seas receded marine creatures and corals were stranded. Their remains were broken down and blown here, forming sand and then dunes over thousands of years. Look around and you'll still see some marine fossils – the likes of coral tubes – embedded in the rock that's interspersed through the dunes.

By the tallest dune, the trackless ride makes a turn back towards the start point, rolling through a few deep sandy dips that are the most challenging moments of the ride – it's a matter of keeping the front wheel pointing straight to avoid it slipping into the sand and turning the outing into a sudden ski trip.

Returning to the start point through the bush, which now seems luxuriant after the emptiness of the dunes, it's a chance to make a transition from bike to board, setting out to the tops of the dunes with a sandboard or toboggan in hand.

The most physical part of the day is this climb to the dune tops, standing high above a scene that feels like it should include the ocean but somehow never does.

Sandboards allow you to stand and ride the dunes in the style of a snowboard, while toboggans provide a seated ride, your weight as far back on the board as you can get it, your hands trailing in the sand to steer or simply hold your line.

Of the two sandboarding adventures covered in this book (the other is at Lancelin in WA, see p.168), this one is the higher and faster, with soft, powder-like sand and two lines of dunes that are primed for boarding. The dune closest to the Adventure Centre office has varying gradients, allowing for gentle runs through to hill hurtles, and it's here that most people are content to stay and play. Walk on another 10min or so, however, crossing through the heart of the dune field, and you come to a higher dune (the tall dune passed on the fat bikes) that's generally cleaner and far-less used. Every time you ascend this dune, you half expect to find a view of the ocean – it's just that kind of landscape – but what you see instead is a sea of bush and sand. Back here, it really does feel almost as remote as the Sahara (without the camels).

Above Biking through the bush *Opposite* Ripple effect

Kangaroo Island's biggest adventure is the Kangaroo Island Wilderness Trail, a five-day, 61km hike along the island's south-west edge, taking in the likes of the Remarkable Rocks, Cape du Couedic and Sanderson Bay. The trail was severely impacted by the 2019-20 bushfires, and at the time of writing had reopened only to licensed tour operators, with none of the purpose-built campsites yet to reopen. Keep up to date on the trail's progress online (parks.sa.gov.au/experiences/kiwt).

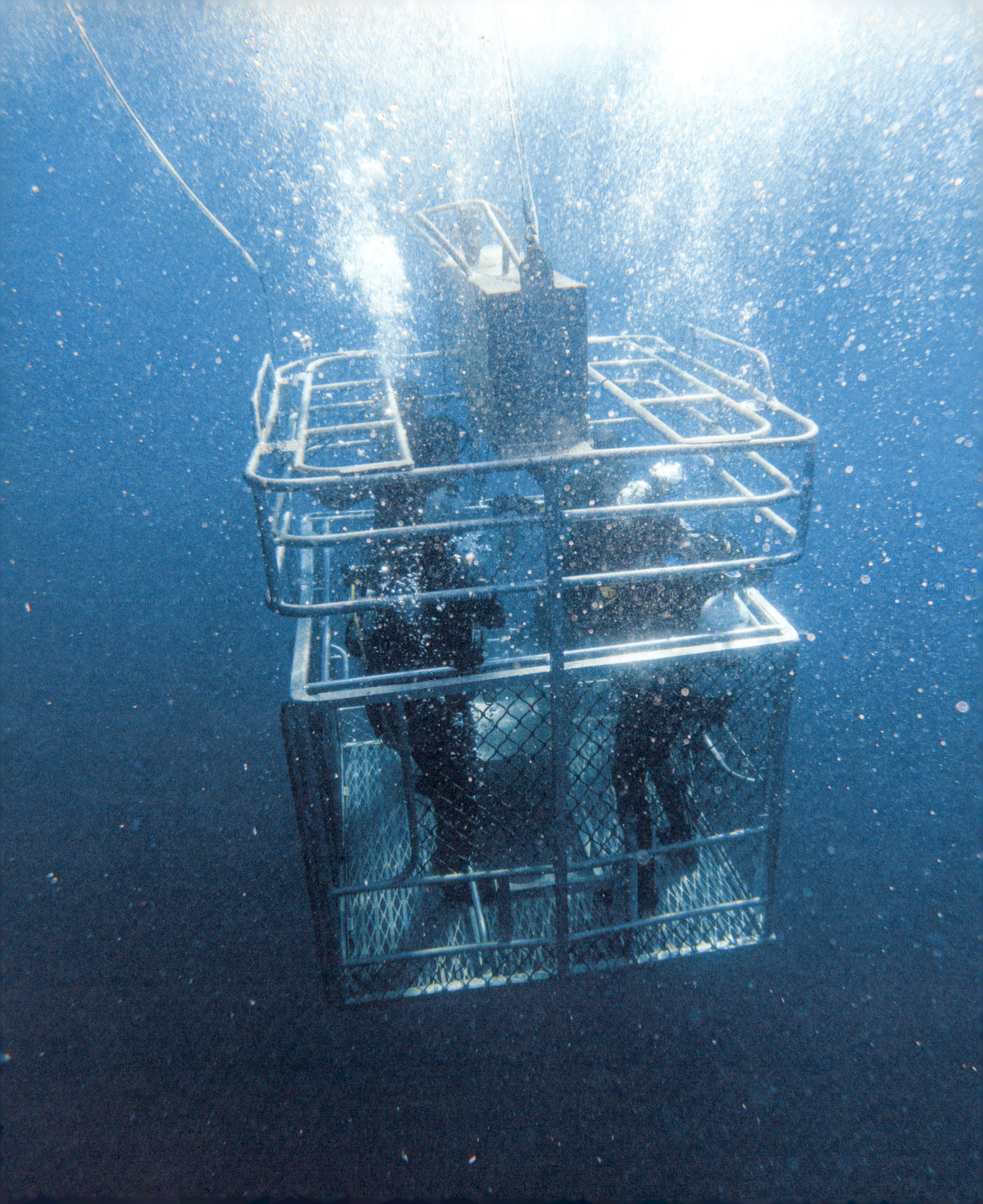

Stare fear – and beauty – in the face as you slip into the world of the ocean's greatest predator.

Diving with great white sharks, off Neptune Islands

Unknown Country

Contributed by Justin Meneguzzi

WHY IT'S SPECIAL

Few animals have captured the population's imagination as nightmarishly as the great white shark. When Steven Spielberg's *Jaws* hit the silver screen in 1975, it delivered a toothsome villain with an ominous film score so traumatic that initial filmgoers were tearing the seats out of the cinema in terror. Nearly 50 years on, the film still taps into our primal fear of being eaten and our fear of the unknown.

Cage diving with great white sharks is an opportunity to flip the script and unmask the villain for what it really is – a beautiful animal full of surprising grace and power. There are few places in the world where you can safely observe the sharks in their habitat, but the Neptune Islands, 70km off the coast of Port Lincoln, are a local hotspot for the species. The islands' craggy coves are home to long-nosed fur seals, a favourite meal for great whites, making it a reliable place to find the sharks.

Because of their geographic isolation, the Neptune Islands can only be reached by charter boat, with about half a day of sailing before the first of the scattered islands starts to come into view. Once the boat has anchored and the cages are lowered into the water, the only thing left to do is muster your courage and dive in.

Where
Trips depart from Port Lincoln, which is 651km west of Adelaide/Tarndanya. Direct flights are available from Adelaide to Port Lincoln.

When
Shark cage diving is available year-round, however sharks are more reliably seen during early summer and late autumn/early winter. Ocean temperatures can be as low as 15°C in winter and as high as 19°C in summer. Expeditions will also vary in length depending on the season, being shorter in summer and longer in winter to account for reduced daylight hours and time in the water.

Do it
Rodney Fox Expeditions runs live-aboard shark-diving experiences and offers a variety of itineraries, from two to eight nights. Its boats regularly host scientists, wildlife photographers and conservation documentary makers (rodneyfox.com.au).

You can participate in this adventure in a surface cage without needing diving qualifications but to do the seafloor cage, you'll need PADI or Open Water certification.

Fitness: ●●○○○

Fear factor: ●●●●●

Expertise required: ●○○○○

Opposite In a flurry of bubbles and adrenaline, divers descend to the seabed

THE ADVENTURE

Wave goodbye to Port Lincoln and admire the passing sand dunes of Lincoln National Park as you sail into Spencer Gulf. Keep an eye out for the ring-shaped tuna farms that helped put Port Lincoln on the map and made the town's early migrant fishermen obscenely rich.

As the boat motors south, you'll get a chance to stop in at islands and swim with some of the local seals. Never fear, the waters around these islands are too shallow for sharks to enter, so have fun playing hide and seek in the seaweed with these curious critters. It's also a good opportunity to try on the wetsuit and mask you'll need later.

Leaving your new friends behind, the boat continues to the South Neptune Islands. The seas can be choppier here, so best come prepared with ginger, seasickness tablets, or other remedies if you're prone to turn green around the gills.

Once the boat arrives at the Neptune Islands, the crew will prepare the two dive cages and provide a safety briefing. Spoiler alert: don't stick your arm out of the cage!

The boat carries two types of cages: a seafloor cage for qualified divers and a surface cage for those who aren't qualified. The surface cage is tethered to the boat's stern, with a ladder to climb down and an onboard pump supplying oxygen via multiple regulators. This cage is available all day and you can choose to go in as many times as you like, so long as there is a regulator free. Non-divers are given priority in this cage ahead of divers.

The seafloor cage is lowered 20m to the seafloor using a crane. This is done multiple times each day, with guests allocated a session for their dive. Up to three guests with PADI or Open Water certification, accompanied by a Dive Professional, can use the cage during each session, which can last up to an hour.

Even though the Neptune Islands are a regular haunt for great white sharks, South Australian regulations permit the use of tuna berley as an attractant, though it is illegal for operators to intentionally feed the sharks. Research has found the use of tuna berley does not alter shark behaviour and the sharks continue to forage as they normally would.

As with any wildlife encounter, it's important to remember there is no guarantee that you will see a shark.

Right A curious great white shark inspects the surface dive cage

Diving with great white sharks, off Neptune Islands

South Australia

130

After pulling on your wetsuit and goggles, climb into your cage of choice and get ready for the thrill of a lifetime. At first, you'll gasp at the jolt of cold water as you're lowered into the sea, then you'll gasp again at the surprising amount of activity underwater. Schools of yellow-finned kingfish huddle right under the ship, seagulls make brief cameos as they dive in and out of the water, and rays ripple their way along the seabed.

Then the real star of the show arrives. Slowly and silently, a 3.5m great white shark emerges from the blue gloom and sizes you up, sending an exhilarating shiver down your spine. If you're lucky, you might have upwards of five sharks circling you before they disappear again into the great blue. You'll need to keep your wits about you as sharks can sneak up behind the cage at any time without warning.

Once the initial thrill of seeing these apex predators wears off, take a moment to observe how they interact with their environment. See how they peacefully swim across the seabed, neither seeking a fight nor eating everything in sight – despite living in an underwater buffet. The surrounding animals aren't scared of them, either. After multiple dives, you'll start to see the sharks as individuals, with distinguishable scars and facial patterns that tell a story.

The experience continues back onboard with educational seminars about great white shark behaviour, ecology and conservation, giving you a more nuanced understanding of these creatures and their role in our oceans. By the time the ship pulls up its anchor, you'll leave these islands with a very different perspective of one of Hollywood's most enduring icons.

The *Tacoma*, an 84ft wooden tuna clipper originally built in 1951, was Port Lincoln's first commercial tuna fishing boat and it helped pioneer the region's thriving fishing industry. The clipper no longer operates commercially, but she is lovingly maintained by the *Tacoma* Preservation Society, which frequently re-creates live-aboard fishing expeditions from the 1950s using original fishing methods with live bait and bamboo poles. The expeditions can go as far as Coffin Bay and the Neptune Islands in search of southern bluefin tuna. Places are limited to just 12 adventurous fisherfolk, with all equipment supplied. Head online to find out more (tacoma.org.au).

Right A great white eyes off a potential snack. Tuna berley is used to attract sharks to the boat *Opposite top* Every shark has its own story – look closely for scars and battle wounds *Opposite bottom left* Trying on a wetsuit during an introductory swim with seals *Opposite bottom right* Most sharks aren't looking for a fight. Instead, you'll find them clocked off and cruising the seabed alongside rays and schools of kingfish

Walk through an ancient landscape and a private conservancy, with fine food and stargazing swags at each day's end.

Hiking the Arkaba Walk, Ikara-Flinders Ranges

Adnyamathanha Country

WHY IT'S SPECIAL

Across Australia, there's now an entire genre of guided multi-day walks sprinkled with luxurious touches. On around a dozen walks (*see* p.305), you can spend each night in private huts or villas with fine food and wine, showers and comfy beds (and even massages along some walks), and while each one might qualify as an Ultimate Adventure, there's something singularly special about days and nights in the company of the Ikara-Flinders Ranges mountains and skies on the Arkaba Walk.

Crossing through Wilpena Pound/Ikara and then striding out across the untracked private lands of the 260sqkm Arkaba Conservancy, the Arkaba Walk journeys through rough, tough country but with the edges softened by the need to carry little gear and by the permanent camps with elevated swags, fire-heated showers and chef-prepared meals.

Every day on the walk, it's like stepping into a Hans Heysen painting, with Wilpena's crowning peaks and the Elder Range rising over the conservancy. Some of the most amazing views in the entire Ikara-Flinders Ranges are found here, and they can only be seen on this walk.

Where
Arkaba Conservancy is around 400km north of Adelaide/Tarndanya, immediately south of Wilpena Pound/Ikara.

When
The Arkaba Walk runs weekly from March to Oct.

Do it
Book at Wild Bush Luxury (arkabawalk.com).

Fitness: ●●●○○

Fear factor: ●○○○○

Expertise required ●●○○○

South Australia

Opposite Camp life, but not as you know it

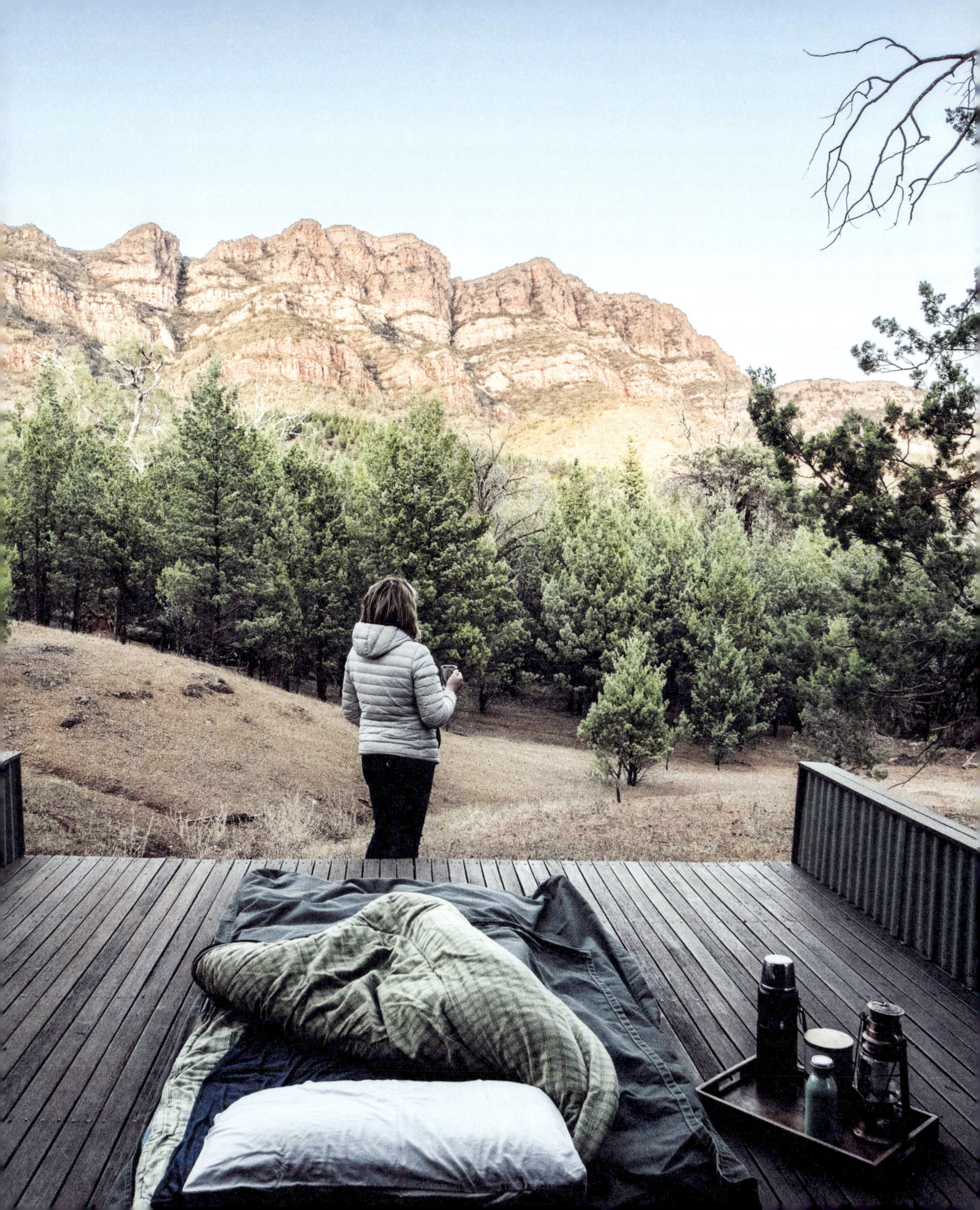

South Australia

THE ADVENTURE

In 1851, two brothers, William and John Browne, both doctors, staked claim to a parcel of land immediately south of Wilpena Pound/Ikara. They were only the second European settlers in the region, and within five years they'd built a five-bedroom homestead on Arkaba Station. Today, that homestead is the starting point for the Arkaba Walk, with walkers spending a night within its stone walls before setting out on foot across the station-turned-conservancy.

After a night in this setting that's Australiana from floor to ceiling – from the corrugated-iron roof, to the wallaby skins on the floor, and the wool bales that serve as bedside tables – it's a short transfer to the edge of Wilpena Pound/Ikara and the beginning of the three-day walk back to the homestead.

Stepping into the Gap, the lone break in the Pound, the trail is lined with river red gums, twisted and tortured into a variety of shapes. Wilpena's popularity means that the walk inevitably begins in a crowd, at least until Hills Homestead, a stone cottage built by the Hill family, who farmed grain in the Pound from 1899 to 1914 (the clearings you'll pass are the paddocks that once grew the wheat). At times it's like walking through a bowling green – or at least a bowling green with kangaroos incuriously watching walkers as they pass, and emus darting about like hedges on legs – until you hit the start of the climb up the Pound's wall towards Bridle Gap.

From this pass atop the Pound, where the walk leaves Ikara-Flinders Ranges National Park, the view extends overland to the Elder Range and everything between where you stand and there is the Arkaba Conservancy. Mountains stand in lines, like waves rippling across the country, and you might sight the distant white haze of Lake Torrens, looking like a cloud touched down on Earth.

As you step off Bridle Gap, you're entering the conservancy, stepping into classic South Australian outback country, with green cypress pines set against orange cliffs, and vegetation dotted onto the slopes as though the landscape was painted onto the earth.

Left Ridgetop hiking in the Arkaba Conservancy

Hiking the Arkaba Walk, Ikara-Flinders Ranges

A serpentine path weaves down onto the plain and finally into a break in the hills named Black's Gap. Here, 13km from the walk's start, is the first of the Arkaba Walk's two standing camps, with low wooden sleeping decks rolled out with swags that look up at the craggy southern face of the Pound, its grey rock eroded to reveal fissures of orange. A campfire is likely to be burning, heating water for the shower, and bottles of wine sit on a crisp white tablecloth. Lanterns hang in readiness for the evening, and there might be rainbow bee-eaters zipping across the sky like sparks.

After dinner, you'll find a hot-water bottle inside your swag as you lie back to view a night sky strewn with stars as the Pound fades to a silhouette.

The next morning, the walk sets out through Black's Gap, tunnelling through the land. For most of the next two days, it's a journey through trackless country. Beyond your group, there's not another person in sight – it's a true wilderness experience, even if softened by wine and brie.

The walk heads up over rocky peaks and down into barren hollows. The land is so open that you're always on track, even though you're literally off-track, going wherever the fancy takes, but always south towards the next camp.

Meandering more than the creeks, the walk has no set course, though when I walked here we stopped to snack beside a lonely windmill in a dry creek bed. Corellas watched down from the treetops, and the multicoloured Elder Range rose beyond the windmill. Around the mill, life was in full swing, with swallows and galahs drinking from its pumped waters.

Your own watering hole this night is Elder Camp, 14km from Black's Gap, and another night in the open-air of a swag before setting out on the final stage back to the homestead. Arkaba Creek is the guiding line for part of this last day, walking downstream even if there's no actual stream in its dry creek bed. There are cliffs layered like pastry, and Arkaba's guides continue to read and interpret the land, telling stories of ancient rock, modern floods and hours-old animal activity.

Part of the contemporary story is about the destocking of the station and its transformation into a conservancy. When the current owners bought Arkaba Station in 2009, there were 2500 sheep on the property (it once ran 28,000 sheep), the last of which were removed in 2013. Efforts continue to reduce the numbers of feral goats, cats and foxes. What's clear to see as you walk is that as the goats have been eradicated, the bush has responded. Cypress pines have returned in their

South Australia

Above The timeless landscape of the Ikara-Flinders Ranges *Opposite* Arkaba Homestead

thousands, and at times it's like walking through a Christmas tree plantation. Kangaroos abound, and a population of near-threatened yellow-footed wallabies has returned to the ranges.

Once again, there is only a general goal – the homestead – in mind. No track, no markers. Just heading east through seasonal carpets of wildflowers. The plains are covered in kangaroos, emus, galahs, corellas and ring-necked parrots. It's like walking through an open-range zoo, not an outback station.

Tasmania is the standard bearer for Australia's luxury guided walks. Of the 12 walks in the Great Walks of Australia portfolio, five are in the island state, including the pioneering Cradle Mountains Hut Walk and Freycinet Experience Walk, which were the first of their kind in the country when they launched in 1987 and 1992, respectively. The Bay of Fires Lodge Walk, Maria Island Walk and Three Capes Lodge Walk have since been added to Tasmania's luxe offerings.

Other private walks around the country with a bent towards comfort and gastronomy include the Murray River Walk (SA), Twelve Apostles Lodge Walk (Victoria), Scenic Rim Trail (Queensland), Seven Peaks Walk (Lord Howe Island) and Cape to Cape Walk (WA).

Hiking the Arkaba Walk, Ikara-Flinders Ranges

Roam across untracked land in remote country north of Blinman, with the burden eased by the presence of hardy camels.

Hiking with camels, Ikara-Flinders Ranges

Adnyamathanha Country

WHY IT'S SPECIAL

In the northern Ikara-Flinders Ranges, the desert-like earth is gloriously track-free. The only lines here are the dry creek beds and the animal tracks that crisscross through the dust. They are creeks that function as guiding lines and literal beds, providing a place to sleep each night as you trek through this open and wondrous landscape.

It's a scene that invites you to choose your own path, no longer bound by lines scratched into the ground, but how to do so when there's so little water and you're out here for days on end? That's where your hiking companions come in – a train of camels, plodding along beside you on their frisbee-sized feet, with water cans and other gear strapped to their backs. Their presence gives you the freedom to wander where and when you please, traversing the harshly beautiful country in a manner befitting of Robyn Davidson's travel classic, *Tracks*.

Where
Blinman is 500km north of Adelaide/Tarndanya, and 60km north of Wilpena Pound Resort.

When
Trips runs from April to Sept, through the coolest time of year in the Ikara-Flinders Ranges.

Do it
Check Flinders and Beyond Camel Treks (flindersandbeyondcamels.com.au) for each season's departures. There are also set seven-day trips that can be booked through World Expeditions (worldexpeditions.com) and nine-day trips through Park Trek (parktrek.com.au), both operated by Flinders and Beyond Camel Treks.

Fitness: ●●●○○

Fear factor: ●●○○○

Expertise required ●●○○○

Above Making camp in a creek bed *Opposite* A head's up

South Australia

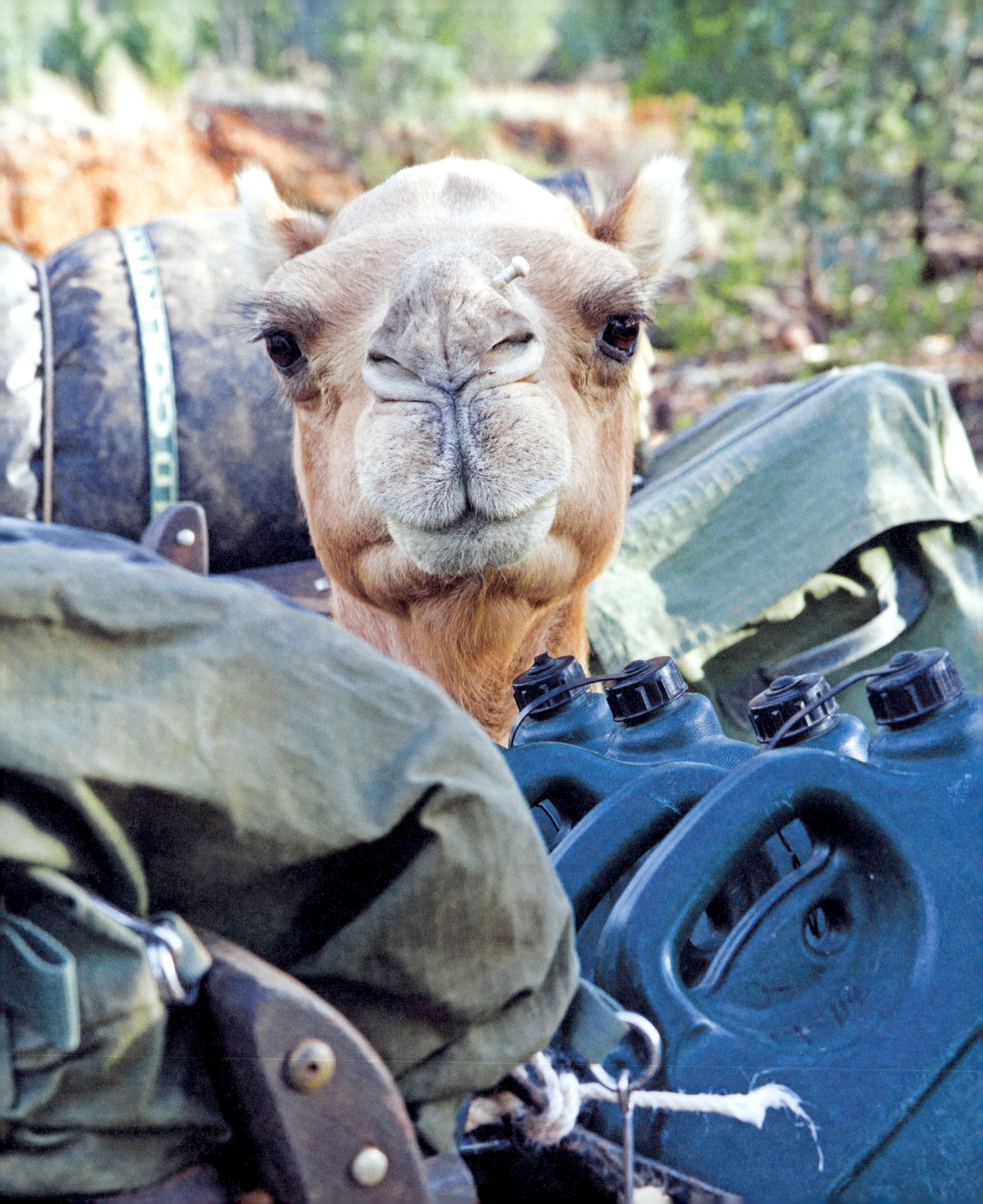

South Australia

THE ADVENTURE

Head north through Ikara-Flinders Ranges, and Blinman is pretty much the end of civilisation. The town of 43 people is anchored by the regulation outback pub, but little else. Look closely beyond the fences and you might wonder if camels almost outnumber people.

The Blinman home of Ryan McMillan, your guide and cameleer, is the starting point for these remote treks, which are as individual as the camels' personalities. You can spend as few as three days on a trek, or up to three weeks bound overland for the likes of Lake Torrens, while there are regular seven-day loops out from Blinman. It was this latter trip that I came to experience.

It's a week in which to pack away agendas and ambitions, with daily itineraries that read as simply as 'travelling through large gum-lined creeks' and 'through valleys and rolling hills'. The days take you where the days want to take you, a style of walking that becomes meditative. Unlike most treks, it doesn't involve defined features or goals. It's overland travel that's entirely about the walking and the camels. Creek lines snake through anonymously beautiful country that's part mountains and part desert.

On my trip, we set out with a train of seven camels, walking side by side with them, each one loaded with saddlebags, swags and water. Morning one was a slow start – it was 10.30am before we were on the trail – and even by the second morning we were less amateurish, knocking an hour off the packing time.

As the trek heads out of town, it follows wheel tracks to begin, but within a couple of kilometres, it turns away, setting out across untracked country. It could be the last time you see a trail for days.

The terrain lends itself to this sort of roaming freedom. Tree cover is sparse, the hills are low and unnamed creek beds are the defining lines in the land, bending through the hills and occasionally flourishing into gorges. It's like stepping off the map.

At day's end, you make camp in the soft sand of these creek beds, rolling out swags and unsaddling the camels before letting them roam off in search of trees to graze through the night – the camels intuitively stay near. With hills rising above the creeks, there's always the chance to wander to a low summit, where the silence is heavy and the views are vast.

Left The open camel road

Cameleer Ryan was first introduced to camels nearly 20 years ago while working at Arkaroola in the far-northern Flinders Ranges, where he talked his way into helping out on a desert camel trek. Soon he would acquire his own team of camels, and would work as a cameleer on the set of the 2013 film adaptation of *Tracks*, which also starred three of his animals. Watching him work with the camels, he exudes the confidence of someone who's done so for two decades.

For most of the trek, it's a journey between or along the ephemeral waterways. River red gums rise like arboreal archways, and wedge-tailed eagle nests balance in the forks of branches. At times, the trek cuts overland, crossing between creeks and following fence lines as unfailing as compasses. For all its uniformity, there's also surprising diversity in the country – white hills sitting side by side with rust-coloured crags; sheets of green rock settled among berry-coloured soils.

The route feels random, though it's not. The hills here are broken by just a few gorges, which, for the camels, are the only way through. The camels and trekkers weave between and through these gorges, like a connect-the-dots puzzle. The most spectacular of the gorges is one of the few places out here that bears a name: Nildottie Gap. With its slanting red walls dotted with spinifex clumps, Nildottie is like a piece of the Pilbara transplanted into South Australia. Its red gums are planted like an avenue of honour, and the creek bed is a mosaic of purple, pink and white stones.

Swinging back towards Blinman – still likely a couple of days' walking away – the terrain naturally funnels into another stunning gorge, where red walls angle down to a grey creek bed. It's prime habitat for yellow-footed wallabies, so scan the cliffs, though often all that seems to move are the camels, wild goats, your feet and, often, the wedge-tailed eagles that drift along behind the group, following the camels because they stir up rabbits.

Place names return as you step into the sandy bed of Eregunda Creek, where maps show waterfalls pouring from the cliffs, though the land is likely to be as dry as the paper of the map. That's at least until you pass the largest of the week's springs, which trickles along beside you. In this environment, it's cooling just to look at it.

The creeks continue to guide the journey until, rising up a ridge, you're suddenly looking down onto the Angorichina woolshed, built in the 1850s and thought to be the oldest shearing shed in the Flinders. Blinman is now just a few camel steps away.

> Blinman might sit removed from the world, but it's no stranger to adventure activities. Two of Australia's premier long-distance trails finish (or start) in Parachilna Gorge, just outside of the town. The Heysen Trail (heysentrail.asn.au) is South Australia's longest walking route, covering 1200km from southerly Cape Jervis to Parachilna Gorge, while its mountain-biking companion piece is the 900km Mawson Trail (southaustraliantrails.com/trails/mawson-trail), beginning at the foot of the Adelaide Hills and reaching all the way to Parachilna Gorge.

Left Hilltop view on sunset *Opposite top* Outback train
Opposite bottom Day's end in a dry creek bed

Hiking with camels, Ikara-Flinders Ranges

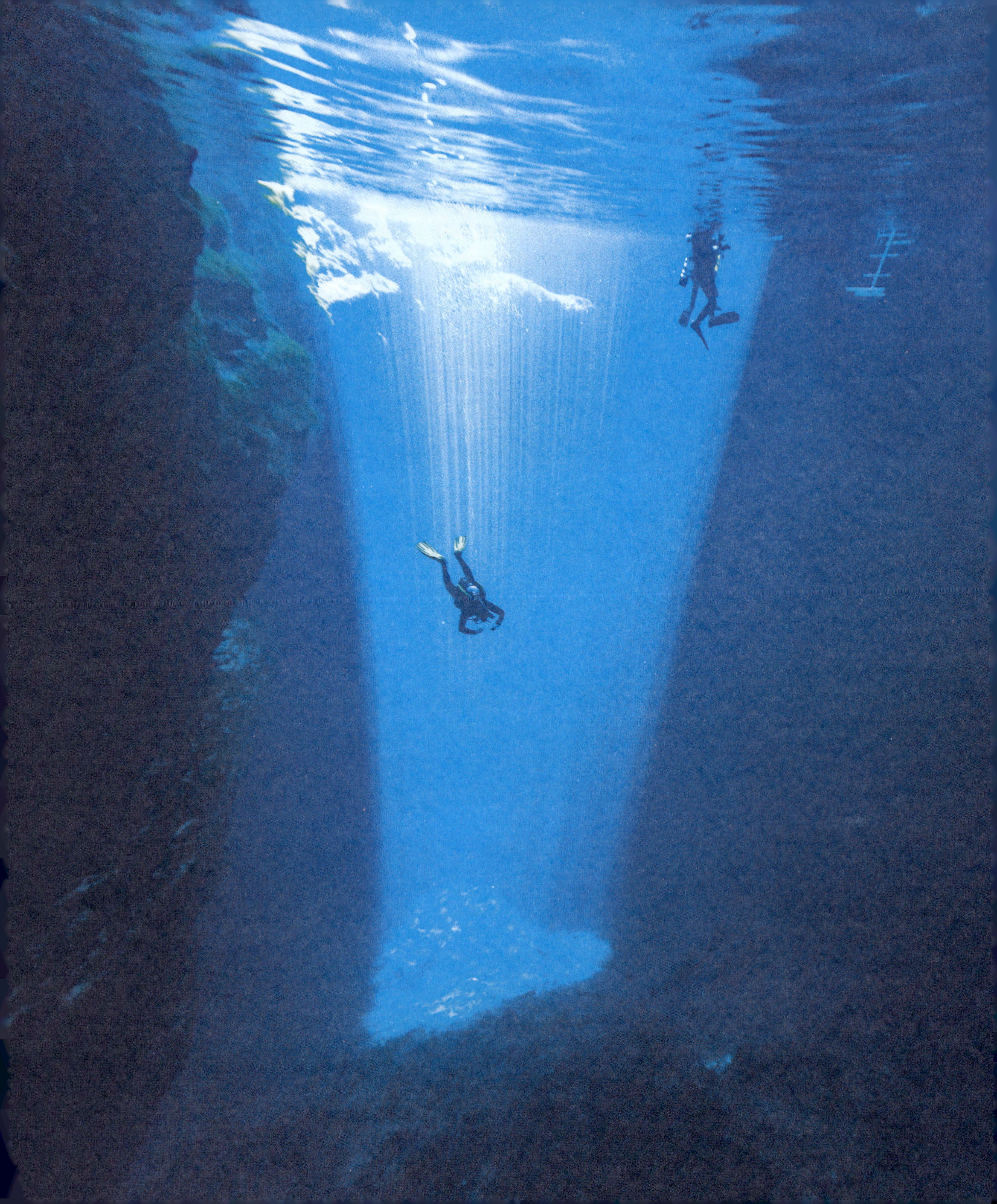

Slip into gin-clear water to snorkel through the sinkholes and ponds that dot the Limestone Coast.

Sinkhole snorkelling, Mount Gambier

Bungandidj Country

WHY IT'S SPECIAL

Mount Gambier's most famous feature is a large watery hole in the ground. The vividly coloured Blue Lake (best seen in summer) fills a deep crater blasted out of the earth by the most recent volcanic activity in Australia, but its vibrant presence overshadows a very different collection of subterranean water features. The limestone lands surrounding South Australia's second largest city are punctured with caves and sinkholes, looking as though somebody went through the country with a hole punch. Many of the sinkholes are filled with water that, filtered through the porous limestone, has a clarity found in few places in the world. And it's inside these sinkholes that you'll find some of the best water adventures in Australia.

Dip into these sinkholes, and the ponds around them, with a snorkel and mask and you'll find water almost as transparent as air. To snorkel here is to feel as though you're flying on water, peering down onto submerged landscapes almost 30m below you and yet seeing them in intense detail and luminosity.

Kilsby Sinkhole, a 15min drive outside of Mount Gambier, is the perfect introduction. Set in the middle of a sheep farm, this sinkhole has stepped from the realms of a spy thriller to become one of the area's most accessible snorkelling sites.

Just as enticing are Ewens Ponds and Picaninnie Ponds, which are also noted for their clarity, and are arguably the region's two most famous snorkelling and diving locations.

Where
Kilsby Sinkhole is on Sisters Rd, 15km south-east of Mount Gambier. Ewens Ponds Conservation Park is 30km south of Mount Gambier - take the B66 to see where the road had to split to get around another sinkhole in the small town of Allendale East.

When
The water in the sinkholes remains a fairly constant and cool 15°C, making summer the most comfortable time to be snorkelling.

Do it
Bookings are required to snorkel at Kilsby Sinkhole and Ewens Ponds. Book Kilsby online (kilsbysinkhole.com), while slots at Ewens Ponds should be booked through the National Parks and Wildlife Service website (parks.sa.gov.au and search for Ewens Ponds Conservation Park). A minimum of two people (and maximum six) is required at Ewens Ponds, and you must wear a full-length wetsuit, fins, mask and snorkel. Wetsuits can be hired from the Allendale East General Store and Dive Shop, but bring your own fins, mask and snorkel. Weight belts aren't permitted for snorkellers.

Fitness: ●●○○○

Fear factor: ●●○○○

Expertise required ●●○○○

Opposite Kilsby Sinkhole: Let there be light

THE ADVENTURE

Draw a circle 15km around Kilsby Sinkhole, and inside it you will find 95 per cent of Australia's sinkholes. These form when rainwater seeps into cracks and weaknesses in the Gambier limestone, slowly eroding these openings until they collapse, leaving a hole in the ground.

Such collapses are plentiful in the area around Mount Gambier, and provide an ascending scale of activities, from walks to swims and scuba dives into dark depths and caverns. Diving at most sites requires certification from the Cave Divers Association of Australia, making snorkelling a happy (and spectacular) medium for plunging into this remarkable water world.

Kilsby Sinkhole has been in the Kilsby family for 130 years, and for 17 years through the 1970s and '80s, it was also used as a research site for the development of the Barra Sonobuoy, a monitoring device dropped from aircraft to detect and locate submarines and ships. Today it continues to be used as a training ground for South Australia's police divers and, more recently, it has opened for snorkelling and diving tours.

The weapons research team's old workshop is now the office for Kilsby's tourism operation. Step out onto its rear deck and you're suddenly staring down into the deep sinkhole. After suiting up in 7mm wetsuits, gloves and hoodies – ample protection against the 15°C chill of the water – you head out across this deck and down through a cutting to a pontoon atop the water, 15m below the cliff-tops. The cutting was carved by the Kilsby family in the 1980s for the then-purpose of using the sinkhole to irrigate the farm.

The visible chamber represents around 25 per cent of the sinkhole's area. Beneath the southern rim of the cliffs, the sinkhole continues further underground, tunnelling beneath the office and carpark. Its deepest point – around 70m – is directly beneath the carpark.

After fitting your fins, mask and snorkel, you enter the water from the pontoon. Snorkelling is limited to the visible chamber, but you're free to explore at will for an hour. At one end, the pool extends into the cliffs, creating a cave-like enclosure. This is the sinkhole's shallowest end – around 12m deep – but through this crystalline water it looks no deeper than 4m or 5m. And not all of the beauty inside this overhang is below the water. At one point, I rolled over onto my back, looking up to the white ceiling of rock furnished with swallow nests, watching the birds fly in and out.

Elsewhere, as the sun shines into the sinkhole, rays of light bore into the water like lasers through the perfect blue. The bubbles from other duck-diving snorkellers rose like diamonds floating through the water.

Along the edge of the sinkhole, algae and grasses grow where sunlight penetrates through the cutting. In nooks and crevices, tiny cincarads – shrimp-like creatures endemic to Mount Gambier's sinkholes – might be seen. The only other life here is a single long-necked turtle, a native creature that was once a Kilsby family pet and now resides in the sinkhole, often resting on ledges as you swim about.

Near the southern cliffs, the sinkhole reaches its deepest point: 27m, a depth that has made Kilsby Sinkhole a favourite training ground for freedivers. But even from the surface, nothing is lost in the underwater view, with the sinkhole floor surreally visible 27m beneath you. Look up from a duck dive and it's like viewing the world through a fish-eye lens. Property owner Graham Kilsby recalls a time diving here and looking up from 25m below the surface to see a wedge-tailed eagle cruising overhead.

Much of this underground water that fills sinkholes, and lurks further beneath, squeezes back to the earth's surface as springs near far-southerly Ewens Ponds and Picaninnie Ponds, before flowing out into the sea. These two ponds require pre-booking through the National Parks and Wildlife Service for hour-long snorkelling slots.

My favourite among the pair is Ewens Ponds, where Eight Mile Creek has carved a hidden water world through the surrounding dairy farms. These ponds, which range in depth

Top Preparing to dive in Kilsby Sinkhole *Bottom* Kilsby Sinkhole bathed in light *Opposite* Divers enter the water at Kilsby Sinkhole

Above **Ewens Ponds** *Opposite* **Bubble trouble**

from 6.5m to 11m, are a trio of flooded dolines (shallow, funnel-shaped depressions in the ground), wrapped in reeds and connected by channels. A snorkelling outing here takes you into all three ponds and through the channels, drifting with the current as you seemingly hover suspended in the glassy water.

The entry point into Ewens Ponds is a wooden pier just a few steps from its carpark. From the pier, you slip into pond 1, the deepest of the trio. The bed of the pond, with its jagged limestone, is almost reef-like and there's a range of fish you might spot, such as the eel-like pouched lamprey and the endemic Ewens pygmy perch, though it's mostly small galaxids darting about the surface.

At pond 1's end, Eight Mile Creek narrows into a reed-lined channel, with the cold current carrying you 50m downstream to pond 2. The shallow channel is lined with reeds and river grasses, and sunlight strobes through the water to the bed of the channel. It's a tight confine, with your body brushing through the grasses. The world closes in, looking green and lush compared to the barren, stone-floored pools. The current is just strong enough that you drift downstream without effort – there's barely a need to kick.

Pond 2 is the shallowest of the trio, and it leads to a second channel. Drifting again without effort, as though in a slipstream, you're transported 125m downstream, brushing again over river grasses, to the final pond, which arrives like a blue abyss – the water is as blue as a summer sky as you emerge from the channel, floating above an overhang and into the 9m-deep pool.

Eight Mile Creek continues flowing on to the sea, just a couple of kilometres away, but snorkellers climb out at a pontoon, walking back to pond 1 on a grassy track through the reeds. In an hour, you can likely fit in two or three swim-throughs of the ponds.

All told, there are around 50 sinkholes in the immediate area around Mount Gambier. Wander into dry, garden-filled sinkholes inside the city limits at Umpherston Sinkhole/Balumbul and Cave Gardens, while Little Blue Lake (unrelated to, and far older than Blue Lake), 20km south of the city, all but doubles as the local public pool on hot days – the 8m-high cliffs serve as the high-diving board. Take short walks into portentously named Hell Hole and Sisters Sinkhole, which is a rare example of a double sinkhole (and contains the wrecks of four trucks beneath its surface).

Sinkhole snorkelling, Mount Gambier

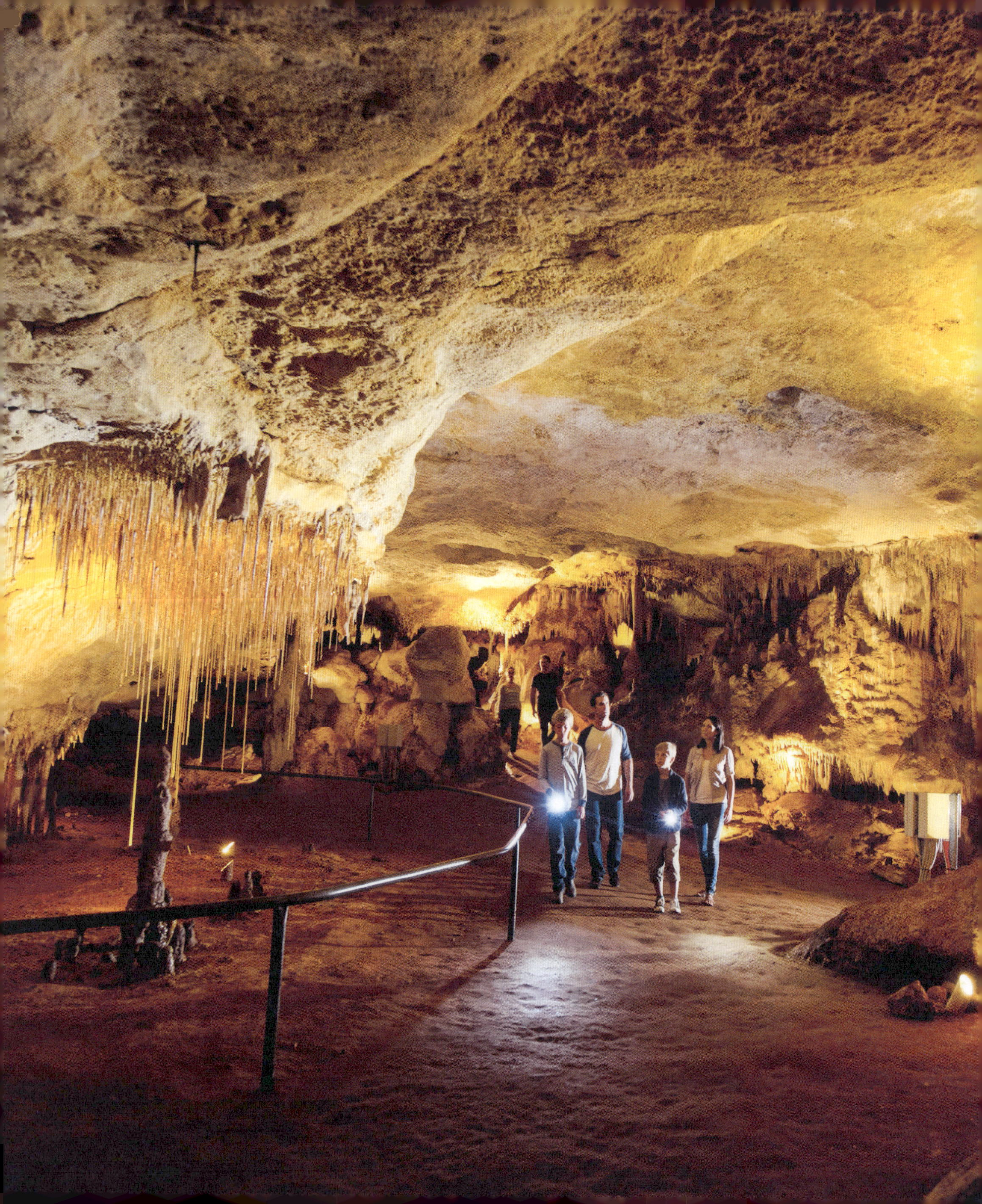

Burrow into the earth at one of the world's great fossil sites, squeezing and squirming your way through dark, narrow tunnels and chambers.

Caving, Naracoorte Caves National Park

Potaruwutij, Jardwadjali, Bungandidj, Meintangk Country

WHY IT'S SPECIAL

Open any discussion on the world's top fossil sites, and the Naracoorte Caves are invariably high in the conversation. Described by UNESCO as one of the world's 10 greatest fossil sites, this network of 28 caves is one of the planet's richest and best-preserved deposits of vertebrate fossils. When you imagine the megafauna world that existed in South Australia's only World Heritage Site – the likes of marsupial lions and diprodotons (a giant wombat-like creature growing to 1.8m in height) – it begins to feel like a subterranean *Jurassic Park*.

Almost as wild is the experience of adventure caving through the network, wiggling and wriggling your way underground. To go caving at Naracoorte Caves National Park is to pass the most impressive of the subterranean fossil beds and then crouch, crawl and squirm into narrow tunnels and holes. Begin with a cave that is one of Australia's most perfect introductions to spelunking, and then progress to wilder things.

Where
Naracoorte Caves National Park is 10km south of Naracoorte, which is a 350km drive south-east of Adelaide/Tarndanya.

When
Adventure caving trips run year-round and, being underground, are less subject to weather vagaries, so any time of year is good.

Do it
Caving trips are led by park rangers at Naracoorte Caves National Park. Details are on the park's official website (naracoortecaves.sa.gov.au); follow the 'Discover' and 'Under the ground' links. Tours run on demand.

Fitness: ●●●○○

Fear factor: ●●●○○

Expertise required ●○○○○

Family friendly

Above Look up! Don't miss the stunning stalactite limestone formations
Opposite Exploring the impressive network of 28 caves

Above **A steep stairway leads you down to the wonders of the caves below**

THE ADVENTURE

Three of Naracoorte's 28 caves are used for ranger-led adventure caving tours, but all participants, regardless of their spelunking experience, must begin with a trip through Stick-Tomato Cave, the entrance to which sits right beside the park's entry road. It takes just a few minutes to get kitted out in overalls, knee pads, helmet and torch, and then you're quickly descending a set of metal stairs into the cave.

This curiously titled cave is named for its two entrances: one known as Stick because people used to throw sticks into it, and the other called Tomato because of a tomato bush that once grew in it. It's the simplest of all of Naracoorte's caves, with a self-guided walk through a section of the cave open to all visitors, but adventure caving tours go far beyond the well-trodden path.

The way into the cave is through the Tomato entrance, a collapsed doline (a shallow, funnel-shaped depression in the ground) that formed when a thin sheet of limestone over the cave broke and crashed down into it. In turn, these 'roof windows' are believed to have acted as pitfalls, with animals falling into the caves, creating Naracoorte's treasury of bones – the remains of nearly 200 species of vertebrate animals have been found in the caves.

Stick-Tomato's public path leads down to a large chamber, where there is a first challenge – a testing ground of sorts – before you delve deeper into the cave. The Baby Crawl is a small horseshoe-shaped tunnel, requiring you to crawl through on elbows and knees. Its ceiling is almost as low as anything ahead, making it a good measure of your spelunking capability.

The cave is lit to this point, but things are about to get dark as you head further into the cave, stepping through a safety barrier and dropping to your knees, commando crawling into the earth through a natural tunnel perhaps 60cm in height.

At the tunnel's end, you emerge deep inside Stick-Tomato Cave. With its two entrances, this cave differs from most of its neighbours, with the air flow between the entrances limiting the ability of stalactites, stalagmites and other cave features to develop. But in their place come a couple of fun squeezes, including the Eye in the Needle soon after you've risen back to your feet.

This postbox-like slot in a wall looks almost too small to fit a human body. You need to push your arms through it, turn your head sideways and push your shoulders through. Inevitably, you will get stuck at the hips, requiring some deft movements to release. Not everybody will fit through, but part of the joy of Stick-Tomato Cave is that every challenge can also be walked around – you can squirm and spelunk as much or as little as you like.

Ahead now, rays of sun pour into the cave through the Stick entrance, where tiny ferns and moss greedily soak up the light. Sprinkled around the cave floor, there might be more modern fossils – the bones of roos, possums or, as on a day I was here, even a mummified frog – and as you step beneath this entrance, the cave continues into another chamber, featuring the well-named Keyhole for another chance to squeeze through a tiny slot in the wall. Here too, there's a passage beneath the cave – almost a cave within a cave – and you begin your return (if you're willing) by squirming through it, contorting around boulders and rubble in an impromptu underground game of Twister.

Only once you've completed Stick-Tomato can you progress to the other adventure caves in the system: Starburst Chamber and Fox Cave. The little-visited latter features some magnificent cave features as well as high chambers and low crawls, but it's the former that beckons most alluringly because it's buried deep within Naracoorte's showpiece cave, the Victoria Fossil Cave.

Set apart from the main cluster of caves, Victoria Fossil Cave begins simply with a concrete path descending through the earth to the fossil chamber. Here, laid out below the path is the caves' main excavation site, strewn with bones. Among them are remains from creatures such as the marsupial lion and short-faced kangaroos, which had a koala-like face. About 20 species of extinct megafauna have been found in this extraordinary deposit of ancient life.

General cave tours proceed no further than this chamber, but adventure caving tours continue through the cave. At first you can walk upright, then stooped, then crawl on hands and knees and, finally, flat on your stomach, crawling on your elbows and toes through a long, narrow tunnel towards the so-called Great Hall.

The contrast between the tunnel and the Great Hall is almost beyond measure – from the tiny confines of the burrow-like approach to the enormity of a chamber perhaps 10m high and 30m wide. At the Great Hall's far end there is a tiny hole, perhaps the narrowest of all the caves' tunnels, and this is the way through to the Starburst Chamber, which takes its name for the beauty of its stalactites, glistening like starbursts. The only way through this tunnel is to stretch your arms overhead Superman-style, suck in your chest and shoulders and push at the floor with your toes to propel you through the first metre or two. Then it opens wider, if not higher, but bear in mind that getting through the passage this way is the easy part. The design and dimensions somehow make the tunnel feel even tighter and trickier when you squirm back through it on the return from the chamber.

The darkness is absolute by the time you emerge at Starburst, with its elaborate decorations. There's a chance to admire nature's artistry by torchlight, and then you retrace your steps (or slide marks, in this case) back through the tight tunnels and the Great Hall to the fossil chamber, almost certainly emerging back above ground stained, as they call it here, 'Starburst red' – the colour of the soil and mud smeared across your knees, hands and overalls.

There are also gentler ways to head underground at the Naracoorte Caves, with standard tours running through four of the caves. Each cave has its own character and attraction. Victoria Fossil Cave is the spot to discover Naracoorte's fossil backstory, with full skeletons of a marsupial lion and short-faced kangaroo on show beside the fossil excavation site. The Naracoorte Caves are one of only two known breeding sites for the tiny, critically endangered southern bent-wing bat, which can be seen on the Bat Tour through Blanche Cave and the Bat Observation Centre. For sheer beauty, delicacy and range of cave features - stalagmites, needle-like stalactites, helectites and twisted columns - Alexandra Cave is the pick of the caves.

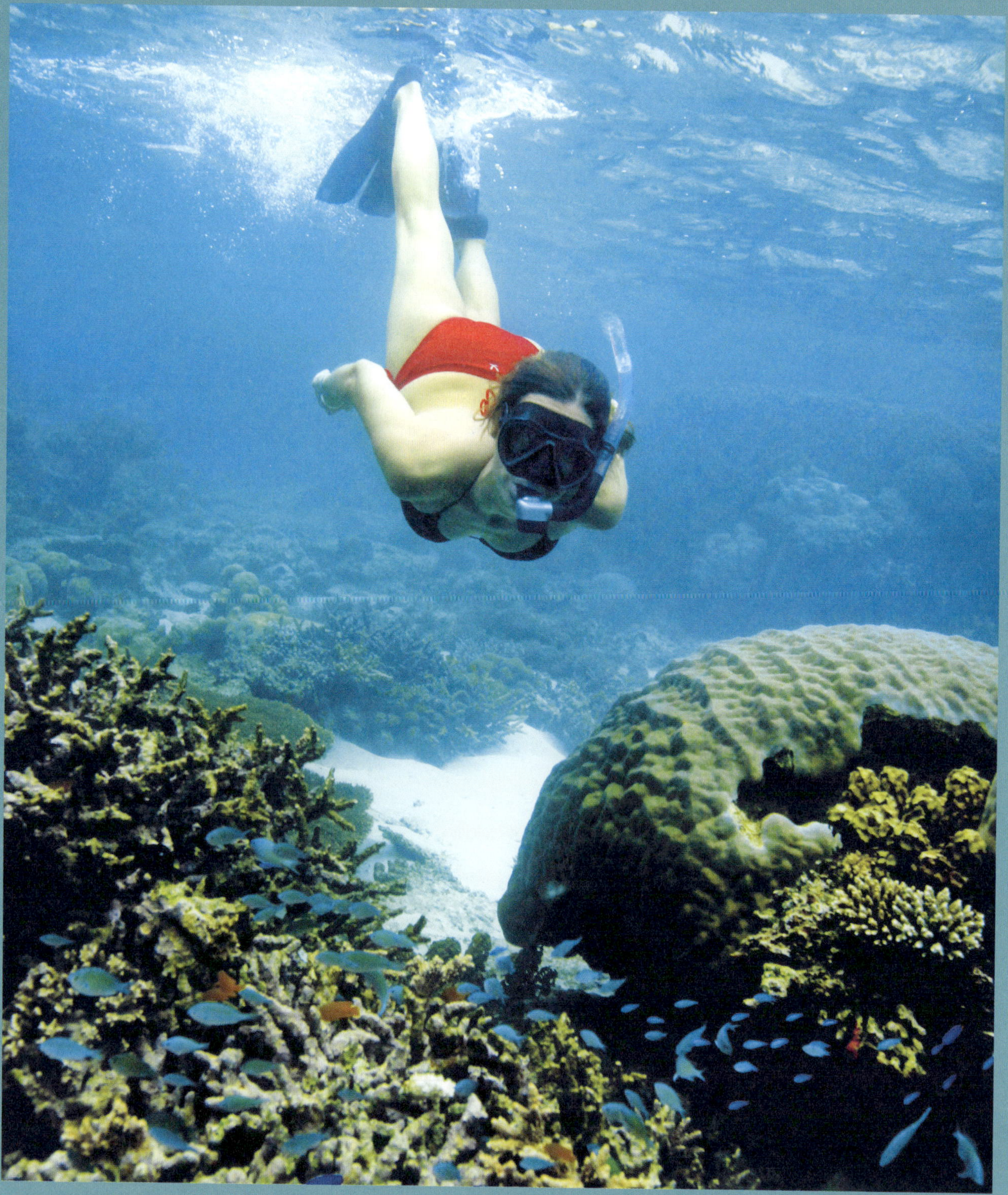

Western Australia

*Australia's largest state delivers the world's biggest fish,
deep gorges and massive tides.*

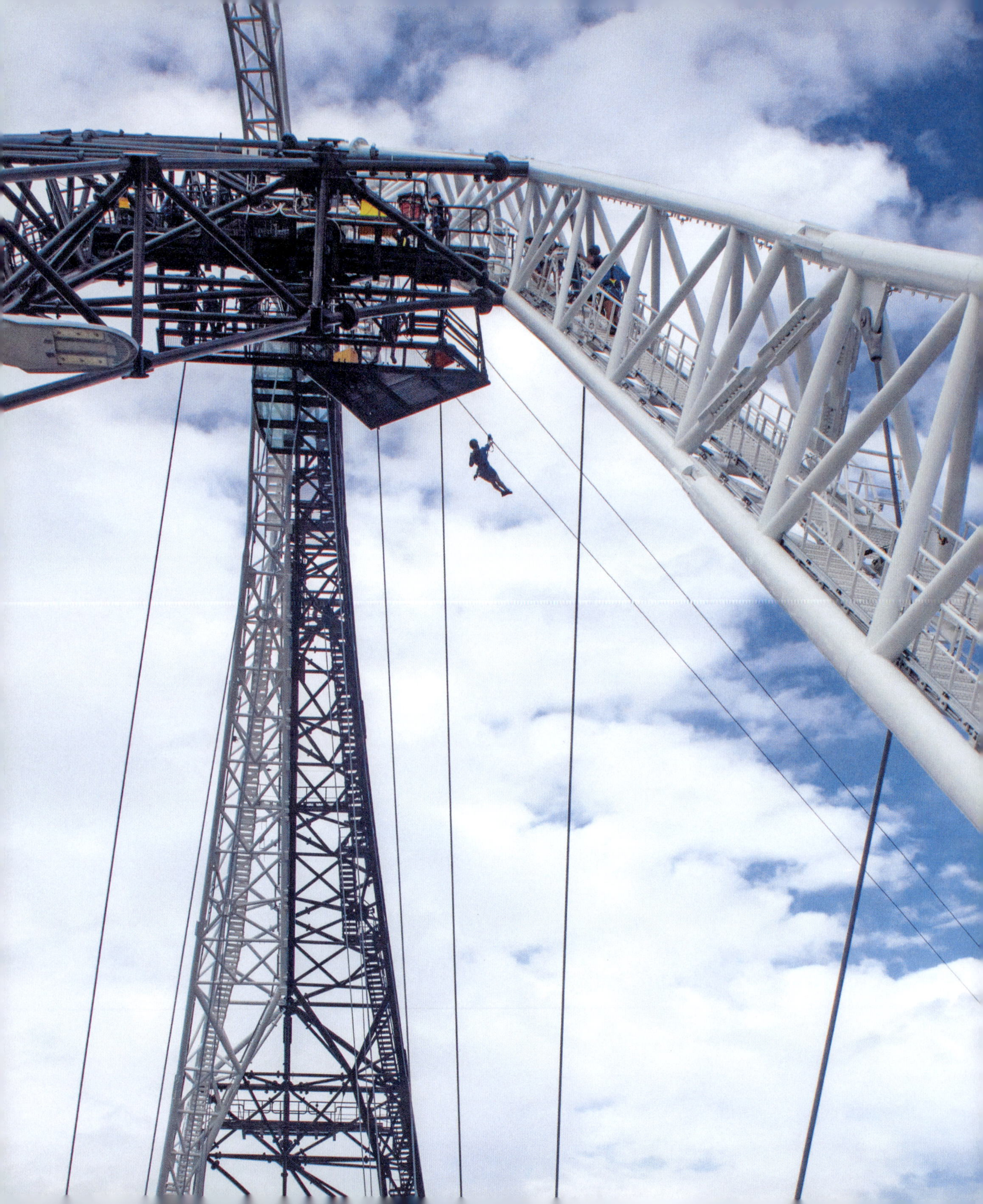

A bridge climb and a zip-line over the city's lifeblood, the Swan River.

Matagarup Zip+Climb, Perth/Boorloo

Whadjuk Noongar Country

WHY IT'S SPECIAL

Australia is no stranger to the concept of bridge climbs. The Sydney Harbour Bridge (*see* p.3) and Brisbane's Story Bridge can both be scaled for heady city views, but on Perth/Boorloo's Matagarup Bridge, opened in 2018 to provide pedestrian access to Optus Stadium, there's a bridge climb with an extra party trick.

Launched in 2020, Matagarup Zip+Climb sees climbers ascend the arches of the bridge to a glass deck 72m above the Swan River. To get down, they clip into a zip-line and hurtle 400m across the river at speeds of up to 75km/h. Effort up, adrenaline down.

Where
Matagarup Bridge crosses the Swan River at the end of Nile St in East Perth, connecting to the Burswood Peninsula.

When
Matagarup Zip+Climb trips run year-round. There are day and twilight climbs.

Do it
For bookings, head online to Matagarup Zip+Climb (zipclimb.com.au).

Fitness: ●●○○○

Fear factor: ●●●○○

Expertise required ●○○○○

Above High above the Swan River *Opposite* Unzipping from Matagarup Bridge *Previous* Underwater discoveries at Ningaloo Reef

THE ADVENTURE

Like all such structure climbs, Matagarup Zip+Climb begins with a safety briefing and a fit-out of harnesses and helmets. What's unique about this particular bit of kit is a small backpack, inside which you carry the trolley device for the zip-line, with a set of zip-line 'handlebars' strapped to its outside. At a glance, the bars look every bit like an ice axe, so that as groups set out walking across the Burswood Peninsula parkland towards the bridge, they appear as though they're striding out on some urban mountain climb.

This 'mountain' – Matagarup Bridge – is just 72m in height, but it comes at gradients worthy of a climbing peak. From the bridge walkway, the group steps through a hidden gate and onto the bridge's maintenance steps, which run inside the curving arches, descends one flight and then begins the steep ascent, which reaches a gradient of around 49 degrees.

The two rollercoaster-like arches – one white, one black – are one of the bridge's most notable design features. Straddling the Swan River, the arches represent the intertwined necks of a black swan and a white swan, while the colours symbolise the meeting of cultures: First Nations and European.

The curving lines of the arches further represent the flowing shape of Wagyl, the rainbow serpent that carved the Swan River in the Noongar creation story.

From the steps, take a moment to give thanks that the bridge went well over its construction budget, with the original plan being to enclose the bridge's arches in wooden cladding, mirroring that on adjoining Optus Stadium. If this bridge that takes its name from a Noongar place name meaning 'where the river is only leg deep, allowing it to be crossed' (even though that shallow bit of water is actually a short distance downstream, by Heirisson Island) had been completed as planned, this view and this climb would never have existed.

Ascending the neck of the black swan, the river falls away beneath you, just as Perth/Boorloo's city towers rise into view. Beneath your feet, pedestrians, cyclists and roller-skaters criss-cross the bridge, some oblivious to what's taking place above them, others stopping to watch. Look out a little further and you're likely to see two types of swans: the mud-brown Swan River and black swans on its surface, like nature imitating architecture.

Right The best seat in the house - zip-lining off Matagarup Bridge

Matagarup Zip+Climb, Perth/Boorloo

Western Australia

Just beneath the point where the necks of the bridge's arches intersect, you step out onto a glass-floored platform. Here you unclip from the bridge, with the chance to wander freely around the platform, taking in the view: the city and Gloucester Park racecourse to one side, the Burswood Peninsula and Optus Stadium to the other. Clad in bronze sheets in colours representing the minerals in Western Australia's earth, Optus Stadium was judged the world's most beautiful stadium in UNESCO's 2019 Prix Versailles awards. What's most beautiful about the stadium is the parkland and gardens around it, including the Chevron Parkland, a spit of riverside land featuring gardens inspired by the six seasons of the Noongar year. In the distance, Perth/Boorloo's hills abbreviate the view, but look down and you'll be peering onto the cables of the zip-line – your fast-track way off the bridge.

Another set of steps descends to the zip-line platform. Reattached to the bridge, you walk down 150 steps – about halfway down the bridge – through a section where the girders are so low and awkward that it's like a yoga class, bending, squatting and contorting to get past them. On so many other bridge and structure climbs, your helmet is little more than a safety regulation, but on this climb it's a vital piece of the kit. Look away from your task for a moment – and you will want to look away to keep enjoying that view – and there's every chance that your helmet clatters into a beam.

On twilight climbs, the sun will likely now be tumbling into the city towers, with the day darkening and yet colouring at the same time as the sky flares with sunset tones. Optus Stadium too begins to light up, emitting flickering lines of light intended to mimic the movement of Wagyl the serpent.

Not to be outshone, Matagarup Bridge's own lights begin to switch on at the same time, producing an ever-changing kaleidoscope of colours. There's 900m of LED strip lighting along the arches of the bridge, and it's claimed that this lighting has 16 million potential colour combinations.

On the zip-line platform, 35m above the river, the trolley and handlebars are removed from your backpack and you're fitted to the 90mm-thick steel cable. Sitting down into your harness, you get a 3-2-1 count, and you're away. There's a moment of trepidation as you first detach from the 2200 tonnes of surety of the bridge, but then it's 400m of pure enjoyment, skidding fast over the river with a metallic hum that can be heard right across the bridge and beyond.

There are two zip-line cables side-by-side, and two people attached to them, so it's a race back to earth until you hurtle over the top of a pond and slam to a halt against a braking puck on the cable. Depending on your weight and the wind speed and direction, you can reach speeds of up to 75km/h, and one Matagarup staff member stands with a radar speed gun, calling out your speed as you finish. The day I was here, most people were clocking speeds of between 45km/h and 55km/h before braking to sudden stops. The zip is down.

> Head just 30km outside of Perth/Boorloo and you come to the start of two of the world's great long-distance trails. The Bibbulmun Track (bibbulmuntrack.org.au) is a 1000km bushwalking trail that leaves Perth's hill to find its way through the tall southern forests – a world of endemic karri, tingle and jarrah trees – to finally finish in coastal Albany. Mirroring its route, but on separate paths, is the Munda Biddi Trail (mundabiddi.org.au), an off-road cycling trail between Mundaring and Albany. Both tracks are dotted with purpose-built campsites featuring sleeping shelters, picnic tables and water tanks (and bike storage shelters on the Munda Biddi).

Above Speeding into the riverbank *Opposite* Lighting up on Matagarup Bridge

Take an easy bike ride around a holiday island strung with beaches and reefs.

Cycling, Rottnest Island/ Wadjemup

Whadjuk Noongar Country

WHY IT'S SPECIAL

Picture an island garlanded with 63 beaches and ringed with reefs. You're pedalling a bike and there's barely a hill of any note across the entire island. The roads are empty of traffic except a single bus and a swarm of other cyclists. Some carry surfboards, others carry fins, masks and snorkels. Idyllic enough? Welcome to Rottnest Island, known to the Whadjuk Noongar People as Wadjemup, meaning 'the land across the sea where the spirits are'.

Rottnest offers the best island cycling in Australia, blessed with sun, sand, flatness and those ridiculously cute quokkas. In a day on a bike, you can loop around the entire island, which is only 11km long and 4.5km across at its widest point, though all those beaches, many with bike racks, are likely to slow your pace to 'Rotto' time.

Where
Rottnest Island/Wadjemup is around 20km off the coast of Perth/Boorloo, connected by three ferry services: Rottnest Express (rottnestexpress.com.au), Rottnest Fast Ferries (rottnestfastferries.com.au) and Sealink (sealinkrottnest.com.au).

When
Rotto is Perth's summer playground, and even the hottest summer days are cooled by all those beaches. Wind is one of the biggest cycling challenges on the island, making autumn - the season with the lightest breezes - a good option.

Do it
Bike hire options are plentiful. All three ferry services have bike-hire packages (and snorkelling gear), while Pedal and Flipper (rottnestisland.com/pedalandflipper) on the island has an extensive fleet of bikes, including e-bikes and bikes with baby seats and child trailers.

Fitness: ●●○○○
Fear factor: ●○○○○
Expertise required ●○○○○
Family friendly

Above Pedalling past Porpoise Bay *Opposite* Bike parking at Salmon Bay

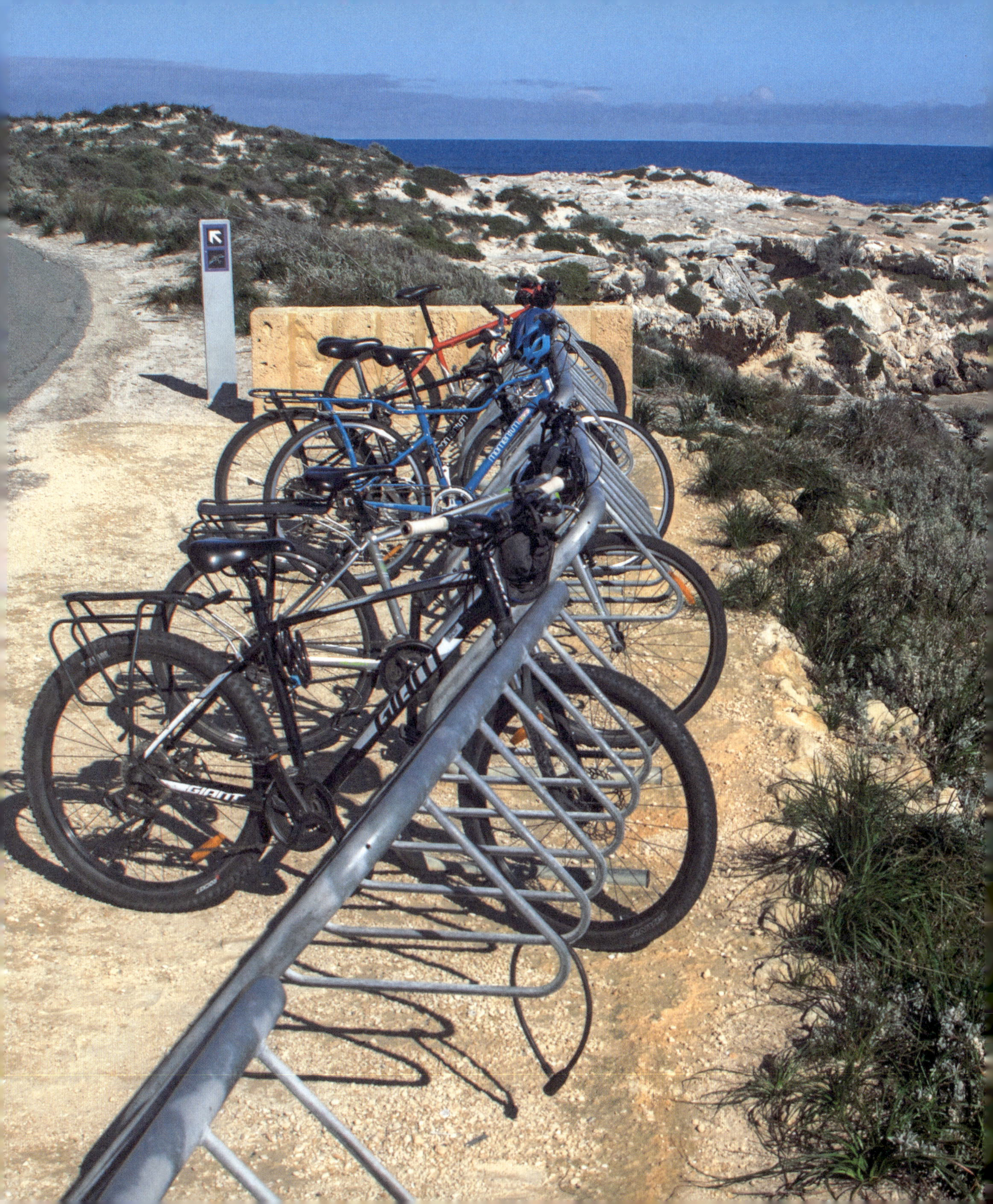

THE ADVENTURE

Ferries from Perth/Boorloo and Fremantle dock at The Settlement, the heart of Rottnest Island/Wadjemup's tourism scene. Visitors and quokkas mingle along the shores, while a wave of bicycles begins a westward migration on the sealed roads that are almost their exclusive domain (were it not for Rottnest's lone bus service).

There are three promoted cycling loops on the drumstick-shaped island: a 4km Rotto Mini Loop; a 10km Beaches, Lighthouses and Lakes ride; and a circuit of the entire island, which, depending on your curiosity, can cover anything from 22km to 28km. To get the best of the island, stretch your day out to the full island loop.

Heading clockwise, the ride crosses a point to Henrietta Rocks on Rotto's south coast, and a first look at the island's limestone coastline. Reefs sit like patches in the sea, creating a dangerous mosaic that's claimed three of the island's known 12 shipwrecks.

From here, it's a chance to stretch out your legs along Porpoise Bay, where the road runs as close to the coast as it does anywhere on the island. Parker Point and Little Salmon Bay are near to being Rottnest's southernmost shores, and it's well worth the short detour down to Little Salmon Bay, which is one of the most popular swimming spots on the island. If you're carrying snorkelling gear, this is the place to bust it out, with the bay featuring a snorkel trail with 10 buoys and information plaques embedded into the sea bed.

Little Salmon Bay swells into bigger Salmon Bay, Rottnest's longest beach, and the road soon passes beneath Wadjemup Lighthouse, standing tall atop the island's highest point, just 46m above the ocean. A side road ascends to the base of the lighthouse if you want something resembling a climb in your day.

The ride west squeezes between Strickland Bay – revered as one of WA's best surf spots – and Rocky Bay, passing through a landscape of dunes, low limestone cliffs and shrubbery pruned almost to bonsai by the Indian Ocean winds. Even the few trees that survive near this western tip grow almost horizontal, bowing to the power of the prevailing winds.

Right Fish Hook Bay, at the western end of the island

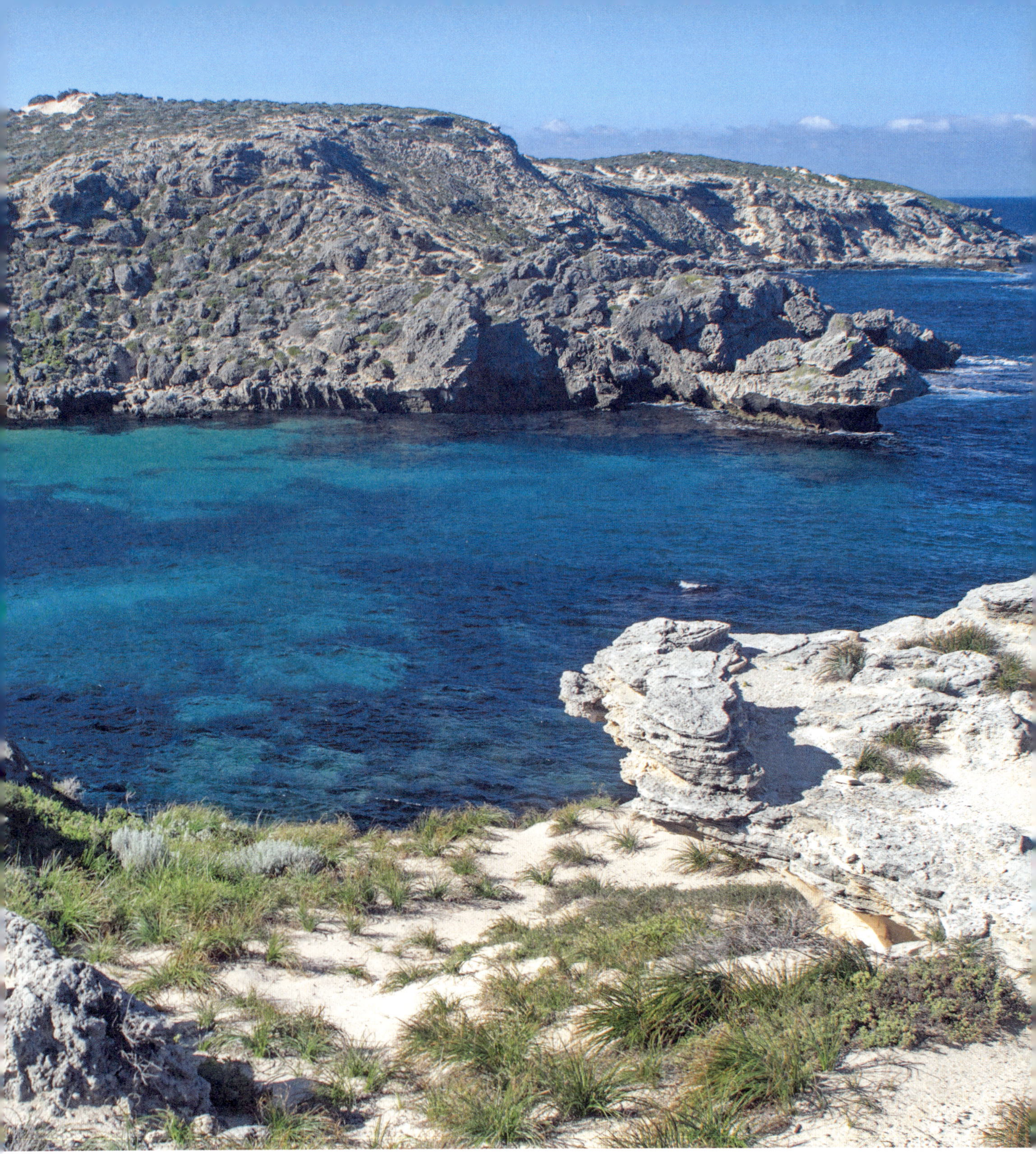

Western Australia

In classically Australian simplicity, the west end of the island is known as West End, and the ride finishes at its far-western point – the more exotically named Cape Vlamingh, where a short walk leads to a colony of New Zealand fur seals around Cathedral Rocks. Dolphins are also regular visitors, so keep an eye further out to sea.

Fuel up at Cape Vlamingh's coffee van and begin the return, retracing your tyre tracks past Rocky Bay to the Bovell Way road, turning away here towards the north coast (signposted to Geordie Bay).

Small bays beckon along this coast, slowing your return more effectively than brakes, at least until Geordie Bay, where you hit the edge of Rottnest's accommodation spread, its apartments racked behind the beach.

The most beautiful way back to The Settlement is along the coast, turning left beside the island's wind turbine to the ever-popular Basin. It's worth pulling out the snorkel and fins here, with this beach's hollowed-out reef home to more than 400 fish species.

Expect a guard of honour of quokkas as you head back towards The Settlement, and keep an eye for the Quod as you pedal towards the ferry for an insight into the tragic side of Rottnest's history. The island was used as an Aboriginal prison and labour camp for almost a century from 1838, with more than 4000 men and boys incarcerated, typically for minor crimes. More than 370 of these men and boys died in custody, and were buried in unmarked graves. The Quod was the main prison building. To learn more about this (and the rest of the island's) history, park up and take the time to visit the Wadjemup Museum.

Cycle through town to wrap up this day of perfect pedalling.

Above Quokka time *Opposite top* Heading for home past Lake Vincent *Opposite bottom* What's a good bike ride without a good coffee van? Cape Vlamingh delivers.

While cycling is the best way to explore Rottnest Island/Wadjemup in a day, the most immersive way to experience the island is on foot. Wadjemup Bidi is a series of five connected walking tracks, covering most of the island along its combined 45km length. Each trail focuses on a different area of the island, from the 9.5km Gabbi Karniny Bidi loop out from The Settlement, to the 8.5km Ngank Wen Bidi circuit around the West End. Pick up an island map at the visitor centre at The Settlement.

Wax up and hurtle down some of the state's highest dunes on a sandboard.

Sandboarding, Lancelin

Yued Noongar Country

WHY IT'S SPECIAL

Drive 90min north of Perth/Boorloo and you come to Lancelin, a low-slung town where the only things higher than the homes are the Norfolk pines, a pair of water towers and, tallest of all, a collection of sand dunes that are claimed as the biggest in Western Australia.

Standing as high as three-storey buildings, this 2km-long field of dunes has become a mighty natural playground. Quad bikes and 4WDs motor about in the hollows between the dunes, but it's on the dunes themselves that the fun really begins. With slopes as steep as 45 degrees, these dunes are a sandboarding favourite, with an established boarding area, providing careering runs in sight of the Indian Ocean and all but looking down onto the roofs of the town. Sitting, standing or kneeling on your board, the sense of speed and sand is brilliant.

Where
Lancelin is 125km north of Perth/Boorloo. Entry to the dunes is off Beacon Rd, at the northern end of town.

When
Try to avoid coming immediately after rain, when the wet dunes can make for a slow and sluggish ride. The dunes are officially open 8am to 7pm, but winds are typically lightest (and thus the boarding is most comfortable) in the morning.

Do it
Book boards online (lancelin.com.au), with the option to hire for 2.5hr or 3hr. Boards are then picked up from a participating business in town - the exact location will be noted in a confirmation email.

Fitness: ●●○○○

Fear factor: ●●○○○

Expertise required ●○○○○

Family friendly

Opposite **The high march to the top**

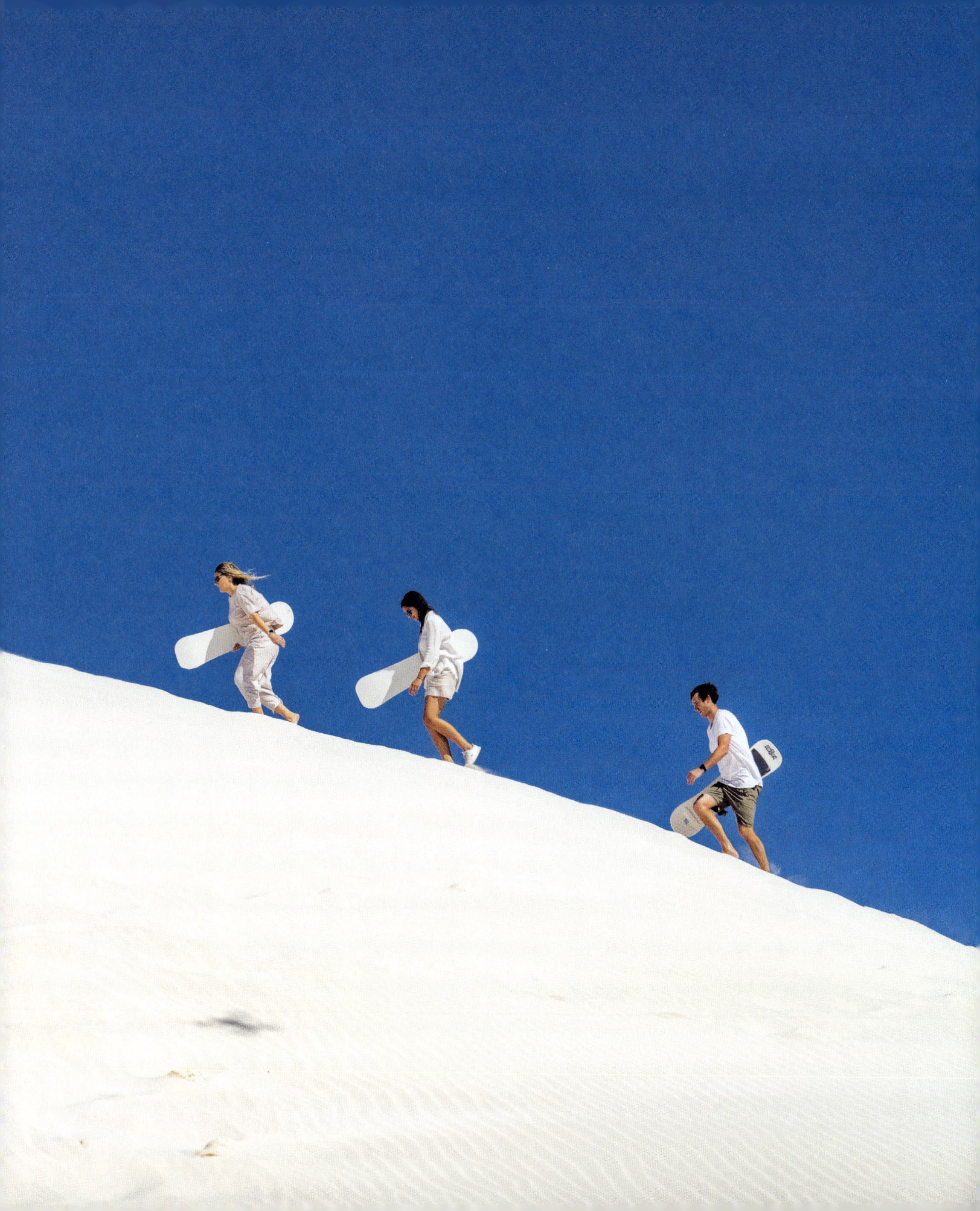

THE ADVENTURE

From near Perth/Boorloo's northern edge, sand country marches north through Nambung National Park, aka the Pinnacles, to Jurien Bay. Coastal scrub covers much of it, but occasionally it bursts open into bare patches of sand. Behind the back of Lancelin is one of the most prominent of these patches – a towering field of dunes looking as though somebody spilled white-out through the bush.

These are coastal dunes that don't quite sit on the coast, with the narrow town separating them from the ocean. As you enter the dune field at the edge of town, a 2WD track heads a couple of hundred metres over hard-packed sand to a makeshift carpark near the base of the dunes (if you're nervous about driving on the sand, you can also park by the entrance – near the quad-bike tour operators' trucks – and walk into the dunes, but watch for vehicles). From here, sand dunes of a range of heights and angles rise immediately ahead. These are shifting dunes, so change is their only constant, but the main sandboarding area, on one of the dunes' steepest slopes, is usually betrayed by the presence of footprints.

The general premise of sandboarding is simple – sit or stand (or lie down, or kneel) on a board (you can hire them in Lancelin, see p.168) and try to ride it all the way to the base of a dune. The most challenging part of each run is the climb to the top of the dunes, which stand up to 15m high. Once you're standing atop a dune, you realise it's just a small piece of a far greater expanse of dunes, heading almost to the horizon in all directions except to the town and sea.

If you've hired a sandboard, there will have been a choice of two options: a bare board for sitting on, and another board with straps for your feet, designed to be ridden standing like a snowboard. If you're not already a proficient snowboarder, the former can be the best choice, since you can also stand on them. The hire boards also come with a stick of wax (in this case, a simple candle) and when you scribble wax over the base of the board, the dynamics of the run change entirely, turning a sand hill into a sand hurtle, as slippery as a slide.

Finding the best run is a question of assessing angles, slopes and degrees, carving a line through the sand towards the Indian Ocean or off the back of the dunes into a limestone hollow, and steering by dragging your hands through the sand like a paddle or rudder. You can go slow, or you can wax the board to a slick finish and plunge like an avalanche.

As you climb back to the top of the dunes, you'll likely find yourself pausing regularly to take in the view (or at least pretending to take it in as you catch your breath) over these bone-white sands beside gleaming blue seas. And then it's down again, as fast as you care or dare.

> Sandboarding on the Lancelin dunes isn't the only adventure you can have in the sand country north of Perth/Boorloo. Continue an hour north from Lancelin and the highway enters the small town of Jurien Bay, a typical coast town of shacks and fishing rods, but also one of the most scenic skydive centres in the country. You can pitch yourself out of a plane on a tandem skydive from 10,000 feet or 14,000 feet – the former comes with 35 seconds of freefall, and the latter with 60 seconds. Head online to Skydive Jurien Bay (skydivejurienbay.com) for details.
>
> At ground level, Jurien Bay is also the start and finish point of the Turquoise Way Trail, a 14km (one way) walking and cycling path through the coastal dunes south of town to the Hill River inlet. Or you can simply drive the loop at the Pinnacles in Nambung National Park, stopping to wander among the limestone pillars that spear out of the sands.

Above Dune perfection *Opposite* The quick way down

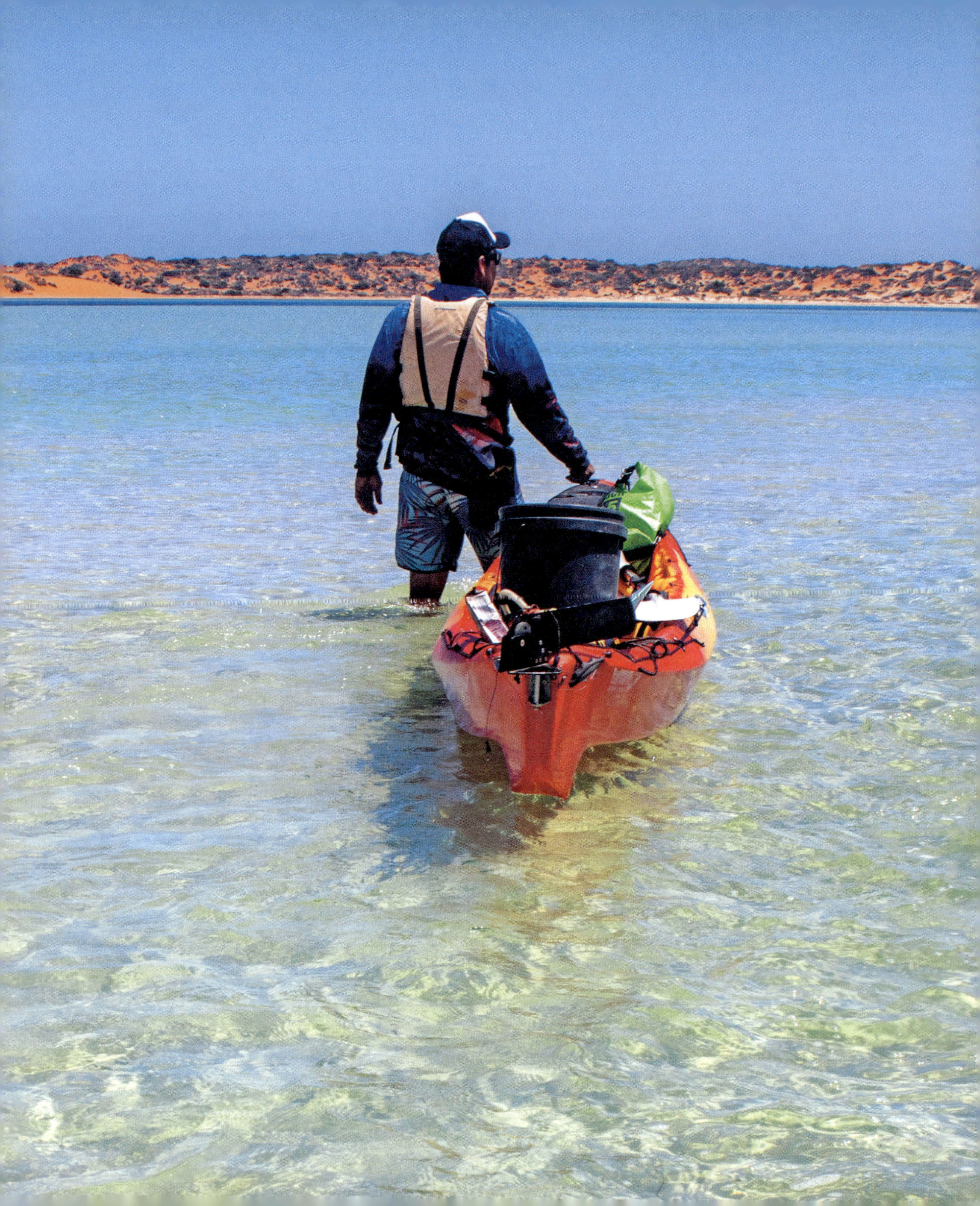

Paddle across a stunning lagoon in a World Heritage setting with a rich First Nations history and abundant wildlife.

Kayaking, Shark Bay

Malgana, Nhanda Country

WHY IT'S SPECIAL

In the lagoons of Francois Peron National Park, the water is so clear it's as though kayaks hover rather than float. Beneath the kayaks, moving like shadows in the sandy shallows, spotted whiptail rays and nervous sharks (a species, not an affliction …) dart about the shallows, and the sandy shores are as red as Australia's centre.

In this coastal national park at the heart of the Shark Bay World Heritage Area, there are more famous creatures than these rays and sharks – such as dugongs and the dolphins of Monkey Mia – but wherever you look, there's life. This 1500km of coastline, known to the Malgana, Nhanda and Yingkarta peoples as Gathaagudu, meaning 'two waters' (for the two bays that actually make up Shark Bay), might easily be considered the world's biggest aquarium. It would also be one of its best stocked. Shark Bay is home to some 10,000 dugongs – around 10 per cent of the world's population – grazing on its 400,000ha of seagrass meadows. Around 35 per cent of Australia's bird species have been recorded in the area, and 70 per cent of the loggerhead turtles found in Western Australia lay their eggs here. Suitably, Shark Bay is also home to 28 species of shark.

In a kayak, in these clear waters, surrounded by dunes both red and white, it all feels so visible and alive. Paddle with Wula Gura Nyinda Eco Cultural Adventures and you can also learn how Shark Bay has sustained the Traditional Owners for over 40,000 years.

Where
Kayaking trips depart from Denham, which is 830km north of Perth/Boorloo. There are daily flights from Perth to Denham.

When
Trips run year-round - even in July the average maximum temperature in Shark Bay is 22°C - but the heat of summer is an encouragement to be on the water.

Do it
Trips are run by Denham-based Wula Gura Nyinda Eco Cultural Adventures (wulagura.com.au), which also operates stand-up paddleboard tours, 4WD tours and a Didgeridoo Dreaming Night Tour.

Fitness: ●●○○○

Fear factor: ●●○○○

Expertise required ●○○○○

Family friendly

Opposite Darren Capewell in the gin-clear waters of Big Lagoon

THE ADVENTURE

Kayaking trips with Wula Gura Nyinda Eco Cultural Adventures take place on Big Lagoon, a long, sheltered tidal inlet about an hour's drive into Francois Peron National Park from Denham. Getting here is part of the adventure, four-wheel driving through the red coastal desert with company owner Darren 'Capes' Capewell. The Nhanda man is a stalwart of local tourism – even the morning coffee is acquired from a store owner who came to Shark Bay 13 years ago, took a tour with Capewell and was convinced by him to stay.

Francois Peron National Park is a land resurrected. The former sheep and goat station once ran up to 15,000 head of livestock, but was gazetted as a national park in 1993. The knee-high scrub and dune-lined coast are slowly recovering from their grazed days, and the landscape is dotted with dry lagoons that Malgana and Nhanda stories credit to the footsteps of creation beings. Near the park entrance, the old station homestead remains, now preserved as the Peron Homestead Precinct. Behind it is a natural artesian pool that was drilled in 1922 and continues to fill a concrete tub with 40°C water.

'That'll be your recovery session,' Capewell promises his group.

Big Lagoon, which stretches around 10km north to south, is a stunning palette of colours. Its waters are customarily as blue as the sky, and it's ringed by red and white sand dunes that further brighten with wildflowers in spring. On its shores, the kayaks are removed from the trailer, and each paddler tosses a handful of sand into the water as a sign of respect for the lagoon. Then they are away, kayaking across the lagoon's single deep channel.

For most of the crossing to the dunes 2km opposite, the water isn't deep at all – fall out here and you're more likely to be standing than swimming. Dark seagrass patches – the foundations of Shark Bay's remarkable dugong population – pass beneath the kayaks, and it's not long until Capewell has his guests climbing out of the kayaks into the water, walking through the thigh-deep shallows rather than paddling.

'It's not all about kayaking,' he says. 'We say this Country looks good, but it feels better. It's about our connection to the place. We don't just want people to fill up their eyes, we want them to feel it in here.' He points to his torso. 'To fill up their guts.'

Right Parked up on Big Lagoon

Kayaking, Shark Bay

Western Australia

As the group wades, towing their kayaks behind them, Capewell talks passionately – informative when needed, irreverent when not – about Country and culture, the old people and the old land. Then the shallows end at another section of the channel, and the paddle continues towards the dunes that appeared so distant a short time ago and now look so near.

The day I was here, we glided ashore beneath the line of dunes, and a spotted whiptail ray swam to the water's edge to check out these new arrivals, soon joined in its audience by a shovelnose shark. Capewell pointed at the dunes and noted that they were one long, ancient midden.

'This is where our ancestors camped for thousands of years,' Capewell said. 'All along here are burial sites, too. Our ancestors were buried on the sides of sandhills so they could keep an eye out over Country.'

The paddle back across the lagoon takes a very different line, nudging along the shores and making regular stops ashore. In the shallows, rays and small sharks are suddenly in abundance – at times side by side, swimming on ahead of the kayaks, their shadows like torpedos.

In one corner of the lagoon, Capewell leads a short walk up onto the red dunes for a view over the entire lagoon, snaking through the land as a brilliant-blue beauty spot. Behind the reddest of the dunes, a highway of kangaroo tracks criss-crosses the sand, leading to two holes scratched deeply into the lowest point by roos that sensed water here. Capewell drops to his knees, digging deeper, until water again begins to fill the holes.

Back at the kayaks, there's time for a swim beside these red dunes. In the hyper-saline water, it's an effortless exercise to float on the surface of the lagoon. The water might be cold, but there's an antidote ahead. The end of the paddle – back where it began – is in sight across the lagoon and the therapy of 40°C artesian waters, soaking away the day's efforts, awaits at the Peron Homestead Precinct on the drive back to Denham.

Above Swim stop *Opposite top* Casting a line in Big Lagoon
Opposite bottom Typically perfect paddling conditions

> They call it Monkey, but it's all about dolphins. A 20min drive from Denham, skirting the southern edge of Francois Peron National Park, Monkey Mia has long been famed for its dolphin-feeding experience. Things have changed a little in the post-pandemic world, with visitors no longer permitted to enter the water and join the hand feeding, but you can still line the ocean's edge to watch these beautiful creatures arrive up to three times a day for a small feed of fish.

Kayaking, Shark Bay

Plunge into one of Australia's most endearing wildlife encounters, swimming beside the largest fish on the planet.

Swimming with whale sharks, Ningaloo Reef

Jinigudera Country

WHY IT'S SPECIAL

Around Ningaloo Reef, the world's largest fringing coral reef, a miracle birth occurs every year. One week after the full moon in March or April, coral along the 260km-long reef begins to spawn, filling the sea with millions of eggs and oodles of sperm. It's a phenomenon that attracts swarms of feasting krill and plankton and, in hungry pursuit of those tiny creatures, the world's largest fish – the whale shark.

Swimming beside these gentle giants is one of the big-ticket items in West Australian travel. During the whale shark season, boats head out daily through the World Heritage–listed reef in search of what they locally call 'our spotted fish'.

The world is transformed when you slip into the ocean and begin swimming beside these slow-moving sharks larger than great whites. It is, without question, one of the most thrilling and humbling wildlife encounters in the country.

These harmless sharks of mystery – where they go after they leave Ningaloo each year is unknown, and they've never been observed giving birth – are the stars of the show, but they could also be a ticket into a world of other whales and sharks. Reef sharks are commonly sighted among the coral bommies inside the reef, and from July to Aug the whale shark season intersects with the humpback whale migration along the WA coast, bringing the very real possibility of whale sightings.

Where
Trips depart from Exmouth, 1250km north of Perth/Boorloo. There are direct flights to Exmouth from Perth/Boorloo and Melbourne/Naarm.

When
The whale shark season opens after the coral spawning in March or April, and runs through until around the end of Sept, though sightings become less certain through Aug and Sept.

Do it
Exmouth Dive & Whalesharks runs daily whale shark trips from March through Sept. Book online (exmouthdiving.com.au).

Fitness: ●●○○○

Fear factor: ●●○○○

Expertise required ●○○○○

Family friendly

Opposite The Cape Range coast and Ningaloo Reef

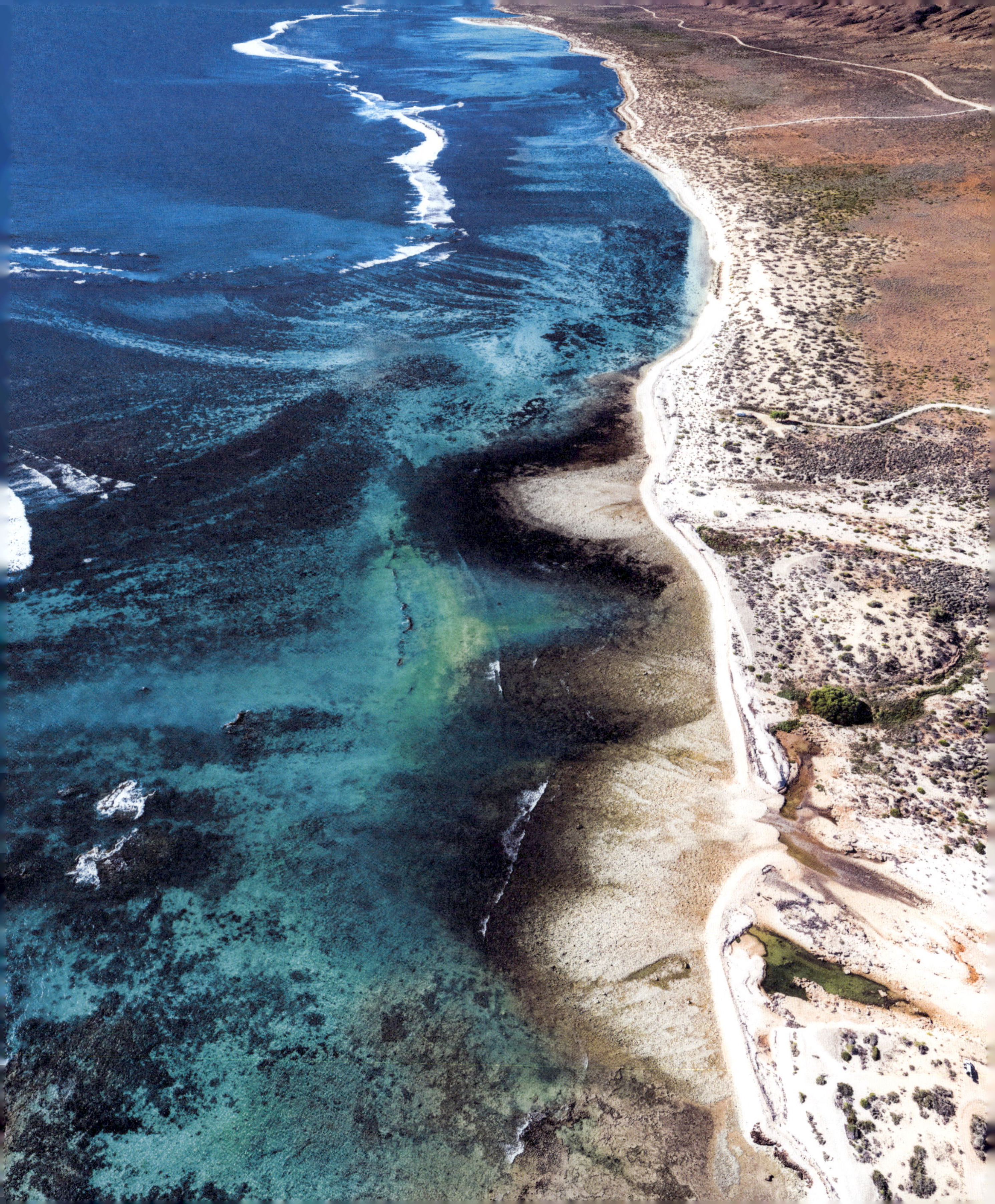

THE ADVENTURE

In the tourist town of Exmouth, they have a unique verb: 'whale sharking'. To go whale sharking is to head out into the Indian Ocean, slip off the back of a boat and swim beside the largest fish on the planet.

One of Ningaloo Reef's most appealing qualities is its proximity to shore. In places, the reef runs just a few hundred metres from the coast, visible from the shores as a white line of breaking surf. Inside the reef, the lagoon is furnished with a plethora of coral bommies (outcrops of coral), and whale shark boats typically make a first stop among these bommies for a trial snorkel. These few minutes in the water give you the chance to fit and test snorkels, mask and fins, while drifting over bommies and among the marine life that gathers around them – fish as colourful as paint charts, and the menacing shapes (but not menacing natures) of black- and white-tip reef sharks.

Whale sharks aren't found among the bommies. These giants stay outside the reef, blithely hoovering up plankton, so whale shark boats punch out into the Indian Ocean through one of three breaks in the reef, and the search for sharks is on.

Spotter planes are employed to locate whale sharks swimming at the surface of the ocean. Often, it's just minutes before the skipper gets word from the sky: whale sharks ahoy.

Entering the water is akin to a military manoeuvre. As the boat stops near the whale shark, you sit at the stern, fins and mask fitted, ready to plunge. A call of 'go, go, go' comes from a deckhand, and you slide into the ocean, waiting on the surface as the exact position of the shark is ascertained. When you do then pop your face into the water, the giant fish will likely be swimming past just metres away.

The whale sharks seen around Ningaloo Reef are typically mere teenagers. These herculean fish grow up to 12m in length (though the largest recorded was 18.8m), while those seen at Ningaloo are more commonly around 3m to 8m.

The day I was here, the first whale shark encountered was around 6m in length. To put that into perspective, it was a fish more than three times the length of the average person. As you swim beside a fish like this, remind yourself that it's as large as the biggest great white shark ever recorded. And here you are, drifting peacefully side-by-side. What a difference a fish's temperament can make.

For a few minutes you swim beside this fantastic fish. Whale sharks typically move slowly, so it's fairly easy to keep pace as their tails flick languidly, their gills ripple, their postbox-like mouths open to draw in water and plankton, and an entourage of small fish hitchhike along beside. The sharks swim so near to the surface that you can often raise your head above water and see their enormous shadow on the water. Equally surreal is the sight of the North West Cape coastline so close by.

Regulations (as well as common sense and respect) decree that you remain at least 3m from the shark, though as with all wildlife encounters, the animals don't always abide by rules – whale sharks have been known to be drawn to the bubbles made by swimmers' fins, mistaking them for plankton, creating an adrenaline-pumping moment of dodge the fish.

Eventually, swimmers drop away from the whale shark and return to the boat, which motors on ahead of the animal and you slide back into the water for another few minutes in the presence of greatness. Then it's back into the boat; rinse and repeat. I ended up swimming beside the same gentle giant four times before word came of a second whale shark in the vicinity, and a new fish friend was made. This smaller whale shark, 3m to 4m in length, swam even slower, and at times I barely needed to kick to keep up as I simply drifted beside it, a land mammal and an ocean fish somehow at peace together in the Indian Ocean.

Top Preparing to swim *Bottom* In the company of natural greatness *Opposite* A classic Ningaloo entourage

There's another grand creature in Ningaloo's almanac of marine experiences. Manta rays are also drawn to the reef by the spawning of the coral, creating another swimming experience for visitors. Coral Bay, at the southern end of the reef, is the main centre for swims with these graceful, highly intelligent fish that are the world's largest rays, with wingspans of up to 4m. Boat trips to swim with mantas operate year-round out of Coral Bay.

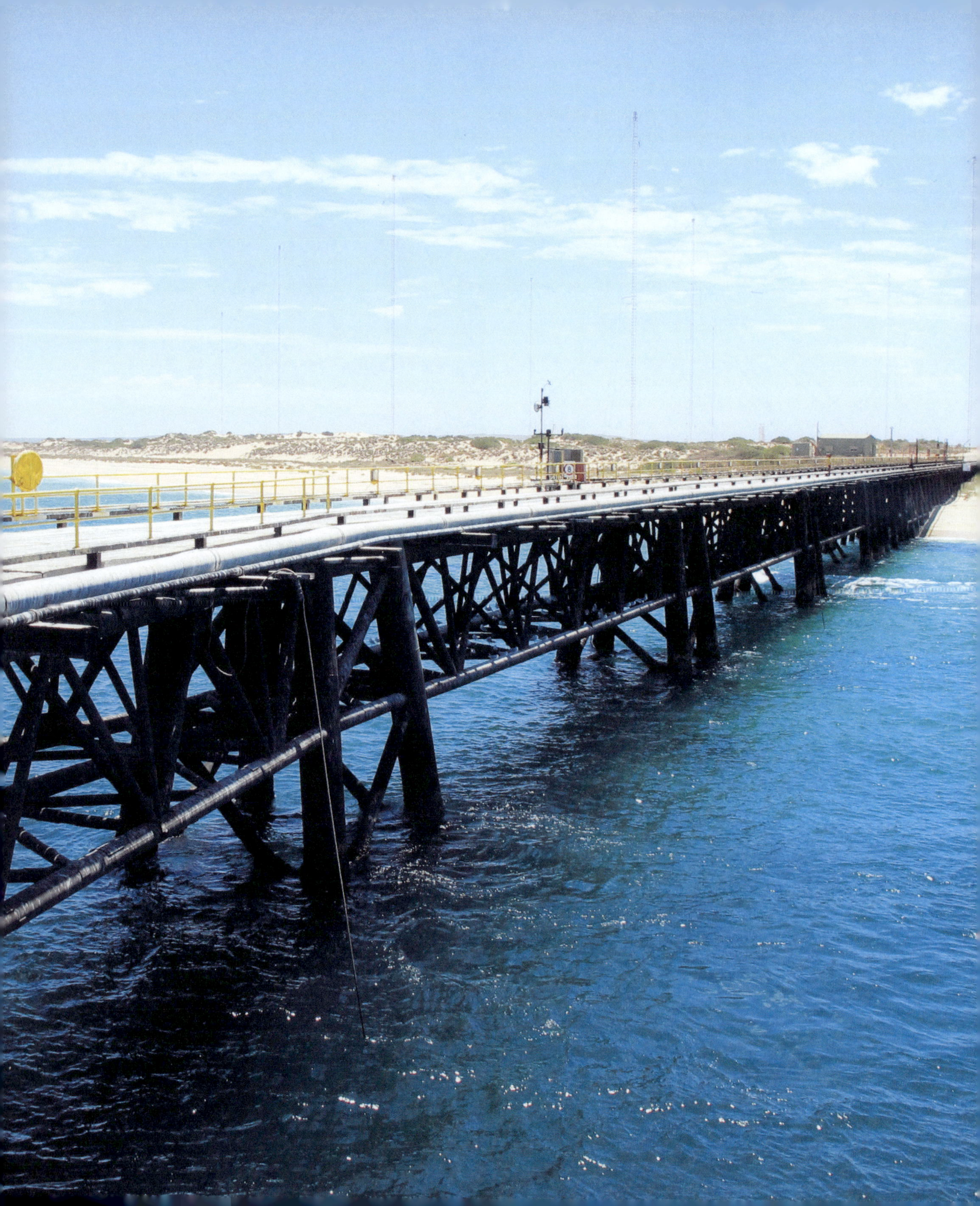

One of the world's top shore dives takes place beneath a jetty inside an operational navy base turned sanctuary zone filled with marine life.

Diving, Exmouth Navy Pier

Jinigudera Country

Contributed by Cathy Finch

WHY IT'S SPECIAL

The Exmouth Navy Pier dive has the enviable reputation of being one of Australia's best dives, and arguably one of the world's top 10 shore dives. Located within a sanctuary zone on Western Australia's remote North West Cape, off Point Murat in Ningaloo Marine Park, it is one of the world's only operational naval bases that allows civilian non-commercial divers access onto a working Commonwealth Defence pier, controlled by the Australian Federal Police. Diver numbers are limited to a maximum of 20 people on the pier at one time.

As a restricted area that maintains high camera surveillance and monitoring, the pier is not accessible to the general public. Beachgoers are allowed to walk beneath the pier, but must not stop or loiter. Snorkelling and fishing around the pier are not permitted, and as a result this area has become a safe haven for a huge diversity of marine life – it teems with more than 200 species of fish. It is a privilege to gain access to this site that offers close-up encounters with a staggering selection of resident marine life, concentrated beneath the shadowy legs of the pier.

Above and opposite A diving site without peer... Exmouth Navy Pier

Where
Exmouth Navy Pier is located 14km north of Exmouth, 1270km north of Perth/Boorloo. There are direct flights to Exmouth from Perth/Boorloo and Melbourne/Naarm.

When
Diving is possible year-round, with March to Nov being the most popular time.

Do it
Dive Ningaloo has the only permit to dive Exmouth Navy Pier, though this may change as the licence goes out periodically to tender. Book directly online (diveningaloo.com.au), or contact the Ningaloo Visitor Centre (ningaloocentre.com.au).

As well as the cost of the dive, an additional $50 fee is to be paid on the day for entry onto the pier. This charge covers the Commonwealth annual licence fee, maintenance, administration, and security costs associated with allowing civilian divers onto a restricted Defence establishment.

Fitness: ●●●●○

Fear factor: ●●○○○

Expertise required ●○○○○

THE ADVENTURE

From Exmouth, divers are transferred by bus to the Navy Pier, which is a 15min drive away. Passengers must carry photo ID such as a passport or driver's licence for spot-check identification purposes if required by the Navy.

A great amount of planning goes into calculating the optimum time of day to dive this pier. Due to the area's large tidal range, strong currents can create poor visibility and challenging conditions. Therefore, it can only be dived on slack water, which occurs at the top and bottom of the tides. Moon phases and varying height differences between tides are also taken into consideration, meaning daily dive times will change, along with the 'time window' that dictates the ability to complete either a single or double dive on that day. While tidal access does tend to limit diving activity, it is also one of the valuable reasons why the Navy Pier maintains its superb biomass, with currents adding to the rich variety of marine life found here.

Although snorkelling is not permitted, non-divers don't need to miss out on this underwater aquarium, with the opportunity to experience a 'Discovery Dive', led by a qualified scuba instructor. Certified divers are free to navigate their own dive, though they are required to have logged at least one dive in the previous 12 months or, alternatively, need to undertake a short refresher course. While the maximum depth on this dive is a comfortable 15m, visibility can be as little as 3m ranging up to 10m. As the marine life shows virtually no fear of divers, and is extremely prolific, low visibility should not be a barrier to experiencing all that this dive has to offer. During my last dive here, I had to virtually fan through healthy schools of colourful fish to see the huge gropers and other critters hiding behind them. Night dives are also offered, but generally only once a month. For these, you need to be an Open Water diver and have logged a minimum of 10 dives.

Personal fitness also needs to be measured if you're considering diving at Navy Pier, as its entry and exit may prove challenging for some. Divers are asked to be fit enough to perform a giant stride entry from the lower platform of the pier and, most importantly, be capable of exiting the water by climbing up a 3m ladder in full gear. Sometimes a beach entry may also be required and, if this is the case, you will be required to walk 150m from the bus to the water through soft sand, in full gear, returning the same way.

After entering the water, navigation of the T-shaped pier is easy, with 300m of length to explore and a further 110m at the top of the T, formed by two square attached outlying 'dolphins' (platforms for larger ships to tie up to).

Diving into this underwater oasis, you will likely meet huge schools of barracuda, trevally, sweetlip and snapper, as well as colourful reef fish such as coral trout, Moorish idol, butterfly, angel, clown fish, scorpion fish, toadfish, rabbit fish, bannerfish, fusiliers and the graceful firefish, to name just a few. You may also eyeball solitary species such as huge Queensland groper, moray eels, octopus, tasselled wobbegongs, whitetip reef sharks and inquisitive sea snakes.

My personal favourites in diving here have been the seven grey nurse sharks I encountered, grinning at me from the depths of the shadowy pylons. The most favourable time to dive to see these docile creatures is March to Nov, the cooler months when many grey nurse sharks come to shelter at the jetty – as the water warms to more than 24°C between Dec and Feb, they move into cooler ocean.

Many delicate corals have also attached themselves to the pier, and macro lovers will find prolific invertebrate life to photograph and admire. Superb sponges thrive, utilising the currents to feed, while the crowd-favourite nudibranchs flounce their intricate patterns and ornately coloured bodies in a wild indulgence of colour that only Mother Nature could create.

> It would be crazy to leave this area without diving on the World Heritage-listed Ningaloo Reef, the longest fringing reef in the world. There are several dive operators in Exmouth, including liveaboard vessels, running trips to this remarkable underwater world. With over 500 species of fish and 200 species of coral, you will be sure to meet many of the reef residents, such as trumpetfish, flutemouths, cod, blennies, wrasse, gobies, damselfish and surgeonfish. Ningaloo Reef is also home to the elusive dugong, four of the world's seven species of sea turtle, and many species of ray and shark, including graceful manta rays (*see* p.181). Some of the most popular Ningaloo Reef dive sites are Bundegi Reef, Lighthouse Bay and Muiron Island.

Opposite top Stare into the eyes of a grey nurse shark, a creature that likes to hang out with divers under the pylons of the pier
Opposite bottom left and right Nose into the current with schools of sweetlip and barracuda, taking shelter under the pier

Diving, Exmouth Navy Pier

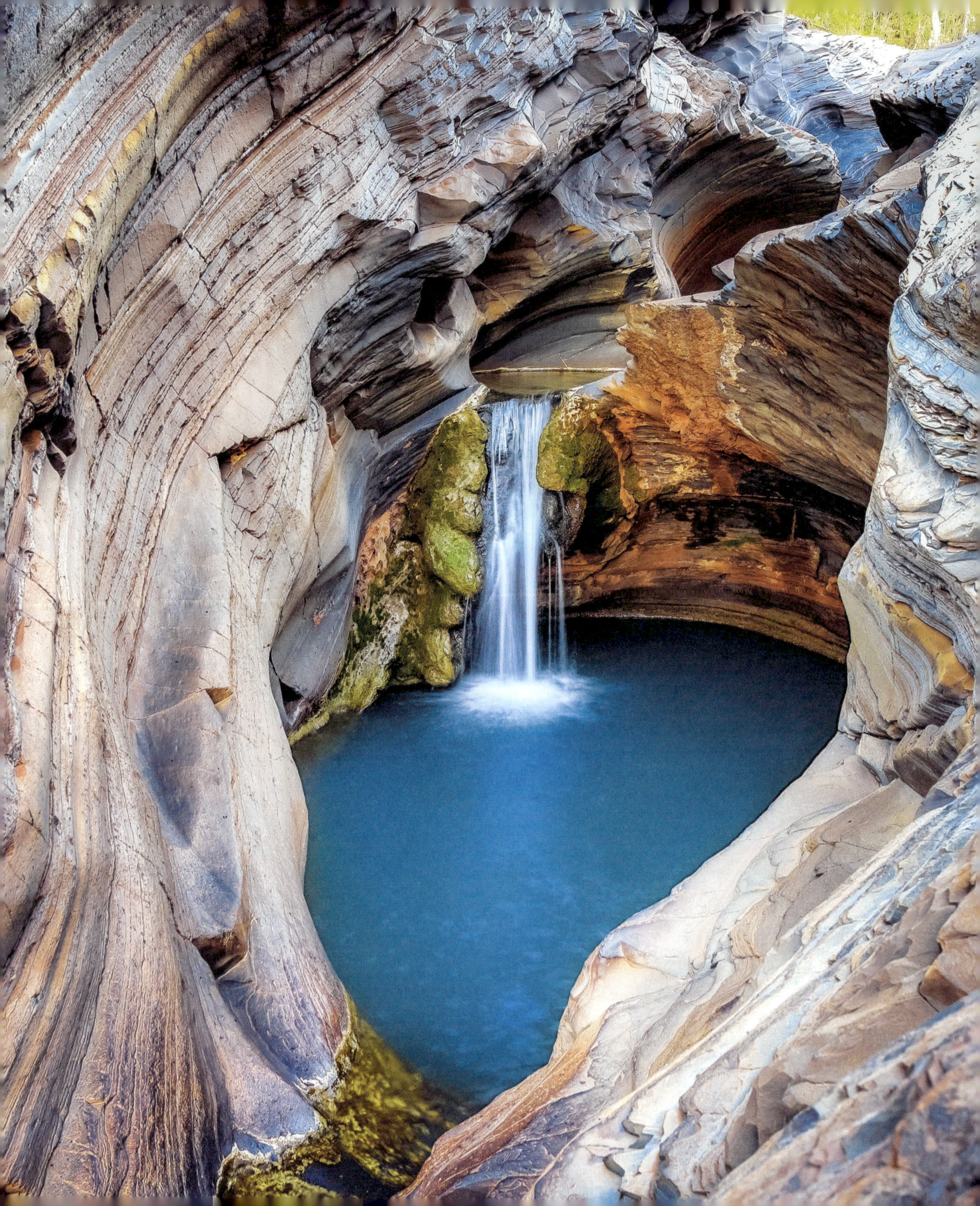

Delve into deep slots in Australia's most beautiful collection of outback gorges.

Exploring gorges, Karijini National Park

Banyjima, Kurrama and Innawonga Country

WHY IT'S SPECIAL

Deep in the Pilbara, a natural masterpiece is etched into the earth. Running like veins through the red-raw mountains of the Hamersley Range is a network of deep gorges that, as a collective, might well be the most beautiful in Australia. Together they form the centrepiece of Karijini National Park.

Western Australia's second largest national park – almost one-tenth the size of Tasmania – is a place I first came to 20 years ago, making a 600km detour by bicycle simply to see a park I'd repeatedly heard exalted as I pedalled along the WA coastline. By the time I left, Karijini had crystallised in my mind as my favourite national park in the country. A repeat recent visit only reaffirmed that love.

It's a park that contains Western Australia's highest mountains, and a landscape furnished with termite mounds, white-limbed gum trees and some of the oldest rock on the planet. But all those are just side dishes to Karijini's gorges, slashed deep and dark into the earth. These are gorges that blur the lines between hiking and canyoning. Collectively, they provide an array of minor challenges – from steep and loose walking trails, to acrobatic scrambling manoeuvres, to swim-through passages – and a wealth of major scenery.

Take your pick from seven gorges or, better yet, stay a while and delve into every one of them.

Where
Karijini National Park is around 1400km north of Perth/Boorloo; the nearest airport is Paraburdoo, which has direct flights to Perth/Boorloo.

When
Visit Karijini in the dry season, around April to Oct.

Do it
Find Karijini's official website at Parks and Wildlife WA (exploreparks.dbca.wa.gov.au).

Life's an Adventure walking holidays (lifesanadventure.com.au) runs a seven-day Karijini National Park Walk trip that explores most of the gorges and includes a climb of Mount Bruce, WA's second highest mountain.

Fitness: ●●●○○

Fear factor: ●●●○○

Expertise required ●●○○○

Family friendly

Opposite Spa Pool in Hamersley Gorge/Minhthukundi

THE ADVENTURE

In Karijini National Park, the best things happen in the cracks. Look across the deep-red plains and you barely notice the multitude of gorges that fracture the earth, but descend into them and they are places of wonder. Each gorge here is distinct – different challenges, different degrees of drama, different by (and in) nature, different swimming holes – but collectively they can be loosely divided into two groups: those gorges that can be explored on pure walks, and those gorges that stray into the world of scrambling and canyoning. Prime among the former are Dales Gorge/Ngirribungunha, Kalamina Gorge/Nhamurrunha and Hamersley Gorge/Minhthukundi, which are great starting points, especially if you're exploring with kids.

When hiking here, stick to the known routes, keep away from cliff-edges and be careful about where and how you enter water – accidents and hypothermia are all-too-common occurrences in this park.

Dales Gorge is the setting for Karijini's only permanent waterfall, and features a cliff-top rim trail as well as a path along the floor of the gorge. Follow the rim trail out to Circular Pool, ringed by cliffs, and then descend steeply into the gorge at Three Ways, where Dales Gorge fragments into a trio of gorges. Overhead, white snappy gums lean out from the gorge edge, and high banded iron cliffs stand sentinel over deep blue pools.

The pool at the base of permanent Fortescue Falls/Jubula provides a good swimming spot, or you can simply watch the water action from above on the ledges of the grandstand-like rock faces that surround the falls. A few minutes' walk upstream, past some magnificent rock fig trees, is Fern Pool/Jubura. A swimming platform was installed here in 2022, but please treat the pool and area with respect as this is a site of immense significance to the Banyjima, Kurrama and Innawonga Peoples – it's said that the rainbow serpent Thurru resides here, having travelled inland from the Gascoyne coast, creating the waterways and gorges as it came.

Kalamina Gorge/Nhamurrunha is one of the less-heralded of Karijini's gorges and, at first, appears one of the least spectacular. A short trail descends into the gorge at a point where it's wide and open, with a base as flat as a barge. Turn downstream, however, and walk the unmarked 1.5km route to Rock Arch Pool, and the cliffs close in, with pools and the streams between them reflecting the red glow of the gorge walls.

Right The deep-red walls of Karijini National Park

Exploring gorges, Karijini National Park

Hamersley Gorge/Minhthukundi sits apart in the park's northwest corner and is like a showpiece for the forces of nature. It's an easy walk down into the gorge, but look around at the colourful cliffs and you'll notice that the bands of rock that form them resemble folds of pastry – swirling and curving lines of rock. There's a good cliff-lined swimming hole at the base of the gorge's low waterfall, but Hamersley's standout feature is Spa Pool, a small, teardrop-shaped pool at the head of a larger pool above the waterfall. It's reached by swimming across the larger pool, or by scrambling around the base of the cliffs above that pool.

Speaking of scrambling ... to get the best out of Karijini's other gorges (Knox, Joffre, Hancock and Weano), a bit of literal handiwork is required, using hands and feet to scramble through the gorges.

Knox Gorge doesn't begin this way. Initially, it appears to be one of the most ordinary of the gorges but, like a good thriller, develops into one of the most magnificent. A steep, loose trail descends into the gorge, where the floor is covered in reeds and paperbarks, with cliffs so straight-edged they look almost bulldozed into the earth.

The walk downstream is short – just 1km to near its junction with Red Gorge – zig-zagging past a series of blue pools. The high cliffs keep you wondering: what's around that bend? And the next bend ...?

At one of the sharpest of these bends, Knox produces its cliff-hanging moment, sending walkers scrambling onto low ledges along the base of the cliffs, their chests pressed hard to the cold rock as they edge around the cliffs above a deep pool.

As the gorge nears its end, both the vegetation and the gorge thin, finally coming to a pool inset into the floor of the gorge beneath towering cliffs and buttresses. Beyond it, Knox Gorge disappears into a slot and plunges away into Red Gorge – a chain at the pool's end marks the furthest point visitors are allowed. If I have a favourite spot in Karijini, this is it.

A few minutes' drive from Knox Gorge is Joffre Gorge/Jijingunha, one of the deepest of Karijini's chasms. A walking track descends into the gorge from beside the rim-top lookout platform (or there's a track for guests from the adjoining Karijini Eco Retreat, run by the Gumala Aboriginal Corporation, serving the Traditional Owners), and reaches the floor of the gorge down a long series of metal ladders fixed to the cliff walls.

There's a pool to satisfy most visitors at the base of the ladders, but turn upstream and you can scramble along cliff ledges into a wide and spectacular amphitheatre at the base of Joffre's high, seasonal waterfall. Downstream, it's a scramble into the next pool, inching along tiny ledges and then plunging into the water – the only way to continue from here is to swim.

'I once swam for 40 minutes and still didn't reach the end of the gorge,' one guide tells me.

Karijini's popstar gorges are Hancock and Weano, which are home to the stunning Kermits Pool and Handrail Pool, respectively. To reach these two pools requires deft foot and hand work.

Kermits Pool hides atop a ledge deep inside Hancock Gorge. To get here, you must swim through a channel (or make a lengthy scramble along the cliffs beside it) and then squeeze into a narrow, polished chute that's akin to a natural slippery slide. Using your hands and feet like a bridge between the narrow rock walls, with the stream flowing below you, it's quickly clear why this section is known as the Spider Walk.

Kermits Pool is one of Karijini's most photographed spots, but that may only be because Handrail Pool is too vast to capture on most cameras. Like Knox Gorge, the approach through Weano Gorge gives little sense of the extraordinary chamber ahead. One moment the walk is in a shallow and open gorge, the next it's narrowed into a polished chute that feels like a paper cut in the earth. A short distance along, the stream tips into Handrail Pool as a waterfall, while walkers descend the cliff using the namesake handrail built into the rock.

It's a chilly swim inside this cliff-shaded cavity, but it's also one of Karijini's most delightful moments. As the pool disappears downstream into a narrow chamber, you can seemingly swim into the earth, following its journey between narrowing rock walls, clambering over rock bars and swimming through the pools between.

Banded cliffs stand as tall as city buildings, and sunlight dances ethereally through the gorge, bouncing between the cliffs and the water, creating art out of rock and air. Down here, Karijini really is a masterpiece.

Above Waterfall pouring into Fern Pool/Jubara *Opposite* Dales Gorge

Having explored the depths of Karijini, head for the heights by climbing one of the park's less-heralded mountains. Western Australia's tallest peak, 1249m Mount Meharry/Wirlbiwirlbi, stands at the park's far-eastern edge, but Meharry's remoteness means that the second highest mountain, Mount Bruce/Punurrunha, draws most of the attention. Just 15m lower than Mount Meharry, Mount Bruce is a 9km-return walk, heading up a craggy ridge overlooking the enormous Marandoo iron-ore mine and a vast swathe of the Pilbara. There's one moment of scrambling around a bluff (with a fixed chain for assistance) but otherwise it's a pure hike.

Exploring gorges, Karijini National Park

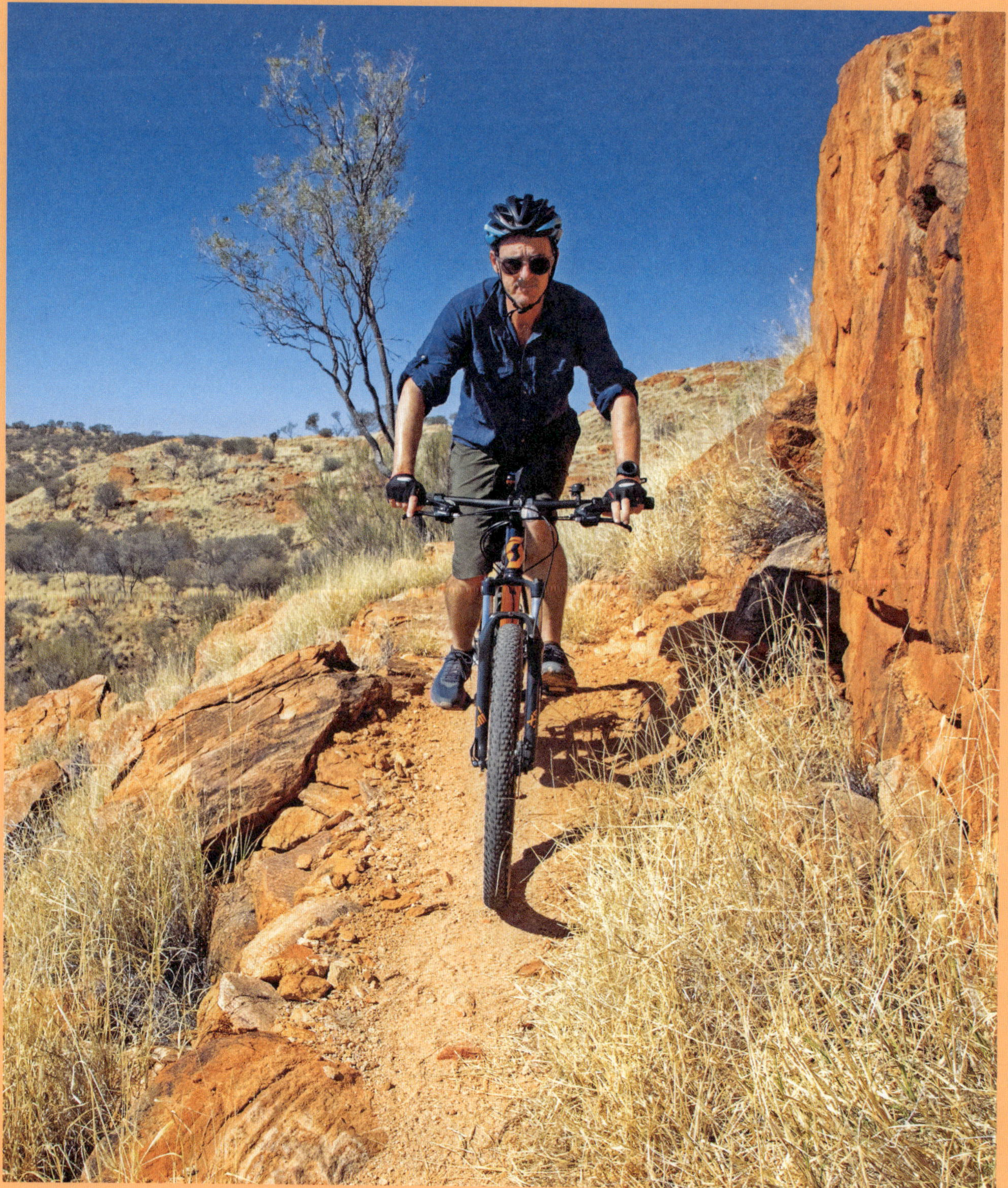

Northern Territory

*Take a dip with crocs, or a long march
across the Red Centre desert on foot.*

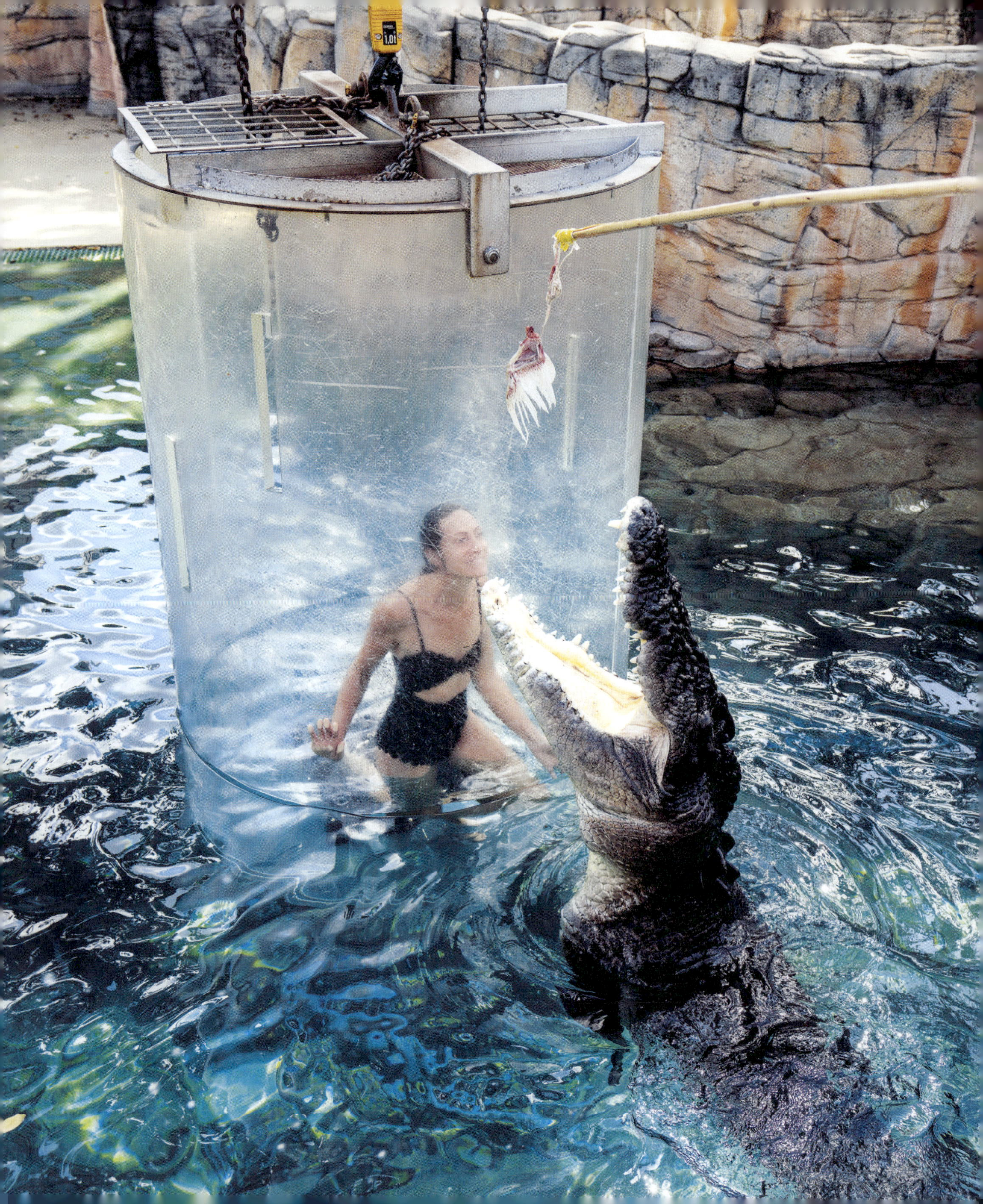

Go nose to nose with a 5m crocodile, from the safety of a perspex tube.

Swimming with a crocodile, Crocosaurus Cove

Larrakia Country

WHY IT'S SPECIAL

Wander along Mitchell St in Darwin/Garramilla CBD and it's tempting to believe that all of the city's wildlife is in the pubs and bars. But tucked away on this central party street is Crocosaurus Cove, a wildlife centre featuring the world's biggest collection of Australian reptiles and some of the largest saltwater (or estuarine) crocodiles found outside natural waterways.

In Australia's extensive catalogue of big and bitey creatures, salties rank high among the most fearsome. There are few ways to safely get close to these reptiles that grow up to 6m in length and 1000kg in weight, which makes the so-called Cage of Death at Crocosaurus Cove a rare and nervous experience, going eye to eye with one of the most powerful animals on the planet.

Stand and watch this experience and it might look a little hokey, but climb inside the 'cage', with just a few centimetres of perspex to keep you from becoming lunch, and it's a raw and rare look into the teeth of danger.

Where
Crocosaurus Cove is at 58 Mitchell St in the heart of Darwin/Garramilla.

When
Cage of Death experiences operate daily.

Do it
Book the Cage of Death online (crocosauruscove.com). Cages can hold one or two people.

Fitness: ●○○○○

Fear factor: ●●●●○

Expertise required ●○○○○

Opposite Crocodiles and adventure go hand in hand *Previous* Mountain biking on Road Train trail, Alice Springs/Mparntwe

THE ADVENTURE

When you enter Crocosaurus Cove, stairs ascend to the World of Crocs display and an ominous foretaste of what's ahead as you pass a couple of former Cages of Death, their perspex surfaces scratched and gouged from previous crocodile activity. Couple this with your first sight of the 5m-long crocodiles and it's a moment of trepidation ahead of being dipped like a meal bag into one of these enclosures.

There are four side-by-side crocodile enclosures into which the Cage of Death might be lowered (along with a couple of other enclosures that are home to the likes of Burt, the crocodilian star of *Crocodile Dundee*), depending on the crocs' levels of activity at the time – the more active the crocodile, the more likely it'll be your companion.

In one enclosure there's the royal pairing of crocs named William and Kate, a 4.6m male and 2.8m female. In another is the 5.1m, 600kg Baru, with a third enclosure containing the Cove's largest croc, 5.5m Wendell. The animal I ended up sharing the water with was Leo, a heavyweight champion – 5m in length and 750kg in weight – with a previous penchant for attacking cattle. It was for this reason that Leo was captured and relocated in the 1980s. When he was first resettled at the Darwin Crocodile Farm, he earned a reputation for chasing the crocodile handlers. He should be fine company for the next 15min.

Your time as croc prey begins in Baru's enclosure, climbing down a ladder into the cylindrical 'cage'. If your lunch date is going to be one of the other beasts, the cage is winched out of the water and shifted, cable-car-like, to another enclosure, where it's lowered into the water. Through tiny holes in the floor and sides of the cage, water pours in, rising to around the level of your chest. Donning a pair of swimming goggles, you breathe in courage and duck your head beneath the water – it's cold at first, but temperature is quickly forgotten when 5m of crocodile comes swimming towards you.

Each encounter is individual and at the whim of the crocodile, but when my cage touched the water, Leo was immediately on the move, swimming straight to the cage and nudging it with his nose. I was suddenly staring into the mouth of the animal with the strongest bite on Earth and the biggest set of teeth I'd ever seen – all 66 of them – many of them broken from a lifetime of hunting.

It was menacing and intimidating, and yet somehow surreal – this killer crocodile just 2cm to 3cm from my fingertips and yet I was as safe as if I was watching the scene on a TV screen.

Above Feeding the crocs *Opposite* Underwater snacks

For a true look at the crocodile, dive down, holding yourself underwater in a skydiving position – hands pressed against one side of the cage, feet against the other – watching the animal from beneath as it glides slowly around the cage. When you rise for breath, its yellow eyes will quite likely be watching you, with the bumps, or scutes, along its back passing by the cage like the teeth of a dangerous bandsaw. As it drifts in slow circles around the cage, it's quite clearly stalking you. To this animal rippling with prehistoric power, you surely look like tinned meat.

After 10min with your crocodile, the cage is raised so that the water now reaches only to knee level. You sit on the floor and watch as the croc is fed bits of chicken on a long stick. Typically, the animal uses its powerful tail to leap for the chicken, often rocking the cage as it crashes down against it. But wildlife behaves however wildlife wants to behave, and when I was in the cage, Leo remained more intent on me than those chicken nibbles. Pressing his nose against the perspex, he continued to stare. When he finally leaped for the chicken, he slammed down against the cage, mouth wide open, teeth on full show.

Even as I was winched out, Leo wouldn't leave the cage.

'They have the intelligence of five-year-olds,' a handler explained. 'And they're just as stubborn.'

So we sat in an impasse for 10 more minutes – the tinned me and the taunting crocodile – before finally Leo was enticed away by chicken.

I'd stared into the eyes of death, and I liked it.

The Top End has a couple of sure-fire locations in which to observe saltwater crocodiles in the wild. Kakadu National Park is said to be home to 10,000 crocodiles, or around 10 per cent of all crocs in the Northern Territory. They're readily sighted on boat tours along East Alligator River (kakaduculturaltours.com.au) and in the Yellow Water/Ngurrungurrudjba wetlands (kakadutourism.com), or you can simply watch the virtual crocodile soup from viewing areas at Cahills Crossing, a causeway into Arnhem Land across the East Alligator River.

Just as reliable is the Daintree River in far-north Queensland, where several operators run croc-spotting boat trips.

Swimming with a crocodile, Crocosaurus Cove

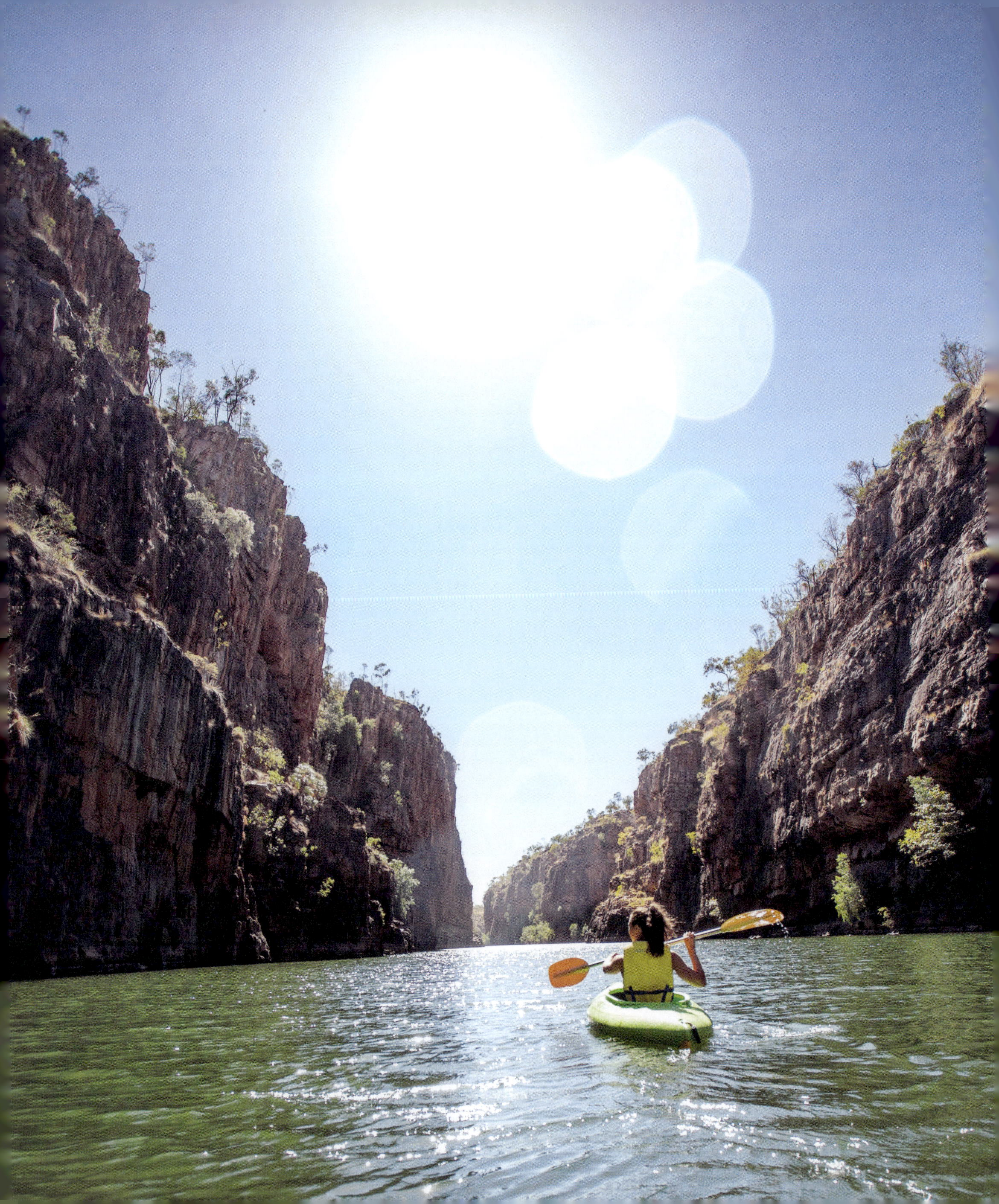

Disappear into one of Australia's most impressive gorges as you paddle and portage through a chain of connected gorges.

Canoeing, Nitmiluk National Park

Jawoyn Country

WHY IT'S SPECIAL

Deep inside Nitmiluk/Katherine Gorge, tall red cliffs frame a perfect Top End scene. Atop the cliffs, a buzz-cut of low eucalypts and yellow grasses hint at the aridity and heat above, but inside the gorge, a towering sandstone buttress known as Smitt Rock stands like a sphinx over the river, with sandy beaches radiating from its base. On a fine day, nothing seems to stir except for an occasional canoe that, in this immense environment, looks barely bigger than an insect.

Etched into the escarpment of the Arnhem Plateau, Nitmiluk was carved by the Katherine River, creating a series of 13 connected gorges. Each one has a character and shape of its own, and canoes can get as far as the 9th gorge, around 9km – and yet seemingly world's away – from the launch point in the 2nd gorge.

Canoe hire inside the gorge is for half-day, full day or two days, and with numerous (and often long and tiring) portages over rock bars, a two-day hire, camping in either the 4th, 6th or 9th gorge, is the best way to get the full feeling for Nitmiluk.

Nitmiluk National Park is on Jawoyn Country, and was returned to the Traditional Owners in 1989. Nitmiluk – a Jawoyn name that means Cicada Place – is jointly managed by the Jawoyn People and the Parks and Wildlife Commission of the Northern Territory, with Jawoyn-owned Nitmiluk Tours managing all commercial activities in the park, including canoe hire.

Where
Nitmiluk National Park is 28km north-east of Katherine, and 345km south-east of Darwin/Garramilla.

When
Canoe trips are only possible in the dry season, from around May to Oct.

Do it
Read the 'Nitmiluk NP Canoeing Guide' at Parks NT (nt.gov.au). Type 'nitmiluk canoeing' into the search bar and hit the 'Canoes, boats, bike trails and fishing in Nitmiluk National Park' link. Hire canoes ahead of your visit from Nitmiluk Tours (nitmiluktours.com.au). If staying overnight in the gorge, be sure to book your campsite ahead (parkbookings.nt.gov.au).

Fitness: ●●●○○

Fear factor: ●●○○○

Expertise required: ●●●○○

Opposite Another world; paddling through the gorge

THE ADVENTURE

All canoe trips in Nitmiluk begin effortlessly, cruising through the 1st gorge in a tour boat, and then making the short walk across a rock bar into the 2nd gorge, where a pontoon is strung with canoes. These are not your classic, deep-tubbed Canadian canoes; they're shallow plastic canoes with limited room for camping and other gear, so pack wisely and sparingly.

An armada of canoeists sets out from the 2nd gorge twice a day, but most will be on the river for just half a day, or one full day, meaning that few will get beyond the 4th gorge. As I paddled out from the 2nd gorge, I was one of only two bookings to be on the river overnight.

The 2nd gorge is the longest of Nitmiluk's sections (2.4km), providing a chance to settle into the routine and rhythm of paddling. At this lower end of the gorge, the cliffs are low and set back from the river, with beaches that seem almost to leak out from their base. The very first beach is also a freshwater crocodile nesting area, but take heart from the fact that crocodiles are no real threat inside this gorge. At the start of the dry season (April), rangers spend six weeks patrolling the gorge for saltwater crocodiles before the gorge is opened to paddlers. In the two days I paddled here, I saw a lone freshwater crocodile, and that was in the 1st gorge, from the tourist boat.

In these early stretches, there are a couple of enticing walks. At a major bend in the river in the 2nd gorge – the deepest point (30m) in the entire Nitmiluk gorge and said to be home to Bolung, the rainbow serpent – a trail heads up a side gully sliced like a razor cut into the cliffs. Known as Butterfly Gorge, it's thick with forest and swirling with butterflies.

In the 3rd gorge, reached on the paddle's easiest portage, across a small rock barrier, there's a second walking trail, heading through the cliffs to Lily Ponds, a deep pool at the base of a tall, wet-season waterfall. The pool at its base lasts through the dry season, providing excellent swimming.

Right Deep beneath the cliffs of the 2nd gorge

Canoeing, Nitmiluk National Park

By the time you reach the 4th gorge, you're in rare territory. Few day paddlers continue into this gorge, discouraged by the arduous, 800m-long portage at the end of the 3rd gorge. Dragging kayaks over rocks and boulders, broken by the respite of small pools, it can take up to an hour to make this transition between gorges. Is it worth the effort? Nitmiluk comes into its own in the 4th and 5th gorges, where it becomes a place of spectacle and wonder.

Here, the cliffs close in, as though the gorge is inhaling. Near the end of the 4th gorge is the short section that is arguably Nitmiluk's most beautiful, passing beneath Smitt Rock, an imposing buttress of rock splitting the gorge in two, its cliffs so smooth and sheer it's as though they were cut by a machine.

The first of the gorge's campsites is immediately beyond Smitt Rock, staring back onto the rock from atop a beach. There are two campsites here – the one on the northern bank is exclusively for canoeists, while the other is shared with walkers. The 5th gorge is a ruler-straight tunnel between the cliffs, like a trench carved into the land. After the run of portages, it's a relief to paddle a long stretch again, with towering cliffs beside. The respite from the effort of portaging is temporary, however, with a trio of rock bars dividing the 5th and 6th gorges. Each one is covered in boulders, adding to the effort of dragging canoes across, but just a few metres ahead, into the 6th gorge, there is a sandy beach filling a break in the cliffs that forms the next campsite. Looking across at cliffs stained like an enormous rock painting, it's one of the most beautiful campsites I've found in Australia.

Nitmiluk changes character again in the 6th gorge, with the high cliffs fading into a wider, drier section of gorge. The 7th and 8th gorges are short, with taxing portages, before Nitmiluk finally narrows again in the 9th gorge – the end of the watery road on one of Australia's greatest canoe trips.

Canoeing through the gorge is only Nitmiluk National Park's second-most-famous adventure. Stretching across the park – beginning from the bank of the Katherine River and following the line of the escarpment north to Leliyn (Edith Falls) – is the 62km Jatbula Trail. Typically walked over five days, the trail is a journey between spectacular waterholes and waterfalls, camping each night beside a cooling swim. A major highlight along the trail is the Amphitheatre, a chasm filled with monsoon forest and spectacular Jawoyn rock paintings. You must book your walk ahead of time; for more information and bookings, go online to Parks NT (nt.gov.au/parks/find-a-park/nitmiluk-national-park/nitmiluk-national-park-jatbula-trail).

Above Perfect moments of solitude *Opposite* Canoeing beneath Smitt Rock

Walk one of Australia's greatest long-distance trails, following the line of the Tjorita/ West MacDonnell Ranges, past waterholes and gorges and onto desert peaks.

Hiking the Larapinta Trail, Tjoritja/ West MacDonnell National Park

Arrernte Country

WHY IT'S SPECIAL

Few walks in the world have made a desert setting quite as approachable as the Larapinta Trail. Beginning at Alice Springs/Mparntwe's edge and stretching the length of the Tjorita/West MacDonnell Ranges, the Larapinta (which takes its title from the Arrernte name for the Finke River) is a Red Centre highlights reel on foot, hopping between the gorges and waterholes that sprinkle the mountains. Days in the desert heat wash away in the waterholes, and the trail travels beside, atop and through this most spectacular of red ranges, meandering so wildly that it takes 223km to cover 120km of ground.

To walk the Larapinta is a commitment of around two weeks, filled with reward throughout. Completed only in 2002 after more than a decade of construction, it's fast become one of Australia's most popular long-distance trails, and with very good reason.

Where
The Alice Springs Telegraph Station is 4km north of the town centre, with walking trails connecting the two. Redbank Gorge, the closest road point to Mount Sonder/ Rwetyepme, is 150km west of Alice.

When
April to Sept is the most comfortable and safest time to be on the Larapinta Trail. Don't even consider a summer hike, with temperatures routinely topping 40°C.

Do it
The dedicated Larapinta Trail website (larapintatrail.com.au) will help you plan the sections and your food and water needs.

You need to book to walk the trail ahead of time (nt.gov.au/parks/find-a-park/tjoritja-west-macdonnell-national-park/larapinta-trail/plan-larapinta-trail-walk).

If hiking independently and making food drops, you'll need to get a key to the storage rooms from the Tourism Central Australia visitor centre in Alice Springs/ Mparntwe. You can make the drops yourself, or pay one of the trail shuttle services to drop them off for you. Shuttles along the trail are run by Larapinta Trail Trek Support (treksupport.com.au) and Larapinta Transfers (larapintatransfers.com.au).

For guided end-to-end hikes, try World Expeditions (worldexpeditions.com) or Trek Larapinta (treklarapinta.com.au).

Fitness: ●●●●○

Fear factor: ●●○○○

Expertise required ●●●●○

Above Euro Ridge *Opposite* Hikers at the mouth of Standley Chasm/ Angkerle Atwatye

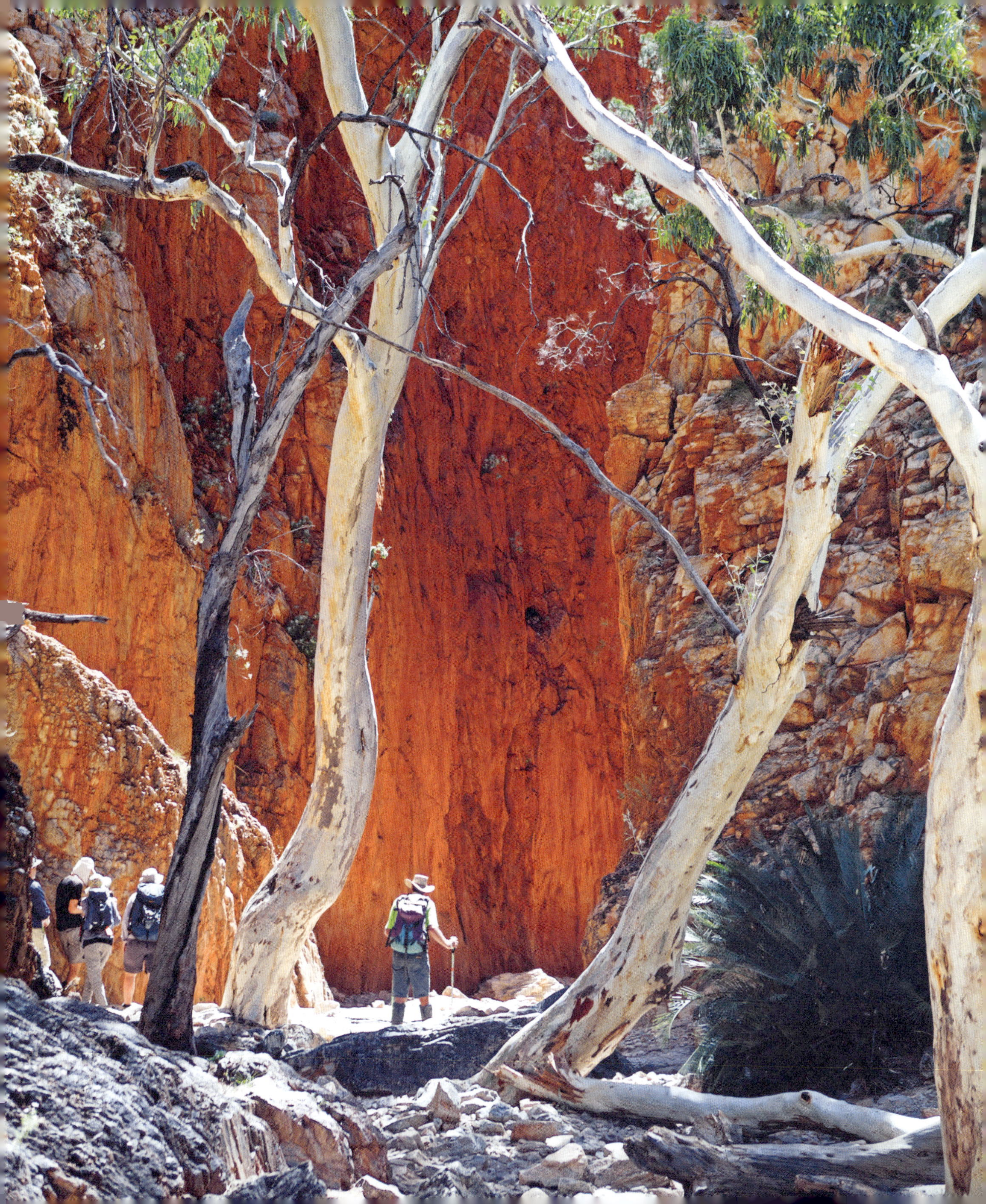

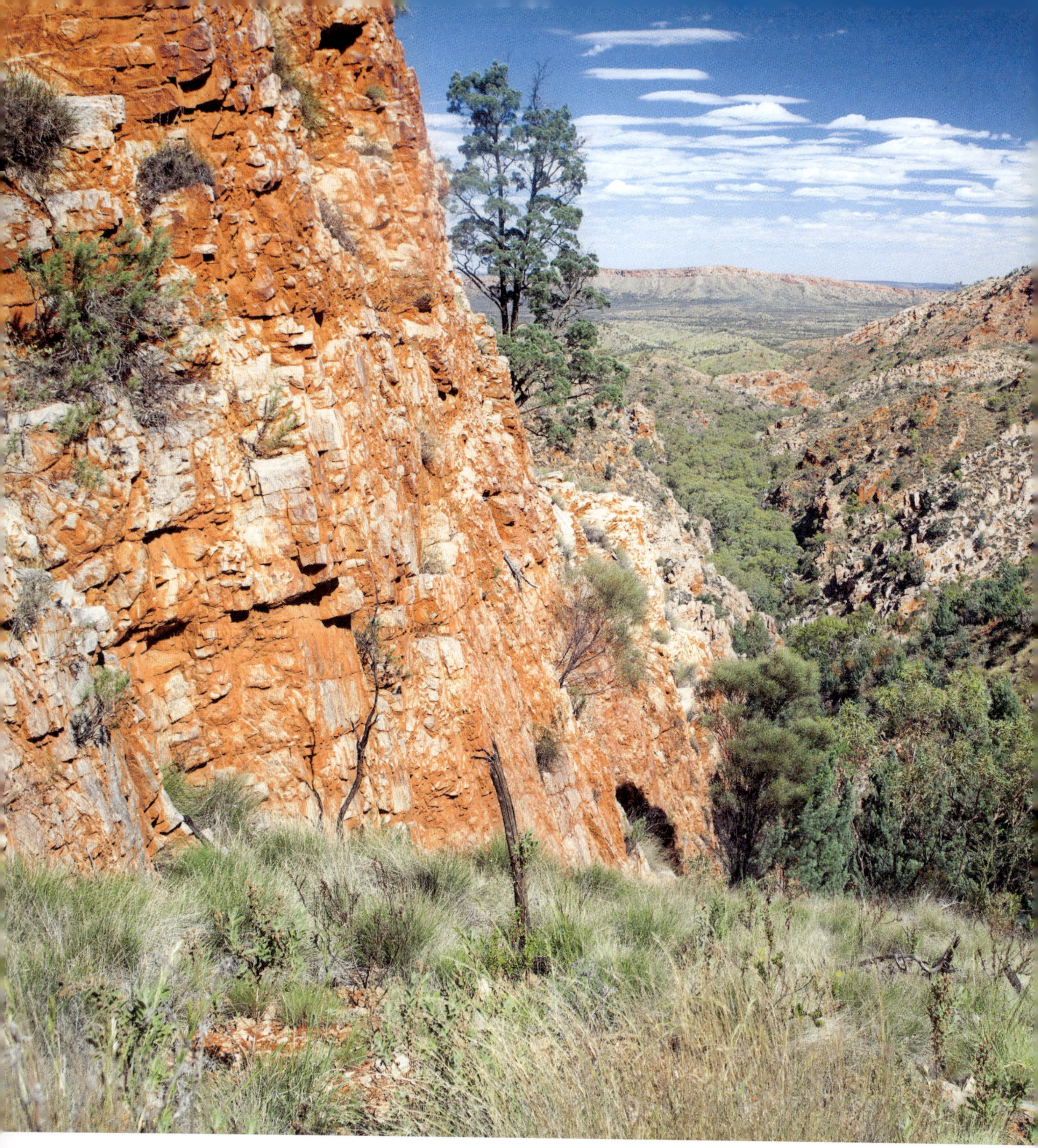

THE ADVENTURE

Larapinta logistics begin even before you set foot on the trail – it can be walked in either direction, and almost every Larapinta hiker has a preference, but they're not always the same. Some prefer to begin at Mount Sonder/Rwetyepme, making the long walk into Alice Springs/Mparntwe, while others prefer to set off into the desert from Alice, which has the benefit of placing the sun at their backs for most of the coming fortnight.

Carrying two weeks of food through a desert is a task worthy of Atlas, so plan to use the food-storage points dotted along the trail. Parks authorities have constructed storage rooms at Ellery Creek South, Serpentine Gorge and Ormiston Gorge, while similar arrangements can also be made with the operators at Standley Chasm/Angkerle Atwatye. It means you likely need carry no more than four days of food at a stretch. Dividing the days and selecting campsites is made pretty simple by the fact that the trail is partitioned into 12 sections, from 9km to 29km in length. All can be walked in a day, though some are more comfortably broken up into smaller sections. There are 26 campsites dotted along the trail, making it a simple task to chart your days between them.

In the east, the trail begins at the Alice Springs Telegraph Station, where Alice itself began in 1871, soon crossing the Stuart Hwy and the Adelaide-Darwin railway and rising onto Euro Ridge – the start of the West Macs. Keep an eye out and it'll likely become clear how the ridge earned its name, with euros (a species of kangaroo) bounding about.

The heartbeat of the Larapinta is its gorges and waterholes, which split the range into portions and provide regular walking goals. It's an unusual natural design – the rivers running through the mountains rather than between them – and an indication of the age of some of these waterways, which were here before the mountains. The Finke River, which has its headwaters in Tjorita/West MacDonnell Ranges and is crossed near the western end of the trail, is often claimed to be the world's oldest river, flowing (or usually not flowing) for more than 350 million years. It puts two weeks of walking into perspective.

Left Ascending above Standley Chasm/Angkerle Atwatye

The first of these breaks in the range is Simpsons Gap/ Rungutjirpa, typically reached at the end of the first or second day, depending on how you get out of the blocks. It's a fine welcome to West Macs life, with a large pool (swimming is not allowed here) pinched between burnt-orange cliffs, white-trunked gums angling out of a sandy creek bed, and rare black-footed wallabies ambling about its bouldery slopes.

Such scenes become common, but never commonplace, as the Larapinta nudges west through the ranges in search of just such cooling sites. At the start of section 4, it steps into Standley Chasm/Angkerle Atwatye, a dry, envelope-thin fracture in the range, squeezing through a crowd of day visitors and climbing beyond them to the summit of Brinkley Bluff – a red bubble of rock atop the range – and where you'll stand atop a peak for the first time. It's a climb that marks the start of the Larapinta's most difficult, remote and arguably most rewarding stretch – sections 4 and 5 – balancing across the well-named Razorback Ridge and descending into Hugh Gorge, which sits isolated and far from the ranges' more heavily trafficked gorges.

The contrast is absolute the next day as the trail sets off across the Alice Valley, switching between ranges on the Larapinta's longest and flattest section. It's almost 30km before it hits the mountains again, passing through a low saddle to the pool at Ellery Creek Big Hole, continuing the trail's now-comforting rhythm – gorge to mountain to gorge.

A day ahead, as the trail marches on into section 8, the beauty goes into overdrive as the trail ascends Heavitree Range to Counts Point, the Larapinta's signature lookout. It's a view across country as dry as bones to a Who's Who of Central Australian features – Gosse Bluff, Mount Giles, Glen Helen Gorge and, rising into distant view now, unmistakable Mount Sonder/Rwetyepme, the walk's high finish. If Sonder's 'sleeping woman' profile looks familiar, the mountain was a regular subject for famed Arrernte artist Albert Namatjira.

Dropping back off the range, be sure to take the short detour to the Ochre Pits, where the colourful banks – white, purple, yellow, orange – of a dry creek have long been mined for ochre by the Arrernte People.

Squeezing through the dry gulch of Inhalanga Pass, filled to the brim with cycads, it's a journey on towards Ormiston Gorge/Kwartatuma, one of the Larapinta's major natural features. If too much walking isn't enough, stick around to walk the side-trail lap through Ormiston Pound, a circular, mountainous beauty spot on the landscape.

The end is now nigh. Crossing the Finke River/Larapinta (you're very unlikely to get wet feet out here ...) and stopping in at Glen Helen Gorge, there's one more overland stage into Redbank Gorge at the foot of Mount Sonder/Rwetyepme. In one sense, you've already completed the Larapinta Trail because to climb Sonder, you have to return to Redbank, a narrow, polished chute that looks strikingly like an offcut from Karijini National Park in Western Australia (*see* p.187), but there's a ritual worthy of a pilgrimage attached to the final day (or first day, if setting out from here).

Tradition dictates that Sonder is climbed in darkness, reaching its summit in time for sunrise. Hikers ascend through the pre-dawn chill, with head torches lighting their way. First light arrives and on they march, standing atop the 1380m mountain – the fourth highest peak in the Northern Territory – as the sun rolls into view. Mountain ranges point like arrows to the horizon, and the red country all around brightens even more, aglow in the first light. The long walk is over and the day has barely started.

> Dropping life for two weeks to walk through a desert isn't a time luxury available to everyone. Fortunately, the Larapinta's popularity has resulted in a number of companies running shorter walking tours along the trail, typically ranging from three days to nine days. These hikes focus on highlight sections, including Ormiston Pound, Counts Point and Mount Sonder/Rwetyepme, driving you between each day's walk and camping along the base of the range.

Opposite top Ridgetop walking towards Counts Point *Opposite bottom* Exploring Ormiston Pound

Hiking the Larapinta Trail, Tjoritja/West MacDonnell National Park

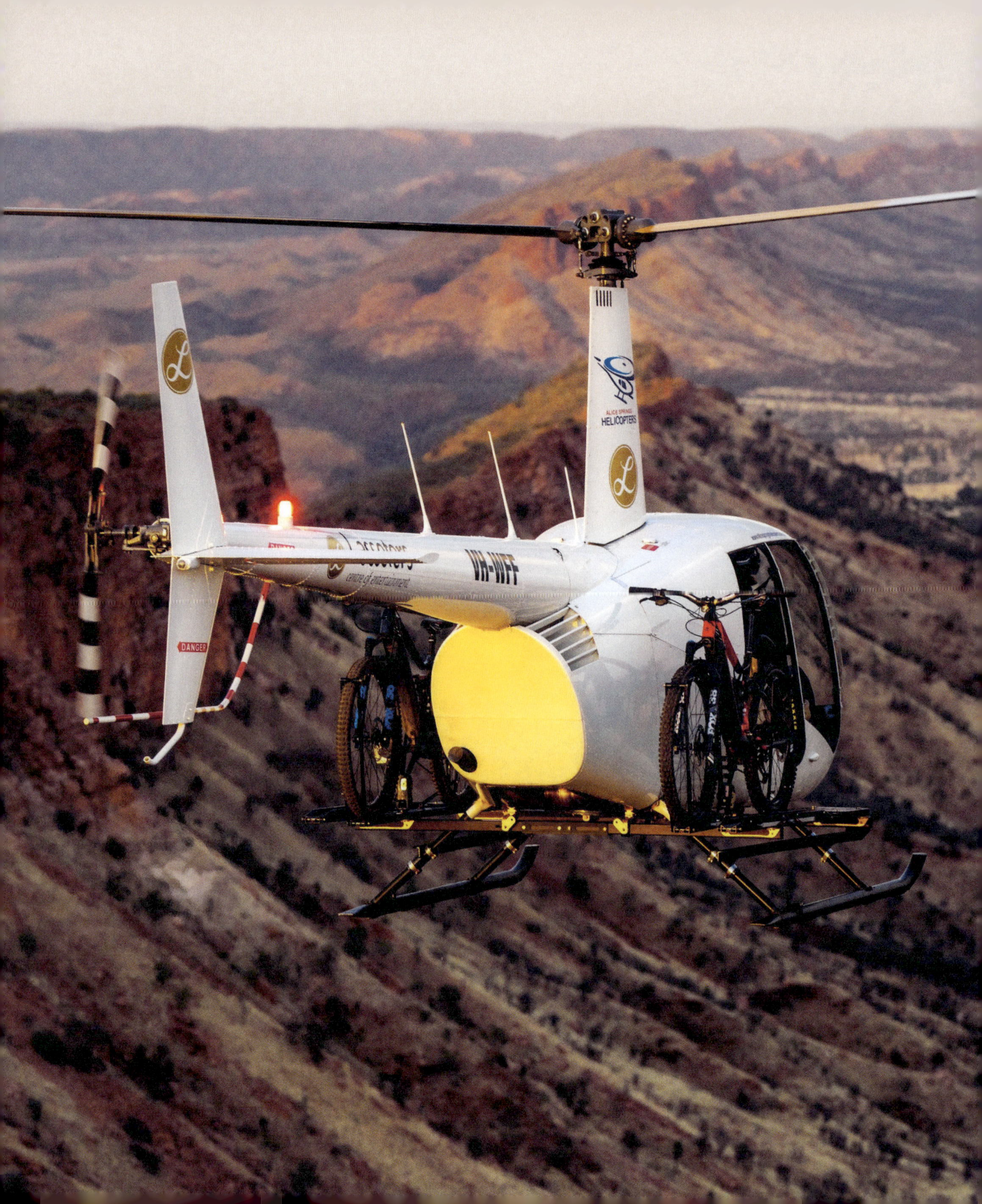
ALICE SPRINGS HELICOPTERS
VH-WFF
DANGER

Drop into one of Australia's best mountain-bike trail networks by helicopter.

Helibiking, Alice Springs/ Mparntwe

Western Aranda/Arrernte Country

WHY IT'S SPECIAL

Alice Springs/Mparntwe's emergence as a top mountain-biking destination has been natural, in all ways. With more than 100km of trails looping out from the town's edge, riding here is as much an exploration of the desert surrounds as a bike ride. The Tjorita/West MacDonnell Ranges loom beside and beneath the singletrack trails, the trunks of ghost gums flicker past like fluorescent white rods, and the rock outcrops appear as perfectly arranged as art installations.

In this natural setting, the trail network has largely found natural lines, with technical features such as berms (banked turns) and tabletop jumps shunned in favour of lines onto exposed rock slabs, over rust-red boulders and through sandy creek beds.

About the only thing that bucks this organic approach to riding is the rare chance to access the trails by helicopter, taking to the skies with your bike before settling back to earth at one of three points along the network. It's a chance to view the desert country you're about to ride, and almost a spy-like way to begin some of the country's most appealing mountain biking at some of its more remote points.

Where
The trail network is largely to Alice Springs/ Mparntwe's immediate north, with trails radiating out from the Alice Springs Telegraph Station, 4km outside of town.

When
Make it a winter bike migration for the most pleasant trail conditions when average maximum temperatures dip to around 20°C. Don't even think about a summer ride; conditions are brutal.

Do it
Heli transfers are operated by Alice Springs Helicopters (alicespringshelicopters.com.au), with choppers able to carry four mountain bikes or two ebikes.

Bikes can be hired from Red Centre Adventures (redcentre.fun) and the Alice Springs MTB Trail Map can be downloaded from its website.

Fitness: ●●●○○

Fear factor: ●●●○○

Expertise required ●●●○○

Opposite Getting air... literally.

THE ADVENTURE

Alice Springs/Mparntwe's airport sits south of the town, separated from it by the Heavitree Range, and for mountain bikers taking the decadent approach to their day in the saddle – accessing the trails by helicopter – this is to their advantage. Alice's trail network is to the north of town, meaning that, with bikes fitted atop the skids of the chopper, the flight begins up and over the range. From the air, you're looking down into Heavitree Gap/Ntaripe, where the mountains appear almost to have snapped in two around the Stuart Hwy, and then onto the rooftops of the town.

For 20min, the mountain biking is secondary as, beneath the helicopter, the West MacDonnells stretch across the earth one way, and the East MacDonnells head in the other, with desert disappearing over the horizon wherever you look.

There are three possible drop sites along the trail network for mountain bikers: beside the Road Train trail; partway along Hell Line; and at the Bronco Yards at Hell Line's westernmost point (the furthest spot in the network from town). Bikes are removed from the skids, the helicopter disappears over the horizon, and you're on your own in the desert. Time to get pedalling.

The trail network is split into two parts: Westside and Eastside. Road Train is pretty much the line between the two. The 5.5km blue (intermediate) trail cuts the thinnest of lines through the desert grasses, crossing a couple of dirt roads and rising through low hills, balanced at times above precipitous drops. The road it soon encounters is the largest of all out this way: the Stuart Hwy. There's the rare mountain-biking-experience of crossing a national highway – perhaps even between the trail's namesake road trains – before the ride nudges up against the Adelaide to Darwin railway.

Road Train turns south here, and you ride pinched between the highway and railway before intersecting with the long-distance Larapinta Trail (see p.204). While the majority of this 223km hiking trail is off-limits to bikes, the small section east of Road Train is shared-use – open to walkers and mountain bikers. You can finish this day and disingenuously boast that you completed the Larapinta Trail.

A more likely riding scenario if you've gone to the trouble and expense of the helicopter transfer, is to turn off Road Train onto Hell Line at the point where the trail meets the railway line.

Hell Line (also blue) is the longest, most remote and most committing of Alice's mountain-bike trails, making a 15km horseshoe-shaped semi-loop that incorporates the Tjorita/ West MacDonnell Ranges. It starts out climbing – not steeply, though Hell Line did take its name from the rockiness of its terrain (much of it cleared away now, mercifully) – and there's a chance to gather breath 4km into the trail at a seat (with a bike rack) atop a rise commanding views across the desert to Heavitree Gap/Ntaripe.

Past the potential helicopter drop point, Hell Line continues west, rounding an old cattle yard – the final helicopter drop option – that sits hauntingly in the middle of nowhere. After the climbs and bumps of the outward journey, Hell Line's return east is more flowing, threading between hills and following the vein-like lines of the ephemeral waterways.

The Larapinta Trail is passed again (bike access isn't permitted here) before Hell Line merges into Locomotive (yep, blue), a title that reflects its course beside the railway, a couple of kilometres south of Road Train.

After an initial climb, Locomotive builds up steam like the proverbial runaway train, providing some of the network's fastest riding before it rises onto a knife-edge ridge peering directly down onto the railway line – if you're riding on a Thursday afternoon, you might even get to watch the *Ghan* scuttle past.

Locomotive ends at a spaghetti junction of trails, and you can turn any which way, riding loops around Nturrerte or Mulga Bill, or heading straight down Atetherre towards town. But, alas, unlike your arrival onto the trails, you do have to finish this day under your own pedal power.

Not everyone is going to want (or be able) to drop into the trail network in a big bird, and it's certainly not required. The hub of the network is the Alice Springs Telegraph Station - the raison d'etre for Alice's establishment in 1871 - with the Eastside trails spiralling off from here and the likes of Apwelantye and Road Train setting out to connect to Westside. Of the 24 trails in the network, 18 are rated as blue (intermediate), with three green (easy) and three black (difficult).

Below Riders approaching the Telegraph Station from Alice Springs/Mparntwe *Opposite* Heavenly riding on Hell Line

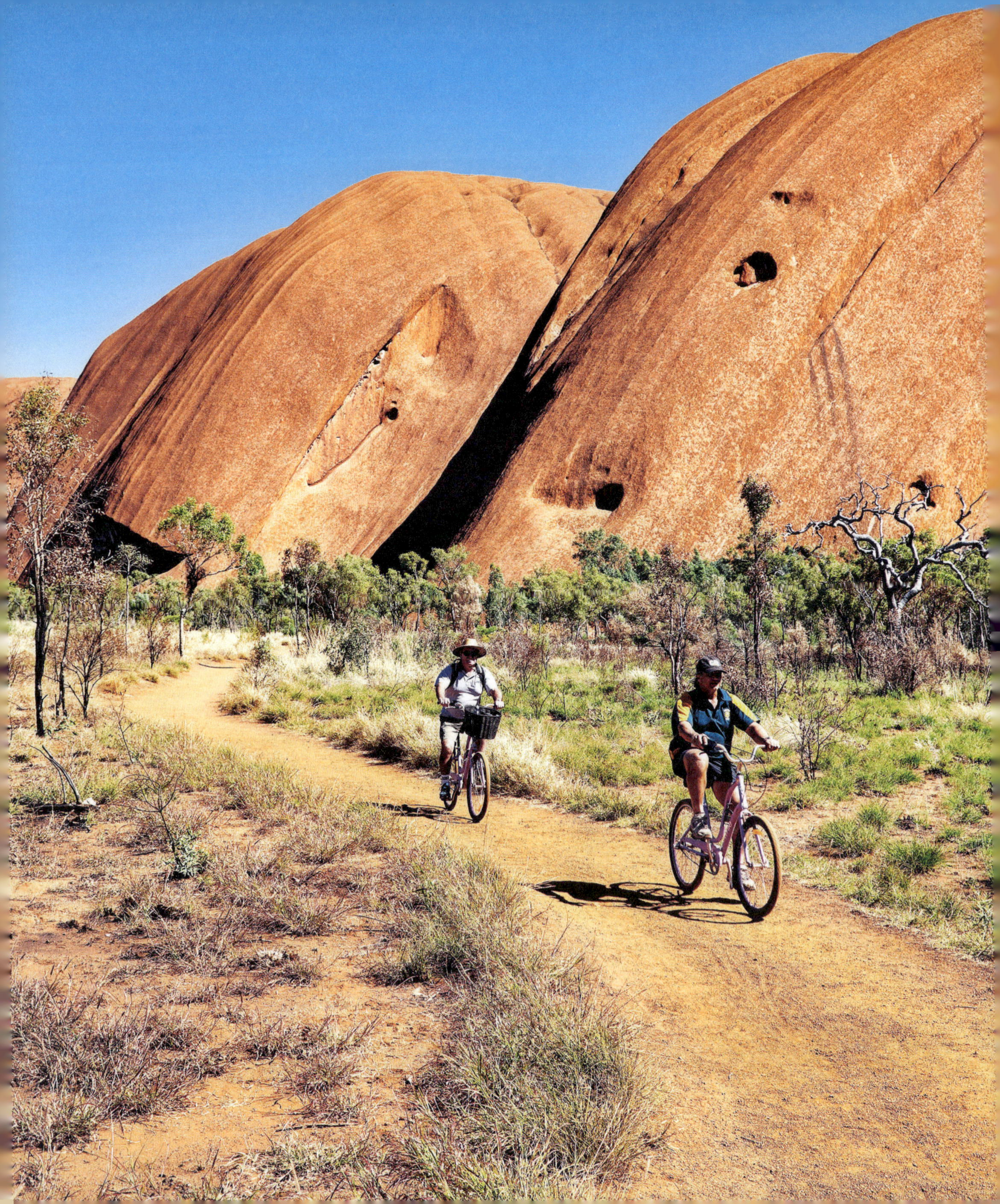

Pedal a lap around the mighty rock that holds Australia's heart and so many cultural stories.

Cycling, Uluṟu
Aṉangu Country

WHY IT'S SPECIAL

With apologies to other natural wonders, Uluṟu – the great red rock at the great red heart of Australia – is surely the country's most impressive natural icon. Rising 348m out of the desert sands, and extending an estimated 2.5km below the ground, it's taller than the Eiffel Tower, redder than Lenin, and is one of the world's greatest and truest rock stars.

To get adventurous here once meant to climb the rock, though this culturally inappropriate practice was finally banned in October 2019 after many years of campaigning by the Traditional Owners to respect the rock as a sacred site. Today, you can walk into various points around Uluṟu (or all the way around it), tootle along its trails on a Segway tour or, best of all, cycle a lap around the rock on a bike.

Uluṟu's base walk is shared between walkers and cyclists, and to pedal it has several advantages: it limits your time in the central Australian heat (the walk is flagged by park authorities to take around 3.5hr), and it allows you to spend as much time as you wish at the rock's key stops and features, with the ability to move quickly between them.

Uluṟu-Kata Tjuṯa National Park is a World Heritage Site and jointly managed by its Traditional Owners, the Aṉangu, and Parks Australia.

Where
Uluṟu is 470km south-west of Alice Springs/Mparntwe. There are direct flights to Uluṟu from Sydney/Warrang, Melbourne/Naarm and Cairns/Gimuy.

When
Winter is the most pleasant time to be on a bike at Uluṟu, with average maximum temperatures settling at around 20°C. Avoid summer at all costs, when average temperatures along this shadeless ride nudge 37°C.

Do it
Bike hire is available for 3hr timeslots from Outback Cycling at the Uluṟu Cultural Centre. Book a bike ahead online (outbackcycling.com).

Fitness: ●●○○○

Fear factor: ●○○○○

Expertise required ●○○○○

Family friendly

Opposite Roll 'n' rock

THE ADVENTURE

The recommended starting point for any loop around Uluru, whether on foot or bike, is the Mala carpark at the rock's western edge, though most cyclists will hire their bikes from Outback Cycling, which sets up each day beside Uluru's Cultural Centre. From here, it's a 2km ride through low scrub to the base of the rock at Mala. Look up at Uluru's slopes here and you'll see the lingering scar from the wear and tear of decades of climbers on the rock. Plaques at the base of the old route tell of some of the 37 deaths – the most recent in 2018 – that occurred on the climb before the long-overdue ban.

Park authorities recommend that walkers set out clockwise from Mala on the 10.6km track around Uluru, with cyclists pedalling anticlockwise, so that each one can see the other approaching, limiting the potential for accidents. The loop can easily be pedalled in less than an hour, though you'll want to stretch that out to fully enjoy the rock.

By riding anticlockwise, cyclists have the immediate advantage of heading first towards Mutitjulu waterhole, one of Uluru's most beautiful nooks. Across the desert sand, the trail is as naturally red as some painted city bike paths, and Uluru slopes down to almost meet the trail in parts. Right beside the path, flakes of rock lie along the monolith's base, shed like sunburnt skin, and the proximity of the rock provides a chance to touch, feel and absorb its beauty and power.

Park up at the bike racks beside the Kuniya walk and head the short distance on foot into Mutitjulu waterhole, one of the few permanent water sources around Uluru, with pockets of lush bush and the possible presence of bush foods such as bush tomatoes, bush plums and figs. Tucked in beside the Kuniya walk is Kulpi Mutitjulu, where generations of Anangu camped, and ancient rock art remains.

Through the bloodwood trees and kangaroo grass, the ride continues east, ducking in beneath the rock as it briefly arches over the trail in a petrified wave, and coming to its eastern tip at Kuniya Piti. This is the furthest point of the rock from Mala, the ride's starting point, so you can expect to see few people out here, bringing a sense of remoteness and magnificence appropriate to the next section of cycling.

At Kuniya Piti (where there's drinking water available, if you need a top-up), the ride rounds the rock, beginning back west along Uluru's north-east face. Like the rest of the trail, this stretch is ruler flat, with only the potential heat offering any difficulties.

Rock formations along this north-east face have particular cultural significance, and the trail begins to shift away from the rock, running a respectfully wide arc around the sacred Taputji rock. Riding a few hundred metres from Uluru, the view opens up wide, taking in the entire red monolith, while the peaks of Kata Tjuta rise over the horizon as a blue silhouette. Note that the Anangu request that no photos be taken along this north-east-face stretch.

Slowly the trail edges back towards Uluru, coming to a second bike rack outside Kantju Gorge. It's a 400m walk into the gorge, offering another moment of greenery, shade and relief from the inevitably hot day to complement the early stop at Mutitjulu waterhole. Look for the ephemeral rivulets on the rock itself, which flow only in the immediate wake of rain. If you're on your own bike, this is a wonderful spot to linger for sunset, when the rock blazes with the day's last light.

This two-wheeled journey around the big red rock concludes along the Mala walk, again skirting close to Uluru on a 2km section of trail where culture feels as tangible and strong as nature. Slow your pace and discover a series of caves that served as ancient gathering places for the Anangu. Tjilpi Pampa Kulpi, with its ceilings blackened by the smoke of fires, is where the old people would come and sit, while Kulpi Minymaku was a kitchen cave where women, girls and small children would camp – smooth sections of the cave floor reveal where seeds were pounded into flour. Most prominent of the caves is art-covered Kulpi Nyiinkaku, the teaching cave, where Anangu Elders would instruct boys about hunting and travelling through the country. The art on the rock was used by the Elders to teach the boys how to track and hunt.

A few more pedal strokes and the Mala carpark comes into sight. The magnificence of Australia's beating red heart falls behind as you turn for the Cultural Centre. It's been the finest kind of revolution.

Above Interpretation boards provide information along the loop
Below Skimming along Uluṟu's base

Aṉangu culture is a vital part of any Uluṟu visit, so park up the bike and spend some time learning about their connection to the place. The Cultural Centre, right beside the Outback Cycling bike-hire operation, provides a grounder into Aṉangu culture and the natural environment of the national park. There's a host of ranger-led activities, including presentations at the Cultural Centre and a daily guided walk along the Mala walk section of the loop trail. Maruku Arts (maruku.com.au) runs a variety of tours and experiences, from dot painting with an Aṉangu artist to cave art tours.

Cycling Uluṟu

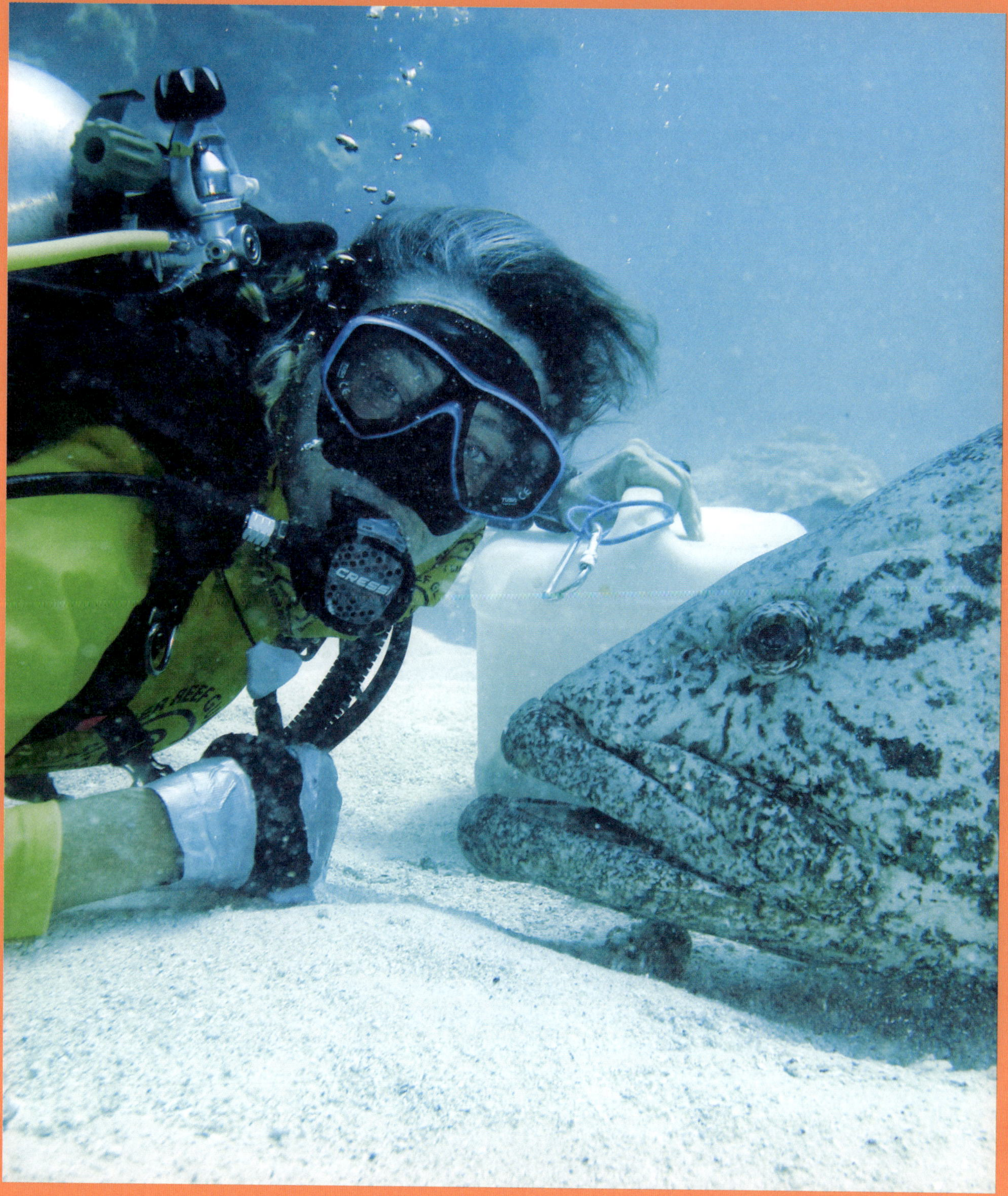
CRESSI

Queensland

*Wet and wild times on the reef, wrecks,
islands and raging rivers.*

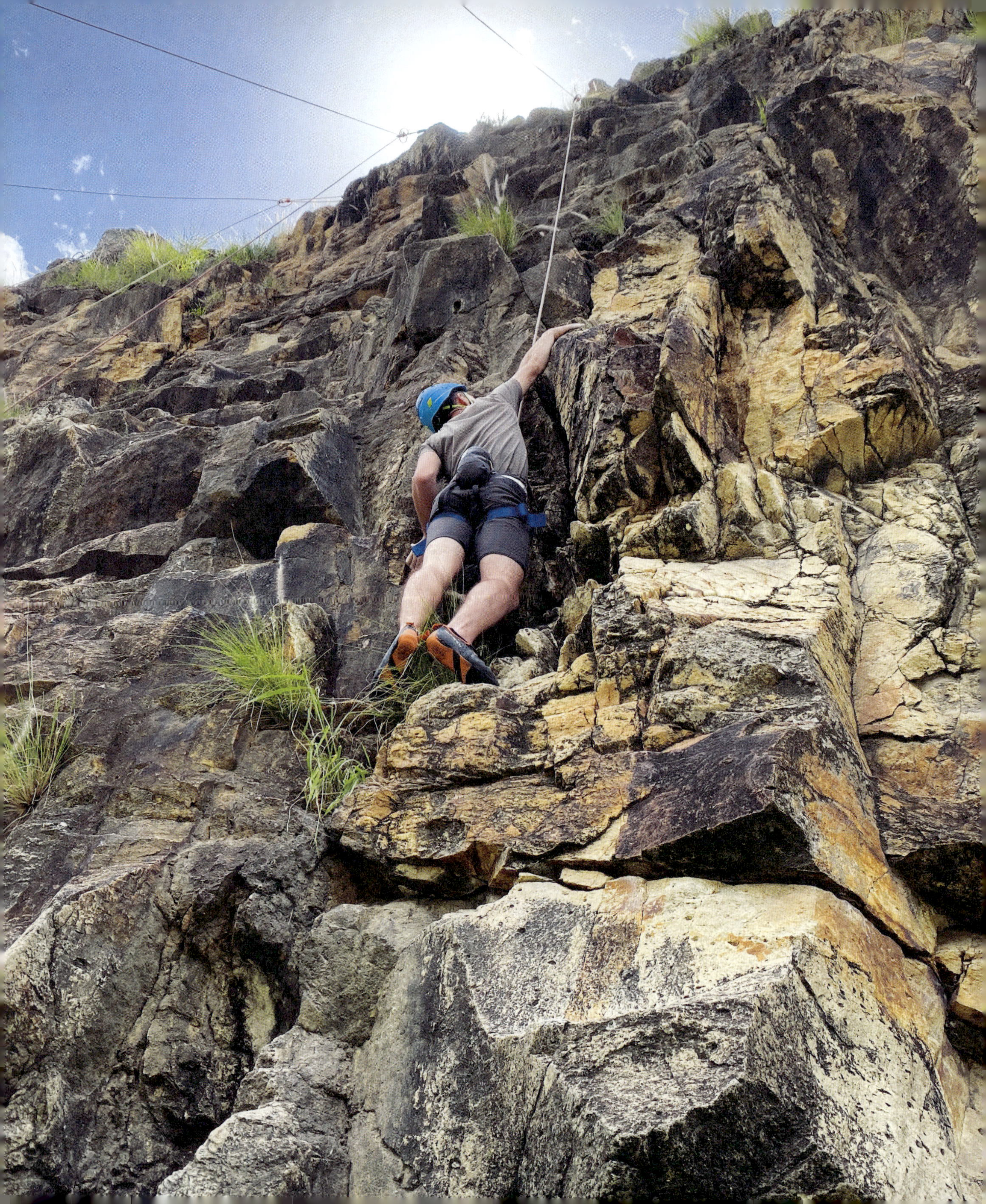

Discover Australia's best urban climbing on riverside cliffs just a few minutes' walk from Brisbane/Meanjin's city centre.

Rock climbing, Kangaroo Point, Brisbane/Meanjin

Turrbal, Jagera Country

WHY IT'S SPECIAL

In central Brisbane/Meanjin, it isn't only stairs and buildings that get climbed. Look across the Brisbane River to the finger-like peninsula of Kangaroo Point, and you'll spy a low line of cliffs that doubles as the best and most central urban rock-climbing site in the country.

Composed of a volcanic rock known as Brisbane Tuff, the 'KP' cliffs are strung with around 300 climbing routes, all scaling a quarry mined by convicts in the 19th century. The rock from this quarry, which operated for almost 50 years, was used to construct major city buildings, such as St John's Cathedral, St Stephen's Cathedral and the Commissariat Store (now a convict museum).

Today it's ropes and harnesses rather than leg irons that attach people to the riverside cliffs, which average around 20m in height. Adding to their appeal, the cliffs are lit at night, providing the chance to climb in the cool of evening. As you do climb, pause and look around – the view across the river to the city centre is one of the best in town, enhanced by the realisation that you're clinging to a cliff.

Where
Kangaroo Point Cliffs Park is immediately opposite Brisbane/Meanjin's city centre, on the western side of Kangaroo Point.

When
While the climbing can be good at any time of year, it's best in the early morning or late afternoon, away from direct sun on the cliffs. There are 62 lightboxes along the base of the cliffs, making evening climbing popular.

Do it
Based at the north end of the Kangaroo Point cliffs, Riverlife (riverlife.com.au) runs 2hr guided climbing tours each weekend, with all equipment supplied. Daytime climbs operate on Sat and Sun, with twilight climbs taking place on Fri and Sat evenings. A good resource for KP climbing routes is The Crag website (thecrag.com/en/climbing/australia/kangaroo-point).

Fitness: ●●○○○

Fear factor: ●●●○○

Expertise required
●○○○○ (guided)
●●●●○ (independent)

Family friendly

Opposite Life on the ledge at Kangaroo Point *Previous* Meeting the locals on the Great Barrier Reef

THE ADVENTURE

On a weekend morning, Kangaroo Point Cliffs Park is where Brisbane/Meanjin seemingly comes to play. Bikes whirr along trails, dogs walk their owners, and activewear seems the only uniform along the riverside strip of paths and lawns. Along the cliffs, beneath the babble of a cafe, climbing ropes hang like ponytails.

Climbing at KP, as the cliffs are known to local climbers, has an ease you find at few Australian sites. From the CBD, you simply need cross a bridge and wander along the riverbank (construction of the Kangaroo Point Green Bridge, slated for completion in 2024, will make access from the city even quicker) to find yourself at the base of the cliffs.

All routes are single-pitch (up a single span of rope), and bollards atop the cliffs mean that most climbs can be top-roped (the climbing rope attached from above). Identifying climbs is simple, with the initials of each route painted onto the rock along the base of the cliffs.

The bulk of KP's routes are graded around 14 to 17, making this a great spot for novice and intermediate climbers to work on their trade (to find out more about the climbing grading system, *see* boxed text p.75). There are more than 100 climbs graded 20 and above to also keep more experienced climbers content (the toughest Kangaroo Point climb is the grade 27 Sinister Pathway).

Though the climbs are arranged along a continual cliff-face, KP is typically divided into three areas: Left Main Wall and Right Main Wall (which begin immediately south of the stone stairway beside Joey's cafe) and KP North, with the small, separate Nursery Cliff (to the south) featuring around 20 routes suited to beginner climbers. Left Main Wall and Right Main Wall contain the majority of the climbs (around 250 of them), and it's here that climbers gravitate – on a typical weekend morning, there can be dozens of climbers on the Main Walls, their numbers thinning only as the sun hits the cliffs around the middle of the morning, turning them into baking stones.

Left Main Wall is the most inviting area for newcomers or social climbers, with less taxing ascents such as Date Anatomy (grade 12), the Lemur's Femur (14), and the adjoining crack climbs of Cornflake Crack (14) and Slime Fresh (16) to really give your fingers a climbing workout. Also here is the large overhang of Dinosaur (23).

Right Main Wall, where the cliffs are smoother, with fewer holds, presents the most difficult climbs, with nearly half of its routes graded 20-plus. Popular climbs in this area include Idiot Wind (21) and the side-by-side beer-inspired climbs of Brisbane Bitter (24) and XXXX (25).

Wherever you climb, the Kangaroo Point cliffs have a relaxed, welcoming atmosphere. On busy days, climbers ascend just a metre or two apart, and belayers perform their duty sitting back on the low metal fence that divides the cliffs from the bike path. On the cliffs, some climbers struggle and grind their way to the top (or sometimes to little more than a couple of metres off the ground), while others flow as easily as the river behind them. All the while, the city looks down on them, rising like a concrete forest across the city's namesake river.

Top The belay relay *Opposite* The view from the cliffs

To climb in a city usually means heading to an indoor climbing gym, but that doesn't have to be the case around Australia's capitals. Standing sentinel above Hobart/nipaluna, on the high slopes of kunanyi/Mount Wellington, is the Organ Pipes escarpment. Climbs on these prominent dolerite columns, which are as tall as 120m, favour the brave.

In Adelaide/Tarndanya's southern suburbs, Onkaparinga River National Park has a dedicated climbing area on the 30m-high cliffs of a gorge, while Morialta Conservation Park, along the foot of the Adelaide Hills, has more good climbing.

In Sydney/Warrang, head out to the Blue Mountains, which are stitched with a seemingly endless array of climbing routes, while Canberra/Ngambri/Ngunnawal is granite country, with one of Australia's best climbing areas at Booroomba Rocks.

Melbourne/Naarm has the unusual treat of the Burnley Bouldering Wall, notched beneath the Monash Fwy on the banks of the Yarra River/Birrarung.

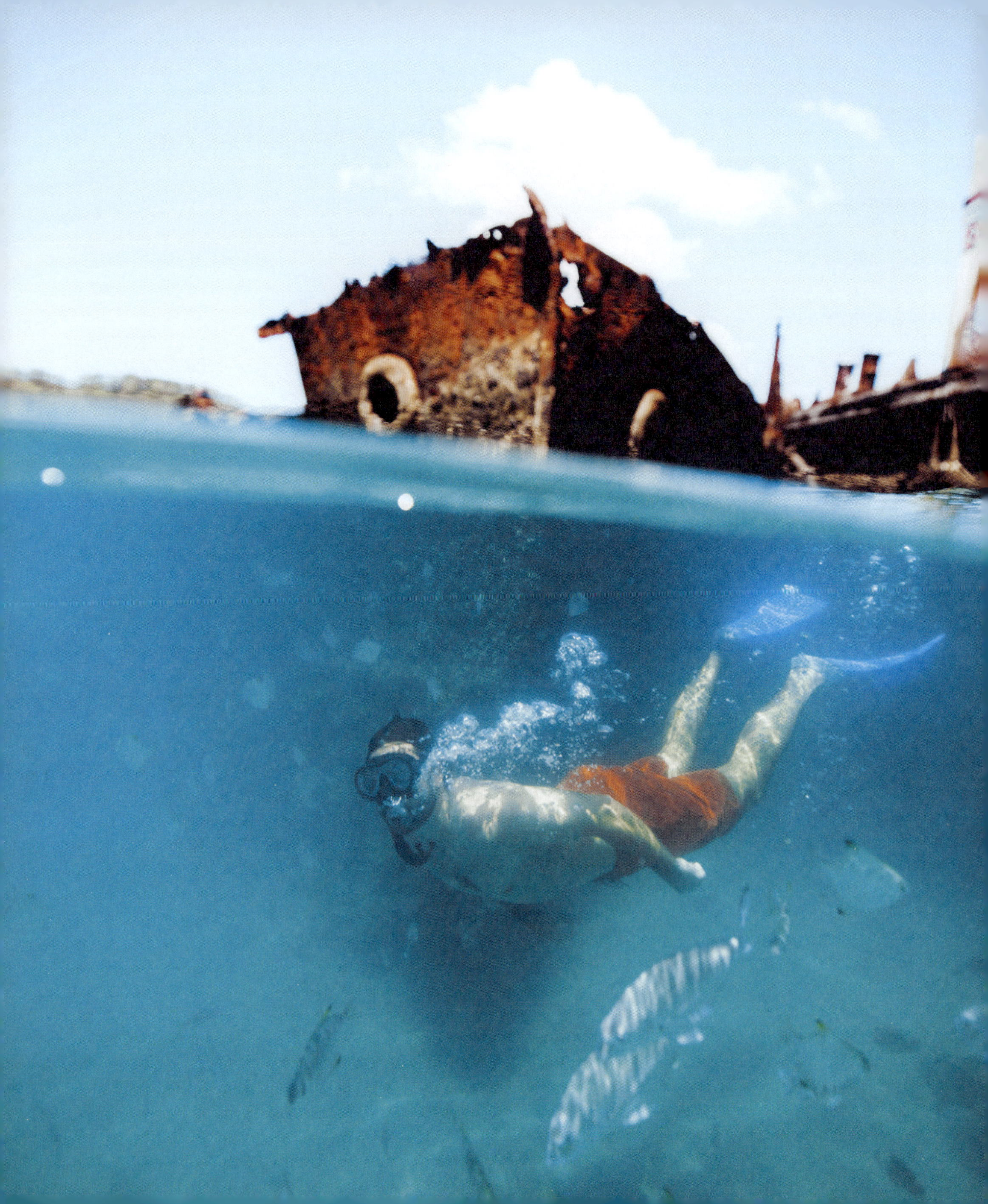

Explore shipwrecks and coral as you snorkel among shoals of fish, turtles and other marine life close to shore.

Snorkelling, Tangalooma Wrecks, Moreton Island/ Mulgumpin

Quandamooka Country

WHY IT'S SPECIAL

To snorkel reefs and wrecks in Australia typically means heading far offshore and a long way from major settlements, but immersing yourself in the colourful marine life along the Tangalooma wrecks of Moreton Island/ Mulgumpin requires only a ferry ride from Brisbane/Meanjin. Scuttled through the 1960s, '70s and '80s to create a safe anchorage for boats, the 15 wrecks have bloomed into a thriving reef less than 100m off the shores of the world's third largest sand island.

Snorkelling among these shipwrecks rivals many sites on the Great Barrier Reef, with the wrecks home to more than 100 tropical fish species, plus big-ticket visitors such as dolphins, green sea turtles, wobbegongs and even dugongs. You can visit the wrecks on a snorkelling tour from the nearby Tangalooma Island Resort, or snorkel independently, wandering into the sea at will from the long strip of beach to the resort's immediate north.

There's nothing particularly difficult or challenging about the snorkelling, but there can be strong currents running between the beach and the wrecks, so aim to snorkel around an hour either side of low or high tide – during the slackwater – when the current is at its most gentle.

Where
The Tangalooma wrecks are on the west coast of Moreton Island/Mulgumpin. There are two ferries to the island from Brisbane/Meanjin: a 75min passenger ferry to the resort, and a 90min vehicle ferry that docks on the beach beside the wrecks.

When
Snorkelling is good year-round. Aim to snorkel as close to high or low tide as possible. Check tide times online (tangalooma.com/moreton-island/weather-tides).

Do it
Book snorkelling tours through Tangalooma Island Resort (tangalooma.com/activities-tours/snorkel-shipwrecks). Snorkelling gear can also be hired through the resort, or at a Sunset Safaris truck (sunsetsafaris.com.au) parked on the beach beside the wrecks.

Fitness: ●○○○○

Fear factor: ●●○○○

Expertise required ●●○○○

Family friendly

Opposite Immersed in the Tangalooma wrecks.

THE ADVENTURE

Stand on the beach north of the Tangalooma Island Resort, and a line of rusted shipwrecks rises like a craggy outcrop from the sea. Seen like this, they appear like debris but head out into the water and they are transformed into magnificent aquariums. Though you're on one of the world's largest sand islands, with the planet's tallest coastal sand dune (Mount Tempest), it's these rusted wrecks that are Moreton Island/Mulgumpin's star feature.

If you're part of a snorkelling tour from the resort, you'll arrive at the wrecks by boat, which drops you right beside the ships, straight into the marine action. If you're snorkelling independently, which allows you to spend as much time as you like in the water, it's a 20min walk along the beach from the resort to the wrecks.

At low tide, the narrowest point between the beach and the wrecks is just 30m, making it a simple swim into this oceanic wonderland. In the far distance, Brisbane/Meanjin's city towers stand like sticks on the horizon, and the silhouetted peaks of the Glass House Mountains rise like the back of a sea monster. Most impressive of all are the enormous freighters cruising past in a channel just beyond the wrecks on their way in or out of the city's port.

The best approach to snorkelling the wrecks is to start from one end of the ships and drift along their line in the current. Swimming out from the beach, the sandy seabed quickly falls away and for a few minutes the world consists of nothing but a blue void of water. The first indication that you're nearing the wrecks is typically the sight of a fish, then a few, and then a colourful cloud of them. My own introduction to the wrecks was a pair of lionfish, their 'manes' all puffed and proud as they drifted over coral just a metre below where I swam at the southern tip of the wrecks.

In the four to six decades since the ships were scuttled, the wrecks have effectively morphed into giant pot plants of coral. As the ships revert back to nature, the coral grows over them like bouquets that form the foundations of the area's marine life, with fish of every colour, stripe and dot darting around – tiny streaks of neon blue, butterfly fish floating about and Moorish idols with their fins trailing like bridal veils.

Right Rusted beauty

Snorkelling, Tangalooma Wrecks, Moreton Island/Mulgumpin

Above The narrow channel separating the wrecks from the island *Opposite* Decked out for snorkelling

In some wrecks you can swim over the deck or even into the hull. As I snorkelled one time atop the sand-covered deck of a ship at the southern end, a wobbegong – a bottom-dwelling carpet shark – swam stealthily beneath me, disappearing into the metal ribcage of the wreck.

At their deepest points, the hulls of the ships fall away into the sea like steel cliffs, reaching depths of up to 12m. Wherever you look as you drift alongside or inside the ships, there are fish, often just a few centimetres away, unconcerned by these strange masked humans suddenly swimming among the shoal. Fish, both large and small, nibble at the hulls, and feed from the corals that now grow from them like hanging gardens, or swim beside and around you – I've seen fish here form virtual vortexes, swirling and circling around snorkellers.

The stars of the show, if they make an appearance, are green sea turtles, one of the five turtle species (of the world's seven turtle species) found around Moreton Bay – this is one of the closest places to a capital city in the world where large populations of turtles are found. I spent two days snorkelling the wrecks without sighting a turtle. Then, as I waited for the vehicle ferry back to Brisbane/Meanjin, I decided on one quick, final snorkel, swimming out from the beach to the southern end of the wrecks, where the largest ships take their eternal rest, their hulls turned into habitats. As I swam above one ship's deck, a green sea turtle emerged from beneath a coral outcrop, floating beneath me for a couple of minutes before surfacing for air right beside me and then silently slipping away. As a farewell from the Tangalooma wrecks, it was perfect – a brief audience with marine royalty.

While most visitors come to Moreton Island/Mulgumpin to snorkel the Tangalooma wrecks, you can delve deeper by joining a diving tour, exploring the parts of the ships that aren't visible to snorkellers.

Another popular dive site is Flinders Reef, around 5km north of the island. The closest true coral reef to Brisbane/Meanjin, Flinders is noted for the clarity of its water, its turtle cleaning station (where green sea turtles come to be cleaned by surgeonfish and cleaner wrasse) and the diversity of its fish and coral – 175 fish species and more varieties of coral than any single reef along the Great Barrier Reef.

On land, Moreton Island/Mulgumpin gets active with sandboarding in the Tangalooma Desert, a bare patch of dunes ringed by bush a short walk from the Tangalooma Island Resort.

Snorkelling, Tangalooma Wrecks, Moreton Island/Mulgumpin

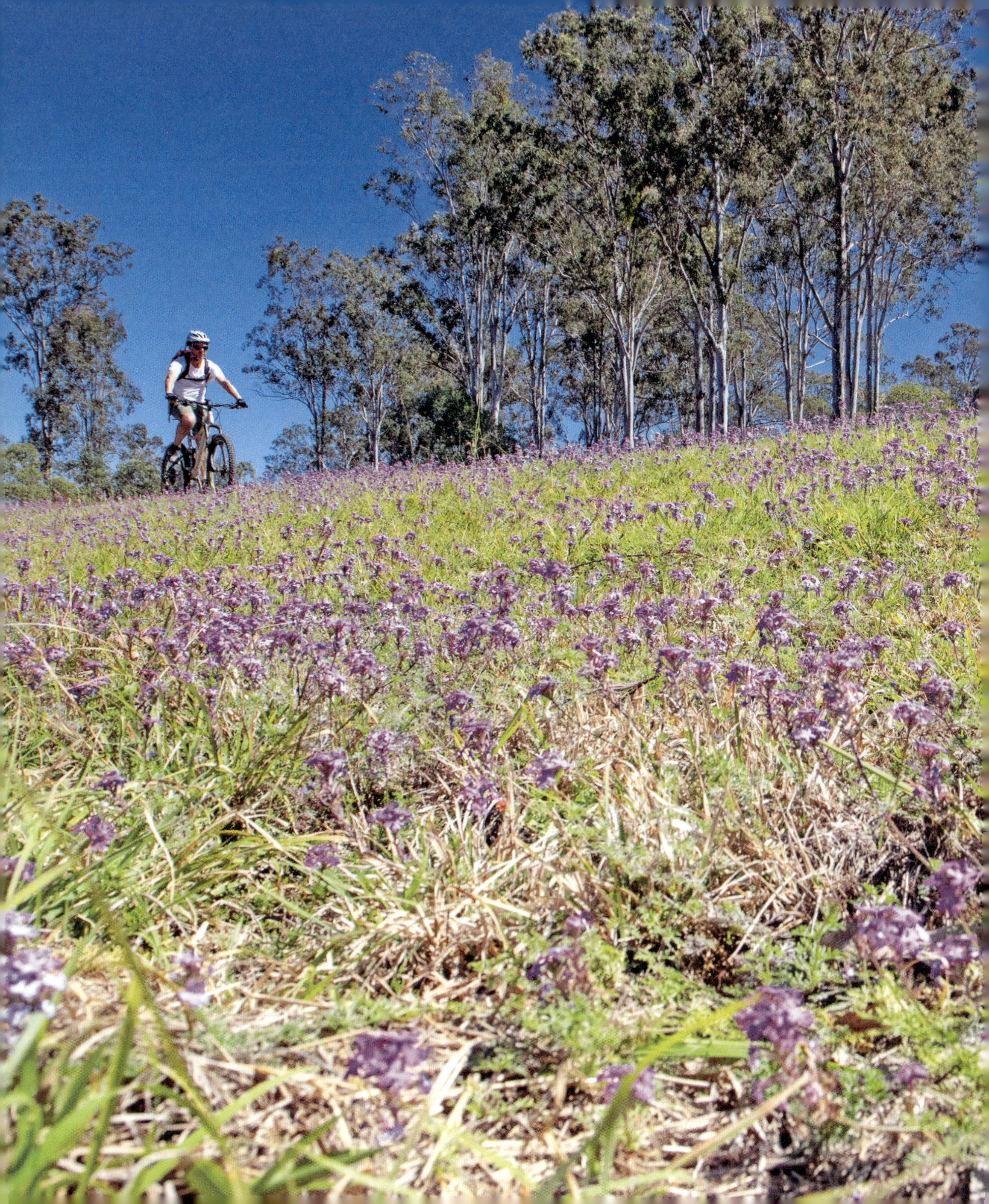

Ride Australia's longest rail trail, passing through classic country towns and outback-like landscape, even with Brisbane/Meanjin just out of sight.

Cycling, Brisbane Valley Rail Trail

Jagera, Yuppera, Yuggera, Ugarapul, Jinibara and Kabi Kabi Country

WHY IT'S SPECIAL

Australia is stitched with rail trails – more than 100 at last count – and while the vast majority of them are in the southern states (Victoria alone has more than 30 rail trails), the longest of them all is on Brisbane/Meanjin's doorstep.

The Brisbane Valley Rail Trail (BVRT) stretches for 161km from Yarraman, just south of Kingaroy, to Wulkuraka, on the edge of Ipswich. Brisbane hovers just over the horizon, but the ride is largely through the sort of rural landscape that makes the presence of a city seem fanciful.

Inaugurated from Wulkuraka to Lowood in 1884, the Brisbane Valley rail line expanded in stages: Lowood to Esk in 1886, Esk to Toogoolwah in 1904, Toogoolwah to Linwood in 1910 and, finally, all the way to Yarraman in 1913. Trains operated until 1989, after which the line sat idle until 2003 when it reopened, once again in sections, as the BVRT.

A comfortable three-day ride (that some cyclists power through in one or two days), the BVRT is sprinkled with rural towns (the largest gap between settlements is just 24km), making it easy to plan nightly stops and find reasons to linger – stop in at local museums, such as the one in Blackbutt celebrating tennis great Roy Emerson, find an art gallery in Australia's oldest condensed milk factory in Toogoolwah, and refresh and, umm, rehydrate in a string of country pubs.

This is one of the few bike rides in Australia that develops the sort of cyclist fraternity you find on long-distance rides abroad, with riders often setting out together and intersecting all the way along the trail.

Where
Yarraman is 175km by road north-west of Brisbane/Meanjin, with Wulkuraka 50km south-west of the capital.

When
April to Sept provides the most comfortable riding climate, though Sept also brings the prospect of spring's swooping magpies.

Do it
The Brisbane Valley Rail Trail website (brisbanevalleyrailtrail.com.au) is the complete resource on the ride, featuring maps, a distance calculator and information about accommodation and food.

Out There Cycling (outtherecycling.com.au) runs a shuttle service along the trail, and offers self-guided tours and bike hire. It also has bike shops along the trail in Moore, Toogoolwah and Esk. Tour de Vines (tourdevines.com.au) also operates self-guided tours.

Fitness: ●●●○○
Fear factor: ●○○○○
Expertise required ●●○○○

Opposite The many colours of the Brisbane Valley Rail Trail

THE ADVENTURE

For most people, the decision about which direction to cycle the BVRT is a simple one, with Yarraman situated 350m higher than Wulkuraka – show me a cyclist who doesn't like a downhill trend. The Yarraman trailhead is a couple of hundred metres from the old train station (double back to it if you feel the need to go point to point between the BVRT's bookending stations), and the unsealed trail disappears immediately into bush interspersed with the sort of rural scenes that persist for much of the coming three days. As the trails zigzags beside and beneath the D'Aguilar Hwy, log trucks and cars are like vehicles from another world on this traffic-free trail.

Most of the trail's descent comes in a single pinch from Benarkin, 24km into the ride, as the BVRT pushes through hills to reach the Brisbane Valley. The pace picks up as the trail slices through a series of cuttings and begins to encounter what will become a familiar feature of the ride – deep dips in and out of gullies that were once bridged by the railway but have no such kindness for cyclists.

This long descent concludes at Linville, where rolling stock lingers as a reminder of the trail's origins. Linville, 42km from Yarraman, is a popular first night's stop, with its refurbished pub the most enticing of all the hotels along the trail. There are hammocks on the upstairs verandah, cold beer on tap, and undercover locked parking for bikes.

Though the ride has now reached its namesake, the Brisbane Valley, which it will follow all the way to Wulkuraka, the low hills roll on, and the land remains furrowed by ever-deeper gullies – don't be surprised if you're pushing out of them by now. Railway trestle bridges stand like games of pick-up sticks, but they are akin to museum pieces, with the trail swooping around them rather than over them.

The last of the BVRT's steep hill pinches (still almost 100km from the ride's finish) is immediately outside the tiny town of Harlin, where the trail climbs into the 100m-long Yimbun Tunnel – the only tunnel along the railway line and hence now the trail.

All the climbs that remain now are nothing more than gentle reminders to slow down and savour the scenery, and the land seems to grow wider with every pedal stroke. It only closes in again as the BVRT approaches Esk, a town squeezed between hills, including the dramatic Mount Glen Rock.

Esk is a logical second night's stop, 52km from Linville and with 67km still to ride to Wulkuraka. Beyond Esk, across a low line of hills, the trail runs as flat as an airfield towards Lowood, riding for one of the few times beside the Brisbane River, which has until now been largely so near and yet so far.

After 156km of gravel beneath your tyres, the trail morphs into a concrete bikeway as it enters Wulkuraka, squeezing between housing estates and coasting to its finish at the Wulkuraka train station. The city has felt so removed throughout the ride, and yet here it is, so close after all. One hour by train and you can be walking the city streets of Brisbane/Meanjin.

Left Cycling near Harlin *Opposite top* Climbing out of a gully beyond Linwood *Opposite bottom* Trail hazards from above

The BVRT might already be the longest rail trail in Australia, but it can easily be turned into an even longer ride. A 55km signposted cycling route connects Yarraman to Kingaroy on backroads, meeting a second rail trail - the Kilikivan to Kingaroy Rail Trail - in the latter. This 88km trail travels through the fertile red earth of Kingaroy's farm country into drier cattle country at the Kilkivan end. It's sealed for half of its journey (from Kingaroy to Murgon) and unsealed and significantly rougher than the BVRT from Murgon to Kilkivan. Ride the pair together and it's a 304km cycling tour, taking around six days.

WARNING - Magpie territory

Magpies nest in this area and may swoop on intruders. This is normal defensive behaviour during the breeding season and lasts up to six weeks.

To protect yourself:
- Avoid areas defended by a Magpie
- Move quickly through area - don't run
- Or walk in a group as less likely to swoop
- Wear a hat or carry an umbrella over your head
- Bike riders - dismount and walk
- Never deliberately provoke or harass a Magpie as this usually makes them more defensive
- Remember - they are only protecting their young

The Magpie is a protected species under the Nature Conservation Act 1992. In dangerous situations, an authorised relocator with a permit from the Department of Environment and Science (DES) may assess, remove and relocate a particular bird.

Paddle across the mirrored waters of one of only two everglade systems on Earth.

Kayaking, Noosa River
Kabi Kabi Country

WHY IT'S SPECIAL

On a good day along the Noosa River – and there are many such days here – it can feel as though the world has stopped. The river seems barely to move, and its surface is so reflective that it mirrors the beauty of the Noosa Everglades that rise from its surface. The only things that disturb the reflections are the occasional dive from a kingfisher and the regular splash of your paddles. It's a scene as still as a photograph, with only the faint drone of mosquitoes to remind you that nowhere is paradise.

The Noosa River, sometimes referred to as the River of Mirrors, might be overshadowed by the fashionable resort town that borrows its name, but it's a unique Australian landscape and one of the finest flatwater paddling destinations in the country. The everglades – submerged marshlands – are an ecosystem found only here and in Florida, and to be here in a kayak, gliding through your own reflection, is a privilege you won't forget in a hurry.

Where
Elanda Point is a 29km drive north-west of Noosa Heads, and 160km north of Brisbane/Meanjin.

When
Spring and autumn are the best times on the river, with average maximum temperatures around 26°C. Spring is the time of lowest rainfall.

Do it
Kanu Kapers (kanukapersaustralia.com), based on the shores of Lake Cootharaba, hires out kayaks for multi-day paddles. Its self-guided trips include maps and notes, camping equipment (if needed), dry bags and an esky for food storage.

Fitness: ●●●○○

Fear factor: ●●○○○

Expertise required ●●○○○

Above Your ride awaits *Opposite* Kayaking through the Everglades

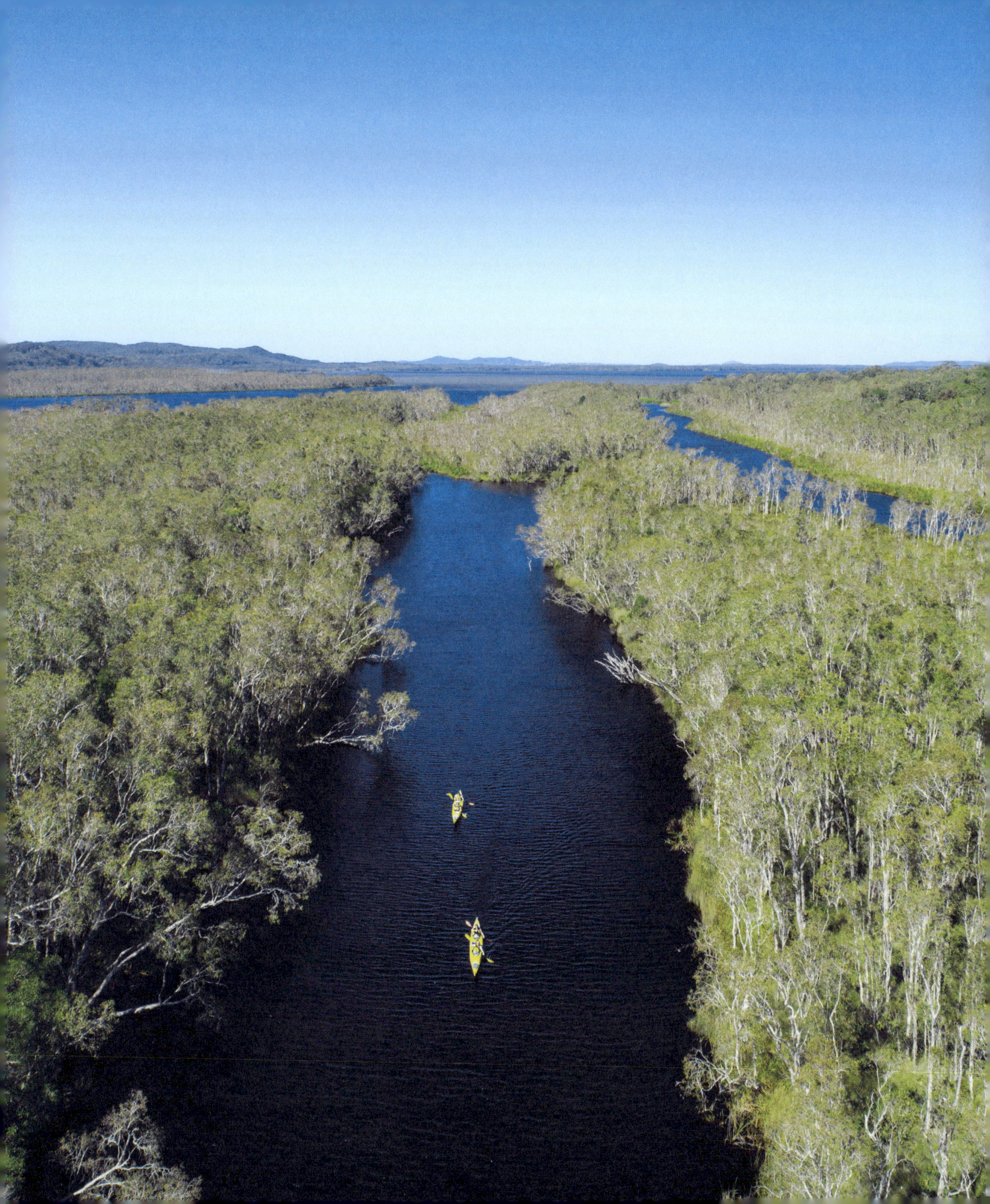

THE ADVENTURE

As it pours into the Pacific Ocean, the Noosa River balloons into a series of lakes, the largest of which – 10km long by 5km wide – is Lake Cootharaba, where most kayaking journeys to the upper Noosa River begin. The canoe and kayak launch is at Elanda Point, from where it's 4.5km to the head of the lake at Kinaba. This is the most exposed section of the paddle, with the lake often stirred into waves by the wind. As you cut across the lake, your paddle might even be scraping the sandy bed, so shallow is this broad body of water, reaching a maximum depth of little more than 1.5m.

The lake ends abruptly at Kinaba, seemingly devoured by an unbroken bank of forest. The unmanned Kinaba visitor information centre provides a chance to pause and browse up on the wetlands and its birdlife – more than 40 per cent of Australia's bird species have been recorded here – before taking a final look back on the lake and preparing to disappear.

Between the mainland and Kinaba Island, Lake Cootharaba is left behind and the river entered through a channel so narrow you almost feel compelled to inhale as you paddle through. It's just a foretaste of what's ahead, with the river quickly inflating once more into Fig Tree Lake, and then finally entering the well-named Narrows.

It's in the Narrows that you feel as though you've truly entered the river, as the melaleuca swamp closes in tight around you. It's a special place, claimed as the only river system in Australia that has its entire upper catchment protected in national park. However stirred up the lakes behind might have been, conditions almost certainly calm inside this tight embrace of trees. Pandanus palms hang over the river, and sedge grasses grow from its waters, but the most impressive feature is invariably the river's celebrated reflections. The water is ink-black, darkened and polished by the tannins from the melaleucas, and the reflections across its surface are as precise as etchings. One day I was here, I looked across at my paddling partner and could see his reflection blinking. At times, without discussion, we stopped paddling, compelled by an unspoken need not to disturb this canvas of water. Trees seemingly grow upwards and downwards, and clouds move across the sky and also across the water. It's dizzying, at times bordering on vertigo-inducing, but entirely mesmerising.

It's 5km through the Narrows to Harry's Hut, the first campsite along the upper Noosa. Beyond here, there are nine more campsites (confusingly named Camp 1, 2, 3, 4, 5, 8, 9, 13 and 15) in a 21km stretch of river. It's a remarkably large selection of options for such a short waterway (the Noosa River begins flowing in the dunes of the Cooloola section of Great Sandy National Park and barely leaves the park before washing into the sea). The longest gap between campsites is 3.5km, providing a wealth of camping options for paddlers.

The river connects these campsites like a black squiggle through the sandy landscape. In between, it continues its sluggish flow, moving like black mercury. As you paddle, expect to be drawn naturally to the middle of the river, paddling as far from each bank as you can to avoid the mosquitoes that await whenever you near land.

You'll want to take to the land, however, at camp 3, almost 8km beyond Harry's Hut and 20km from Elanda Point. At this campsite, the river intersects with the multi-day Cooloola Great Walk, and there's the chance to secure your kayak and set out on foot for the Cooloola Sandpatch, a 12km-return walk to a bare, 2km-long sandblow incongruously set into the forest like a white brush stroke.

It's another 13km upstream to camp 15, hidden high up the river, but the chain of campsites allows you to turn back whenever you wish – paddle up, camp, paddle back. It's another chance to reflect, and be one of the reflections, on the beauty of a remarkable river.

> Delve deeper into the Cooloola section of Great Sandy National Park with an extended hike on the Cooloola Great Walk. One of Queensland's 10 Great Walks, the 102km hike connects the Noosa North Shore to Rainbow Beach along the Cooloola dunes, one of Queensland's largest accumulations of wind-blown sand. The walk is divided into a natural five-day outing by four walker campsites. Highlights of the walk include crossing the Cooloola Sandpatch and Carlo Sandblow, passing perched lakes (similar to those on K'gari) such as Poona Lake, and hiking along the bank of the Noosa River.

Top The lower reaches of the Noosa River *Bottom* Plenty of time to reflect *Opposite* Adrift on the Noosa River

Kayaking, Noosa River   237

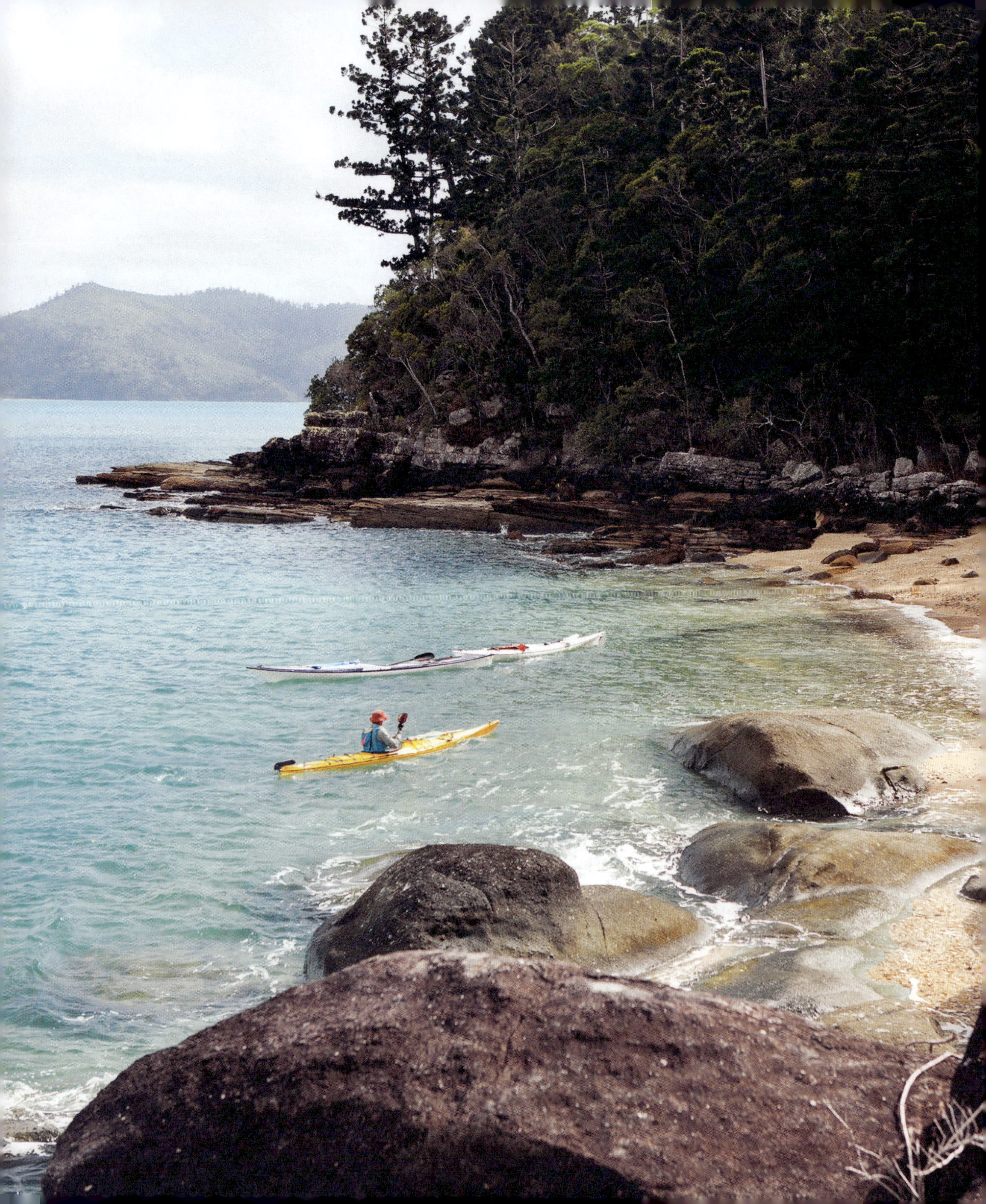

An island-hopping paddle through the Whitsunday Islands, stopping in at beaches and bays and walking short trails.

Kayaking, Whitsunday Ngaro Sea Trail

Ngaro Country

WHY IT'S SPECIAL

Queensland's Great Walks program is a curated collection of 10 multi-day bushwalks across the state. The Whitsunday Ngaro Sea Trail is one of these Great Walks, but it has a distinct point of difference. This 'walk' through the Whitsunday Islands is primarily a kayak journey, paddling between islands with five short walking trails sprinkled across them.

Setting out from Shute Harbour, 10km east of Airlie Beach, the trail makes a loose circuit around Whitsunday Island (home to the famed white sands of Whitehaven Beach), calling in to tracks on South Molle and Hook islands as it goes.

The entire loop covers around 110km, with more than half a dozen campgrounds dotted along its course, but it can be tailored in myriad ways. It's the least you'll ever use your legs on a multi-day walking trail.

Where
The Whitsunday Islands sit offshore from the popular holiday town of Airlie Beach, 1100km north of Brisbane/Meanjin. There are direct flights to nearby Whitsunday Coast Airport near Prosperine from Brisbane/Meanjin, Sydney/Warrang and Melbourne/Naarm.

When
The best time to kayak the Ngaro Sea Trail is from May to Sept.

Do it
Shute Harbour-based Salty Dog Sea Kayaking (saltydog.com.au) runs tours through the Whitsunday Islands, and also hires out single and double sea kayaks.

Book campsites ahead through the Queensland National Parks Booking Service (qpws.usedirect.com).

Scamper (whitsundaycamping.com.au) is a local water taxi service that can drop you and kayaks at campsites on South Molle, Whitsunday and Hook Islands.

Fitness: ●●●●○

Fear factor: ●●○○○

Expertise required ●●●●○

Opposite Heading into camp

THE ADVENTURE

Out of Shute Harbour, the Whitsunday Islands dot the Coral Sea like stepping stones, which is exactly what they are for kayakers on the Whitsunday Ngaro Sea Trail. Queensland's most famous island group consists of 74 islands, strung along the coast between Proserpine and Bowen, with the Ngaro Sea Trail focussing principally on three of the islands: Whitsunday, South Molle and Hook. Short deviations are also possible to the likes of Hamilton (a night of resort comfort, anyone?), Cid, Henning, Daydream and North Molle islands.

The complete route heads first to South Molle Island and then across the Whitsunday Passage to the southern shores of Whitsunday Island and Whitehaven Beach. From the northern tip of Whitsunday Island, it crosses narrow Hook Passage to Hook Island and returns to the mainland across the Whitsunday Passage.

Like so many decisions on the water, it's possible that the ultimate route may be determined more by conditions than planning. When I paddled the Sea Trail, persistent 20-knot easterlies blew over the Whitsundays, making it a fight against wind and waves to reach the ocean, windward side of Whitsunday Island, so we kayaked a 70km inner loop instead, along the western, land-facing shores of Whitsunday Island.

From Shute Harbour, it's less than 5km to South Molle Island, making for an easy opening day of kayaking. The island's 11.5km network of walking tracks has two entry points – Sandy Bay and the suitably named Paddle Bay – both accessible to kayaks.

Walking options range from a low-tide stroll across a spit from Paddle Bay to Mid Molle Island, just 150m across the water, to an ascent of South Molle's highest peak (195m Mount Jeffreys). Another goal is Spion Kop, with tracks passing Balancing Rock (a huge boulder with more purchase than its name suggests) to a rocky peak that stands around 40m lower than Mount Jeffreys, with a view across the Whitsunday Passage to Whitsunday and Hook islands. It's a sight line of the days ahead.

Right Ocean perfection in the Whitsundays

Kayaking, Whitsunday Ngaro Sea Trail

Queensland

The Whitsunday Passage separates South Molle Island from Whitsunday Island, the largest island in the Whitsunday group, and is the longest crossing between islands – it's a paddle of around 10km from South Molle to Cid Harbour on Whitsunday Island. The white dazzle of Whitehaven Beach is Whitsunday Island's headline feature and the obvious goal for kayakers, but two of the island's best walking trails are elsewhere.

From Dugong Beach, on the island's western shores, a trail ascends 437m to Whitsunday Peak. The hour-long walk to the island's highest point first crosses to adjoining Sawmill Bay and then funnels up a gully bearing remnants of the island's sawmilling days. Higher up the slopes, the few hoop pines that eluded the loggers stand tall, bursting through the canopy. From the summit, there's a view down onto Sawmill Beach and Cid Harbour, filled with yachts that resemble bath toys from this height.

The finest of the island's three walking trails heads to Whitsunday Cairn, a distinctive anvil-shaped rock that's visible as you paddle across the Whitsunday Passage. Setting out from Cairn Beach at the island's northern tip, the steeper 4km-return climb ascends through rainforest and hoop pines to a ridge covered in large grass trees. Though almost 100m lower in elevation than Whitsunday Peak, the Cairn presents a more spectacular view over the surrounding islands and sea.

From Cairn Beach, Hook Island is deceptively near, with just the thread-thin Hook Passage separating the pair. The passage is as narrow as 400m, but a massive amount of water funnels through it, making it one of the most notorious stretches of water in the Whitsundays, with tides often creating a virtual whitewater course through its centre.

Hook Island's southern edge is scored with two deep inlets, the furthest of which is Nara Inlet. The most popular mooring in the Whitsundays, it's also the compelling conclusion to the Ngaro Sea Trail's terrestrial stops. The inlet is lined with weathered, scoured rock that's scrawled in the graffiti of visitors from half a century ago, but this isn't the art you paddle here to see. Towards the head of the inlet, a tiny beach on the right marks the start of a short walking trail to the Ngaro Cultural Site. One of the oldest-known First Nations sites on Australia's east coast, the cave contains rock art from the seafaring Ngaro People, who have inhabited the Whitsundays for at least 9000 years.

Opposite top The view from Whitsunday Cairn
Opposite bottom Hugging the shores

The Cultural Site is the last of the Ngaro Sea Trail's walks, but some of the paddle's most memorable sights aren't on land. On this 'Great Walk', marine life is likely to be your most regular companion. In my own journey here, turtles surfaced around us with clockwork regularity, and dolphins cruised beside the kayaks along the shores of Whitsunday Island. On our final day, we followed a pair of humpback whales out of Nara Inlet, playing as they went in displays of fins and flukes and geyser-like blasts of water (humpbacks migrate through this area from around June to Sept).

There's truly no 'walk' in Australia like it.

Prefer your Great Walk to be an actual walk? The other nine Great Walks in Queensland are the K'gari Great Walk (90km), Gold Coast Hinterland Great Walk (54km), Conondale Range Great Walk (56km), Cooloola Great Walk (102km), Sunshine Coast Hinterland Great Walk (58.8km), Carnarvon Great Walk (87km), Mackay Highlands Great Walk (56km), Conway Circuit (27km) and the Wet Tropics Great Walk (broken into two sections: Wallaman Falls and the Juwun and Jambal walks).

Disappear into a hidden slot for the rare experience of stand-up paddleboarding through the outback.

Stand-up paddleboarding, Cobbold Gorge

Ewamian Country

WHY IT'S SPECIAL

Slashed into the north Queensland savannah, a 6hr drive west of Cairns/Gimuy, Cobbold Gorge is a geological paper-cut in a dry and dusty landscape. Around the gorge, termite mounds spear from the ground like quills, and Brahman cattle languidly graze the parched land. It's not the sort of place you come expecting to find water activities.

'Discovered' by station owners only in 1992 – though long known to the Ewamian Traditional Owners – Cobbold Gorge is Queensland's youngest gorge, forming just 12,000 to 14,000 years ago. In the three decades since the gorge was unearthed and opened to visitors on the private station, it has become one of outback Queensland's tourism stars.

In 2019, Australia's first fully glass bridge was built across the gorge, and there are daily boat and walking tours into and around the gorge, as well as scenic helicopter flights over it. The most intriguing way to explore the gorge, however, is on a stand-up paddleboard (SUP), gliding between its 30m-high cliffs and among its population of freshwater crocodiles.

Where
Cobbold Gorge is a 460km drive south-west from Cairns/Gimuy, and a 490km drive west from Townsville. Cobbold Village, the tourist complex that has sprung up to service visitors to the gorge, contains campsites, cabins, restaurant, an infinity pool, a dam with kayaks, and various tours, including helicopter flights.

When
The one-hour SUP tours run twice-daily, with morning and late-afternoon departures.

Do it
Tours are run out of Cobbold Village. Follow the Tours link at the Cobbold Gorge website (cobboldgorge.com.au).

Fitness: ●●○○○

Fear factor: ●●○○○

Expertise required ●○○○○

Family friendly

Above The deep chasm of Cobbold Gorge *Opposite* Get up, stand up

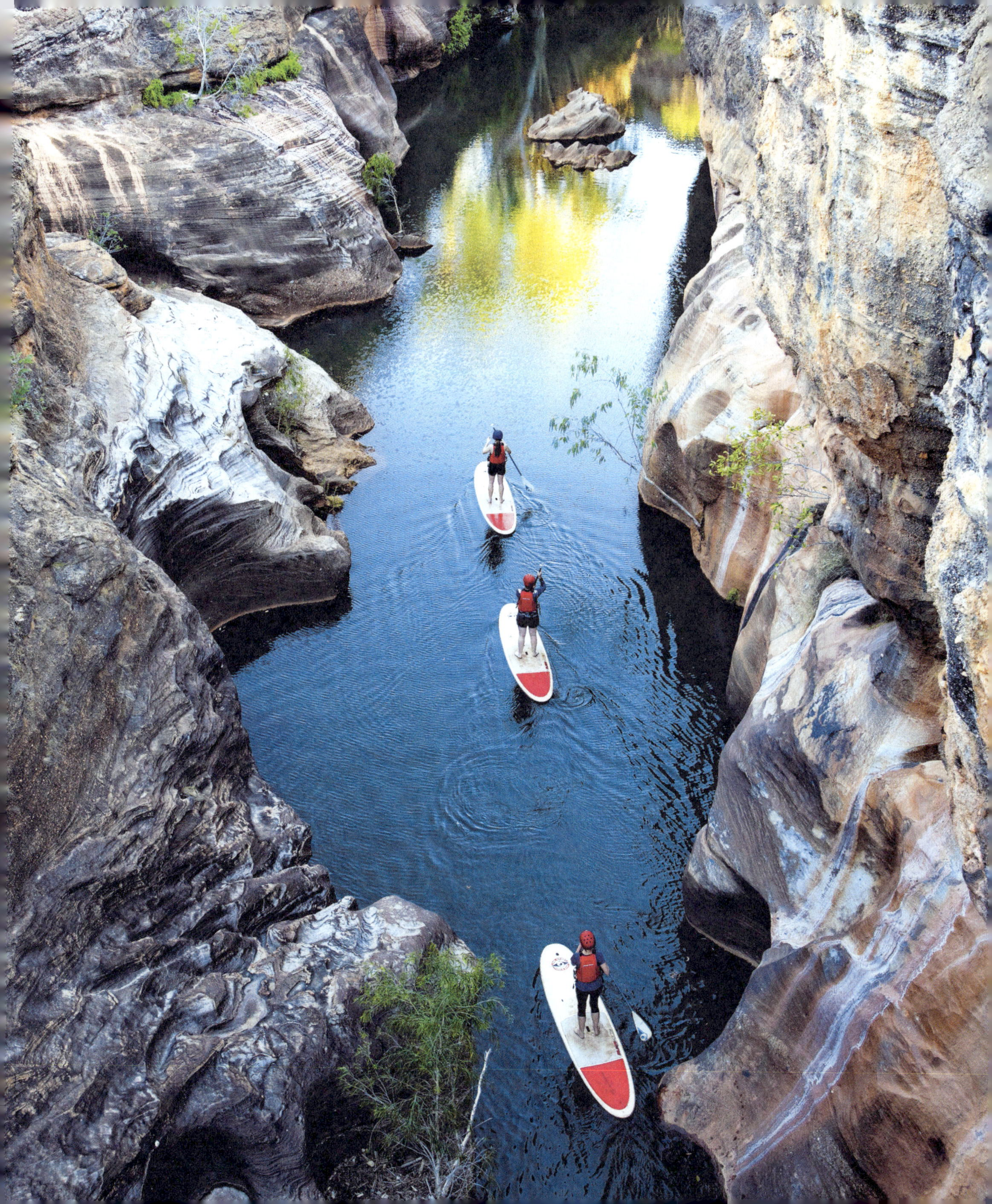

Queensland

THE ADVENTURE

Stand-up paddleboards (SUPs) are a common sight along Australia's coastline and estuaries, but they're an oddity in the arid outback ... unless you're at Cobbold Gorge. Here, on the permanent, spring-fed waters of Cobbold Creek, SUPs float between the gorge's spectacular cliffs, gently stirring the water as they pass beneath Australia's first fully glass bridge and between the narrowing walls of this elusive natural feature.

Like all activities at the gorge, which is located on the 320sqkm Howlong Station, a cattle property about 80km south of Georgetown, SUPing is only possible on guided tours. Buses make the 10min drive from Cobbold's campground and accommodation village, crossing the seemingly dry bed of the Robertson River, though this 'upside down' river has enough water flowing beneath the parched surface to supply all of the village's year-round needs.

Flowing into the Robertson River is Cobbold Creek, where station owners and stockmen watered cattle for nearly a century before current station owner Simon Terry steered a tinnie upstream in 1992, wondering what lay beyond. Cobbold Gorge revealed itself.

It's only when you see it from the air that you can begin to imagine how this gorge remained hidden for so many years. Cobbold Gorge is notched into the edge of an 80sqkm sheet of sandstone. The movement of a fault line that runs beneath Robertson River has shifted and broken the sandstone country in myriad places, slicing thousands of parallel cracks through it. It's impassable country – for that first century after European settlement, Cobbold Gorge was literally lost in the cracks.

Beside a pontoon at the mouth of the gorge, SUPs stand racked against a paperbark tree, with paddlers donning lifejackets and helmets before stepping out on the wide paddleboards and beginning the peaceful journey into the gorge. Near its mouth, scratched carelessly into the orange cliffs, is the name and date 'J.E. Clark. 1900', a graffitied hint of how close James Clark, the first owner of what was then Robin Hood Station, came to uncovering the gorge.

The navigable section of Cobbold Gorge, which sits inside a nature refuge excised from Howlong Station, is around 850m in length, and at this northern end it's wide and open. Rock bars rise above the creek's surface, and there are patches of

Left The sandstone country that long hid Cobbold Gorge

Stand-up paddleboarding, Cobbold Gorge

riverbank on which freshwater crocodiles are regularly sighted – the gorge is said to be home to up to 15 crocs – though with SUP tours setting out in the early morning and approaching sunset, the sun-loving reptiles are less likely to be spotted than on the daytime boat tours. The day I paddled here, I sighted five crocodiles from the daytime boat, but none from the evening SUP.

Cobbold Gorge begins to narrow, and its walls darken, as you pass beneath the glass bridge – a 13m-long structure with 41mm-thick glass, 17m above the surface of the creek. In just a few hundred metres, the chasm slims to a point that you can almost stretch your arms wide and touch both cliffs. Thousands of wet seasons have sculpted the walls into an array of shapes: calligraphic curls, thin fins of rock, scoured potholes. High overhead, the sky is all but obscured by the cliffs, and the only sounds come from the depths – the splash of paddles, errant SUPs occasionally scraping against the cliffs, and any chatter that hasn't been silenced by the awe of the setting.

At a blockage in the gorge, paddlers turn their boards to go back downstream, drifting almost effortlessly with the imperceptible flow. It's a change to ponder Cobbold Gorge anew. From down here, deep in the cracks of the earth, it feels like a major natural feature, a grand canyon of its own, and yet Australia's new wave – the European settlers who pushed out into the Ewamian People's land at the end of the 19th century – knew nothing of it for such a long time. There's a palpable sense of natural secrecy that's as rare as the sight of these SUPs in the outback.

> From the edge of the town of Mossman, WindSwell Kitesurfing and Standup Paddleboarding (windswell.com.au) runs half-day SUP tours along the gin-clear river, passing beneath enormous fig trees and drifting through a slice of rainforest paradise. You'll notice a crocodile warning sign as you carry your SUP to the water's edge at Mossman River on Kuku Yalanji Country, but you'll quickly realise that the waters in this landmark north Queensland river are so transparent that the only biting things you probably need worry about are mosquitoes - wear insect repellent. The Mossman River flows faster than Cobbold Creek, making paddleboard balance more of a challenge, but even a tumble off the board is welcome in the tropical Mossman heat.

Above Paddling through scoured chambers in the gorge *Opposite* Cobbold Gorge's glass bridge

Stand-up paddleboarding, Cobbold Gorge

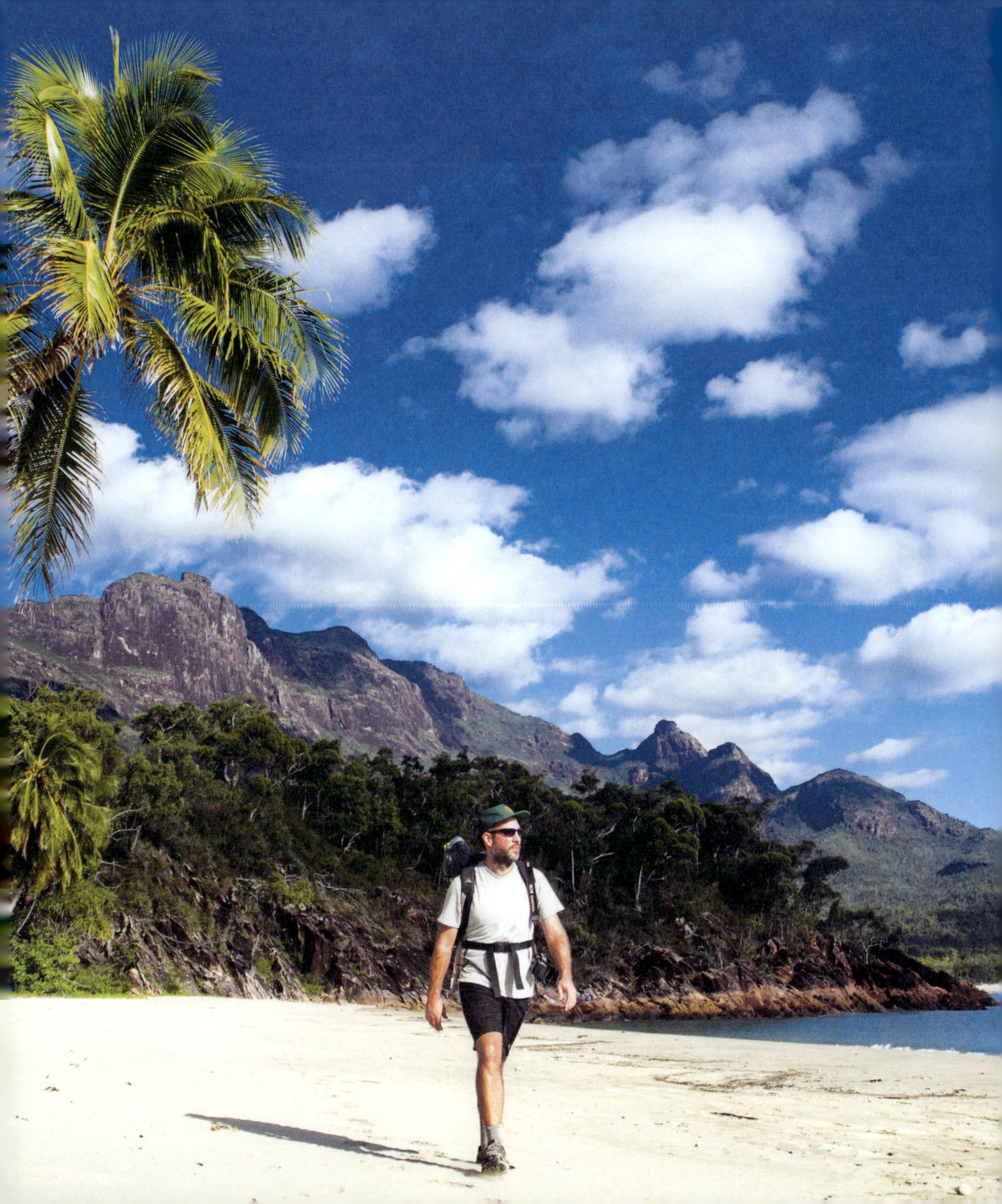

Tropical-island dreams don't typically involve a pair of hiking boots, but on Australia's largest island national park they sure do.

Hiking the Thorsborne Trail, Hinchinbrook Island/ Munamudanamy

Bandjin, Girramay Country

WHY IT'S SPECIAL

Australia's largest island national park is also one of the most dramatically spectacular places in the country. On Hinchinbrook Island/ Munamudanamy, craggy summits rise more than 1km above the Coral Sea, and coconut palms arch over empty beaches. Unseen waterfalls rush through rainforest, and where one of Australia's largest expanses of mangroves ends, beaches as white as snow begin.

Through it all threads a single path, the Thorsborne Trail, stitching together beaches, lookouts, cooling swimming holes and waterfalls along the island's east coast. It's a multi-day bushwalk with a difference, short on discomfort and high on distraction. Stretching for 32km, it's usually walked over four days, meaning a daily average of just 8km – by the standards of Australian bushwalking, it's positively lethargic, leaving ample time each day for swims and even snoozes.

Where
Hinchinbrook Island/Munamudanamy is immediately offshore from Cardwell and Lucinda, midway between Townsville and Cairns/Gimuy.

When
Hike in the dry season, from around April to Sept, for the most comfortable conditions. Water can get scarce on the island late in the dry season.

Do it
Plan well ahead for a Thorsborne Trail hike. Only 40 hikers are allowed onto the trail at a time, and permits book out quickly; bookings can be made up to six months in advance. Book your spot on the trail through the Queensland National Parks Booking Service online (qpws.usedirect.com/qpws).

Absolute North Charters ferry business (absolutenorthcharters.com.au) operates a ferry to the start and finish points from Lucinda, while Hinchinbrook Island Cruises (hinchinbrookislandcruises.com.au) run out of Port Hinchinbrook in Cardwell.

Fitness: ●●●○○

Fear factor: ●●○○○

Expertise required ●●●○○

Family friendly

Opposite Hiker at Little Ramsay Bay

THE ADVENTURE

As the ferry from Lucinda noses through the narrowing mangrove-lined channels near Hinchinbrook Island/Munamudanamy's northern end, the last thing you might expect is a sandy beach. But it's just a few steps from the ferry landing onto the sweeping white arc of Ramsay Bay, where the Thorsborne Trail begins as it intends to continue, hopping between beaches. Ahead, Mount Bowen, the highest peak on any Australian island (outside of far-distant Heard Island), rises more than 1100m into the sky, providing a sense of the dramatic scenery to come over the next four days.

Ramsay Bay's white sands turn briefly to Blacksand Beach's eponymous black sands before one of the few climbs of any real note along the Thorsborne Trail begins. It's no massive climb, ascending only to the shoulder of low Nina Peak, but the tropical heat is its own sapping force, especially if you continue up a side trail to the summit of Nina Peak. It's a highly recommended detour, since it's the only high vantage point anywhere along the hike. From here, little more than 300m above sea level, you peer up to the island's high peaks and down onto its mangrove channels, which run like veins through the island.

Most hikers spend this first night at Little Ramsay Bay, 7km from the start of the trail. For me, this is the most beautiful of Hinchinbrook/Munamudanamy's campsites, set beside a lagoon, with Mount Bowen towering above and the beach a step or two away. Facing east over the Coral Sea, the sunrises are spectacular, lighting up the rock faces of the mountain behind.

The next day is likely your longest on the trail – a 10.5km crossing to Zoe Bay. It's a day in which the island reveals its uncanny ability to be multiple places at once. At the southern end of Little Ramsay Bay, the Thorsborne Trail begins a long headland crossing to Zoe Bay. Partway across the headland, tiny Banksia Falls presents a chance for a restorative swim, washing away the early heat of the day. Beyond here, the island flickers like a field guide: one moment in rainforest, the next in paperbark swamp, then mangroves and back into rainforest. It's like costume changes from nature, which continue until the trail returns to the coast at the trail's midpoint, Zoe Bay.

Right A beach hop disguised as a hike

Hiking the Thorsborne Trail, Hinchinbrook Island/Munamudanamy

Queensland

Zoe Bay is another grand sweep of beach but somehow overshadowed by the waterfall at its back. Zoe Falls is passed early on the walk the next day, but it beckons long before that. With crocodile warning signs lining the beaches, it's freshwater pools such as those at Zoe Falls that promise relief from the heat, and it's a walk of just a few minutes from camp to these falls.

The crocodile signs can be confronting, especially at Zoe Bay, where high tide comes close to camp, but there's never been an attack along the trail, and the most toothy creatures I've ever sighted here are harmless reef sharks. The creatures you more likely need to worry about are the native giant white-tailed rats and fawn-footed melomys, which will chew through pretty much anything if there's a suggestion of food inside (I once heard a story, apocryphal or not, of the rats chewing through a kayak to get at food). For that reason, there are frames from which to hang your backpacks at each campsite. Be sure to use them.

The third day begins with another inland crossing, passing Zoe Falls – grab another swim, or save it for the infinity-like plunge pools at the top of the steep ascent through the cliffs to the head of the falls. It's one of the most beautiful places for a swim that I've ever found in Australia.

The trail rises on, following South Zoe Creek towards the crest of a ridge that drapes down from the island's spine of mountains. With it comes a new view, ahead to Mulligan Bay – the long white stripe of beach that will be your final morning's walk – with Lucinda's sugar-loading jetty poking into the sea behind it. At 5.7km in length, it's the longest jetty in the Southern Hemisphere.

The final campground along the Thorsborne Trail, 7.5km from Zoe Bay, is set right beside Mulligan Falls – so close that you can fall asleep to the purr of the waterfall. Ahead tomorrow is another 7.5km day, a rapid finish along the hard sands of Mulligan Bay (plan to cross Mulligan Creek at low to half tide, if possible) to meet the ferry at George Point, so on this last night settle back and ponder your surrounds – this island, those beaches, that waterfall. Like the pub with no beer, this is the tropical island with no resort, but could it be any better?

For a different (and equally good) angle on Hinchinbrook Island/Munamudanamy, consider a kayaking trip. Week-long expedition-style paddling trips set out from Lucinda, following the island's east coast, where beach stops provide the chance to sample the Thorsborne Trail by walking into the likes of Zoe Falls. From Hinchinbrook's northern end, it's an island hop north to Mission Beach, stopping at the likes of Goold Island, Wheeler Island and Dunk Island along the way. Hinchinbrook paddling trips are operated by Coral Sea Kayaking (coralseakayaking.com) and Southern Sea Ventures (southernseaventures.com).

Right top Cooling off in Diamantina Creek *Opposite top* Breakfast on Little Ramsay Bay *Opposite bottom* Taking in the view over Zoe Bay from the top of Zoe Falls

Hurtle through a deep tropical gorge as you ride the rapids of one of the world's most revered rafting rivers.

Rafting, Tully River

Jirrbal and Gulngay Country

WHY IT'S SPECIAL

The Tully River is a byword for fast and furious whitewater rafting. As the 133km-long river brawls its way through Tully Gorge in far-north Queensland, water bubbles and boils like a cauldron and inflatable rafts toss about like bath toys on its powerful grade IV rapids.

Part of the Wet Tropics World Heritage Area, the gorge is a stunning stretch of water and was the venue for the 2019 World Rafting Championships. Hills rise steeply from its banks, blanketed in thick forest; vines seem to tie the forest together like baling twine; giant strangler figs hang from cliffs; and tall kauri pines burst through the canopy. It's primeval and perfect – a magnificent backdrop to Australia's wildest water ride.

The unruly Tully, which was once named among the world's 10 best rafting rivers by the International Rafting Federation, is one of very few Australian waterways that can be rafted year-round, with flows dictated by releases from the Kareeya Hydro Power Station. A day-long rafting trip here is high octane but not necessarily high energy, with a guide at the rear of the raft doing all the steering and much of the grunt work. Your job is to hold on, paddle as directed, and try – or not, if you want more thrills – to stay in the raft.

Where
The Tully River flows from the Cardwell Range to reach the Coral Sea at Tully Heads. The rafting begins at the top of the Tully Gorge, 50km north-west of Tully, but shuttle pick-ups are from Cairns/Gimuy, Mission Beach or Tully.

When
Rafting trips run year-round, with departure ties determined by water releases from the Kareeya Hydro Power Station.

Do it
Tully River rafting trips are operated by Raging Thunder (ragingthunder.com.au).

Fitness: ●●●○○

Fear factor: ●●●●○

Expertise required ●○○○○

Opposite Hold on and hope

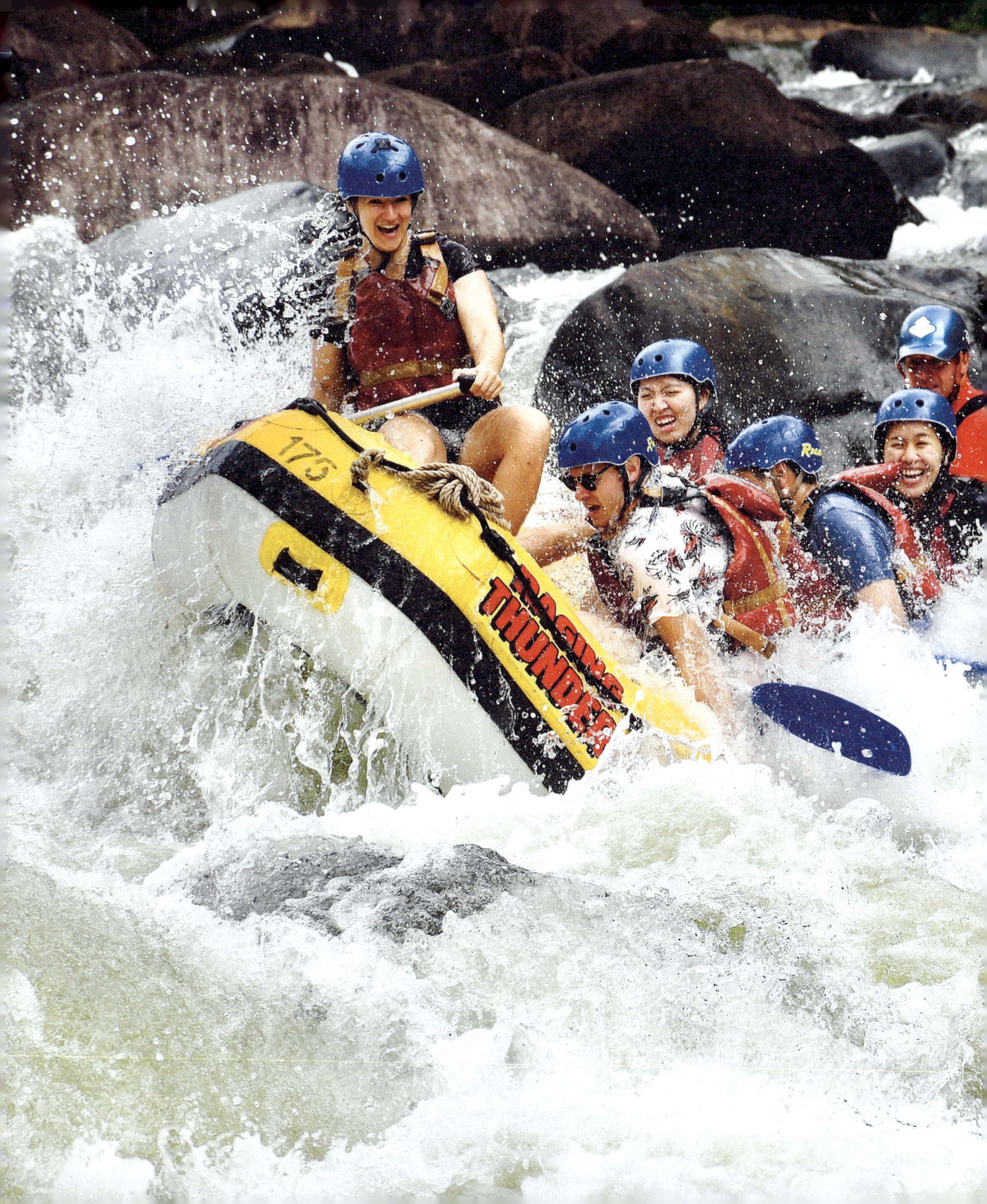
175
THUNDER

Queensland

THE ADVENTURE

On the main street of the north Queensland town of Tully, a giant gumboot commands centre stage. Standing 7.9m tall, the Golden Gumboot is a graphic reminder of the 7.9m of rain that fell on the town in 1950. Water is an integral part of life in Australia's wettest town – the average annual rainfall is around 4.1m – making this a suitable starting point for one of the country's great water trips.

From beside the Golden Gumboot, shuttles set out for the head of Tully Gorge, where rafting trips begin immediately below the Kareeya Hydro Power Station.

On this river respected among rafters the world over, there's little time to settle in. Ahead is 9km to 12km of river and rapids, depending on water conditions, and no sooner do rafts push off from the riverbank than the fight is on. The Tully tumbles immediately into Alarm Clock, a grade IV rapid that is indeed a wake-up call as to what's ahead. Rafts lurch, dive and splash, and quickly you become familiar with the language of rafting as guides bellow orders to their rafters: 'forward paddle', 'back paddle', 'hold on' and, most excitingly, 'get down'. As a start to an adventure, it's both intimidating and nerve-settling.

With the rafts pinballing between granite boulders, the Tully's meanest rapids follow soon after. The well-named Theatre ('it has action, drama, laughing, crying,' says one guide) is a chain of connected rapids, entered through the narrow Ninja Chute, with rafts squeezing between boulders before seemingly diving into a pit and speeding away downstream. It's the crux of the journey, and the Tully's greatest challenge. Guides work to set up safety lines and provide cover for other rafts in event of a flip – tumble out here and you're all but guaranteed a frightening swim through some of the river's wildest moments.

The Tully is a grade IV river, with more than 45 rapids through the gorge, but that doesn't mean that every rapid is big and beastly. Between the largest lurches are grade II and III filler rapids that still speed rafts through the gorge but in less emphatic style.

Then there are the moments between rapids, where the water flattens and flows without menace. These provide a chance to slow and absorb the surrounds of the Wet Tropics World Heritage Area, which is a tangled mess of trees as dense as any forest in the country, creating a sense of wilderness so near to civilisation – Cairns/Gimuy is less than 100km away to the north.

Opposite Dwarfed by rocks and rapids

After Theatre, the river quickly enters a series of rapids called Staircase, which equally exciting but are run quicker, with one rapid leading seamlessly into another. Wet and Moist comes next, providing a drenching as rafts splash and fill with water. Each rafter emerges drenched from this rapid, but it's a mere precursor to what's ahead. A few metres beyond Wet and Moist, Ponytail Falls pour over a low cliff, thundering down onto the surface of the Tully River. It's the most spectacular sight through the gorge, but it's not here just to be looked at. Rafters are invariably set the challenge of paddling through the falls, which pound on the raft and each person's helmet and shoulders with the frantic force of a heavy-metal drummer. Any thought of staying even the tiniest bit dry on this river is now long gone.

The fine margins between safe and perilous on a wild whitewater river become most evident at Cardstone Weir, where the river tumbles over a natural barrier a couple of metres high. It looks innocuous but plunge over this weir anywhere along the line of its main falls and it's a highly dangerous bit of water, pouring into a 30m-deep pool and trapping rafts. Instead, a narrow chute on the far-left side provides a safer line. Rafts turn and reverse over the ledge through this chute, gliding safely on past Champagne Falls, which weep down the columns of a cliff.

Rapids roll on to the trip's end, but the final confronting one is Double D Cup. To get through this rapid, rafts turn sideways, skidding down it with water pouring over the side of the raft. They then turn, filling the other side of the raft with water.

'That's the one rapid that even I get down inside the raft for,' one guide noted. It's also the only rapid in which a rafter fell out the day I ran the river, being briefly sucked back beneath the rapid before floating away downstream to be scooped up by another raft.

From here, the river wraps around Jabba the Hutt, a rock named for an apparent resemblance to its namesake *Star Wars* character, and the end is suddenly nigh. The river flows on, fast and frenetic, but the rafts pull into the riverbank and are eclipsed again by forest.

Not quite ready for the torrent of the Tully? Or prefer a taster that's a touch more mellow? The Tully's companion rafting waterway is the Barron River, at Cairns/Gimuy's northern edge. With grade II to III rapids, it's a smaller, lighter version of the Tully, with fewer potential dangers, and half-day trips that are good for families and anyone a little intimidated by the Tully. Rafting trips on the Barron are also run by Raging Thunder (ragingthunder.com.au).

Choose from a menu of bungy options as you take the brave leap into infinity and beyond from high above the rainforest.

Bungy jumping, Cairns/Gimuy

Yirrganydji Country

WHY IT'S SPECIAL

On the Vanuatu island of Pentecost, there's an annual harvest ritual called naghol, or land diving. From wooden towers that resemble a game of pick-up-sticks, local men dive towards the earth, with liana vines tied around their ankles to break their fall (rather than their skulls). These naghol dives are performed to ask the gods for a bountiful yam harvest.

In the 1980s, naghol caught the attention of two Kiwis named AJ Hackett and Henry van Asch. In 1987, Hackett climbed the Eiffel Tower and leaped from it with an elastic cord secured to his ankles. The resulting arrest didn't deter the pair, who the following year launched the world's first commercial bungy jump on a bridge over the Kawarau River outside of Queenstown, Aotearoa New Zealand.

The phenomenon of bungy jumping has since spread across the planet, with jumps operating in countries as diverse as Switzerland, Nepal and South Africa, along with the requisite half-dozen in Aotearoa New Zealand. Australia has just one bungy jump site, at Skypark Cairns on the city's northern edge in its forested foothills.

Look out to the Coral Sea from atop the bungy tower, breathe in courage, and take the plunge.

Where
Skypark Cairns is 16km north of Cairns/Gimuy, in the suburb of Smithfield.

When
Skypark Cairns is open daily from 10am to 5pm.

Do it
Check out the jump options, and book ahead (skyparkglobal.com/au-en/cairns).

Fitness: ●○○○○

Fear factor: ●●●●●

Expertise required: ●○○○○

Opposite Going down

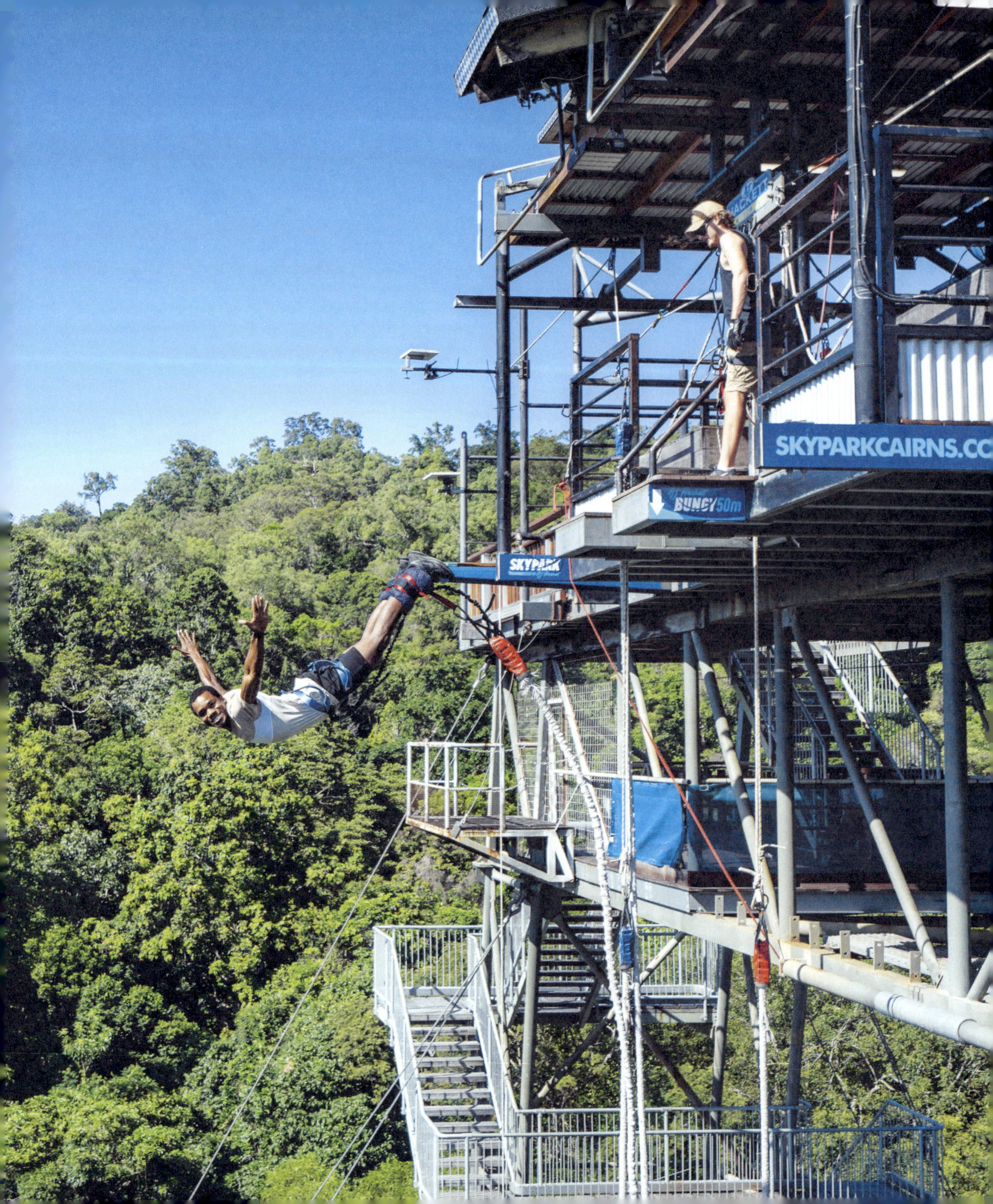
SKYPARKCAIRNS.CO
BUNGY 50m
SKYPARK

THE ADVENTURE

In a tangle of rainforest outside the Cairns/Gimuy suburb of Smithfield, there's a deceptively peaceful path. Past a 'Caution Falling People' sign, it climbs through forest filled with birdsong but also – every now and then – a human bellow or scream. Walk further and the source of these cries reveals itself: people leaping from a 50m-high giant metal frame straddling the forest.

At the path's end you check in at the bungy office and select your jump from a bewildering array of options. Most people simply lean forward into a classic swan dive, but you can choose from another 15 jump options across three levels of difficulties and an ascending scale of gymnastics and imagination. At the less complicated end, there's the likes of a tandem jump and re-creating the famous Kate Winslet pose from *Titanic*. At the other end of the scale, you can begin with a handstand, do a flip, or hang like a fruit bat before gravity has its way with you. You can even ride a BMX bike off the roof of the tower.

And with each jump there's the option of a water dunk, with the bungy cord stretching that little bit further so that you don't bounce back up until your head and shoulders have been plunged into a waterfall-fed lagoon beneath the tower – it's the ultimate high dive.

At the base of the tower is the hub building, featuring the bungy reception and a cafe/bar, and from here paths set out around both sides of the lake. The path to the right heads to the giant swing, into which you (and up to two other people) are fitted by a harness and slowly drawn up into the forest. Poised at the height of the canopy, you pull a release rope and suddenly plunge, swinging over the lagoon at up to 120km/h, flying so low it almost feels as though you're going to crash into the hub building as you skim over its top.

The path to the left leads to the long set of steps onto the bungy tower. For most, it's a long nervous climb up the staircase before stepping out onto the platform, where you're fitted into your harness and your legs are bound together and attached

Queensland

to the bungy cord. If wobbling out to the towers' edge doesn't test your fear of heights, staring out over the forest and Cairns/Gimuy to the coast, pondering the coming few seconds, probably will. It's the ultimate fight-or-flight moment, though it always ends in flight – just over three seconds of terror and freefall, plunging at more than 100km/h, before the bungy cord breaks your fall, propelling you back up towards the sky. After bobbing around like a teabag a few more times, you'll be pulled into a raft, unclipped and returned to land.

Feeling empowered by the experience? A follow-up second jump costs less than half the price of the first jump. Or you can just contentedly head to the bar, which sells champagne by the glass (or bottle if you really need to celebrate big).

Wouldn't mind the view and the vertiginous feeling of the bungy jump, but don't want to actually make the leap? Skypark's newest experience, opened in 2021, is Walk the Plank, which involves edging out onto a narrow platform atop the bungy tower. You can lean back, seemingly about to tumble to earth, but you're secured to the tower by a rope and harness.

Top and opposite left and right: Options aplenty: splash down, ride a bike, share the moment

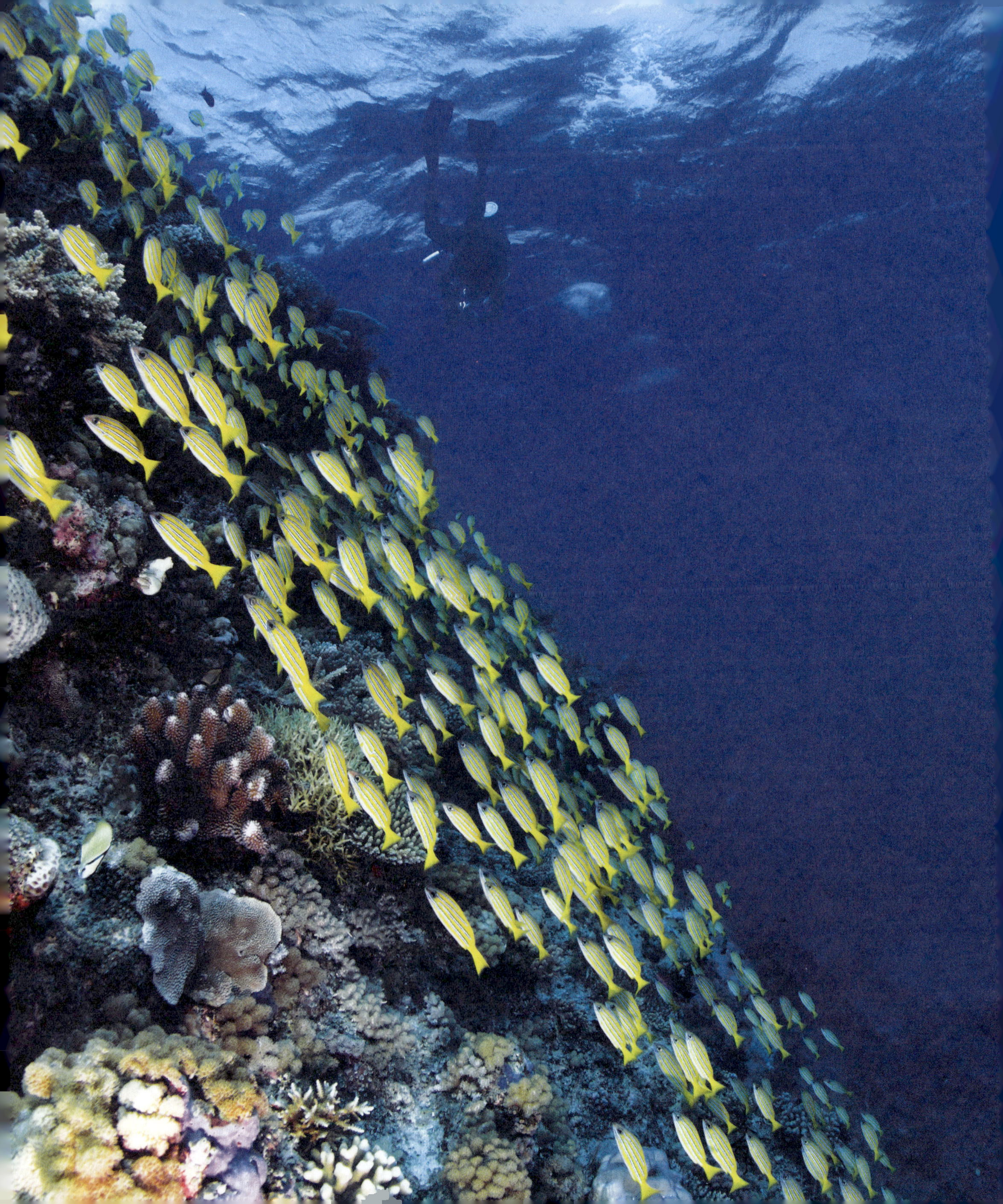

Submerge yourself at a gorgeous section of reef for the world's only chance to swim with dwarf minke whales.

Diving and swimming with minke whales, Ribbon Reefs

Dingaal Country

Contributed by Deborah Dickson-Smith

WHY IT'S SPECIAL

Each Australian winter, the Great Barrier Reef plays host to some very special visitors – dwarf minke whales. This is the only place in the world where you can don a mask and snorkel in warm tropical water and swim with these whales.

Dwarf minke whales visit the northern Great Barrier Reef each June and July, forming the only known predictable aggregation of these whales in the world. The second smallest member of the baleen whale family, growing up to 8m in length, they are only found in the Southern Hemisphere, spending summers feeding in sub-Antarctic waters and migrating to the warm waters of the Great Barrier Reef over winter to breed and give birth. The extroverts of the whale family, dwarf minkes are incredibly inquisitive and often approach boats and snorkellers, sometimes interacting with them for hours.

They are most frequently encountered at the northern end of the Ribbon Reefs, specifically at Ribbon Reef 10, at a site called Two Towers, where the unique position of two isolated pinnacles on the leeward side of the Great Barrier Reef forms a large, protected area: a tailor-made nursery for minke mums and their newborn calves.

The chance of a minke whale encounter is not the only thing that makes a visit to the Ribbon Reefs a special experience. For divers, these reefs are spectacular year-round, with tall pinnacles and dramatic coral formations, covered in vibrant soft and hard corals, teeming with a biodiverse range of marine life, from macro wonders, such as colourful mantis shrimps and nudibranchs, to reef sharks, eagle rays and giant potato cods.

Where
The Ribbon Reefs are around 200km north of Cairns/Gimuy, from where most dive cruises depart.

When
The Ribbon Reefs can be dived year-round, with calm seas and warmer water between Sept and Jan. In June and July, dive boats visiting the Ribbon Reefs can almost guarantee a minke whale encounter. Divers can also expect excellent visibility during those winter months.

Do it
Operating out of Cairns/Gimuy, dive liveaboards Mike Ball Dive Expeditions (mikeball.com) and Spirit of Freedom (spiritoffreedom.com.au) run multi-day trips to the Ribbon Reefs and Coral Sea reefs, such as Osprey, Holmes and Bougainville Reef, every week.

During minke season, they're joined by Pro Dive Cairns (prodivecairns.com) and Divers Den (diversden.com.au), which run three- to four-day trips, offering a mix of diving at the Ribbon Reef's best sites and encounters with dwarf minke whales. These trips are suitable for both divers and snorkellers. For more information and bookings, head online (diveplanit.com).

Fitness: ●●●○○

Fear factor: ●●○○○

Expertise required ●●○○○

Opposite The incredible coral cover at the Ribbon Reefs' Two Towers

THE ADVENTURE

While itineraries vary, dive cruises in minke season usually start by reef-hopping north from Cairns/Gimuy, giving divers an opportunity to take the plunge at Norman, Hastings or Saxon reefs, which are closer to Cairns/Gimuy, then the Agincourt Reefs out from Port Douglas, before steaming north overnight to the Ribbon Reefs.

The next morning, expect to wake up bright and early on the northern Ribbon Reefs, ready to slip quietly into the water not long after sunrise.

On my first minke trip, I didn't need a wake-up call. After a comprehensive briefing the night before, I was fidgeting with anticipation and eager to jump in the water at the earliest opportunity. As soon as I heard the crew in action, I grabbed my mask, snorkel and fins and headed out to the dive deck, where I was told they had already spotted at least 10 minke whales.

After sliding quietly into the water, there was a hushed atmosphere as we waited for our first sighting. At first, some whales appeared and disappeared quickly – nothing more than a brilliant flash of white. They gradually became bolder, swimming closer, until they were cruising by at eye level – if there's a more humbling experience than staring into the eye of a five-tonne mammal on the world's most famous reef, I've yet to find it. It's an encounter you'll remember for years to come.

Even beyond the presence of minke whales, this northern section of the Great Barrier Reef is very special for divers, especially Two Towers at Ribbon Reef 10. The coral cover at Two Towers is beautiful, but it is also a comeback story that gives us hope for the reef.

In 2013 and 2014 this reef was hammered by two cyclones and a devastating crown of thorns sea star outbreak. It was so badly damaged there was hardly any coral cover left at all. Yet when Two Towers was surveyed in the 2020 Great Reef Census, scientists were overjoyed to find it was in considerable recovery. After just six years, the coral cover on this once dead reef was incredible, bringing with it a renewed diversity and density of marine life.

Right Dwarf minke whales are extroverts and often spend hours interacting with snorkellers

Diving and swimming with minke whales, Ribbon Reefs

Above and opposite top This is a passive encounter - snorkellers hold onto a mermaid line, while the minkes come to them
Opposite bottom left and right Encounters with graceful spotted eagle rays and coral trout on the hunt on the pinnacles

Highlights for divers on the Ribbon Reefs include sites such as Pixie Pinnacle, Steve's Bommie, Crackajack, Cod Hole and Challenger Bay, each one a world-class dive in its own right.

Pixie Pinnacle encapsulates everything I love about diving coral reefs, the vibrant colours and teeming marine life. This tall pinnacle on Ribbon Reef 10 descends to around 30m. In the deeper waters, there are enormous gorgonian fans, soft corals and dozens of crinoids. The shallower parts of this pinnacle are even prettier. Here you'll find yourself surrounded by clouds of orange and purple anthias, bright yellow damsels, glass fish, coral trout and anemones.

Rising from 35m to its apex at around 5m, Steve's Bommie never fails to impress with the sheer quantity of schooling fish – jacks, barracuda, snapper – and the pinnacle's dense coral coverage. Look a little closer and you will find more of the reef's masters of camouflage, including leafy scorpionfish and wobbegong sharks.

Crackajack is a tall pinnacle in the middle of the channel between Ribbon 4 and Ribbon 5, descending to the sea floor at around 30m. At its base, you'll find large gorgonian fans and bright-red whip corals, while out in the blue there are schools of fusiliers, jacks and barracuda. In shallower water, from around 15m, you'll find yourself surrounded by colourful anthias, banner fish and damsels, while clouds of glass fish hug the reef, clearing every now and then to reveal lurking coral trout looking for lunch. Look in the nooks and crannies for mantis shrimp, pipefish and banded cleaner shrimp.

At the aptly named Cod Hole, you'll encounter many friendly and enormous potato cods and a few whitetip reef sharks, as well as countless other reef fish and the odd moray eel hiding under a rock. Dive boats have been visiting this site for many years, so the potato cods are completely unfazed by human interaction. In fact, alpha-cod Spot (so named by Spirit of Freedom's master reef guide Michelle Barry) responds to simple hand gestures in the same way a dog would for a few snacks. It makes for great photo opportunities with these gentle giants.

With or without minke whales, diving this section of the Great Barrier Reef is an exhilarating experience.

A code of practice is in place to manage safety for both divers and dwarf minke whales, providing the maximum opportunity to see whales at very close range while ensuring the whales interact on their terms. Abiding by these codes, a maximum of two surface ropes are placed in the water with swimmers then positioned 3m to 4m apart for a safe encounter. The whales control the encounter in that they decide how close they interact.

Most of the Great Barrier Reef tour operators that offer dwarf minke whale expeditions also contribute to scientific research through the Minke Whale Project, and guests are invited to participate. Ongoing research aims to map migratory paths, identifying critical habitats and potential feeding grounds and identify risks and threats beyond the protected waters of the Great Barrier Reef.

Diving and swimming with minke whales, Ribbon Reefs   269

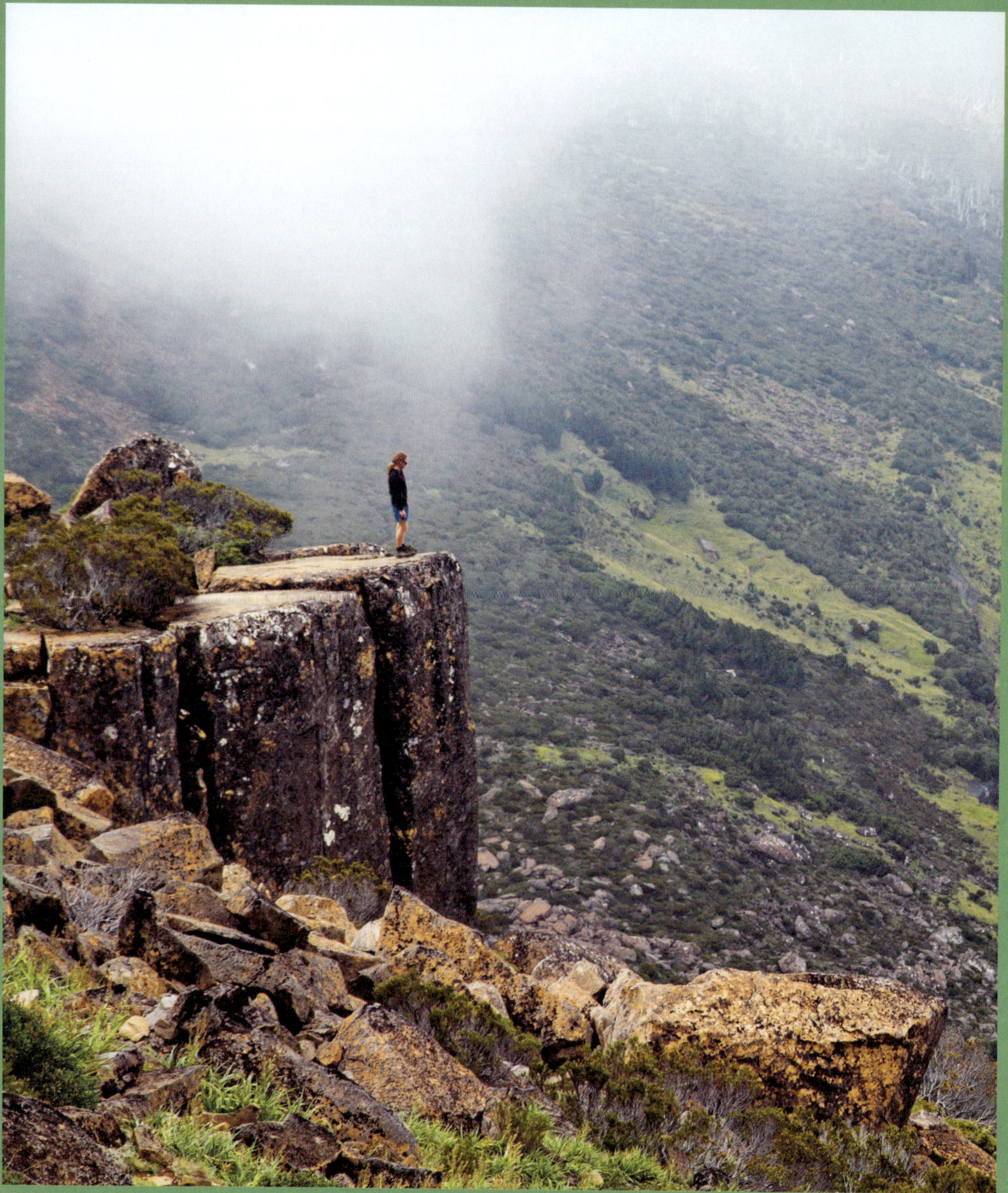

Tasmania

*World-class mountain biking, hiking, canyoning,
rafting and kayaking ... Welcome to adventure island.*

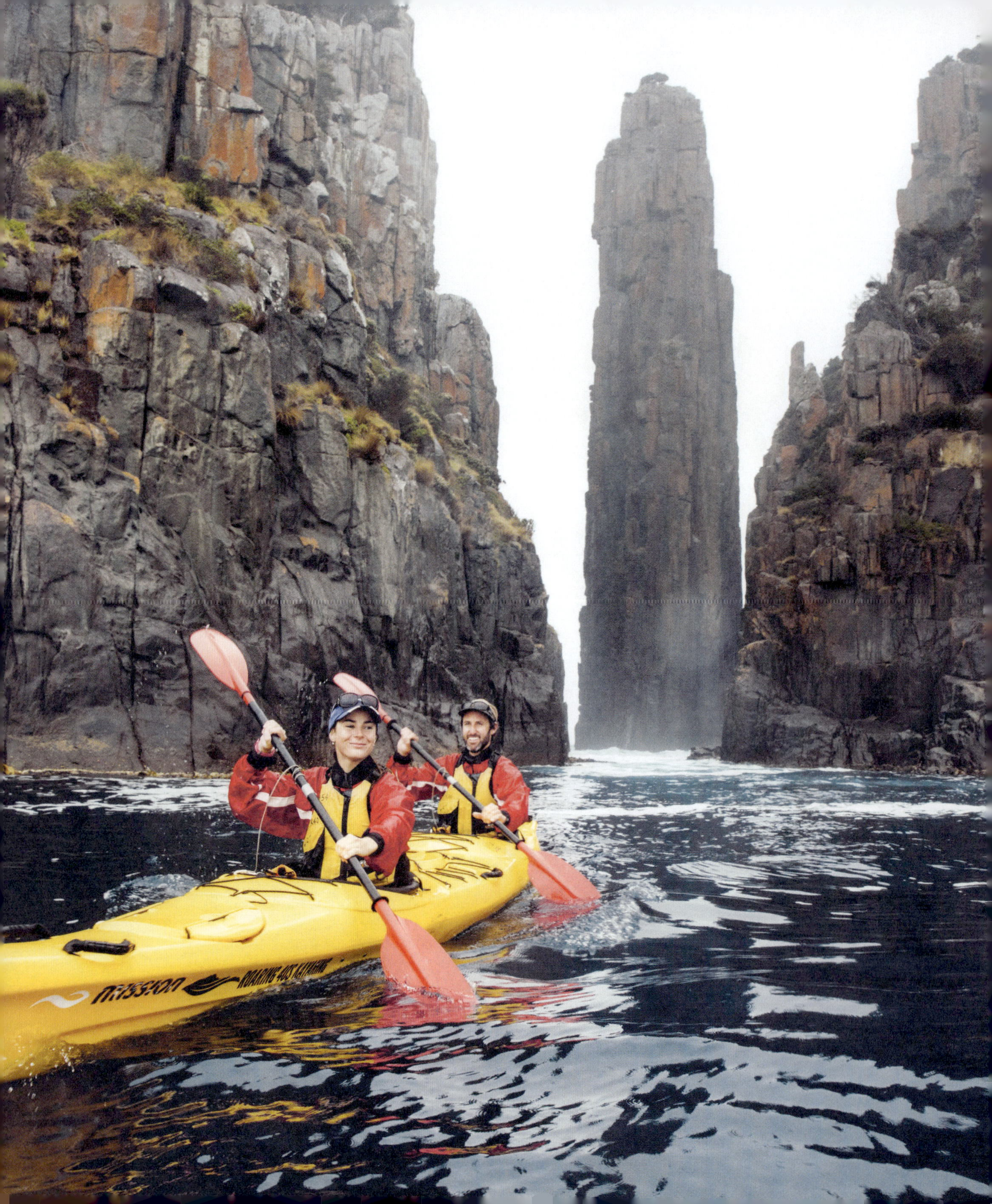
mission
ROARING 40ᴼS KAYAKING

Paddle beneath Australia's highest sea cliffs and a rock icon, as you mingle with fur seals and other wildlife.

Kayaking, Turrakana/ Tasman Peninsula

Palawa Country

WHY IT'S SPECIAL

Chiselled into the coast immediately east of Port Arthur Historic Site, Fortescue Bay has impeccable adventure credentials. It's the finish point of the four-day Three Capes Track, and the start (or finish) of day hikes to the likes of nearby Bivouac Bay and Waterfall Bay. Most famously, it's also the site of the Totem Pole, one of the world's most spectacular coastal rock climbs. But the most enjoyable way to experience Fortescue Bay might well come from the seat of a kayak, paddling far beneath Australia's highest sea cliffs, with fur seals for company and the sort of audience with the Totem Pole that is otherwise only available to the hardiest of rock climbers.

This is unquestionably one of the most beautiful and dramatic kayak daytrips in the country.

Where
Fortescue Bay is 100km south-east of Hobart/Nipaluna, and a 30min drive from Port Arthur Historic Site. Roaring 40s Kayaking's guided trips depart from Cambridge, near Hobart/Nipaluna, or meet at Fortescue Bay.

When
Guided trips operate on Mon and Fri, Nov to April. Southern right whales are sighted from May to Nov, with humpback whales migrating past Tasmania from around May to July and Sept to Nov.

Do it
Book trips with Roaring 40s Kayaking (roaring40skayaking.com.au).

Fitness: ●●●○○

Fear factor: ●●●○○

Expertise required ●●○○○

Above Gliding across Fortescue Bay *Opposite* Kayaking beneath the Candlestick and Totem Pole *Previous* Hiker on the slopes of Mount Ossa, high above the Overland Track

THE ADVENTURE

Make the effort to drive into Fortescue Bay, the longest beach in Tasman National Park, and you'll be greeted by a long white beach that gleams like a smile. For most, this is reason enough to make the 12km detour down a dirt road, but it's really just a pretty preface to more striking natural details further out along the bay's coastline.

The best view throughout the bay is the water view, peering onto the cliffs and coast from a kayak. The launch point for kayak trips, whether independent or on a guided paddle with Roaring 40s Kayaking, is a boat ramp beside the beach's southern end. Come on a fine day and there's a bright welcome from nature, with the bay's sandy shallows gleaming in the clearest, cleanest water imaginable.

The wide bay makes for a natural circuit, setting out along the southern shores, clinging to the cliffs that rise from the water like a bar graph of dolerite. As is common along Tasmania's dolerite coastlines, the cliffs are notched with small caves. If conditions are calm, it's possible to paddle into these caves, backing your kayak up against their rear walls, with each tiny surge of water reverberating like thunder as the swell lifts and lowers you like an elevator.

Back along the shore, strands of kelp from Tasmania's disappearing kelp forests rise above the sea's surface, but round a corner and suddenly what appears to be strands of kelp aren't kelp at all – they're the flippers of fur seals. Near the point of Cape Hauy – one of the two capes in the Three Capes Track (don't ask about the maths …) – is a colony of cohabiting Australian fur seals and New Zealand fur seals. At the base of these cliffs, what appear to be rocks is just as likely to be seals. Don't be surprised to see them slipping into the sea and swimming towards you, as they often seem to be as interested in you as you are in them.

This isn't the only encounter with wildlife that you might experience in this patch of water. Dolphins are often sighted in the bay, and humpback and southern right whales also appear regularly during their migration between Antarctic waters and warmer waters off the Australian mainland.

Right Amazing action above and below water

Kayaking, Turrakana/Tasman Peninsula

Among the seal colony, a narrow channel marks the end of Cape Hauy, separated by just a few metres from a pair of islands known as the Lanterns. Inside this channel, which is a virtual sea canyon, is the area's grandest sight – the tall, slender sea stack called the Totem Pole, which has graced climbing posters the world over and, right beside it, the even taller and larger Candlestick.

Ocean conditions dictate the advisability of paddling into the channel – on a messy day it can be a fierce and dangerous place – but if conditions are kind, it's an extraordinary spot to be in a kayak. With the ocean slapping the cliffs that narrow around you, it's a short paddle past the Candlestick, a wide sea stack more than 100m tall, to the base of the Totem Pole. This 65m-high stack is just 4m wide – the very fact that it's still standing in this wild stretch of sea seems like a miracle in stone – and rises like a needle from among the cliffs.

Pop out past the Totem Pole and things don't get any less dramatic. The Turrakana/Tasman Peninsula coast stretches away south to Cape Pillar, forming a 300m-high wall of sea cliffs that are the tallest in Australia.

Turning around here – either paddling back through the channel or around the Lanterns – it's an open-water crossing to Fortescue Bay's northern shores and into the protected slot of Bivouac Bay. Here, guided trips pause for lunch, sharing the rocky shores with only the few hikers who pass by on the trail from Fortescue Bay to Waterfall Bay.

From Bivouac Bay, it's just 2km back to the boat ramp, but first there's one more worthwhile detour. Immediately along the coast from Bivouac Bay is Canoe Bay, with its entrance guarded by a shipwreck. The *William Pitt* was used in the 1940s to construct the original floating bridge across the River Derwent in Hobart/Nipaluna, and was scuttled in Canoe Bay in 1955 to create a breakwater for moored boats. If you're carrying snorkelling gear in your kayak's hatches, this is the perfect spot to bust it out, ahead of the final paddle back along Fortescue Bay beach to the boat ramp.

Above Beached at Fortescue Bay *Below* Yeah, whatever *Opposite* The rock stars of Cape Hauy: the Totem Pole, Candlestick and the Lanterns.

Turrakana/Tasman Peninsula's long coastline lends itself to extended kayak trips, and there are a couple on offer. Roaring 40s Kayaking also runs a four-day Turrakana/Tasman Peninsula trip exploring the likes of Tasman Arch and the Blowhole around Teralina/Eaglehawk Neck, the waters of Port Arthur, Cape Frederick Hendrick and the cove where Abel Tasman made his only Tasmanian landing in 1642. Southern Sea Ventures (southernseaventures.com) operates a four-day kayak trip that focuses on the migrating whales.

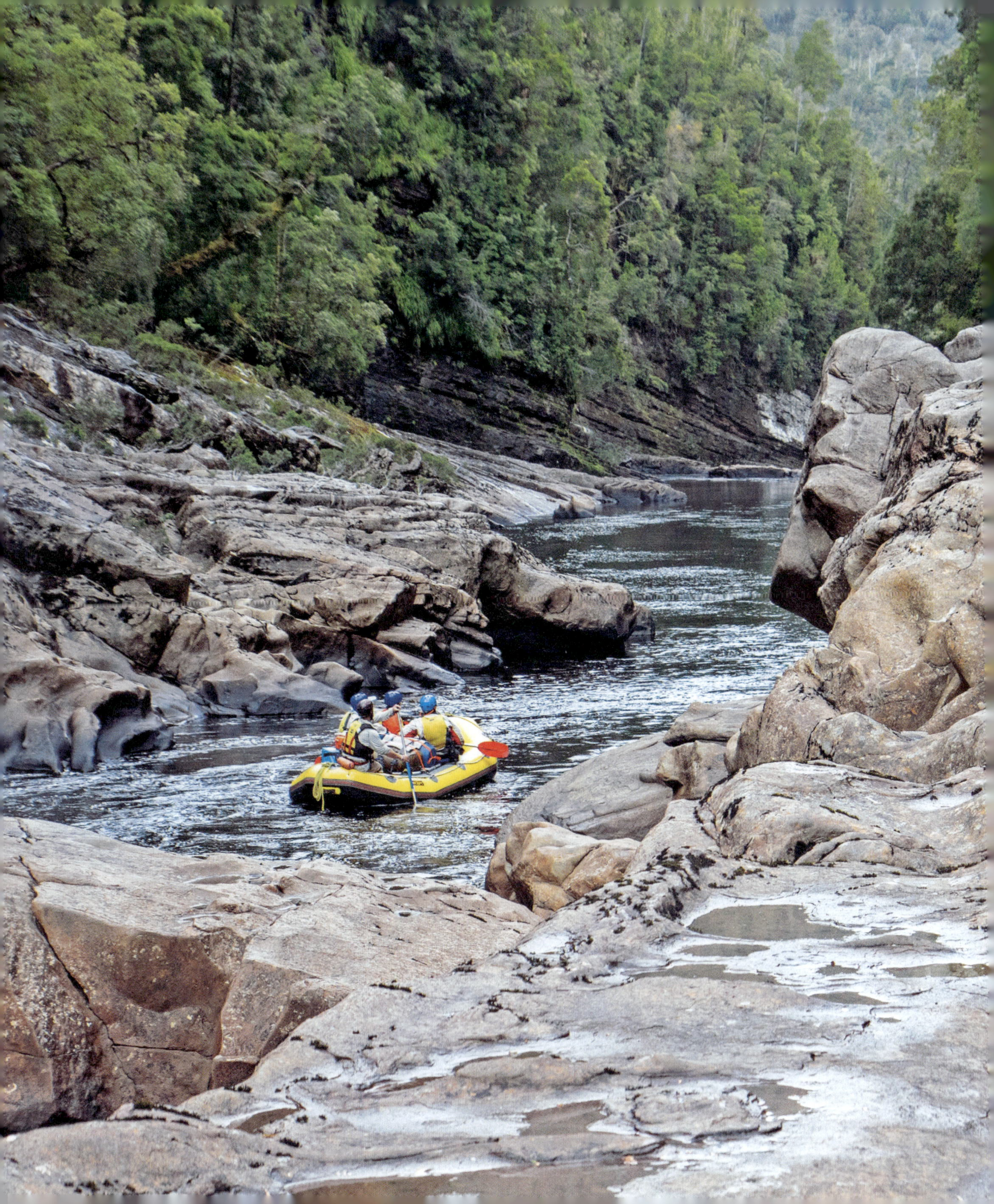

Disappear into the Tasmanian wilderness on a legendary journey along Tasmania's most celebrated river.

Rafting, Franklin River
Palawa Country

WHY IT'S SPECIAL

Some 50 years ago, the Franklin River was a largely unheralded waterway, inaccessible and inhospitable as it flowed through the hidden folds of Tasmania's remote south-west wilderness. Most of its rapids and features hadn't even been named, and fewer than a handful of people had rafted it.

The campaign to prevent the Franklin from being dammed in the early 1980s transformed the river's profile, turning it into one of the most famous waterways in the country. More than 1400 people were arrested during a months-long blockade, and the Hawke federal government was elected with a promise to stop the dams.

Today, the Franklin River flows free, and often furiously, away from humankind's ambitions. Intermittently, its dark waters carry with them small fleets of rafts, on trips that US magazine *Outside* once rated as the world's best river journey.

It's a committing trip – once you launch beneath a highway bridge near Lake St Clair, you're wedded to the river for around eight days. But what a river. This is a waterway that contains not a single patch of cultivated land in its catchment, and not a house or building. There are rapids and stretches of river as intimidating as any in the world, and others with unmatched beauty and serenity, all within 100km of a capital city.

I've spent 25 years travelling the world, writing about outdoor adventures, and I've rafted the Franklin twice, and it remains my most cherished adventure.

Where
The launch point is the Collingwood River bridge, 210km north-west of Hobart/Nipaluna, and 205km south-west of Launceston.

When
Rafting season on the Franklin River runs from around Oct to April.

Do it
The vast majority of people run the Franklin River on guided trips. Deaths have occurred on the river, and therefore only highly experienced paddlers should attempt it independently. Operators include Tasmanian Expeditions (tasmanianexpeditions.com.au), Franklin River Rafting (franklinriverrafting.com) and Water by Nature Tasmania (franklinriver.com). All trips conclude with a pick-up from a yacht, which transports paddlers into Strahan.

Fitness: ●●●○○

Fear factor: ●●●●○

Expertise required
●●○○○ (guided)
●●●●● (independent)

Opposite Exiting Newlands Cascades

THE ADVENTURE

Rafting trips on the Franklin River don't begin on the Franklin. Even though the Lyell Hwy crosses the river between Derwent Bridge and Queenstown, the launch point is on the Collingwood River, another 13km the west. Beneath the highway bridge, rafts are inflated, drums of food and gear strapped aboard and, finally, the rafts are pushed out into the stream and sucked away with the river's flow. The bridge disappears behind – it's pretty much the last that's seen of human endeavour for the next eight days.

A few kilometres downstream, the Collingwood River flows into the Franklin, but how long it takes to get here is less about your efforts and more about conditions. At high water, when the river swells with rainfall, it's a quick sprint to the confluence, but if water levels are low, there's a whole lot of heaving and hauling of rafts over rocks, logs and anything else that intrudes across the river.

On one of my rafting trips, it took us five hours just to cover the 6km to the Franklin. It's a theme that continues down the river – high water can be more intimidating, but low water more tiring. But it can also change quickly here, with rainfall suddenly filling the river and changing the entire dynamic of a trip. It's not uncommon for the river to rise and fall by metres overnight, sometimes stranding rafters for a few days.

Beside the confluence, the honey-coloured waters of the Franklin emerge from a narrow gorge. A few kilometres downstream, the first Huon pines appear, drooping from the banks. One moment there are none, the next they're plentiful as the river wraps around the foot of Frenchmans Cap – one of Tasmania's most prominent mountains (the river runs so close to the mountain that there's a fleeting glimpse at one point along the journey, and then it's never seen again) – entering the first of the Franklin's four major gorges, Descension Gorge.

It was this gorge that foiled the first attempt to kayak the river in 1951, when John Hawkins's kayak was overturned, with the river sweeping him away unconscious. He survived and was rescued, but the trip was over (it would take another two attempts before the river was successfully run for the first time in 1959).

Today, Descension Gorge is just a precursor to bigger and more intimidating things, a chance to feel the rapids ahead of the mighty Great Ravine. But not before the peace of the Irenabyss. Like so many places along the Franklin River, the Irenabyss was named by Bob Brown, the future leader of both the Franklin River blockade and the Australian Greens, who in 1976 was among the first people to raft it. Taken from the Greek words for 'chasm of peace', the Irenabyss is well named, for the river seems to momentarily pause as it flows through the deep and narrow gorge.

A steep hiking trail begins at the Irenabyss, ascending to the summit of Frenchmans Cap, 1200m above, but most groups camp here a night and paddle on.

For two days from the Irenabyss, the Franklin flattens and fills and it's pure pleasure all the way to the Great Ravine, paddling when you wish and not paddling when you prefer. The 60m-high Blushrock Falls pour over a cliff before the river straightens at Inception Reach as if coming to attention for the wild entry into the Great Ravine.

In climbing terms, the Great Ravine is the Franklin River's crux – a string of powerful rapids inside a gorge sunk as deeply as 500m into the mountains. It begins with a set of rapids called the Churn and continues as its starts, crowded with rapids that are like labyrinths around house-sized boulders, logs and disappearing pits of black water.

The first European settler to record sighting the Great Ravine, James Calder, described it as a 'hideous defile' (a description that hadn't improved much by the time Tasmanian Premier Robin Gray called it a 'brown, leech-ridden ditch' during the dam fight), though it's also thought that the first European to sight it might have been escaped convict Alexander Pearce, just before he ate one of his fellow escapees.

The Great Ravine's rapids are so powerful that they require portages. At the Churn, rafters unpack the raft, hauling all their gear – luggage, barrels of food – along narrow cliff ledges, often pulling the rafts along the cliffs behind them. But the Great Ravine is also the yin and yang of the river, with its gut-sinking rapids broken by deep, motionless pools. The first of these is Serenity Reach, just beyond the Churn. This deep stretch of river can be so still as to produce perfect reflections,

Top Pig Trough at Rock Island Bend … beautiful place, awful name *Opposite* The Lost World slot canyon

Rafting, Franklin River 281

Top left, middle and right **Three-step process** - piling out of the raft for a portage, preparing the raft for a rapid, inside the Great Ravine

before the river goes into another white fit through Coruscades rapids. It is indeed a serene pause before tackling the four major rapids still to come through the Great Ravine. It's a curious place where you can hear the violence of Coruscades, but look down onto the still surface of Serenity Reach.

Like all camp spots along this river, rafters roll out sleeping mats onto the bare earth, shielded only by tarpaulins in the event of rain. The unexpected benefit of this is that one night at Coruscades, I discovered myself sleeping beneath a canopy of glow worms – twinkling blue constellations attached to the ferns and forest.

In the morning, the black water suddenly turns white as it dives into Corsucades and beyond. Each time I've been here, it's taken around seven hours to cover the 7km through the ravine, hauling gear over boulders and along the riverbank, dragging and throwing rafts from boulders, piling back into the raft and doing it all again at the next rapid.

The rapids inside the Great Ravine are named like show rides – Sidewinder, Thunderush, the Cauldron – and it's only as the rafts exit the Cauldron that the rapids begin to ease before wearied groups pull up at Rafters Basin for a relieved and restful night.

Another gorge awaits immediately, but Propsting Gorge is the fun after the fury of the Great Ravine. The proposed site of one of the dam walls in the 1980s, Propsting Gorge is now a succession of low rapids, each one runnable. It's the river's most thrilling run, hurtling down the waterway in what feels like the aftershocks of the Great Ravine.

This run concludes at a small waterfall, tipping into Rock Island Bend. If you've only seen one photo of the Franklin River, it's likely to be this spot. In 1982, an image by Peter Dombrovskis of Rock Island Bend became the face of the anti-dam campaign, featuring in double-page political advertisements across Australian newspapers, alerting readers to the sheer beauty of what could be lost.

An overhang along the cliffs just beyond Rock Island Bend serves as a sleeping cave for one of the most beautiful nights of the trip, with Newlands Cascades – the longest rapid on the river – roaring past. It's also one of the final rapids on the river, with the Franklin now flattening and widening as it heads towards its distant confluence with the Gordon River. Its most exciting bits are behind, but there are plenty of river treasures still ahead.

Hidden behind a rack of cliffs halfway between Newlands and the trip's end at Sir John Falls on the Gordon River is Kutikina

Cave, which played a key role in saving the river. Kutikina was occupied by First Peoples from around 20,000 to 12,000 years ago, and an archaeological dig in 1981 found more than 300,000 artefacts – stone tools and bone fragments – in an area of less than one cubic metre inside the cave. It is one of the richest archaeological sites ever found in Australia, and was described by one newspaper in the day as 'the most significant archaeological find in the southern hemisphere'. If the river had been dammed, it would have ended up 50m underwater, but instead it helped the area secure World Heritage status, which was crucial in preventing the dams.

Paddle on and you can drift to the entrance of a hidden canyon known as the Lost World. Here, a large cave narrows into the skinniest of slot canyons, its walls thick with moss in parts, while bare, black and embedded with fossils in others.

As the Franklin washes out into the Gordon River, the waters are dark but the future feels bright. A river was saved, and it flows on, oblivious, continuing its millennia-old passage to the sea and just happening to be one of the world's great river journeys.

> To see Tasmania's wild west coast rivers from a raft without the commitment of eight or nine days, cast your eyes further west to the King River, just outside of Queenstown. Day rafting trips along this river punch through the King River Gorge, which is strung with exciting rapids, before smoothing out into what is essentially a flatwater paddle. Options to vary the trip include a Raft and Steam day, rafting through the gorge and then hopping aboard a steam train on the West Coast Wilderness Railway for the return to Queenstown. Trips are run by King River Rafting (kingriverrafting.com.au).

Rafting, Franklin River

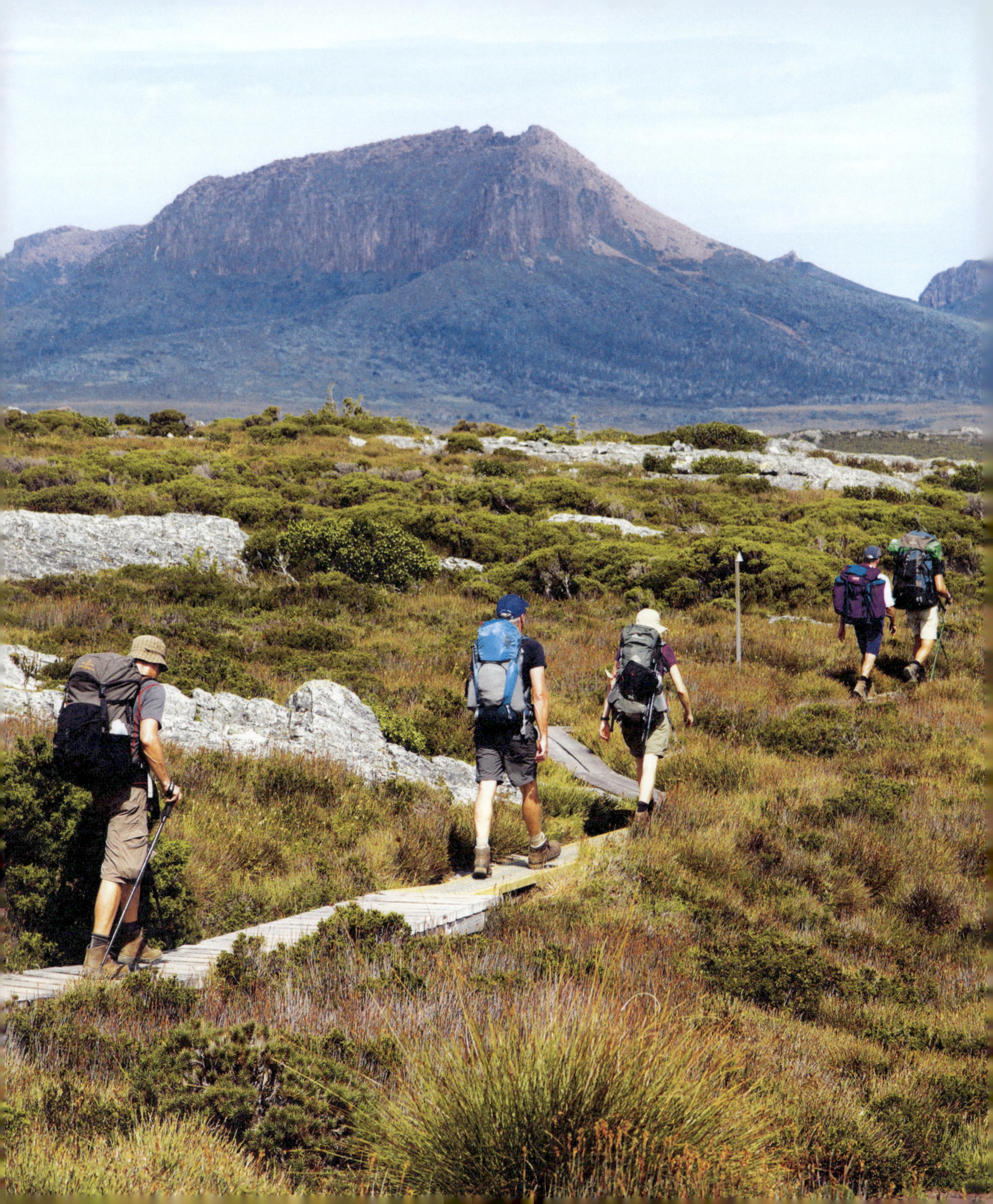

Thread between some of Tasmania's highest and most dramatic mountains on the state's showcase walking trail.

Hiking the Overland Track, Cradle Mountain–Lake St Clair National Park

Palawa Country

WHY IT'S SPECIAL

Long Australia's most famous hike (even if challenged for the title these days by the likes of the Larapinta Trail (*see* p.204) and Three Capes Track), the Overland Track remains the ultimate showcase of Australia's most impressive and abstract collection of peaks. It's a 65km walk (or 82km if you finish along the shores of Lake St Clair, which most hikers skip) through the mountains but mercifully not over the mountains. Instead, it threads through the valleys beneath four of Tasmania's five tallest peaks (with side trails to each one of them), passing alpine lakes, roaring waterfalls and historic huts.

Strung along its course are six hiker huts, neatly spaced to break the walk into manageable portions. Follow the standard six-day itinerary, staying each night in the next hut along the track, and the longest day of walking is just 17km, but more typically between 7km and 10km.

Where
The Overland Track runs between Cradle Mountain and Lake St Clair, the bookends of Cradle Mountain–Lake St Clair National Park. Cradle Mountain is 140km west of Launceston, and 300km north-west of Hobart/Nipaluna. Lake St Clair is 170km south-west of Launceston and 180km north-west of Hobart/Nipaluna.

When
The Overland Track's hiking season is from Oct to May. Summer naturally brings the warmest mountain conditions, while autumn brings the famous changing colours of the fagus, Tasmania's only winter deciduous plant species.

Do it
From 1 Oct to 31 May, permits are required to hike the Overland Track, and it can be walked in only one direction (Cradle Mountain to Lake St Clair). Make bookings at Tasmania Parks & Wildlife Service (parks.tas.gov.au), and plan ahead as there are only 34 spots available to independent hikers each day - they book up fast, especially in summer.

A shuttle service operated by Overland Track Transport (overlandtracktransport.com.au) takes hikers to the start of the track from Launceston, and returns them to Hobart/Nipaluna (or back to Launceston) from the finish.

The Cradle Mountain Huts Walk (taswalkingco.com.au/overland-track) is a luxury guided hike along the track, staying in private huts.

Fitness: ●●●●○

Fear factor: ●●○○○

Expertise required: ●●●○○

Opposite Hiking beneath Pelion West on Pine Forest Moor

THE ADVENTURE

Picture Cradle Mountain and the start of the Overland Track and it's often Dove Lake, pooled so beautifully at the base of the mountain, that comes to mind, but the track's true beginning is a short distance back along the road, at Ronny Creek. The national park's shuttle buses drop hikers at the start of a boardwalk that sets out through classic Tasmanian buttongrass moors, ascends to Crater Lake and then into the steepest section of walking along the entire Overland Track as it rises – aided by chains – to Marions Lookout. The view is a high take on one of the most familiar natural scenes in Tasmania, looking down onto Dove Lake and across to the iconic bowed figure of Cradle Mountain.

Soon, the fin-like summit of Barn Bluff, Tasmania's fourth highest peak, joins the view as the track crosses its most exposed section, skirting the shoulder of Cradle Mountain into Cradle Cirque. On a day of poor weather, nowhere cops it harder than this alpine stretch.

Just beyond Kitchen Hut, a side trail scrambles onto Cradle Mountain's slopes and summit, while there's a second chance to detour away at Barn Bluff. Few hikers will manage to climb both mountains and make the 10.7km walk from Ronny Creek to Waterfall Valley Hut (the first night's accommodation) in a single day. However, it is possible to return to Barn Bluff on the second morning (walking the short distance back from Waterfall Valley to the track junction at Cradle Cirque) and still make it through to stay at Windermere Hut on Lake Windermere that night.

Leaving Windermere Hut on the third morning, you are setting out on the Overland Track's longest day. A big portion of this day is spent crossing Pine Forest Moor, the largest section of buttongrass moorland along the track. A soup of black mud that's easily traversed on boardwalks, it's an empty and barren alpine space, relieved by the views of craggy Mount Pelion West, Tasmania's third highest mountain, and saw-toothed Mount Oakleigh, one of the lower peaks passed on the track but, with its horns of dolerite, also one of the most striking.

If you're looking for a rest day along the track, as many people do, New Pelion Hut is the perfect choice. It's one of the more spacious and best-set of the track's huts. Staring across the Pelion Plains to Mount Oakleigh's column-tipped summit, it contains (like all the huts) sleeping platforms for hikers, tables and a heater. For hardier walkers, or those averse to snoring,

Right Rewarded with iconic views along the track

Hiking the Overland Track, Cradle Mountain-Lake St Clair National Park

Above Mount Oakleigh rising above Pelion Plains *Opposite* Winter wonderland on the summit of Mount Oakleigh

each hut also has wooden tent platforms. Each night it's as though a diverse bush village materialises in and around the huts, dispersing again in the morning.

From New Pelion Hut, you can while away a day wandering out to nearby Old Pelion Hut, built originally for copper miners in the 1890s (there's an old copper mine still hidden behind it), picking through the stones on the bank of Douglas Creek for fossils, or climbing Mount Oakleigh – the endemic pandani bushes high on its slopes are among the tallest I've ever seen. Or you can simply sit out on the deck of New Pelion Hut, savouring the widescreen view of Mount Oakleigh's dolerite columns and saving your strength for the next day, which has potential to be a big one.

If trekkers make only one side trip along the Overland Track, it's often to Mount Ossa, Tasmania's highest mountain. The trail to the 1617m peak deviates from the Overland Track at Pelion Gap, 300 vertical metres above New Pelion Hut and at the end of one of the track's few sustained climbs. Reduce your weight by dropping your pack at Pelion Gap and ascending Mount Ossa with raingear, some warm clothing, a first-aid kit, food and water, but be sure to cover all zips on your backpack as the currawongs on Pelion Gap are seriously adept thieves – it's very common to return from the mountain to find trekkers' gear strewn about the gap by birds.

The Ossa climb can add around four hours – and 500m of vertical ascent – to the walking day, but the lure of standing atop Tasmania's highest point is a siren call for many. The trail skirts adjoining Mount Doris and then ascends steeply between Ossa's cliffs, with some scrambling required. A shorter, less-trafficked side trip from Pelion Gap heads in the opposite direction to 1461m Mount Pelion East. Reaching its rocky, nib-like summit also involves some scrambling, but it's about half the distance and half the time of the Ossa climb, and delivers a view of Mount Ossa and most of Cradle Mountain-Lake St Clair National Park's highest peaks.

If this fourth day of walking is about mountains, the fifth day is pure waterfalls. Past the century-old Du Cane Hut, built by early track guide Paddy Hartnett, the hike burrows into its most impressive stretch of rainforest. Shards of sunlight pierce tiny breaks in the canopy, and a pair of side trails lead away to a trio of waterfalls along the upper reaches of the Mersey River.

The first side trail heads to D'Alton and Fergusson falls, while a short walk ahead is the detour down to Hartnett Falls. Each waterfall has a personality and mood of its own, be it the deep gorge at Hartnett, the ferocity of D'Alton, or the narrow, mossy chasm at Fergusson.

Another day ahead, after rising through Du Cane Gap and spending a night at Bert Nichols Hut, the Overland Track comes to its de facto finish at Narcissus Hut on the northern shores of Lake St Clair, Australia's deepest lake. It's by almost unspoken agreement that the hike ends here, even if the track officially continues along the lakeshore to the park visitor centre at Cynthia Bay. Most people hop onto the lake ferry at Narcissus rather than making the 17.5km haul through rainforest along the length of the lake – in defence of those hikers, it is the longest and most tedious stretch of all, and the finish of choice for only the stubborn. By now, instead, civilisation and post-hike treats – beer, anyone? – are invariably calling. It's hard to refuse the ferry.

> A growing number of hikers are discovering the Overland Track's cold secret: winter. From June to the end of Sept, permits aren't required to hike the track (and it can be walked in either direction). Winter trips aren't to be taken lightly, and are recommended only to highly experienced hikers, but I've hiked it in both seasons and there's a definite magic to a winter crossing. Pack for the worst possible conditions, and consider carrying a pair of snowshoes to make snow travel easier.

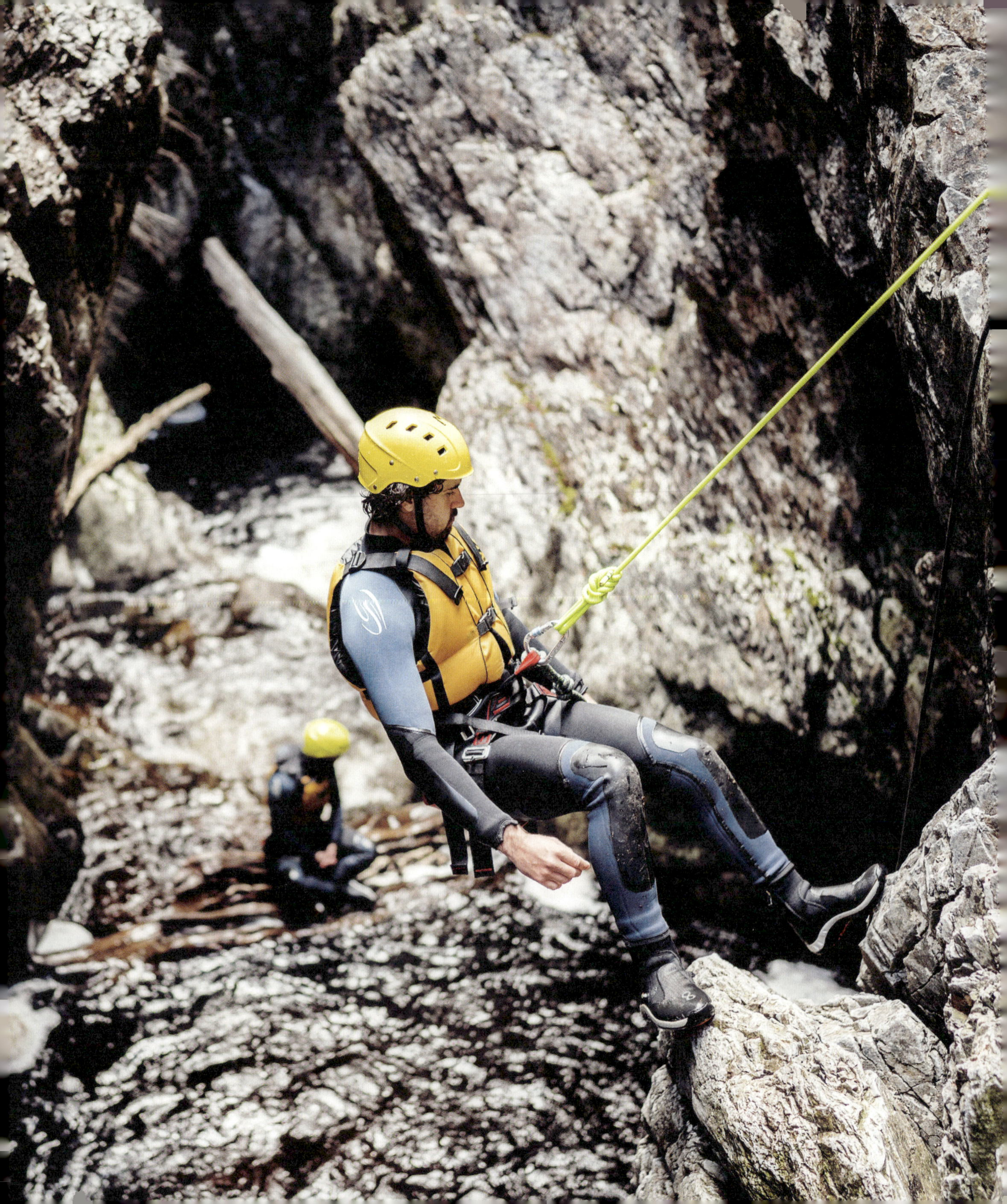

Discover Cradle Mountain's secret underworld as you abseil, swim, slide and leap your way through a narrow canyon.

Canyoning, Cradle Mountain
Palawa Country

WHY IT'S SPECIAL

Most people go to Cradle Mountain and look up, intent on the peak's famously sagging skyline. But there's one very special thing here that can only be found in the cracks of the earth. Flowing out from the much-visited Dove Lake, pooled at the foot of the mountain, is Dove River, carving a deep canyon through the alpine terrain.

To journey through this narrow canyon requires the full set of canyoning party tricks: abseils, high leaps from the tops of waterfalls, swims, wades, slides and traverses over rocky ledges. Dove Canyon is one of the most exciting, easily accessible canyons in Australia, and a chance to see the treasures that Cradle Mountain hides in its cellar.

Where
Trips begin from Cradle Mountain Canyons' office in the Cradle Mountain Visitor Centre, 140km west of Launceston and 300km north-west of Hobart/Nipaluna.

When
Canyoning trips run daily from Nov to April.

Do it
Head to the Cradle Mountain Canyons website for information and to book (cradlemountaincanyons.com.au).

Fitness: ●●●○○

Fear factor: ●●●●○

Expertise required ●○○○○

Above Preps and packing *Opposite* Abseiling into Dove Canyon

Tasmania

THE ADVENTURE

From Cradle Valley, there's a little-used walking track that heads along the top of Dove Canyon, but so narrow is the canyon that you can't ever see into its depths from above. The only way to truly experience this unexpected gash in the earth is to disappear deep within on a guided canyoning trip with Cradle Mountain Canyons.

From the northern entrance to Cradle Mountain-Lake St Clair National Park, the star section of the Tasmanian Wilderness World Heritage Area that blankets around 20 per cent of the state, it's a walk of around 40min to the canyon edge and so-called 'change rock', where you dump packs and climb into wetsuits (this is Tasmania, so there are three layers of wetsuits providing insulation against the canyon's inevitable chill), lifejacket and harness and don a helmet.

From just below 'change rock', the trip begins with its highest abseil – 12m down the canyon cliffs directly into the river, 8km downstream from Dove Lake. The only way out now is through the canyon. Game on.

It's just a few metres downstream to the first leap – a low teaser of things to come. Cliff walls already rise above you, but it's a short wade and walk until you enter the canyon proper, stepping beneath a jam of fallen trees, with the quartzite cliffs suddenly towering up to 50m overhead like the walls of city buildings. You're entering one of the most dynamic places imaginable, changing year by year with the seasonal ebb and flow of the river. Logs shift and water flows change, but always ahead are six major natural features that you must negotiate.

The first of these is Freestyle Falls, soon after you enter the canyon. Here, you find yourself standing at the top of a waterfall, breathing in courage as you face the prospect of the highest jump in the canyon. A dark pool lies 6m below and yet somehow, in this moment, it looks more like 16m. As you stand at the waterfall's edge, it's a step into the unknown. There's an instant where you seem to hang suspended in the air and then you splash down. It's your first big challenge inside the canyon, and one that makes everything ahead seem somehow so much easier.

Left Free falling at Freestyle Falls

Between the six features, you wade or swim downstream through pools and between the narrowing walls. It's a chance to lie back on the surface of the river and look up at the cliffs as they seem to close over you high above. It's a place of pure awe, the tannin-stained waters the colour of tea, but as clean as any water in the world, falling from clouds that arrived from the west, crossing nothing but ocean for thousands of kilometres, and then running down empty mountain slopes. It's worth pausing to drink from it as often as you can.

The cave-like Pit is the next feature, where Jimmy's Falls pours into a dark, narrow slot. On most occasions, you sit at the head of the waterfall and use your arms to push yourself off the ledge, propelling yourself out beyond the waterfall and another deep dive into a pool. At the end of this pool is Dove Canyon's signature feature, the Laundry Chute, which is akin to a slippery slide down a steep ledge. Water has scoured a chute through the rock, and you lie back in this chute, pull in your elbows, take a deep breath and shoot (pun intended ...) away on the stream, luge-style. For canyoners, it's often a favourite moment or a loathed moment – for me, a favourite – plunging them deep into the large pool at its base.

It's a more hectic experience at times of high water, when Jimmy's Falls becomes too powerful to navigate. At these times, you climb to a log wedged between the cliff walls above the Pit and drop around 8m into the water, quickly grabbing a breath before you're sucked through the Laundry Chute.

The canyon is little wider than your hips at the top of the Laundry Chute but opens out wider again at its base, where the final trio of features awaits. They come in quick succession. At Log Jam, so named for the tangle of logs wedged into the base of the canyon, there's a 5m drop into a pool that's too shallow for a safe jump, so a second abseil is required. From atop the highest log, you traverse out across the cliffs and are then unceremoniously dunked into the water as the cliffs recede into an overhang.

Tea Cup Falls are almost as high as Freestyle Falls and, for some people, more intimidating because you leap into a smaller pool. For others, there's no hesitation – it's a chance to step up to the waterfall edge and, emboldened by the challenges already surmounted, confidently leap out into space and water. All fun, no fear.

The final big feature is Horsey Falls, which are slightly lower again but with their own distinct character. The leap lands you in the bubbles at the base of the falls – a soft landing in a cushion of air that allows the nimble and brave to finish acrobatically with a backward or forward flip into the water. Or not.

The canyon ends just beyond another cascade, which provides a gentle slide to finish. To get into this slide, however, you step over a log with a momentous story. When Cradle Mountain Canyons' owner Anthony O'Hern and then business partner Tim Trevaskis first navigated their way through Dove Canyon more than 13 years ago (initially looking to see if it would be suitable for kayaking trips – it wasn't), they believed they might have been the first non-Aboriginal people to do so, but later investigations revealed that they weren't. The journal of James 'Philosopher' Smith, the first person to discover tin in Tasmania and after whom Philosopher Falls, not far west from Cradle Mountain, were named, revealed that he'd passed through Dove Canyon in the mid-19th century, trying to float logs through it to be collected and sold downstream. This final log in the canyon – a massive King Billy pine with an estimated market value of around $60,000 – shows signs of having been felled, and with no real logging in this area, it's likely that it was one of Smith's logs, still wedged here after 160 years of floods and flow.

The world calms beyond here as you wade out of the canyon and back into Tasmanian rainforest. It feels like you've covered kilometres, but you have in fact passed through just 750m of canyon – one of the most adventurous 750m stretches in the country.

Arguably the most physically taxing part of the day now awaits – the climb back out of the canyon to 'change rock' – followed by inarguably the second most physically taxing part of the day: getting out of your wetsuit.

> There are several canyons slashed into the landscape around Cradle Mountain, with three that can be traversed on Cradle Mountain Canyons trips. Higher up the Dove River, the Lost World is a gentler introduction to canyoning – little more than a float – that's family friendly (open to children aged eight years and over). Machinery Canyon presents a string of high abseils down large waterfalls with comforting names like Petrifying Falls. Phoenix Gorge is a step up the chain again, with abseils as high as 30m and zip-line crossings over waterfalls and into pools.

Opposite **Washing through the Laundry Chute**

Canyoning, Cradle Mountain

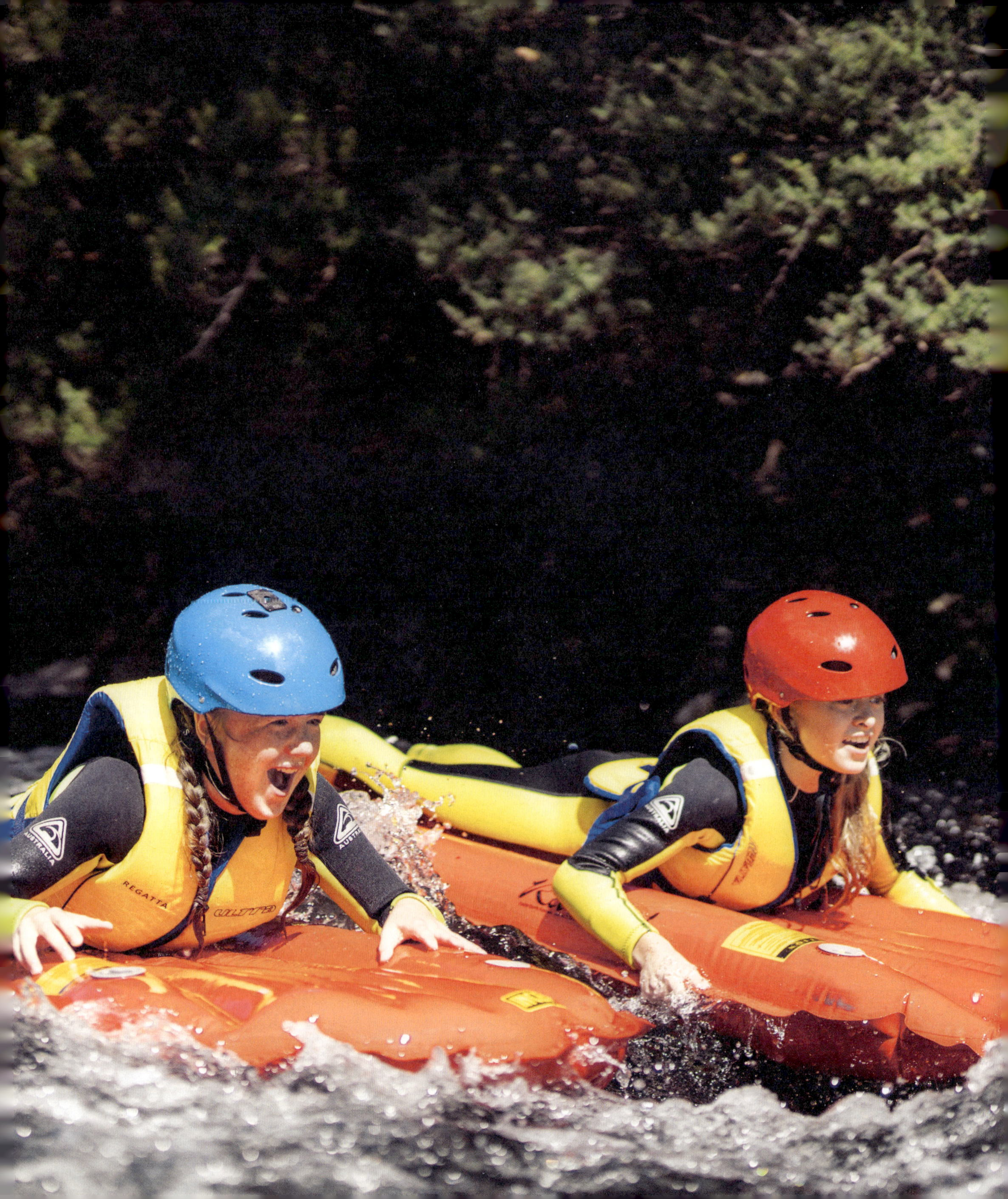
AUSTRALIA
REGATTA

Think rafting for one – hop on a 'sled' and go with the flow through low rapids on the edge of the Tasmanian Wilderness World Heritage Area.

Whitewater sledding, Meander River

Palawa Country

WHY IT'S SPECIAL

In rivers that rage across adrenaline-fuelled countries such as Aotearoa New Zealand, Slovenia, Norway and Zambia, there's an adventure activity known variously as whitewater sledging, river boarding and hydrospeeding. Conceived in the 1970s in the rivers that bleed the glaciers and snowfields of the French Alps, it's akin to whitewater rafting for one, with participants clinging to glorified bodyboards as they splash through wild whitewater rides.

In Tasmania, there's a tamer version of these river runs. On the Meander River, sleds instead of sledges glide through grade I and II rapids that provide just enough churn to feel adventurous, but not enough bump to feel dangerous. River sledding trips skid through a series of small rapids that somehow feel larger because you're eye level with them on this journey along the northern edge of Tasmania's Wilderness World Heritage Area.

Where
Meander is 60km south-west of Launceston, and 200km north-west of Hobart/Nipaluna.

When
Sledding trips on the Meander River operate from Nov to April.

Do it
For information and bookings, head to the Meander Wilderness Experiences website (meanderwildernessexperiences.com).

Fitness: ●●○○○

Fear factor: ●●○○○

Expertise required ●○○○○

Family friendly

Above Flat stretches provide a chance to lie back and enjoy *Opposite* Heading into a rapid

THE ADVENTURE

From Meander, a tiny northern town encased by dairy country, it's a 10min drive to another world. Beyond the pasture's edge, dirt roads narrow to tracks, and trees push high into the sky and tight against the Meander Wilderness Experiences bus as it transports sledders towards the banks of the Meander River.

At a road end about 3km downstream from the Meander Dam, the bus stops and sleds are unloaded from a trailer. Fitted in wetsuits, helmets and life jackets, with a sled tucked under each person's arm, the group follows a narrow track to the river's edge, walking upstream. In just a few minutes, they'll be hurtling back past atop the sleds.

The approach on foot ends beside a small waterfall where there's the option to make a gentle start from below the falls or begin by plunging over the metre-high waterfall. It's a palpably nervous moment – do you really want to start over a waterfall? – but it takes only one or two brave souls to calm the collective tension. The day I sledded the river, all 15 in the group ended up taking the drop, and no-one took a spill.

Ahead now stretches 2km of river to the take-out point, with seven rapids up to 300m in length. Guiding your sled through these rapids is simple. Unlike river boards used elsewhere in the world, which are typically about torso length with handles for steering and grip, the PVC sleds used on the Meander River are body length and reminiscent of li-los. Lying down on them, your arms do all the work, paddling into rapids and steering the sled with a drag of an arm or a change of stroke through the water. As the rapid grabs you, you can hold onto the side of the sled to keep your hands out of the fray, but mostly you keep paddling or use your hands to push off rocks, and to free yourself from the inevitable times that you run aground atop a boulder.

Like the bulk of the rapids, the first one, just a few metres downstream from the waterfall, is a grade I rapid. This is the lowest classification on the international rafting system of rapids, defined as moving water with a few ripples and small waves, and few or no obstructions. In this particular rapid, the river pours over boulders, and it's a dodgem car-like start, with sleds banging into rocks and each other in a fun mess.

The second rapid is the most powerful – the only grade II rapid along this section of river. This denotes rapids that are still at the lower end of the whitewater scale, even if, on a sled, eye to eye with the rapids as they splash in your face, it feels a little wilder.

Below this rapid, the Meander used to split around an island, but a powerful flood in 2014 shifted the shape of the river, moving boulders and blocking one of the channels. Now, the entire river swings right, taking the sleds with it into another rumble strip of rapids.

At the bottom of each rapid, where the river slows and stills, the group regathers. It's a chance to take in the surrounds, with gum trees, wattles and native cherry trees standing tall along the banks.

The most serene moment of all comes at the base of the fourth rapid, on a longer section of flat water that's been suitably christened Flat Zen. Here, sledders are encouraged to lie on their backs on the sleds, staring up into the treetops as they drift gently downstream – a carefree moment in life broken only by the arrival of the next rapid.

After another couple of rapids, the river flows past Fossil Park, a local camping area on a private dairy farm. In contrast to the granite boulders that still fill the river, having washed down from above over millennia, the sedimentary rock here is covered in fossils up to 500 million years of age. It was here that

Above Dodgem cars, whitewater style *Opposite* In the beginning...

Meander Wilderness Experiences owner Daniel Wickham first dreamed up the idea of sledding on the river. While camping at Fossil Park, he'd send fellow campers downstream on li-los, driving into the town of Meander to pick them up a short while later. It was a bit of camping fun that grew into an idea for an adventure business.

Just one more rapid now awaits, and a guide sits at its entrance, pointing out a ruler-straight line through the whitewater to avoid the submerged rocks. Then it's a few more ripples and splashes before you're pulling over to the riverbank and walking back up the slopes, returning to the bus that waits at the edge of the farmland that you might well have forgotten existed in the fun of the river run.

> Want to take a step up from river sledding to river boarding? Head to the Barron River, outside of Cairns/Gimuy, where half-day trips career through Barron Gorge on Australia's only river boarding tour. The section of gorge run by operator Rapid Boarders, beginning just below 250m-high Barron Falls, contains 11 rapids, mostly grade II but stepping up to grade III at the fiercer Cheese Churn. The trip also gives you a chance to try some river surfing by kicking back into standing waves. For details, go to the Rapid Boarders website (rapidboarders.com.au).

Ride the world-class trail network that transformed Australian mountain biking – it's as scenic as it is sensational.

Mountain-biking, Derby
Palawa Country

WHY IT'S SPECIAL

Dial the clock back to 2014 and few people – even mountain bikers – knew that a north-east Tasmanian town called Derby existed. Many might have driven through it on their way between Launceston and the east coast, chuckling at a boulder painted like a fish on its outskirts, but few would even have stopped.

Then something seismic happened. In 2015, the Blue Derby mountain-bike trail network was opened, with a round of the Enduro World Series raced here the same year. Quickly, Blue Derby's trails became the benchmark and blueprint for mountain biking around Australia.

Build a trail network anywhere in the country now – and they've sprouted like mushrooms since Derby's opening – and it's inevitably judged against Blue Derby's trails. And with good reason. Derby's 120-plus kilometres of trails are world-class, curling through rainforest, lapping a lake, squeezing between boulders and flowing as if at one with the terrain and landscape. And at the end of it all, you can always grab a sauna atop the lake.

Tasmania

Where
Derby is around 100km north-east of Launceston, and 300km north of Hobart/Nipaluna.

When
The best riding is outside the wet winter season. Derby fills with bikes through summer and Easter school holidays, bringing a sense of cycling fraternity, though the trails are less crowded outside those holiday times.

Do it
The Blue Derby website (rideblluederby.com.au) has trail and accommodation information.

Shuttle operators in town include Vertigo MTB (vertigomtb.com.au), MTB Express (mtbexpress.com.au), Up Down Around MTB (updownaround.com.au) and MAD MTB (madmtb.com.au).

Shredly's (shredlys.com.au) operates camping-based mountain bike tours in Derby, while the Blue Derby Pods Ride (bluederbypodsride.com.au) is as much about comfort as cycling, staying each night in pods hidden within the trail network.

Fitness: ●●●○○

Fear factor: ●●●○○

Expertise required ●●○○○

Family friendly

Opposite Rolling through a bend on Krushka's trail

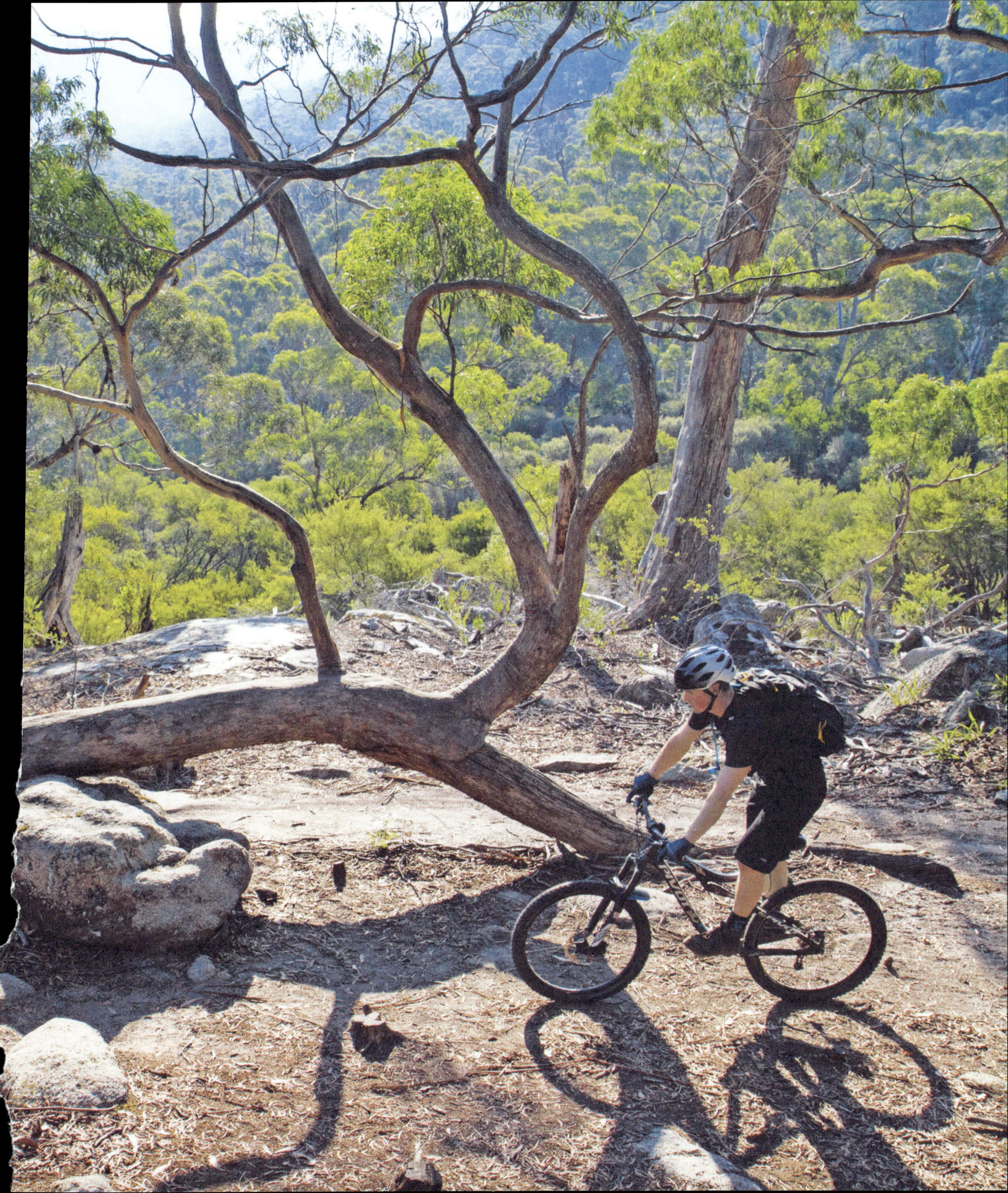

THE ADVENTURE

If your driving maps aren't clear about Derby's location, don't worry. You'll know you've hit the old tin-mining town when the streets fill with more bikes than cars. Storefronts here are either cafes or bike shops, and kids in helmets and an armoury of protection swirl about a pump track beside the Ringarooma River. It's Australia's most bike-filled bike scene.

Blue Derby's major trailheads are in the town itself, making it simple to get riding. At this lower end of the network, a gentle trail crosses the river on a bridge to lap Briseis Hole, a one-time tin mine that suddenly became a lake when it filled with water during a 1929 flood that killed 14 people in Derby.

Back across the river, another green (easy) trail disappears into bush to begin a lap through the Cascade River valley, as well as provide access to most of the lower trails. The much-photographed Twisties creates a dizzying opening, coiling tightly up the slopes, before the trail skims past Tasty Trout Falls in an early heads-up that Derby's mountain biking is as scenic as it is energetic. As this loop works its way back towards town, a side trail plummets down to the Derby Tunnel, built in the 1880s by a miner trying to sneak his tailings out beneath another miner's lease. On a bike, you need to crouch to fit beneath the ceiling of the faintly lit, 600m-long tunnel, freewheeling down a gentle slope as you do. It's one of the most enjoyable moments of mountain biking in the country.

Other trails run like tentacles off this green loop, heading up and into the surrounding hills, but much of the grunt work can be avoided by using Derby's array of shuttle services. Shuttle buses can deliver you to the top of the Blue Tier, the mountains that rise in rainforest-covered slopes to Derby's east; to the Atlas trailhead outside of Weldborough; and to the Black Stump above Derby.

From the Black Stump, a series of blue (intermediate) trails (and a black or two) drape back down the slopes into Derby. Swirl through the berms (banked turns) of Flickety Sticks down one slope, or be guided down another slope by a 120-year-old water race on Kingswall.

Blue Derby's crowning moment comes, literally, atop the Blue Tier, where the Blue Tier trail (blue) provides a remarkable diversity of scenery in just 22km of riding. Setting out across subalpine clearings and traversing the range, it finishes on arguably the network's finest descent, plunging through rainforest and rolling between tall tree ferns like slalom posts. A well-travelled mountain biker once described this Blue Tier ride to me as the best trail in the world.

Above Green and at times mean: Blue Tier trail *Opposite left and right* Boulders and beach: rolling through rock fields on the Bay of Fires Trail ahead of its sandy finish at Swimcart Beach

Complete the descent by meeting a shuttle bus at the Weldborough Hotel, near the base of Blue Tier, and heading out to nearby Atlas trail, where the plunge into Derby continues, quickly passing a lookout over the surrounding hills and then bumping downhill over roots, rocks and berms – the tightest and steepest of these turns are saved until almost the end of the 15km trail. Though also a blue trail, Atlas is a little more technical than Blue Tier, so approach with caution.

Back atop the mountains, at the start of the Blue Tier trail, Derby's mountain-bike trails blur into the St Helens Mountain Bike Trails. Blue Tier trail shares a starting point with the Bay of Fires Trail (blue), St Helens's marathon-length opus on wheels, descending the Blue Tiers's eastern slopes (the opposite side of the range to the Blue Tier trail) to finish 42km later – and 800m lower – on the white sands of Larapuna/Bay of Fires. Though the Bay of Fires trail isn't officially part of the Blue Derby network, it warrants inclusion in any Derby visit, and can be accessed by shuttles from the town.

At the end of it all, there's the Floating Sauna Lake Derby, back atop Briseis Hole, right beside the lakeside trail.

Balanced atop a pontoon, the wood-fired sauna can provide a restorative finish to riding days (or an excuse not to ride). Book ahead online (floatingsauna.com.au), step onto the pontoon, put yourself on a slow boil, then leap into the lake. Rinse and repeat. There's no better end to a Derby day.

Derby's success as a mountain-bike destination has inspired numerous new networks across Australia, and nowhere more so than around Tasmania itself. A veritable peloton of trails has followed in Blue Derby's wheel tracks, beginning at Maydena (maydenabikepark.com), the Southern Hemisphere's largest gravity-focused bike park - 820m of descent from top to tail; and spreading to St Helens (sthelensmtbtrails.com.au); Wild Mersey (ridewildmersey.com.au); the west coast (mtb.westcoasttas.com.au); Penguin; the Dial Range; George Town (georgetownmtbtrails.com.au); and to tracks across the foothills of kunanyi/Mount Wellington in Hobart/Nipaluna.

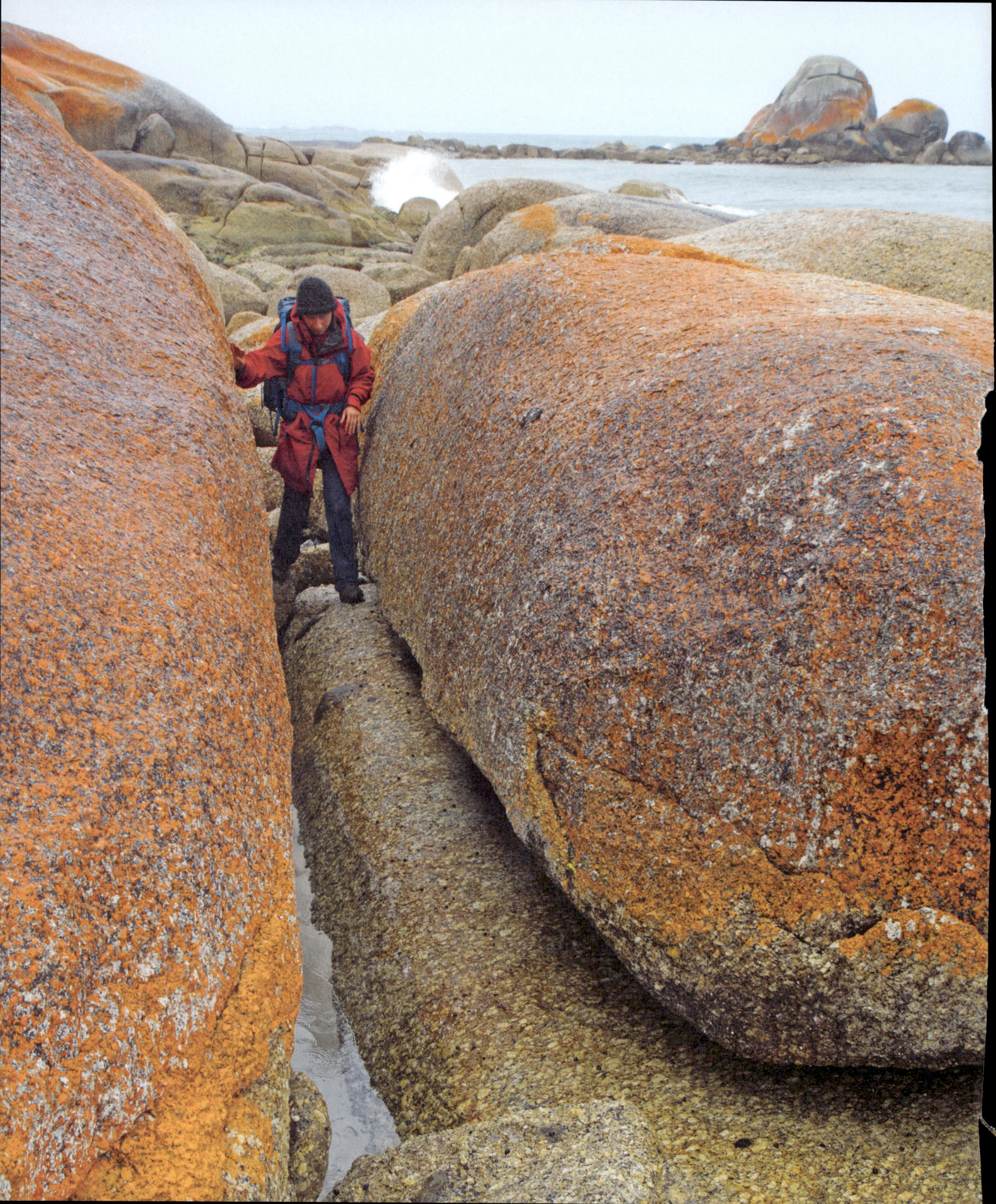

Walk in the footsteps of Tasmania's original inhabitants on a guided Palawa-led hike filled with culture, history and beauty.

Hiking the wukalina Walk, Larapuna/Bay of Fires

Palawa Country

WHY IT'S SPECIAL

On the sands of Larapuna/Bay of Fires, footprints wash away quickly and yet there remain prints of sorts here as indelible as the geology itself. For millennia, Palawa People have lived along this vibrant coastline, which took its European name from the dozens of fires that English explorer Tobias Furneaux saw burning along the coast in 1773.

With its blue seas, white sands and splashes of orange lichen seemingly drizzled over the granite boulders and headlands, Larapuna/Bay of Fires is one of the most beautiful stretches of coastline in Tasmania, if not Australia. In 2018, it became the focus of the first tourism venture from the Palawa community, with the launch of the wukalina Walk. Owned and guided by Palawa People, the four-day hike follows this stunning coastline from near the top of Mount William National Park to Eddystone Point Lighthouse, mixing natural beauty with cultural immersion, from bush tucker, to kelp basket making, creation stories and cultural sites.

Suitably, it's a walk through largely trackless country, guided by long, dazzling beaches in no need of tracks, spending nights in an architecturally designed camp and the cottages of a remote lighthouse.

Where
The wukalina Walk begins at the Elders Council of Tasmania Aboriginal Corporation in Launceston. From here, it's about a 2.5hr drive to Mount William National Park.

When
The wukalina Walk operates from Sept to May.

Do it
Find more info and book at wukalina Walk's website (wukalinawalk.com.au).

Fitness: ●●●○○

Fear factor: ●○○○○

Expertise required ●●○○○

Opposite Lichen this beach walking

THE ADVENTURE

Mount William – 'wukalina' to the Palawa – is a small mountain that rises alone off the plains of Tasmania's north-east, and it's here that the namesake wukalina Walk first gets into step. Rising above grassy plains that fill with wombats and wallabies on dawn and dusk, wukalina/Mount William stands just 215m above sea level, but it's the most significant bump in this uncharacteristically flat corner of Tasmania.

After driving to Mount William National Park from Launceston, the walk begins up its slopes which yield easily – it might take only 45min to reach the summit. Though it's low, the summit affords views across Bass Strait to Truwana/Cape Barren Island and mountainous Flinders Island. From this summit, guides tell, fire signals were sent to the islands – an overland telegraph in smoke.

Returning to the base of the mountain, the walk sets off overland towards the coast, crossing the plain to a cleverly hidden track junction cut specifically for the wukalina Walk. It's easy walking, as it will be on all four days, with the murmur of the ocean calling you forward. Kunzea trees scent the air like butterscotch, and though the bush looks like nothing more than ordinary coastal scrub, you'll learn over the coming hours and days that it's also a rich larder of Traditional foods and medicines.

As the sound of the ocean rises, camp nears, but this is no ordinary camp. The walk's base for the first two nights, krakani lumi, is a stylised, architecturally designed re-creation of Traditional Palawa shelters. The communal area is a dome cut into the design of the camp's hub building, with chairs and bean bags forming a semi-circle on a deck around a fire-pit, on which dinners featuring the likes of wallaby and muttonbird are cooked.

Timber sleeping pods are dotted around the hub, each one with an ingenious winch design that cranks open one of the walls to reveal the entrance to safari tent–style accommodation. The interior of each pod is also dome-shaped, like old Palawa shelters, with wallaby throws across the bed. A classically spectacular Larapuna/Bay of Fires beach is just a 5min walk away.

Right The finish line ahead: Eddystone Point Lighthouse

Hiking the wukalina Walk, Larapuna/Bay of Fires

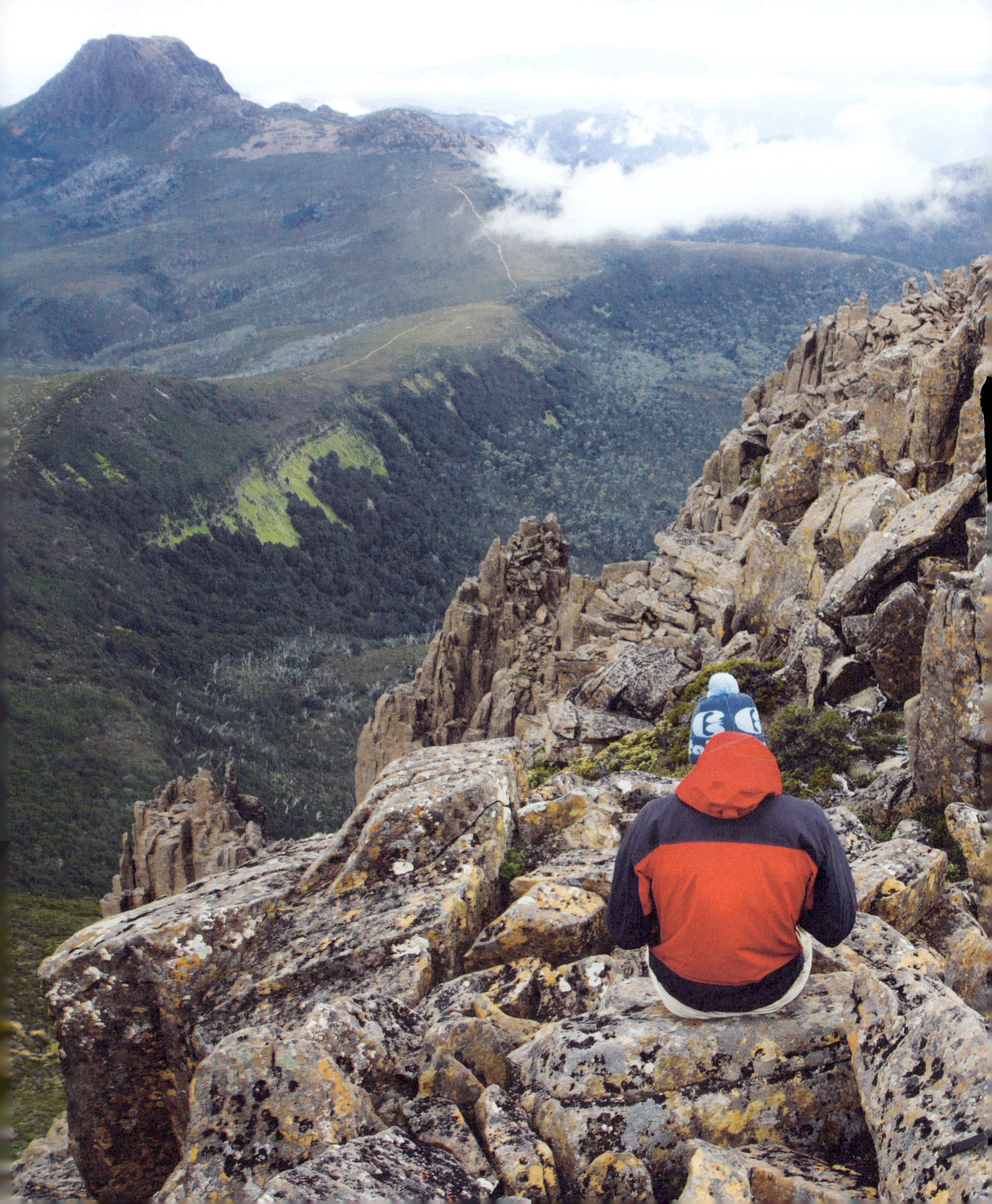

See the state from multiple elevated angles on its premier mountain challenge, climbing the 158 mountains that rise above 1100m with a drop of at least 150m around them.

Climbing the Abels, across Tasmania

Palawa Country

WHY IT'S SPECIAL

In Scotland, there's a much-loved mountain quest called Munro bagging, which sees hill walkers attempting to climb the country's 282 'Munros' – mountains that exceed 3000ft (914.4m) in height. Among Scottish walkers, it's a minor national obsession to climb them all.

Inspired by the Munros, Tasmania has the Abels. Compiled by local bushwalker Bill Wilkinson in the 1990s, the Abels are the Tasmanian mountains that exceed 1100m in height, with a minimum drop of 150m on all sides. Named after Abel Tasman, the first European to sight Tasmania, there are 158 such mountains across the state, from lofty Mount Ossa, Tasmania's highest mountain at 1617m, to barely-made-it Marriotts Lookout at 1100m.

These mountains are the pinnacle of Tasmanian hiking quests. There are books about Abels, decks of cards featuring the Abels, and many minds and feet in pursuit of Abels. You don't have to climb them all to begin to feel the obsession – at the time of writing, just 31 people had completed all 158 peaks – but start out with a plan to climb just a few and you might be surprised where it leads.

Where
The Abels are dotted right across Tasmania.

When
Many of the more challenging and remote peaks are best attempted in late spring, summer or early autumn, while several of the easier-to-reach summits can be scaled in winter.

Do it
The definitive guide to the Abels is the two-volume *The Abels: Tasmania's Mountains over 1100m High*, edited by Bill Wilkinson.

The Abels also have their own website (theabelmountains.com.au), which includes a full list of peaks.

Fitness: ●●●●○

Fear factor: ●●○○○

Expertise required ●●●○○

Opposite Hiker atop Barn Bluff, looking out to Cradle Mountain

THE ADVENTURE

Ask any Abelist, as those who've complete all 158 mountains are called, and they'll tell you that their favourite peaks are the remote and trackless ones, but every quest begins somewhere, and Abels challenges typically start with Tasmania's more accessible mountains.

The prime candidate for an easy first ascent is kunanyi/Mount Wellington, the hulking figure at Hobart/Nipaluna's back. You can drive to the top of this Abel (but do you really want to start that way …?), or rise up its slopes on a web of trails from the city. But kunanyi's Abel ambitions don't stop there. The Wellington Range extends west from the summit, taking in a line of largely unheralded peaks – Collins Bonnet, Trestle Mountain, Mount Marian – that are also Abels, connected by trails that rise up the range from Collinsvale.

A 90min drive out of Hobart/Nipaluna, Mount Field National Park – the oldest national park (along with Freycinet) in Tasmania – encompasses five Abels, making it a rich picking ground. There are defined walking trails to Mount Field East and Mount Field West, while to get to the far-flung latter you have to cross the Rodway Range, itself an Abel. Tick, tick. Florentine Peak is reached by heading off track, detouring off the trail to Mount Field West near K Col, while Mount Lord sits remote and removed, requiring good navigation and off-track skills to reach it.

A perfect way to lock away another cluster of Abels is to combine the effort with an Overland Track hike (*see* p.285). Though the Overland Track threads largely through the valleys between peaks, it's stitched with side trails that lead up to summits. In an extended trip along the Overland Track, you could climb more than a dozen Abels, some near and some far. Popular summits along the track include Cradle Mountain, Barn Bluff, Mount Oakleigh, Mount Ossa, Mount Pelion East and, with a longer detour, the Acropolis.

Right The descent begins on Mount Murchison

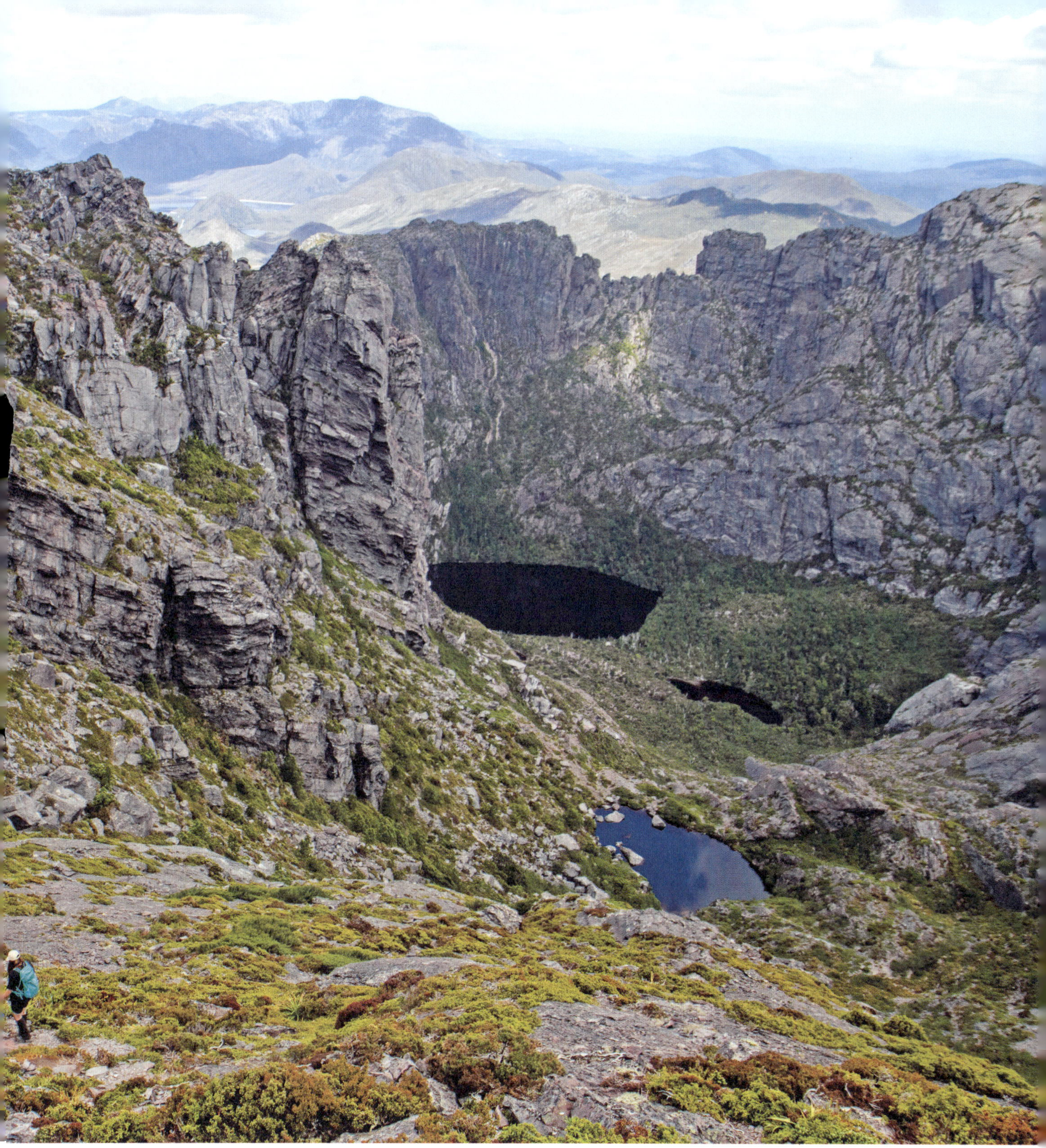

Tasmania

Cradle Mountain can also be climbed on a long day hike from Dove Lake, rounding the lake and scrambling through the cliffs of Tasmania's fifth highest and most famous mountain to a broad view across the Tasmanian highlands and the other peaks strung along the Overland Track. Barn Bluff and Mount Ossa are similarly dextrous climbs, with equally rewarding views. Range out further as you traverse the Overland Track and there are Abels such as Mount Pelion West, Mount Thetis, Mount Emmett, Mount Achilles, Perrins Bluff, Castle Crag, Mount Massif, Mount Gould and Mount Olympus in striking range.

Read in isolation, a list like that one could lead you to think that the Abels are something you might knock off in a summer, but so many of the mountains are difficult to reach and demand years of commitment to the challenge. For every kunanyi, Cradle Mountain or The Needles, near to roads and reachable in a day, there's a Tramontane, West Portal and Federation Peak, requiring demanding multi-day outings. It often takes 15 to 20 years to complete all 158 peaks – I once spoke to an Abelist who felt he'd hurried through them in 12 years, though the record at the time of writing (and likely well beyond) for a full round of all 158 Abels was a remarkable 158 days.

To climb all 158 Abels is to just get started in the Tasmanian mountains. This lumpy state is slathered in peaks - more than 480 of them, to be exact - which has, in turn, created a second mountain challenge for the seriously keen. The Hobart Walking Club has produced a list of every mountain in Tasmania, assigning a point value (between one and 10) to each of them, according to the difficulty of the climb and access. Climb every mountain in the state and it totals 900 points, though if you're just getting started, it's going to take a while to get past even the 200 points needed to become more than a 'Dishonourable Peak-Bagger'. Find the spreadsheet of peaks online at Hobart Walking Club (hobartwalkingclub.org.au, follow the links to Resources and click on 'Peak Baggers List').

Top Scaling a boulder field on the climb to Mount Anne
Opposite top left Pandani and flowering scoparia atop Mount Eliza
Opposite top right Water views from the slopes of Mount Murchison
Opposite bottom Dawn light on the climb to Mount Anne

INDEX

A
Abels, the Tas. 309-11
abseiling, Mount Buffalo Vic. 87-9, 92, 93
Absolute North Charters (ferry) 251
Acropolis Tas. 310
Adelaide/Tarndanya SA 109-11, 117, 118, 223
Adelaide Dolphin Sanctuary SA 113-15
Adelaide International Bird Sanctuary National Park SA 114
Adelaide Oval SA 109-11
Adnyamathanha Country 132, 138
Agincourt Reefs Qld 266
Air Play Hang Gliding 15
Airlie Beach Qld 239
Alarm Clock, Tully River Qld 259
Albany WA 161
Alexandra Cave, Naracoorte Caves National Park SA 153
Alice Springs/Mparntwe NT 204, 207, 211-13
Alice Springs Helicopters 211
Alice Springs Telegraph Station NT 204, 207, 213
Alpine National Park Vic. 98
Alpine Nature Experience 97, 98
Anangu Country/People 215-17
Angaston SA 118
Anglesea Vic. 69
Apwelantye (trail), Alice Springs/Mparntwe NT 213
Arakwal Country/People 37, 41
Arapiles Climbing Guides 71
Arkaba Consrvancy, Ikara-Flinders Ranges SA 132, 135, 136
Arkaba Walk, Ikara-Flinders Ranges SA 132-7
Arrernte Country/People 204, 208
Arthurs Seat Vic. 21
Auburn SA 118

B
Back of Falls climb, Falls Creek Vic. 84, 85
backcountry skiing 47
Guthega, Snowy Mountains NSW 43-7
Baird Bay SA 114
Bairnsdale Vic. 105
Bald Hill NSW 23-5
Balloon Aloft Canberra 55, 56, 57
ballooning, Canberra/Ngambri/Ngunnawal ACT 55-7
Ball's Pyramid, Lord Howe Island NSW 94
Bamurru Plains NT 100
Bandjin Country 251
Banyjima Country/People 187, 188
Barn Bluff Tas. 286, 310, 313
Barngalla Country 120
Barossa Bike 117
Barossa Trail SA 117, 118
Barossa Valley SA 117-19
Barron Falls Qld 299
Barron Gorge Qld 299
Barron River Qld 299
Bass Coast Rail Trail Vic. 105
Bay of Fires Lodge Walk, The Tas. 137
Bay of Fires Trail Tas. 303
Beechworth Vic. 119
Bellarine Peninsula Vic. 61
Bells Beach Vic. 64-9
Bells Track, Bells Beach Vic. 68
Belongil Beach NSW 40-1
Benarkin Qld 232
Bert Nichols Hut, Overland Track Tas. 287
Beyond the Edge trips 91, 92
Beyond Skyway, Blue Mountains NSW 17-21
Bibbulmun Track WA 161
Big Lagoon, Francois Peron National Park WA 174
Bivouac Bay Tas. 273, 276
Blackbutt Qld 231
Blacksand Beach, Hinchinbrook Island/Munamudanamy Qld 252
Blanche Cave, Naracoorte Caves National Park SA 153
Blinman SA 141, 142
Blowhole Tas. 277
Blue Derby mountain-bike trail network Tas. 300-3
Blue Derby Pods Ride 300
Blue Derby website 300
Blue Lake, Mount Gambier SA 145
Blue Mountains Adventure Company 13
Blue Mountains NSW 13-21, 223
Blue Tier trail, Derby Tas. 302, 303
Blues Point, Sydney NSW 9
Blushrock Falls Tas. 280
Boambee Beach NSW 27-9
Boon Wurrung/Bunurong People 61
Boroomba Rocks ACT 223
Bougainville Reef Qld 265
Bowen Qld 240
bridge climbs
Matagarup Zip+Climb, Perth/Boorloo WA 5, 157-61
Story Bridge Adventure Climb, Brisbane/Meanjin Qld 5
Sydney Harbour Bridge NSW 3-5
BridgeClimb tours 3, 4, 5
Bright Vic. 25, 94
Bright Adventure Company 87, 88, 89
Brinkley Bluff NT 208
Brisbane/Meanjin Qld 5, 221-3, 225
Brisbane Valley Rail Trail Qld 231-3
Briseis Hole, Derby Tas. 302, 303
Bronco Yards (trail), Alice Springs/Mparntwe NT 212
Broome WA 307
Brunswick River NSW 41
Bullock Island Vic. 105
Bundegi Reef WA 184
Bundjalung Country 37
Bungandidj Country 145, 151
Bungle Bungle Wilderness Lodge WA 100
bungy jumping, Cairns/Gimuy Qld 260-3
Burnley Bouldering Wall, Burnley Vic. 63, 223
Burrawa Climb, Sydney Harbour Bridge NSW 3-5
Byron Bay NSW 25, 37-41

C
cable cars 21
Cage of Death, Crocosaurus Cove, Darwin/Garramilla NT 195-7
Cahills Crossing, Kakadu National Park NT 197
Cairn Beach, Whitsunday Island Qld 243
Cairns/Gimuy Qld 21, 25, 256, 259, 260-3, 265, 266, 299
Caldwell Qld 251
Cambridge Tas. 273
camel treks, Ikara-Flinders Ranges SA 138-43
Canberra/Ngambri/Ngunnawal ACT 55-7
Canberra Balloon Spectacular ACT 57
Candlestick, Turrakana/Tasman Peninsula Tas. 276
Canoe Bay Tas. 276
canoeing
Glenelg River Vic. 76-9
Nitmiluk National Park NT 199-203
see also kayaking
canyoning
Blue Mountains NSW 13-15
Cradle Mountain Tas. 291-5
Cape Bridgewater Vic. 79
Cape Byron NSW 37, 40, 41
Cape du Couedic, Kangaroo Island SA 125
Cape Hauy Tas. 274, 276
Cape Jervis SA 142
Cape Nelson Vic. 79
Cape Pillar Tas. 276
Cape to Cape Walk WA 137
Cape Vlamingh, Rottnest Island/Wadjemup WA 167
Cardstone Weir, Tully River Qld 259
Carlo Sandblow Qld 237
Carnarvon Great Walk Qld 243
Castle Crag Tas. 313
Cataract Gorge, Launceston Tas. 21
caving
Mount Buffalo Vic. 89
Naracoorte Caves National Park SA 151-3
Champagne Falls, Tully River 259
Charlotte Pass NSW 51, 52
Chinaman's Hat, Port Phillip Vic. 62
Churn, the, Franklin River Tas. 281
Cid Harbour, Whitsunday Island Qld 243
Clare SA 117, 118
Clare Valley SA 117-19

Clare's Riesling Trail SA 117, 118
Clarkes Beach NSW 37, 38
climbing
   the Abels, across Tasmania 309-11
   to the top of Australia, Mount Kosciuszko NSW 48-51
Climbing Cyclist website 80
Cobbold Gorge Qld 244-9
Cobbold Village Qld 244
Cod Hole, Ribbon Reefs Qld 268
Coffin Bay SA 131
Coffs Creek NSW 30
Coffs Harbour NSW 27, 28, 29, 30, 34
Collingwood River Tas. 279, 280
Collins Bonnet Tas. 310
Collinsvale Tas. 310
Conondale Range Great Walk Qld 243
Conway Circuit Qld 243
Cooloola Great Walk Qld 237, 243
Cooloola Sandpatch Qld 237
Cooloola section, Great Sandy National Park Qld 237
Coral Bay WA 181
Coral Sea Kayaking 255
Coruscades, Franklin River Tas. 282
Counts Point NT 208
Crackajack, Ribbon Reefs Qld 268
Cradle Cirque Tas. 286
Cradle Mountain Tas. 285, 286, 291-5, 310, 313
Cradle Mountain Canyons website 291, 293, 294
Cradle Mountain Hut Walk Tas. 137, 285
Cradle Mountain–Lake St Clair National Park Tas. 285-9, 293
crocodiles
   Crocosaurus Cove, Darwin/Garramilla NT 195-7
   Daintree River Qld 197
   Kakadu National Park NT 197
Crocosaurus Cove, Darwin/Garramilla NT 195-7
Crystal Brook Falls Vic. 88, 94

Cycle Hunter Valley map NSW 119
cycling
   7 Peaks, High Country Vic. 80-5
   Barossa and Clare valleys and McLaren Vale SA 117-19
   Brisbane Valley Rail Trail Qld 231-3
   Gippsland Rail Trails Vic. 105
   Kilikivan to Kingaroy Rail Trail Qld 233
   Little Sahara, Kangaroo Island SA 120-5
   Mawson Trail SA 142
   Munda Biddi Trail WA 161
   Rottnest Island/Wadjemup WA 162-7
   Turquoise Way Trail WA 171
   Uluru 215-17
   wine-themed bike trails 119
   see also mountain-biking
Cynthia Bay Tas. 287

D

Daintree River Qld 197
Dales Gorge/Ngirribungunha, Karijina National Park WA 188
D'Alton Falls Tas. 287
d'Arenberg Cube, McLaren Vale SA 119
Dargo Lookout Vic. 97, 98
Dargo Valley Vic. 98
Dartmoor Vic. 78
Darwin/Garramilla NT 195-7
Denham WA 173, 174, 175
Derby Tas. 300-3
Derby Tunnel Tas. 302
Descension Gorge Tas. 280
Dharug Country/People 10, 13, 17
Dhudhuroa People 80
Dial Ranges trail Tas. 303
Dingaal Country 265
Dinner Plain Vic. 83, 84, 97, 98
diving
   Exmouth Navy Pier WA 183-5
   Flinders Reef Qld 228
   Julian Rocks Nguthungulli Nature Reserve NSW 41
   Moreton Island/Mulgumpin Qld 228

Ningaloo Reef WA 184
   sinkholes, Mount Gambier SA 146, 147
   with great white sharks, off Neptune Islands, SA 127-31
   with minke whales, Ribbon Reefs Qld 265-9
Dolphin and Seal Swim Tour, Port Phillip Vic. 61, 62
Dolphin Sanctuary Kayak Tours 113
dolphins 41, 61-3, 104, 113-15, 167, 173, 177, 274
Double D Cup, Tully River Qld 259
Dove Canyon Tas. 291, 293-5
Dove Lake Tas. 286, 291, 313
Down the Rabbit Hole, McLaren Vale SA 119
Dragon's Foot Abseiling Adventure, Mount Buffalo Vic. 89
Du Cane Hut, Overland Track Tas. 287
Dugong Beach, Whitsunday Island Qld 243
Dunk Island Qld 255
Dyuritte Traditional Owners 71

E

East Alligator River NT 197
East Gippsland Rail Trail Vic. 105
East MacDonell Ranges NT 212
Eddystone Point Lighthouse Tas. 305, 306
Eight Mile Creek SA 147-8
El Questro WA 100
Elanda Point Qld 234, 236
Elder Range SA 132, 135, 136
Ellery Creek Big Hole NT 208
Ellery Creek South NT 207
Empress Canyon, Blue Mountains NSW 13-15
Empress Falls, Blue Mountains NSW 15
Esk Qld 231, 232
Ewamian Country/People 244, 248
Ewens Ponds, Mount Gambier 145, 147-8
Ewens Ponds Conservation Park SA 145
Exmouth WA 178, 180, 183-5

Exmouth Dive & Whalesharks 178
Exmouth Navy Pier WA 183-5

F

Falls Creek Vic. 47, 80, 83, 84
Federation Peak Tas. 313
Fergusson Falls Tas. 287
Fern Pool/Juburu, Karijini National Park WA 188
Fig Tree Lake Qld 237
Finke River/Larapinta NT 207, 208
First Nations culture
   Bells Beach Vic. 68
   Byron Bay NSW 41
   Jawoyn rock paintings, Nitimuk National Park NT 203
   Kutikina Cave Tas. 283
   Lurujarri Heritage Trail, Kimberley coast WA 307
   Ngaro Cultural Site, Hook Island Qld 243
   Optus Stadium, Perth/Boorloo WA 111
   Shark Bay WA 173-7
   Uluṟu NT 217
   wukaline Walk, Larapuna/Bay of Fires Tas. 305-7
fishing, Port Lincoln SA 131
Flat Zen, Meander River Tas. 298
Flinders and Beyond Camel Treks 138
Flinders Reef Qld 228
Florentine Peak Tas. 310
Fortescue Bay Tas. 273, 274, 276
Fortescue Falls/Jubula, Karijina National Park WA 188
Fossil Park, Meander River Tas. 298-9
fossil sites, Naracoorte Caves National Park SA 151, 153
Fox Cave, Naracoorte Caves National Park SA 153
Francois Peron National Park WA 173-7
Franklin River Tas. 279-83
Franklin River Rafting 279
Fraser Island Vic. 104
Freestyle Falls Tas. 293
Fremantle WA 164
Frenchmans Cap Tas. 280
Freycinet Experience Walk SA 137

G

Gadigal Country/People 3, 4, 5, 6
Garden Island SA 113, 114
Garigal National Park NSW 10
Gawler SA 117, 118
George Point, Hinchinbrook Island/Munamudanamy Qld 255
George Town Tas. 303
Georgetown Qld 247
Gippsland Lakes Vic. 103-5
Gippsland Lakes Discovery Trail Vic. 105
Girramay Country 251
Glass House Mountains Qld 226
Glen Helen Gorge NT 208
Glenelg SA 114
Glenelg River Vic. 76-9
Glenelg River Canoe Trail Vic. 76
Gold Coast Hinterland Qld 25
Gold Coast Hinterland Great Walk Qld 243
Golden Gumboot, Tully Qld 259
Goolarabooloo Traditional Owners 307
Goold Island Qld 255
Gordon River Tas. 282, 283
Gorge, the, Mount Buffalo Vic. 87, 88, 89, 92
gorge exploration, Karijini National Park WA 187-91
Gosse Bluff NT 208
Great Barrier Reef 265-9
Great Ravine, Franklin River Tas. 280, 281, 282
Great Sandy National Park, Cooloola section Qld 237
Great South West Walk Vic. 78, 79
Great Southern Rail Trail Vic. 105
Great Walks of Australia 137
great white sharks, Neptune Islands SA 127-31
Gulngay Country 266
Gumala Aboriginal Corporation 191
Gumbaynggirr Country/People 27, 30, 33
Gunaikurnai Country/People 80, 97, 103, 104
Gunditjmara Country/People 76, 78
Gundungarra Country 13, 17
Guthega, Snowy Mountains NSW 43-7
Guthega Dam NSW 44

H

Hamersley Gorge/Minhthukundi, Karijina National Park WA 188, 190
Hamersley Range WA 187
Hancock Gorge, Karijini National Park WA 191
Handrail Pool, Karijini National Park WA 191
hang gliding 23 Bald Hill NSW 23-5
HanggglideOZ 23, 24
Harlin Qld 232
Harrietville Vic. 84
Harry's Hut, Noosa River Qld 236, 237
Hartnett Falls Tas. 287
Hastings Reef Qld 266
Hawkesbury Classic Paddle NSW 10
Hawkesbury River Kayaks 10
Heaviree Range NT 208, 212
Heavitree Gap/Ntaripe NT 212
helibiking, Alice Springs/Mparntwe NT 211-13
helicopter flights, Gippsland Lakes 103-4
heliSUP-ing, Gippsland Lakes Vic. 103-5
Hell Hole, Mountain Gambier SA 148
Hell Line (trail), Alice Springs/Mpartntwe NT 212
Henrietta Rocks, Rottnest Island/Wadjemup WA 164
Heysen Trail, The SA 142
High Country Vic.
  cycling 80-5
  snow camping 97-101
  trail-rides 29
hiking
  Bibbulmun Track WA 161
  Cooloola Great Walk Qld 237, 243
  Great South West Walk Vic. 79
  Great Walks Qld 239, 243
  Heysen Trail SA 142
  Jatbula Trail, Nitmiluk National Park NT 203
  Karijina National Park Walk WA 187
  Larapinta Trail, Tjoritja/West MacDonnell National Park NT 204-9, 212
  Mount Bruce/Punurrunha WA 191
  Overland Track, Cradle Mountain-Lake St Clair National Park Tas. 285-9, 310, 313
  Thorsborne Trail, Hinchinbrook Island/Munamudanamy Qld 251-5
  Three Capes Track Tas. 137, 273, 274
  Turquoise Way Trail WA 171
  Wadjermup Bidi, Rottnest Island/Wadjemup WA 167
  wukalina Walk, Larapuna/Bay of Fires Tas. 305-9
hiking (luxury) 137
  Arkaba Walk, Ikara-Flinders Ranges SA 132-7
  Cradle Mountain Huts Walk Tas. 137, 285
hiking (with camels), Ikara-Flinders Ranges SA 138-43
Hill River Inlet WA 171
Hinchinbrook Island/Munamudanamy Qld 251-5
Hinchinbrook Island Cruise 251
Hobart/Nipaluna Tas. 273, 310
Hobart Walking Club 313
Holmes Reef Qld 265
Hook Island Qld 239, 240, 243
Hook Passage Qld 243
horse riding
  Boambee Beach NSW 27-9
  High Country, Vic. 29
Horsey Falls Tas. 294
Hotham Heights Vic. 97
Howlong Station Qld 247
Hugh Gorge NT 208
HWH Stables' beach rides 27, 28

I

Ikara-Flinders Ranges SA 132-43
Ikara-Flinders Ranges National Park SA 135
Inhalanga Pass NT 208
Innawonga Country/People 187, 188
Ipswich Qld 231
Irenabyss, Franklin River Tas. 280

J

Jaadwa Country 71
Jacob's Creek (winery), Roland Flat SA 118
Jadawadjali Country 71
Jagera Country 221, 231
Jaithmathang People 80
Jan Juc Vic. 68
Jardwadjali Country 151
Jatbula Trail NT 203
Jawoyn Country/People 199, 203
Jimmy's Falls Tas 294
Jinibara Country 231
Jinigudera Country 178, 183
Jirrbal Country 256
Joffre Gorge/Jijingunha, Karijina National Park WA 191
Julian Rocks Nguthungulli Nature Reserve NSW 41
Jupagulk Country 71
Jurien Bay WA 170, 171
Juwan and Jambal walks, Wet Tropics Great Walk Qld 243

K

K Col Tas. 310
Kabi Kabi Country 231, 234
Kachoong, Mount Arapiles/Dyuritte Vic. 75
Kakadu National Park NT 100, 197
Kalamina Gorge/Nhamurrunha, Karijina National Park WA 188
Kangaroo Island SA 120-5
Kangaroo Island Wilderness Trail SA 125
Kangaroo Point cliffs, Brisbane/Meanjin Qld 221-3
Kantju Gorge, Uluru NT 216
Kanu Kapers 234
Kareeya Hydro Power Station, Tully Qld 256, 259
Karijini Eco Retreat 191
Karijini National Park WA 187-91
Kartan Country 120

Kata Tjuta NT 216
Katherine NT 199
Katherine River NT 199, 203
Katoomba NSW 13, 17
Katoomba Falls, Blue Mountains NSW 18, 21
Kaurna Country/People 109, 113, 114, 120
kayaking
  Adelaide Dolphin Sanctuary SA 113-15
  Cape Byron NSW 41
  Hawkesbury River NSW 10
  Hinchinbrook Island/Munamudanamy Qld 255
  Noosa River Qld 234-7
  Shark Bay WA 173-7
  Sydney Harbour NSW 6-11
  Turrakana/Tasman Peninsula Tas. 273-5
  Whitsunday Ngaro Sea Trail Qld 239-43
Kermits Pool, Karijini National Park WA 191
K'gari Great Walk Qld 243
Kilikivan to Kingaroy Rail Trail Qld 233
Kilsby Sinkhole, Mount Gambier SA 145, 146-7
Kinaba Qld 236
King River Tas. 283
King River Gorge Tas. 283
King River Rafting 283
Kingaroy Qld 231, 233
Kirribilli Point, Sydney NSW 10
Knox Gorge, Karijina National Park WA 190
Koombana Bay WA 114
Kosciuszko Express chairlift, Thredbo NSW 48, 51
Kosciuszko National Park NSW 48
Kuku Yalanji Country 248
Kulpi Mutitjulu, Uluru NT 216
Kulpi Nyiinkaku (cave), Uluru NT 216
kunanyi/Mount Wellington Tas. 223, 303, 310, 313
Kuniya Piti, Uluru NT 216
Kuranda Qld 21
Kuranda Scenic Railway Qld 21
Kurrama Country/People 187, 188
Kutikana Cave Tas. 282-3

L
Lake Burley Griffin ACT 55, 56, 57
Lake Cootapatamba NSW 52
Lake Cootharaba Qld 234, 236
Lake Mountain Vic. 80, 83
Lake St Clair Tas. 285, 287
Lakes Entrance Vic. 103, 104, 105
Lancelin WA 168-71
Lanterns, Turrakana/Tasman Peninsula Tas. 276
Larapinta Trail, Tjoritja/West MacDonnell National Park NT 204-9, 212
Larapuna/Bay of Fires Tas. 303, 305-9
Larrakia Country 195
Lasletts Vic. 79
Launceston Tas. 21
Lavendar Bay, Sydney NSW 6, 10
Left Main Wall, Kangaroo Point Cliffs, Brisbane/Meanjin Qld 222
Leliyn (Edith Falls), Nitmiluk National Park NT 203
Let's Go Surfing 37
Life's an Adventure walking holidays 187
Lighthouse Bay WA 184
Linville Qld 232
Little Blue Lake, Mount Gambier SA 148
Little Ramsay Bay, Hinchinbrook Island/Munamudanamy Qld 252
Little Sahara, Kangaroo Island SA 120-5
Little Sahara Adventure Centre 120, 123, 124
Little Salmon Bay, Rottnest Island/Wadjemup WA 164
Little Wategos Beach NSW 40
Locomotive trail, Alice Springs/Mparntwe NT 212-13
Lost World, Franklin River Tas. 283
Lost World Canyon Tas. 294
Lower Glenelg National Park Vic. 76, 79
Lowood Qld 232
Lucinda Qld 251, 252, 255
Lurujarri Heritage Trail, Kimberley coast WA 307
luxury guided walks 137

Arkaba Walk, Ikara-Flinders Ranges SA 132-7
Cradle Mountain Huts Walk Tas. 137, 285
Freycinet Experience Walk Tas. 137
Lyndoch SA 118

M
McCormacks Mountain Valley Trail Rides 29
Machinery Canyon Tas. 294
Mackay Highlands Great Walk Qld 243
McLaren Vale SA 117-19
McLaren Vale's Coast to Vines Rail Trail SA 117, 118
Main Beach NSW 37, 38, 40
Mala carpark, Uluru NT 216
Malgana Country/People 173, 174
Mansfield Vic. 84
manta rays, Coral Bay WA 181
Margaret River WA 119
Maria Island Walk Tas. 137
Marino Rocks SA 118
Marriots Lookout Tas. 309
Maruka Arts 217
Matagarup Bridge, Perth/Boorloo WA 5, 157-61
Matagarup Zip+Climb, Perth/Boorloo WA 157-61
Mawson Trail SA 142
Maydena Tas. 303
Meander Tas. 298
Meander River Tas. 297-9
Meander Wilderness Experiences website 297, 298
Meintangk Country 151
Melbourne Skydeck, Melbourne/Naarm Vic. 63
Melbourne/Naarm Vic. 61, 63, 223
Mid Molle Island Qld 240
Middle Harbour NSW 10
Mike Ball Dive Expeditions 265
Milawa Gourmet Region Vic. 119
minke whales, Ribbon Reefs Qld 265-9
Mirimbah Vic. 84
Mission Beach Qld 255, 256
Moleside Landing Vic. 78, 79
Monkey Mia WA 114, 173, 175
Moonee Beach NSW 34
Moonee Creek NSW 30, 33

Moonraker Dolphin Swims 61
Moore Qld 231
Moreton Island/Mulgumpin Qld 114, 225-9
Moriata Conservation Park SA 223
Mornington Peninsula Vic. 61
Mossman Qld 248
Mossman River Qld 248
Mount Achilles Tas. 313
Mount Arapiles/Dyuritte Vic. 71-5
Mount Baw Baw Vic. 83
Mount Beauty Vic. 84, 85
Mount Bowen, Hinchinbrook Island/Munamudanamy Qld 252
Mount Bruce/Punurrunha WA 187, 191
Mount Buffalo Vic. 80, 83, 84, 87-95
Mount Buller Vic. 83, 84
Mount Emmett Tas. 313
Mount Field East Tas. 310
Mount Field National Park Tas. 310
Mount Field West Tas. 310
Mount Gambier SA 145-9
Mount Giles NT 208
Mount Gould Tas. 313
Mount Hotham Vic. 83, 84, 85, 96-101
Mount Jeffreys, South Molle Island Qld 240
Mount Kosciuszko NSW 48-51
Mount Lord Tas. 310
Mount Marian Tas. 310
Mount Massif Tas. 313
Mount Meharry/Wirlbiwirlbi WA 191
Mount Oakleigh Tas. 286, 288, 310
Mount Olympus Tas. 313
Mount Ossa Tas. 286, 287, 309, 310, 313
Mount Pelion East Tas. 287, 310
Mount Pelion West Tas. 286, 313
Mount Richmond Vic. 79
Mount Solitary NSW 18
Mount Sonder/Rwetyepme NT 204, 207, 208
Mount Tate NSW 44
Mount Thetis Tas. 313
Mount Townsend NSW 52
Mount Twynam NSW 44

Index 317

Mount William National Park Tas. 305, 306
mountain-biking 303
   Alice Springs/Mpartntwe NT 211-13
   Derby Tas. 300-3
Mr Mick (winery), Clare SA 118
Mudgee NSW 119
Mueller Pass NSW 52
Mueller Peak NSW 52
Mulligan Bay, Hinchinbrook Island/Munamudanamy Qld 255
Mulligan Falls, Hinchinbrook Island/Munamudanamy Qld 255
Mulron Island WA 184
Munda Biddi Trail WA 161
Mundaring WA 161
Murgon Qld 233
Murray River Walk SA 137
Murray to Mountains Rail Trail Vic. 119
Mutitjulu waterhole, Uluru NT 216

N

Nambung National Park WA 170, 171
Nara Inlet, Hook Island Qld 243
Naracoorte Caves National Park SA 151-3
Narcissus Hut, Overland Track Tas. 287
Narrows, Noosa River Qld 236
Natimuk Vic. 71, 75
Needles, The Tas. 313
Nelson Vic. 78, 79
Nelson Canoe Hire 76
Neptune Islands SA 127-131
New Pelion Hut, Overland Track Tas. 286, 288
Newlands Cascades, Franklin River Tas. 282
Ngadjuri Country 117
Ngarigo Country 43, 48
Ngaro Country/People 239, 243
Ngarrindjeri Country 120
Ngunnawal Country 55
Nhanda Country/People 173, 174
Nina Peak, Hinchinbrook Island/Munamudanamy Qld 252
Ningaloo Marine Park WA 183
Ningaloo Reef WA 178-81, 184

Nitmiluk National Park 199-203
Nitmiluk Tours 199
Noosa Everglades Qld 234
Noosa Heads Qld 234
Noosa River Qld 234-7
Norman Reef Qld 266
North Wall, Mount Buffalo Vic. 87, 88, 92, 94
North Wall Mega Abseil, Mount Buffalo Vic. 89
North West Cape WA 81, 183
Nuriootpa SA 118
Nursery Cliff, Kangaroo Point, Brisbane/Meanjin Qld 222
Nyora Vic. 105

O

Ochre Pits NT 208
Old Pelion Hut, Overland Track Tas. 288
Old Reynella SA 118
O'Leary Walker Wines, Clare SA 118
Omeo Vic. 84, 85
Onkaparinga River National Park SA 223
Optus Stadium, Perth/Boorloo WA 111, 161
Orange NSW 119
Organ Pipes, kunanyi/Mount Wellington Tas. 223
Organ Pipes, Mount Arapiles/Dyuritte Vic. 72, 75
Ormiston Gorge/Kwartatuma NT 207, 208
Ormiston Pound WA 208
Orphan Rock, Blue Mountains NSW 18, 21
Osprey Reef Qld 265
Out There Cycling 231
Outback Cycling, Uluru Cultural Centre 215, 216
Overland Track, Cradle Mountain-Lake St Clair National Park Tas. 285-9, 310, 313
Ozymandias, Mount Buffalo Vic. 88, 89

P

Paddle Bay, South Molle Island Qld 240
Paestan Canoe Hire 76
Palawa Country/People 273, 279, 285, 291, 297, 300, 305-8, 309

Paraburdoo WA 187
Parachilna Gorge SA 142
paragliding, Jan Juc Vic. 69
Pass, The, Byron Bay NSW 38, 41
Peaks Challenge Falls Creek Vic. 85
Pedal and Flipper 162
Pelion Gap, Overland Track Tas. 286
Penguin Tas. 303
Pennicott Wilderness Journeys' Tasman Island Cruise 94
Penwortham SA 11
Peron Homestead Precinct, Francois Peron National Park WA 174, 177
Perrins Bluff Tas. 313
Perth/Boorloo WA 5, 111, 157-61, 162, 164, 170
Picaninnie Ponds, Mount Gambier SA 145, 147
Pine Forest Moor, Overland Track Tas. 286
Pines campground, Mount Arapiles/Dyuritte Vic. 72, 75
Pines Landing Vic. 78
Pinnacles, The WA 170, 171
Pixie Pinnacle, Ribbon Reefs Qld 268
Point Addis Vic. 67, 68
Point Murat WA 183
Polperro Dolphin Swims 61
Ponytail Falls, Tully River Qld 259
Poona Lake Qld 237
Popes Eye, Port Phillip Vic. 62
Porepunkah Vic. 94
Porpoise Bay, Rottnest Island/Wadjemup WA 164
Port Arthur Tas. 277
Port Arthur Historic Site Tas. 273
Port Douglas Qld 266
Port Hinchinbrook Qld 251
Port Lincoln SA 127, 128
Port Phillip Vic. 61-3
Port River SA 113, 114
Port Stephens NSW 114
Port Welshpool Vic. 105
portaledge, Mount Buffalo Vic. 89-95
Portland Vic. 79
Potaruwutij Country 151

Princess Margaret Rose Cave Vic. 79
Propsting Gorge Tas. 282
Proserpine Qld 239, 240

Q

Quandamooka Country 225
Queenscliff Vic. 61, 62
Queenstown Tas. 283

R

rafting
   Barron River, Cairns/Gimuy Qld 259
   Franklin River Tas. 279-83
   King River Tas. 283
   Tully River Qld 256-9
Raging Thunder 256, 259
Ramindjeri Country 120
Ramsay Bay, Hinchinbrook Island/Munamudanamy Qld 252
Ramshead Range NSW 51
Rapid Boarders website 299
Rawson Pass NSW 51, 52
Razorback Ridge NT 208
Red Centre Adventures 211
Red Gorge, Karijina National Park WA 190
Red Rocks Creek NSW 30
Redbank Gorge NT 204, 208
Reef N Beyond Eco Tours 94
Remarkable Rocks, Kangaroo Island SA 120, 125
remote camping 100
   Mount Hotham Vic. 97-101
Rex Point Lookout, Cairns/Gimuy 25
Ribbon Reefs Qld 265-9
Riesling Trail Hire 118
Riesling Trail Bike Hire 117
Rigby Island Vic. 104, 105
Right Main Wall, Kangaroo Point Cliffs, Brisbane/Meanjin Qld 222-3
Ringarooma River Tas. 302
Rip Curl Pro, Bells Beach Vic. 64, 68
river boarding, Barron Gorge Qld 299
River Torrens SA 109, 111
Riverlife 221
Riverton SA 118
Road Train trail, Alice Springs/Mpartntwe NT 212
Roaring 40s Kayaking 273, 274, 277

Robertson River Qld 247
Rock Arch Pool, Karijini National Park WA 188
rock climbing
  Blue Mountains NSW 223
  Boroomba Rocks ACT 223
  Burnley Bouldering Wall, Burnley Vic. 63, 223
  grading system 75
  Kangaroo Point, Brisbane/Meanjin Qld 221-3
  kunanyi/Mount Wellington Tas. 223
  Moriata Conservation Park SA 223
  Mount Arapiles/Dyurrite Vic. 71-5
  Onkaparinga River National Park 223
  Ozymandias, Mount Buffalo Vic. 88, 89
  Totem Pole and Candlestick, Turrakana/Tasman Peninsula Tas. 273, 274
Rock Island Bend, Franklin River Tas. 282
Rockingham WA 114
Rodney Fox Expeditions 127
Rodway Range Tas. 310
Roland Flat SA 118
Ronny Creek Tas. 286
RoofClimb
  Adelaide Oval SA 109-11
  Optus Stadium, Perth/Boorloo WA 111
Rottnest Express 162
Rottnest Fast Ferries 162
Rottnest Island/Wadjemup WA 162-7
Rutherglen Vic. 119

S
SA e-Bikes 117
St Helens Tas. 303
St Helens Mountain Bike Trails Tas. 303
St Hugo (winery), Rowland Flat SA 118
Salopian Inn, McLaren Vale SA 119
Salty Dog Sea Kayaking 239
sandboarding
  Lancelin WA 168-71
  Little Sahara, Kangaroo Island SA 120-5

Tangalooma Desert, Moreton Island/Mulgumpin Qld 228
Sanderson Bay SA 125
Sandy Bay, South Molle Island Qld 240
Sawmill Bay, Whitsunday Island Qld 243
Saxon Reef Qld 266
Scamper (water taxi service) 239
Scenic Rim Trail Qld 137
Scenic Skyway, Blue Mountains NSW 17, 18, 21
Scenic World, Katoomba NSW 17, 18
Sea All Dolphin Swims 61, 62
sea cliffs, Turrakana/Tasman Peninsula Tas. 94
Seal Bay SA 120
Sealink 162
seals 61-3, 104, 114, 120, 128, 167, 273, 274
Serenity Reach, Franklin River Tas. 281, 282
Serpentine Gorge NT 207
Settlement, The, Rottnest Island/Wadjemup WA 164, 167
7 Peaks Ride, High Country Vic. 80-5
Seven Peaks Walk, Lord Howe Island NSW 137
Sevenhill Cellars, Clare SA 118
Shark Bay WA 173-7
shark cage diving, Neptune Islands SA 127-31
Shiraz Trail SA 119
Shredly's 300
Shute Harbour Qld 239, 240
Simpsons Gap/Rungutjirpa NT 208
sinkhole snorkelling, Mount Gambier SA 145-9
Sisters Sinkhole, Mount Gambier SA 148
Skipworth Springs Vic. 79
Skydive Jurien Bay 171
skydiving, Jurien Bay WA 171
Skypark Cairns, Smithfield Qld 260, 263
Skyrail, Cairns/Kuranda Qld 21
sleeping on a portaledge, Mount Buffalo Vic. 91-5
snorkelling
  Ball's Pyramid, Lord Howe Island NSW 94

Canoe Bay Tas. 276
Julian Rocks Nguthungulli Nature Reserve NSW 41
Little Salmon Bay, Rottnest Island/Wadjemup WA 164
Port Phillip Vic. 62
sinkhole, Mount Gambier SA 145-9
Tangalooma Wrecks, Moreton Island/Mulgumpin Qld 225-9
snow camping, Mount Hotham Vic. 97-101
Snowy Mountains NSW 43-51
Snowy Mountains Backcountry Tours 43, 44
Snowy Mountains Main Range NSW 44, 47, 51, 52
Solitary Islands Marine Park NSW 30-5
Sorrento Vic. 61, 62
South Molle Island Qld 239, 240, 243
South Zoe Creek, Hinchinbrook Island/Munamudanamy Qld 255
Southern Sea Ventures 255, 277
Southside Vic. 68, 69
Spion Kop, South Molle Island Qld 240
Spirit of Freedom 265
stand-up paddleboarding
  Byron Bay NSW 41
  Cobbold Gorge Qld 244-9
  Gippsland Lakes Vic. 103-5
  Mossman River Qld 248
  Shark Bay WA 173
  Solitary Islands Marine Park NSW 30-5
Standley Chasm/Angkerle Atwatye NT 207, 208
Stanthorpe to Ballandean Bike Trail Qld 119
Stanwell Park Beach NSW 23, 25
Starburst Chamber, Naracoorte Caves National Park SA 153
Steve's Bommie, Ribbon Reefs Qld 268
Stick-Tomato Cave, Naracoorte Caves National Park SA 152-3
Story Bridge Adventure Climb, Brisbane/Meanjin Qld 5
Strahan Tas. 279

Strickland Bay, Rottnest Island/Wadjemup WA 164
Sunset Safaris 225
Sunshine Coast Hinterland Great Walk Qld 243
surfing
  Bells Beach Vic. 64-9
  Byron Bay NSW 37-41
  Strickland Bay, Rottnest Island/Wadjemup WA 164
  URNBSURF, Melbourne Vic. 63
swimming
  and diving with minke whales, Ribbon Reefs Qld 265-9
  with a crocodile, Crocosaurus Cove, Darwin/Garramilla NT 195-7
  with dolphins and seals, Port Phillip Vic. 61-3, 114
  with whale sharks, Ningaloo Reef WA 178-81
Sydney/Warrang NSW 3-9
Sydney by Kayak 6
Sydney Harbour NSW 4, 6-11
Sydney Harbour Bridge NSW 3-5
Sydney Harbour Kayaks 10
Sydney Opera House, NSW 4, 6, 9

T
Tacoma Preservation Society 131
Tallows Beach NSW 41
Tangalooma Desert, Moreton Island/Mulgumpin Qld 228
Tangalooma Island Resort 225, 226, 228
Tangalooma Wrecks, Moreton Island/Mulgumpin Qld 225-9
Tanunda SA 118
Tasman Arch Tas. 277
Tasman National Park Tas. 274
Tasmanian Expeditions 279
Tasmanian Walking Company's Crescent Bay Camp Tas. 100
Tasmanian Wilderness World Heritage Area 293, 297
Tasty Trout Falls Tas. 302
Taungurung Country/People 80, 87, 91, 97
Tea Cup Falls Tas. 294
Teralina/Eaglehawk Neck Tas. 277

the Abels Tas. 309-11
The Bay of Fires Lodge Walk Tas. 137
the Churn, Franklin River Tas. 281
The Crag website 221
the Gorge, Mount Buffalo Vic. 87, 88, 89, 92
The Heysen Trail SA 142
The Needles Tas. 313
The Pass, Byron Bay NSW 38, 41
the Pines campground, Mount Arapiles/Dyuritte Vic. 72, 75
The Pinnacles WA 170, 171
The Settlement, Rottnest Island/Wadjemup WA 164, 167
Theatre, Tully River Qld 259
Thorsborne Trail, Hinchinbrook Island/Munamudanamy Qld 251-5
Thredbo NSW 47, 48, 51
Three Capes Track Tas. 137, 273, 274
Three Sisters, Blue Mountains 17, 18, 21
Tim Adams Wines, Clare SA 118
Tiptoe Ridge, Mount Arapiles/Dyuritte Vic. 72, 75
Tjilpi Pampa Kulpi, Uluru NT 216
Tjoritja/West MacDonnell National Park NT 204-9, 211, 212
Toogoolwah Qld 231
Torquay Vic. 64, 67, 68
Torrens Island SA 114
Totem Pole, Turrakana/Tasman Peninsula Tas. 273, 276
Tramontane Tas. 313
Treetops Adventure, Belgrave Vic. 63
Trestle Mountain Tas. 310
Tully Qld 256, 259
Tully Gorge Qld 256, 259
Tully River Qld 256-9
Turquoise Way Trail WA 171
Turrakana/Tasman Peninsula Tas. 94, 273-5, 276
Turrbal Country 221
Twelve Apostles Lodge Walk Vic. 137
Two Towers, Ribbon Reef 10 Qld 266

U
Ugarapul Country 231
Uluru NT 215-17
Uluru Cultural Centre NT 215, 216, 217
Uluru-Kata Tjuta National Park NT 215-17
Umpherston Sinkhole/Balumbul and Cave Gardens, Mount Gambier SA 148
Underground River Caving Adventure, Mount Buffalo Vic. 89
URBNSURF, Melbourne Vic. 63

V
Venture Out 103, 104, 105
Victoria Fossil Cave, Naracoorte Caves National Park SA 153
Vivonne Bay SA 120

W
Wadandi Track WA 119
Wadawurrung Country 61, 64
Wadjemup Bidi, Rottnest Island/Wadjemup WA 167
Wadjemup Lighthouse, Rottnest Island/Wadjemup WA 164
Wajaana Yaam Adventure Tours 30, 34
Walgalu Country 48
Walk the Plank, Skypark Cairns Qld 263
Walking SA website 117
Wallaman Falls section, Wet Tropics Great Walk Qld 243
Warrang Bridil's Aboriginal Cultural Tours 111
Wategos Beach NSW 37, 38, 40
Water by Nature Tasmania 279
Waterfall Bay Tas. 273, 276
Waterfall Valley Hut, Overland Track Tas. 286
Watermaarq 61
Watsons' Mountain Country Trail Rides 29
Waywarru People 80
Weano Gorge, Karijini National Park WA 191
Weldborough Hotel Tas. 303
Wellington Range Tas. 310
Wentworth Falls NSW 13, 14
Wergala Country 71
west coast trail Tas. 303
West Coast Wilderness Railway Tas. 283
West End, Rottnest Island/Wadjemup WA 167
West Portal Tas. 313
Western Aranda/Arrernte Country 211
Wet and Moist, Tully River Qld 259
Wet Tropics Great Walk Qld 243
Wet Tropics World Heritage Area Qld 256, 259
Whadjuk Noongar Country 157, 158, 162
whale sharks 178-81
whales 41, 178, 243, 265-9, 277
Wheeler Island Qld 255
Whitehaven Beach Qld 239, 240, 243
whitewater sledding, Meander River Tas. 297-9
Whitsunday Cairn, Whitsunday Island Qld 243
Whitsunday Island Qld 239, 240, 243
Whitsunday Islands Qld 239-43
Whitsunday Ngaro Sea Trail Qld 239-43
Whitsunday Passage Qld 240, 243
Wild Bush Luxury 132
Wild Mersey (trail) Tas. 303
Willunga SA 118, 119
Wilpena Pound/Ikara SA 132, 135, 136
Winaityinaityi Pangkara SA 114
Windermere Hut, Overland Track Tas. 286
WindSwell Kitesurfing and Standup Paddleboarding 248
wine-themed bike trails 117-19
Winki Pop Vic. 68
Winnap Vic. 76
Wire Plain Vic. 97, 98
Wodl Wodl Country 23
Wollumbin (Mount Warning) NSW 41
World Expeditions 204
Wotjobaluk Country 71
wukalina Walk, Larapuna/Bay of Fires Tas. 305-9
Wula Gura Nyinda Eco Cultural Adventures 173, 174
Wulkuraka Qld 231, 232

Y
Yarraman Qld 231, 232, 233
Yellow Water/Ngurrungurrudjba wetlands, Kakadu National Park NT 197
Yingkarta People 173
Yirrganydji Country 260
Yued Noongar Country 168
Yuggera Country 231
Yuppera Country 231

Z
zip lines, Matagarup Bridge, Perth/Boorloo WA 157-61
Zoe Bay, Hinchinbrook Island/Munamudanamy Qld 252, 255
Zoe Falls, Hinchinbrook Island/Munamudanamy Qld 255

ABOUT THE AUTHOR

Andrew Bain has been travelling the planet for 25 years in search of adventures that have seen him cycle a lap around Australia, hike across the United Kingdom and pedal over the Himalayas. He is an award-winning travel writer, and the author of Ultimate Cycling Trips World and Ultimate Cycling Trips Australia, among many other books.

Andrew satisfies his need to be near the mountains by living in Hobart with his children Kiri and Cooper.

ACKNOWLEDGEMENTS

Researching a book about adventures is an adventure itself in a time of La Niña, so it was a treat to have a far-flung cast of hosts as I travelled around the country. For putting up with me - err, putting me up - at various times, a big thanks to Brian and Rosemary Flanagan, Lyn Bain, Darren and Louise Grimsell, Sid and Jill Hosking, and Geoff and Sue Bain.

To each of the operators in the book, a very large thank you for giving me the opportunity to sample an amazing array of activities and experiences. For keeping the fun in the adventures - and being right there during a health hiccup in the midst of it all - eternal thanks to Ali Savage.

A book's journey is only starting once it's written, so I owe immense gratitude to all at Hardie Grant, especially Melissa Kayser, Megan Cuthbert and Alice Barker's ever-keen eye. The book's journey from words to wow is as much yours.

Photography credits

All images © Andrew Bain with the exception of the following:

Front cover: Dylan deHaas; Back cover: Nathan McNeil; Pages ii, 157, 159, 160 Matagarup Zip+Climb; iii, 6, 7, 8, 11 Sydney by Kayak; v, 93 Jo-anne and Jeremy Booth; xvi, 12, 14, 15 Blue Mountains Adventure Company; 2 BridgeClimb Sydney; 4, 5, 31, 35, 36, 38, 39, 40 Destination New South Wales; 16, 19, 20 (bottom) Scenic World; 22 iStock Photo; 24, 25 Hangglide Oz; 32 Wajaana Yaam Adventure Tours; 42, 43, 45, 46, 47 Doug Chatten; 54, 57 Balloon Aloft Canberra; 56, 108, 109, 111, 120, 122, 130 (bottom right), 144, 147, 149, 150, 156, 167, 169, 179, 180, 181, 194, 196, 197, 198, 218, 235, 236, 307 Tourism Australia; 61, 62, 63 Sea All Dolphin Swims; 65, 66, 69, 89 Visit Victoria; 86, 86 Bright Adventure Company; 90, 95 Unleased-Unlimited; 96, 101 (bottom) Travis Leenaerts; 97 Tom Putt; 99 Toshi Pander; 100 Aaron Shum Photography; 101 (top left) Kate Hanton; 101 (top right) Fabio Olivera; 102, 105 Venture Out; 104 Luke Tscharke; 112, 114, 115 (top) Dolphin Sanctuary Kayak; 126, 130 (bottom left), 131 Justin Meneguzzi; 129 Rodney Shark Expeditions; 130 (top) Australian Coastal Safaris; 133, 134, 136, 137 Experience Co; 143 Flinders and Beyonds Camel Treks; 155 (bottom), 190, 214, 217 (top), 234, 237 (bottom) Alamy; 151, 152, 182, 183, 186, 189, 191 Shutterstock; 185 Cathy Finch; 209 (bottom) World Expeditions / Great Walks of Australia; 210 Alice Springs Helicopters; 220, 223 Riverlife Adventure Centre; 222, 224, 226, 228, 229, 237 (top), 241, 245 Tourism and Events Queensland; 257, 258 Raging Thunder; 261, 262, 263 Skypark Cairns; 264, 266, 268, 269 Deborah Dickson-Smith; 272, 273, 275, 276, 277 Roaring 40s Kayaking; 288 Tasmanian Walking Company / Great Walks of Australia; 290, 291, 292, 295 Nic Hansen; 296, 297, 298, 299 Meander Wilderness Experiences.

Published in 2023 by Hardie Grant Explore,
an imprint of Hardie Grant Publishing

Hardie Grant Explore (Melbourne)
Wurundjeri Country
Building 1, 658 Church Street
Richmond, Victoria 3121

Hardie Grant Explore (Sydney)
Gadigal Country
Level 7, 45 Jones Street
Ultimo, NSW 2007

www.hardiegrant.com/au/explore

All rights reserved. No part of this publication may be reproduced, stored in a retrieval system or transmitted in any form by any means, electronic, mechanical, photocopying, recording or otherwise, without the prior written permission of the publishers and copyright holders.

The moral rights of the author have been asserted.

Copyright text © Andrew Bain 2023
Copyright concept, maps and design © Hardie Grant Publishing 2023

The maps in this publication incorporate data from © Commonwealth of Australia (Geoscience Australia), 2006. Geoscience Australia has not evaluated the data as altered and incorporated within this publication, and therefore gives no warranty regarding accuracy, completeness, currency or suitability for any particular purpose.

A catalogue record for this book is available from the National Library of Australia

Hardie Grant acknowledges the Traditional Owners of the Country on which we work, the Wurundjeri People of the Kulin Nation and the Gadigal People of the Eora Nation, and recognises their continuing connection to the land, waters and culture. We pay our respects to their Elders past and present.

For all relevant publications, Hardie Grant Explore commissions a First Nations consultant to review relevant content and provide feedback to ensure suitable language and information is included in the final book. Hardie Grant Explore also includes traditional place names and acknowledges Traditional Owners, where possible, in both the text and mapping for their publications.

Traditional place names are included in *palawa kani*, the language of Tasmanian Aboriginal People, with thanks to the Tasmanian Aboriginal Centre.

Ultimate Adventures: Australia
ISBN 9781741177916

10 9 8 7 6 5 4 3 2 1

Publisher Melissa Kayser
Project editor Megan Cuthbert
Editor Alice Barker
Proofreader Frieda Herrmann
First Nations consultant Jamil Tye, Yorta Yorta
Cartographer Emily Maffei
Design Andy Warren
Initial layout Susanne Geppert
Typesetting Hannah Schubert
Index Max McMaster
Production coordinator Simone Wall

Colour reproduction by Hannah Schubert and Splitting Image Colour Studio

Printed and bound in China by LEO Paper Products LTD.

The paper this book is printed on is certified against the Forest Stewardship Council® Standards and other sources. FSC® promotes environmentally responsible, socially beneficial and economically viable management of the world's forests.

Disclaimer: While every care is taken to ensure the accuracy of the data within this product, the owners of the data (including the state, territory and Commonwealth governments of Australia) do not make any representations or warranties about its accuracy, reliability, completeness or suitability for any particular purpose and, to the extent permitted by law, the owners of the data disclaim all responsibility and all liability (including without limitation, liability in negligence) for all expenses, losses, damages (including indirect or consequential damages) and costs which might be incurred as a result of the data being inaccurate or incomplete in any way and for any reason.

Publisher's Disclaimers: The publisher cannot accept responsibility for any errors or omissions. The representation on the maps of any road or track is not necessarily evidence of public right of way. The publisher cannot be held responsible for any injury, loss or damage incurred during travel. It is vital to research any proposed trip thoroughly and seek the advice of relevant state and travel organisations before you leave.

Publisher's Note: Every effort has been made to ensure that the information in this book is accurate at the time of going to press. The publisher welcomes information and suggestions for correction or improvement.